FREE Study Skills Videos/DVD Offer

Dear Customer,

Thank you for your purchase from Mometrix! We consider it an honor and a privilege that you have purchased our product and we want to ensure your satisfaction.

As part of our ongoing effort to meet the needs of test takers, we have developed a set of Study Skills Videos that we would like to give you for FREE. These videos cover our *best practices* for getting ready for your exam, from how to use our study materials to how to best prepare for the day of the test.

All that we ask is that you email us with feedback that would describe your experience so far with our product. Good, bad, or indifferent, we want to know what you think!

To get your FREE Study Skills Videos, you can use the **QR code** below, or send us an **email** at studyvideos@mometrix.com with *FREE VIDEOS* in the subject line and the following information in the body of the email:

- The name of the product you purchased.
- Your product rating on a scale of 1-5, with 5 being the highest rating.
- Your feedback. It can be long, short, or anything in between. We just want to know your impressions and experience so far with our product. (Good feedback might include how our study material met your needs and ways we might be able to make it even better. You could highlight features that you found helpful or features that you think we should add.)

If you have any questions or concerns, please don't hesitate to contact me directly.

Thanks again!

Sincerely,

Jay Willis
Vice President
jay.willis@mometrix.com
1-800-673-8175

PSAT® 8/9

Prep 2023 with Practice Tests

2 Full-Length Exams

PSAT® 8/9 Secrets Study Guide with Step-by-Step Video Tutorials

6th Edition

Written and edited by the Mometrix College Admissions Test Team

Printed in the United States of America

This paper meets the requirements of ANSI/NISO Z39.48-1992 (Permanence of Paper).

Paperback
ISBN 13: 978-1-5167-2301-0
ISBN 10: 1-5167-2301-5

Dear Future Exam Success Story

First of all, **THANK YOU** for purchasing Mometrix study materials!

Second, congratulations! You are one of the few determined test-takers who are committed to doing whatever it takes to excel on your exam. **You have come to the right place.** We developed these study materials with one goal in mind: to deliver you the information you need in a format that's concise and easy to use.

In addition to optimizing your guide for the content of the test, we've outlined our recommended steps for breaking down the preparation process into small, attainable goals so you can make sure you stay on track.

We've also analyzed the entire test-taking process, identifying the most common pitfalls and showing how you can overcome them and be ready for any curveball the test throws you.

Standardized testing is one of the biggest obstacles on your road to success, which only increases the importance of doing well in the high-pressure, high-stakes environment of test day. Your results on this test could have a significant impact on your future, and this guide provides the information and practical advice to help you achieve your full potential on test day.

Your success is our success

We would love to hear from you! If you would like to share the story of your exam success or if you have any questions or comments in regard to our products, please contact us at **800-673-8175** or **support@mometrix.com**.

Thanks again for your business and we wish you continued success!

Sincerely,
The Mometrix Test Preparation Team

Need more help? Check out our flashcards at:
http://MometrixFlashcards.com/PSAT

Table of Contents

Introduction

Thank you for purchasing this resource! You have made the choice to prepare yourself for a test that could have a huge impact on your future, and this guide is designed to help you be fully ready for test day. Obviously, it's important to have a solid understanding of the test material, but you also need to be prepared for the unique environment and stressors of the test, so that you can perform to the best of your abilities.

For this purpose, the first section that appears in this guide is the **Secret Keys**. We've devoted countless hours to meticulously researching what works and what doesn't, and we've boiled down our findings to the five most impactful steps you can take to improve your performance on the test. We start at the beginning with study planning and move through the preparation process, all the way to the testing strategies that will help you get the most out of what you know when you're finally sitting in front of the test.

We recommend that you start preparing for your test as far in advance as possible. However, if you've bought this guide as a last-minute study resource and only have a few days before your test, we recommend that you skip over the first two Secret Keys since they address a long-term study plan.

If you struggle with **test anxiety**, we strongly encourage you to check out our recommendations for how you can overcome it. Test anxiety is a formidable foe, but it can be beaten, and we want to make sure you have the tools you need to defeat it.

Secret Key #1 – Plan Big, Study Small

There's a lot riding on your performance. If you want to ace this test, you're going to need to keep your skills sharp and the material fresh in your mind. You need a plan that lets you review everything you need to know while still fitting in your schedule. We'll break this strategy down into three categories.

Information Organization

Start with the information you already have: the official test outline. From this, you can make a complete list of all the concepts you need to cover before the test. Organize these concepts into groups that can be studied together, and create a list of any related vocabulary you need to learn so you can brush up on any difficult terms. You'll want to keep this vocabulary list handy once you actually start studying since you may need to add to it along the way.

Time Management

Once you have your set of study concepts, decide how to spread them out over the time you have left before the test. Break your study plan into small, clear goals so you have a manageable task for each day and know exactly what you're doing. Then just focus on one small step at a time. When you manage your time this way, you don't need to spend hours at a time studying. Studying a small block of content for a short period each day helps you retain information better and avoid stressing over how much you have left to do. You can relax knowing that you have a plan to cover everything in time. In order for this strategy to be effective though, you have to start studying early and stick to your schedule. Avoid the exhaustion and futility that comes from last-minute cramming!

Study Environment

The environment you study in has a big impact on your learning. Studying in a coffee shop, while probably more enjoyable, is not likely to be as fruitful as studying in a quiet room. It's important to keep distractions to a minimum. You're only planning to study for a short block of time, so make the most of it. Don't pause to check your phone or get up to find a snack. It's also important to **avoid multitasking**. Research has consistently shown that multitasking will make your studying dramatically less effective. Your study area should also be comfortable and well-lit so you don't have the distraction of straining your eyes or sitting on an uncomfortable chair.

The time of day you study is also important. You want to be rested and alert. Don't wait until just before bedtime. Study when you'll be most likely to comprehend and remember. Even better, if you know what time of day your test will be, set that time aside for study. That way your brain will be used to working on that subject at that specific time and you'll have a better chance of recalling information.

Finally, it can be helpful to team up with others who are studying for the same test. Your actual studying should be done in as isolated an environment as possible, but the work of organizing the information and setting up the study plan can be divided up. In between study sessions, you can discuss with your teammates the concepts that you're all studying and quiz each other on the details. Just be sure that your teammates are as serious about the test as you are. If you find that your study time is being replaced with social time, you might need to find a new team.

Secret Key #2 – Make Your Studying Count

You're devoting a lot of time and effort to preparing for this test, so you want to be absolutely certain it will pay off. This means doing more than just reading the content and hoping you can remember it on test day. It's important to make every minute of study count. There are two main areas you can focus on to make your studying count.

Retention

It doesn't matter how much time you study if you can't remember the material. You need to make sure you are retaining the concepts. To check your retention of the information you're learning, try recalling it at later times with minimal prompting. Try carrying around flashcards and glance at one or two from time to time or ask a friend who's also studying for the test to quiz you.

To enhance your retention, look for ways to put the information into practice so that you can apply it rather than simply recalling it. If you're using the information in practical ways, it will be much easier to remember. Similarly, it helps to solidify a concept in your mind if you're not only reading it to yourself but also explaining it to someone else. Ask a friend to let you teach them about a concept you're a little shaky on (or speak aloud to an imaginary audience if necessary). As you try to summarize, define, give examples, and answer your friend's questions, you'll understand the concepts better and they will stay with you longer. Finally, step back for a big picture view and ask yourself how each piece of information fits with the whole subject. When you link the different concepts together and see them working together as a whole, it's easier to remember the individual components.

Finally, practice showing your work on any multi-step problems, even if you're just studying. Writing out each step you take to solve a problem will help solidify the process in your mind, and you'll be more likely to remember it during the test.

Modality

Modality simply refers to the means or method by which you study. Choosing a study modality that fits your own individual learning style is crucial. No two people learn best in exactly the same way, so it's important to know your strengths and use them to your advantage.

For example, if you learn best by visualization, focus on visualizing a concept in your mind and draw an image or a diagram. Try color-coding your notes, illustrating them, or creating symbols that will trigger your mind to recall a learned concept. If you learn best by hearing or discussing information, find a study partner who learns the same way or read aloud to yourself. Think about how to put the information in your own words. Imagine that you are giving a lecture on the topic and record yourself so you can listen to it later.

For any learning style, flashcards can be helpful. Organize the information so you can take advantage of spare moments to review. Underline key words or phrases. Use different colors for different categories. Mnemonic devices (such as creating a short list in which every item starts with the same letter) can also help with retention. Find what works best for you and use it to store the information in your mind most effectively and easily.

Secret Key #3 – Practice the Right Way

Your success on test day depends not only on how many hours you put into preparing, but also on whether you prepared the right way. It's good to check along the way to see if your studying is paying off. One of the most effective ways to do this is by taking practice tests to evaluate your progress. Practice tests are useful because they show exactly where you need to improve. Every time you take a practice test, pay special attention to these three groups of questions:

- The questions you got wrong
- The questions you had to guess on, even if you guessed right
- The questions you found difficult or slow to work through

This will show you exactly what your weak areas are, and where you need to devote more study time. Ask yourself why each of these questions gave you trouble. Was it because you didn't understand the material? Was it because you didn't remember the vocabulary? Do you need more repetitions on this type of question to build speed and confidence? Dig into those questions and figure out how you can strengthen your weak areas as you go back to review the material.

Additionally, many practice tests have a section explaining the answer choices. It can be tempting to read the explanation and think that you now have a good understanding of the concept. However, an explanation likely only covers part of the question's broader context. Even if the explanation makes perfect sense, **go back and investigate** every concept related to the question until you're positive you have a thorough understanding.

As you go along, keep in mind that the practice test is just that: practice. Memorizing these questions and answers will not be very helpful on the actual test because it is unlikely to have any of the same exact questions. If you only know the right answers to the sample questions, you won't be prepared for the real thing. **Study the concepts** until you understand them fully, and then you'll be able to answer any question that shows up on the test.

It's important to wait on the practice tests until you're ready. If you take a test on your first day of study, you may be overwhelmed by the amount of material covered and how much you need to learn. Work up to it gradually.

On test day, you'll need to be prepared for answering questions, managing your time, and using the test-taking strategies you've learned. It's a lot to balance, like a mental marathon that will have a big impact on your future. Like training for a marathon, you'll need to start slowly and work your way up. When test day arrives, you'll be ready.

Start with the strategies you've read in the first two Secret Keys—plan your course and study in the way that works best for you. If you have time, consider using multiple study resources to get different approaches to the same concepts. It can be helpful to see difficult concepts from more than one angle. Then find a good source for practice tests. Many times, the test website will suggest potential study resources or provide sample tests.

Practice Test Strategy

If you're able to find at least three practice tests, we recommend this strategy:

Untimed and Open-Book Practice

Take the first test with no time constraints and with your notes and study guide handy. Take your time and focus on applying the strategies you've learned.

Timed and Open-Book Practice

Take the second practice test open-book as well, but set a timer and practice pacing yourself to finish in time.

Timed and Closed-Book Practice

Take any other practice tests as if it were test day. Set a timer and put away your study materials. Sit at a table or desk in a quiet room, imagine yourself at the testing center, and answer questions as quickly and accurately as possible.

Keep repeating timed and closed-book tests on a regular basis until you run out of practice tests or it's time for the actual test. Your mind will be ready for the schedule and stress of test day, and you'll be able to focus on recalling the material you've learned.

Secret Key #4 – Pace Yourself

Once you're fully prepared for the material on the test, your biggest challenge on test day will be managing your time. Just knowing that the clock is ticking can make you panic even if you have plenty of time left. Work on pacing yourself so you can build confidence against the time constraints of the exam. Pacing is a difficult skill to master, especially in a high-pressure environment, so **practice is vital**.

Set time expectations for your pace based on how much time is available. For example, if a section has 60 questions and the time limit is 30 minutes, you know you have to average 30 seconds or less per question in order to answer them all. Although 30 seconds is the hard limit, set 25 seconds per question as your goal, so you reserve extra time to spend on harder questions. When you budget extra time for the harder questions, you no longer have any reason to stress when those questions take longer to answer.

Don't let this time expectation distract you from working through the test at a calm, steady pace, but keep it in mind so you don't spend too much time on any one question. Recognize that taking extra time on one question you don't understand may keep you from answering two that you do understand later in the test. If your time limit for a question is up and you're still not sure of the answer, mark it and move on, and come back to it later if the time and the test format allow. If the testing format doesn't allow you to return to earlier questions, just make an educated guess; then put it out of your mind and move on.

On the easier questions, be careful not to rush. It may seem wise to hurry through them so you have more time for the challenging ones, but it's not worth missing one if you know the concept and just didn't take the time to read the question fully. Work efficiently but make sure you understand the question and have looked at all of the answer choices, since more than one may seem right at first.

Even if you're paying attention to the time, you may find yourself a little behind at some point. You should speed up to get back on track, but do so wisely. Don't panic; just take a few seconds less on each question until you're caught up. Don't guess without thinking, but do look through the answer choices and eliminate any you know are wrong. If you can get down to two choices, it is often worthwhile to guess from those. Once you've chosen an answer, move on and don't dwell on any that you skipped or had to hurry through. If a question was taking too long, chances are it was one of the harder ones, so you weren't as likely to get it right anyway.

On the other hand, if you find yourself getting ahead of schedule, it may be beneficial to slow down a little. The more quickly you work, the more likely you are to make a careless mistake that will affect your score. You've budgeted time for each question, so don't be afraid to spend that time. Practice an efficient but careful pace to get the most out of the time you have.

Secret Key #5 – Have a Plan for Guessing

When you're taking the test, you may find yourself stuck on a question. Some of the answer choices seem better than others, but you don't see the one answer choice that is obviously correct. What do you do?

The scenario described above is very common, yet most test takers have not effectively prepared for it. Developing and practicing a plan for guessing may be one of the single most effective uses of your time as you get ready for the exam.

In developing your plan for guessing, there are three questions to address:

- When should you start the guessing process?
- How should you narrow down the choices?
- Which answer should you choose?

When to Start the Guessing Process

Unless your plan for guessing is to select C every time (which, despite its merits, is not what we recommend), you need to leave yourself enough time to apply your answer elimination strategies. Since you have a limited amount of time for each question, that means that if you're going to give yourself the best shot at guessing correctly, you have to decide quickly whether or not you will guess.

Of course, the best-case scenario is that you don't have to guess at all, so first, see if you can answer the question based on your knowledge of the subject and basic reasoning skills. Focus on the key words in the question and try to jog your memory of related topics. Give yourself a chance to bring the knowledge to mind, but once you realize that you don't have (or you can't access) the knowledge you need to answer the question, it's time to start the guessing process.

It's almost always better to start the guessing process too early than too late. It only takes a few seconds to remember something and answer the question from knowledge. Carefully eliminating wrong answer choices takes longer. Plus, going through the process of eliminating answer choices can actually help jog your memory.

Summary: Start the guessing process as soon as you decide that you can't answer the question based on your knowledge.

How to Narrow Down the Choices

The next chapter in this book (**Test-Taking Strategies**) includes a wide range of strategies for how to approach questions and how to look for answer choices to eliminate. You will definitely want to read those carefully, practice them, and figure out which ones work best for you. Here though, we're going to address a mindset rather than a particular strategy.

Your odds of guessing an answer correctly depend on how many options you are choosing from.

Number of options left	5	4	3	2	1
Odds of guessing correctly	20%	25%	33%	50%	100%

You can see from this chart just how valuable it is to be able to eliminate incorrect answers and make an educated guess, but there are two things that many test takers do that cause them to miss out on the benefits of guessing:

- Accidentally eliminating the correct answer
- Selecting an answer based on an impression

We'll look at the first one here, and the second one in the next section.

To avoid accidentally eliminating the correct answer, we recommend a thought exercise called **the $5 challenge**. In this challenge, you only eliminate an answer choice from contention if you are willing to bet $5 on it being wrong. Why $5? Five dollars is a small but not insignificant amount of money. It's an amount you could afford to lose but wouldn't want to throw away. And while losing $5 once might not hurt too much, doing it twenty times will set you back $100. In the same way, each small decision you make—eliminating a choice here, guessing on a question there—won't by itself impact your score very much, but when you put them all together, they can make a big difference. By holding each answer choice elimination decision to a higher standard, you can reduce the risk of accidentally eliminating the correct answer.

The $5 challenge can also be applied in a positive sense: If you are willing to bet $5 that an answer choice *is* correct, go ahead and mark it as correct.

Summary: Only eliminate an answer choice if you are willing to bet $5 that it is wrong.

Which Answer to Choose

You're taking the test. You've run into a hard question and decided you'll have to guess. You've eliminated all the answer choices you're willing to bet $5 on. Now you have to pick an answer. Why do we even need to talk about this? Why can't you just pick whichever one you feel like when the time comes?

The answer to these questions is that if you don't come into the test with a plan, you'll rely on your impression to select an answer choice, and if you do that, you risk falling into a trap. The test writers know that everyone who takes their test will be guessing on some of the questions, so they intentionally write wrong answer choices to seem plausible. You still have to pick an answer though, and if the wrong answer choices are designed to look right, how can you ever be sure that you're not falling for their trap? The best solution we've found to this dilemma is to take the decision out of your hands entirely. Here is the process we recommend:

Once you've eliminated any choices that you are confident (willing to bet $5) are wrong, select the first remaining choice as your answer.

Whether you choose to select the first remaining choice, the second, or the last, the important thing is that you use some preselected standard. Using this approach guarantees that you will not be enticed into selecting an answer choice that looks right, because you are not basing your decision on how the answer choices look.

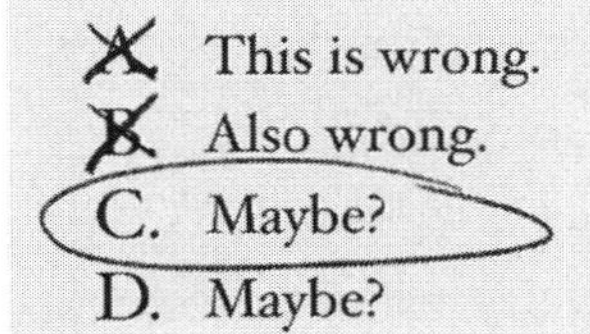

This is not meant to make you question your knowledge. Instead, it is to help you recognize the difference between your knowledge and your impressions. There's a huge difference between thinking an answer is right because of what you know, and thinking an answer is right because it looks or sounds like it should be right.

Summary: To ensure that your selection is appropriately random, make a predetermined selection from among all answer choices you have not eliminated.

Test-Taking Strategies

This section contains a list of test-taking strategies that you may find helpful as you work through the test. By taking what you know and applying logical thought, you can maximize your chances of answering any question correctly!

It is very important to realize that every question is different and every person is different: no single strategy will work on every question, and no single strategy will work for every person. That's why we've included all of them here, so you can try them out and determine which ones work best for different types of questions and which ones work best for you.

Question Strategies

☑ Read Carefully

Read the question and the answer choices carefully. Don't miss the question because you misread the terms. You have plenty of time to read each question thoroughly and make sure you understand what is being asked. Yet a happy medium must be attained, so don't waste too much time. You must read carefully and efficiently.

☑ Contextual Clues

Look for contextual clues. If the question includes a word you are not familiar with, look at the immediate context for some indication of what the word might mean. Contextual clues can often give you all the information you need to decipher the meaning of an unfamiliar word. Even if you can't determine the meaning, you may be able to narrow down the possibilities enough to make a solid guess at the answer to the question.

☑ Prefixes

If you're having trouble with a word in the question or answer choices, try dissecting it. Take advantage of every clue that the word might include. Prefixes can be a huge help. Usually, they allow you to determine a basic meaning. *Pre-* means before, *post-* means after, *pro-* is positive, *de-* is negative. From prefixes, you can get an idea of the general meaning of the word and try to put it into context.

☑ Hedge Words

Watch out for critical hedge words, such as *likely, may, can, sometimes, often, almost, mostly, usually, generally, rarely*, and *sometimes*. Question writers insert these hedge phrases to cover every possibility. Often an answer choice will be wrong simply because it leaves no room for exception. Be on guard for answer choices that have definitive words such as *exactly* and *always*.

☑ Switchback Words

Stay alert for *switchbacks*. These are the words and phrases frequently used to alert you to shifts in thought. The most common switchback words are *but, although*, and *however*. Others include *nevertheless, on the other hand, even though, while, in spite of, despite*, and *regardless of*. Switchback words are important to catch because they can change the direction of the question or an answer choice.

✓ Face Value

When in doubt, use common sense. Accept the situation in the problem at face value. Don't read too much into it. These problems will not require you to make wild assumptions. If you have to go beyond creativity and warp time or space in order to have an answer choice fit the question, then you should move on and consider the other answer choices. These are normal problems rooted in reality. The applicable relationship or explanation may not be readily apparent, but it is there for you to figure out. Use your common sense to interpret anything that isn't clear.

Answer Choice Strategies

✓ Answer Selection

The most thorough way to pick an answer choice is to identify and eliminate wrong answers until only one is left, then confirm it is the correct answer. Sometimes an answer choice may immediately seem right, but be careful. The test writers will usually put more than one reasonable answer choice on each question, so take a second to read all of them and make sure that the other choices are not equally obvious. As long as you have time left, it is better to read every answer choice than to pick the first one that looks right without checking the others.

✓ Answer Choice Families

An answer choice family consists of two (in rare cases, three) answer choices that are very similar in construction and cannot all be true at the same time. If you see two answer choices that are direct opposites or parallels, one of them is usually the correct answer. For instance, if one answer choice says that quantity x increases and another either says that quantity x decreases (opposite) or says that quantity y increases (parallel), then those answer choices would fall into the same family. An answer choice that doesn't match the construction of the answer choice family is more likely to be incorrect. Most questions will not have answer choice families, but when they do appear, you should be prepared to recognize them.

✓ Eliminate Answers

Eliminate answer choices as soon as you realize they are wrong, but make sure you consider all possibilities. If you are eliminating answer choices and realize that the last one you are left with is also wrong, don't panic. Start over and consider each choice again. There may be something you missed the first time that you will realize on the second pass.

✓ Avoid Fact Traps

Don't be distracted by an answer choice that is factually true but doesn't answer the question. You are looking for the choice that answers the question. Stay focused on what the question is asking for so you don't accidentally pick an answer that is true but incorrect. Always go back to the question and make sure the answer choice you've selected actually answers the question and is not merely a true statement.

✓ Extreme Statements

In general, you should avoid answers that put forth extreme actions as standard practice or proclaim controversial ideas as established fact. An answer choice that states the "process should be used in certain situations, if…" is much more likely to be correct than one that states the "process should be discontinued completely." The first is a calm rational statement and doesn't even make a definitive, uncompromising stance, using a hedge word *if* to provide wiggle room, whereas the second choice is far more extreme.

⊘ Benchmark

As you read through the answer choices and you come across one that seems to answer the question well, mentally select that answer choice. This is not your final answer, but it's the one that will help you evaluate the other answer choices. The one that you selected is your benchmark or standard for judging each of the other answer choices. Every other answer choice must be compared to your benchmark. That choice is correct until proven otherwise by another answer choice beating it. If you find a better answer, then that one becomes your new benchmark. Once you've decided that no other choice answers the question as well as your benchmark, you have your final answer.

⊘ Predict the Answer

Before you even start looking at the answer choices, it is often best to try to predict the answer. When you come up with the answer on your own, it is easier to avoid distractions and traps because you will know exactly what to look for. The right answer choice is unlikely to be word-for-word what you came up with, but it should be a close match. Even if you are confident that you have the right answer, you should still take the time to read each option before moving on.

General Strategies

⊘ Tough Questions

If you are stumped on a problem or it appears too hard or too difficult, don't waste time. Move on! Remember though, if you can quickly check for obviously incorrect answer choices, your chances of guessing correctly are greatly improved. Before you completely give up, at least try to knock out a couple of possible answers. Eliminate what you can and then guess at the remaining answer choices before moving on.

⊘ Check Your Work

Since you will probably not know every term listed and the answer to every question, it is important that you get credit for the ones that you do know. Don't miss any questions through careless mistakes. If at all possible, try to take a second to look back over your answer selection and make sure you've selected the correct answer choice and haven't made a costly careless mistake (such as marking an answer choice that you didn't mean to mark). This quick double check should more than pay for itself in caught mistakes for the time it costs.

⊘ Pace Yourself

It's easy to be overwhelmed when you're looking at a page full of questions; your mind is confused and full of random thoughts, and the clock is ticking down faster than you would like. Calm down and maintain the pace that you have set for yourself. Especially as you get down to the last few minutes of the test, don't let the small numbers on the clock make you panic. As long as you are on track by monitoring your pace, you are guaranteed to have time for each question.

⊘ Don't Rush

It is very easy to make errors when you are in a hurry. Maintaining a fast pace in answering questions is pointless if it makes you miss questions that you would have gotten right otherwise. Test writers like to include distracting information and wrong answers that seem right. Taking a little extra time to avoid careless mistakes can make all the difference in your test score. Find a pace that allows you to be confident in the answers that you select.

⊘ Keep Moving

Panicking will not help you pass the test, so do your best to stay calm and keep moving. Taking deep breaths and going through the answer elimination steps you practiced can help to break through a stress barrier and keep your pace.

Final Notes

The combination of a solid foundation of content knowledge and the confidence that comes from practicing your plan for applying that knowledge is the key to maximizing your performance on test day. As your foundation of content knowledge is built up and strengthened, you'll find that the strategies included in this chapter become more and more effective in helping you quickly sift through the distractions and traps of the test to isolate the correct answer.

Now that you're preparing to move forward into the test content chapters of this book, be sure to keep your goal in mind. As you read, think about how you will be able to apply this information on the test. If you've already seen sample questions for the test and you have an idea of the question format and style, try to come up with questions of your own that you can answer based on what you're reading. This will give you valuable practice applying your knowledge in the same ways you can expect to on test day.

Good luck and good studying!

Three-Week PSAT 8/9 Study Plan

On the next few pages, we've provided an optional study plan to help you use this study guide to its fullest potential over the course of three weeks. If you have six weeks available and want to spread it out more, spend two weeks on each section of the plan.

Below is a quick summary of the subjects covered in each week of the plan.

- Week 1: Reading Test
- Week 2: Writing and Language Test
- Week 3: Mathematics Test

Please note that not all subjects will take the same amount of time to work through.

Two full-length practice tests are included in this study guide. We recommend saving any additional practice tests until after you've completed the study plan. Take this practice test timed and without any reference materials a day or two before the real thing as one last practice run to get you in the mode of answering questions at a good pace.

Week 1: Reading Test

Instructional Content

First, read carefully through the Reading Test chapter in this book, checking off your progress as you go:

- ❑ Information and Ideas
- ❑ Rhetoric
- ❑ Synthesis
- ❑ Reading Passages
- ❑ Final Warnings

As you read, do the following:

- Highlight any sections, terms, or concepts you think are important
- Draw an asterisk (*) next to any areas you are struggling with
- Watch the review videos to gain more understanding of a particular topic
- Take notes in your notebook or in the margins of this book

After you've read through everything, go back and review any sections that you highlighted or that you drew an asterisk next to, referencing your notes along the way.

Practice Test #1

Now that you've read over the instructional content, it's time to take a practice test. Complete the Reading Test section of Practice Test #1. Take this test with **no time constraints**, and feel free to reference the applicable sections of this guide as you go. Once you've finished, check your answers against the provided answer key. For any questions you answered incorrectly, review the answer rationale, and then **go back and review** the applicable sections of the book. The goal in this stage is to understand why you answered the question incorrectly, and make sure that the next time you see a similar question, you will get it right.

Practice Test #2

Next, take the Reading Test section of Practice Test #2. This time, give yourself **55 minutes** (the amount of time you will have on the real PSAT 8/9) to complete all of the questions. You should again feel free to reference the guide and your notes, but be mindful of the clock. If you run out of time before you finish all of the questions, mark where you were when time expired, but go ahead and finish taking the practice test. Once you've finished, check your answers against the provided answer key and as before, review the answer rationale for any that you answered incorrectly and go back and review the associated instructional content. Your goal is still to increase understanding of the content but also to get used to the time constraints you will face on the test.

Week 2: Writing and Language Test

Instructional Content

First, read carefully through the Writing and Language Test chapter in this book, checking off your progress as you go:

- ❑ Expression of Ideas
- ❑ Standard English Conventions
- ❑ Agreement and Sentence Structure
- ❑ Punctuation
- ❑ Common Errors

As you read, do the following:

- Highlight any sections, terms, or concepts you think are important
- Draw an asterisk (*) next to any areas you are struggling with
- Watch the review videos to gain more understanding of a particular topic
- Take notes in your notebook or in the margins of this book

After you've read through everything, go back and review any sections that you highlighted or that you drew an asterisk next to, referencing your notes along the way.

Practice Test #1

Now that you've read over the instructional content, it's time to take a practice test. Complete the Writing and Language Test section of Practice Test #1. Take this test with **no time constraints**, and feel free to reference the applicable sections of this guide as you go. Once you've finished, check your answers against the provided answer key. For any questions you answered incorrectly, review the answer rationale, and then **go back and review** the applicable sections of the book. The goal in this stage is to understand why you answered the question incorrectly, and make sure that the next time you see a similar question, you will get it right.

Practice Test #2

Next, take the Writing and Language Test section of Practice Test #2. This time, give yourself **30 minutes** (the amount of time you will have on the real PSAT 8/9) to complete all of the questions. You should again feel free to reference the guide and your notes, but be mindful of the clock. If you run out of time before you finish all of the questions, mark where you were when time expired, but go ahead and finish taking the practice test. Once you've finished, check your answers against the provided answer key, and as before, review the answer rationale for any that you answered incorrectly and then go back and review the associated instructional content. Your goal is still to increase understanding of the content but also to get used to the time constraints you will face on the test.

Week 3: Mathematics Test

Instructional Content

First, read carefully through the Mathematics Test chapter in this book, checking off your progress as you go:

- ❑ How to Approach the Math Questions
- ❑ Foundational Math Concepts
- ❑ Heart of Algebra
- ❑ Problem Solving and Data Analysis
- ❑ Passport to Advanced Math
- ❑ Student Produced Response

As you read, do the following:

- Highlight any sections, terms, or concepts you think are important
- Draw an asterisk (*) next to any areas you are struggling with
- Watch the review videos to gain more understanding of a particular topic
- Take notes in your notebook or in the margins of this book

After you've read through everything, go back and review any sections that you highlighted or that you drew an asterisk next to, referencing your notes along the way.

Practice Test #1

Now that you've read over the instructional content, it's time to take a practice test. Complete the Mathematics Test section of Practice Test #1. Take this test with **no time constraints**, and feel free to reference the applicable sections of this guide as you go. Once you've finished, check your answers against the provided answer key. For any questions you answered incorrectly, review the answer rationale, and then **go back and review** the applicable sections of the book. The goal in this stage is to understand why you answered the question incorrectly, and make sure that the next time you see a similar question, you will get it right.

Practice Test #2

Next, take the Mathematics Test section of Practice Test #2. This time, give yourself **20 minutes** to complete the No-Calculator questions and **40 minutes** to complete the Calculator questions. You should again feel free to reference the guide and your notes, but be mindful of the clock. If you run out of time before you finish all of the questions, mark where you were when time expired, but go ahead and finish taking the practice test. Once you've finished, check your answers against the provided answer key, and as before, review the answer rationale for any that you answered incorrectly and then go back and review the associated instructional content. Your goal is still to increase understanding of the content but also to get used to the time constraints you will face on the test.

Command of Evidence

Understanding a Passage

One of the most important skills in reading comprehension is the identification of **topics** and **main ideas**. There is a subtle difference between these two features. The topic is the subject of a text (i.e., what the text is all about). The main idea, on the other hand, is the most important point being made by the author. The topic is usually expressed in a few words at the most while the main idea often needs a full sentence to be completely defined. As an example, a short passage might be written on the topic of penguins, and the main idea could be written as *Penguins are different from other birds in many ways*. In most nonfiction writing, the topic and the main idea will be **stated directly** and often appear in a sentence at the very beginning or end of the text. When being tested on an understanding of the author's topic, you may be able to skim the passage for the general idea by reading only the first sentence of each paragraph. A body paragraph's first sentence is often—but not always—the main **topic sentence** which gives you a summary of the content in the paragraph.

However, there are cases in which the reader must figure out an **unstated** topic or main idea. In these instances, you must read every sentence of the text and try to come up with an overarching idea that is supported by each of those sentences.

Note: The main idea should not be confused with the thesis statement. While the main idea gives a brief, general summary of a text, the thesis statement provides a **specific perspective** on an issue that the author supports with evidence.

Review Video: Topics and Main Ideas
Visit mometrix.com/academy and enter code: 407801

Supporting details are smaller pieces of evidence that provide backing for the main point. In order to show that a main idea is correct or valid, an author must add details that prove their point. All texts contain details, but they are only classified as supporting details when they serve to reinforce some larger point. Supporting details are most commonly found in informative and persuasive texts. In some cases, they will be clearly indicated with terms like *for example* or *for instance*, or they will be enumerated with terms like *first*, *second*, and *last*. However, you need to be prepared for texts that do not contain those indicators. As a reader, you should consider whether the author's supporting details really back up his or her main point. Details can be factual and correct, yet they may not be **relevant** to the author's point. Conversely, details can be relevant, but be ineffective because they are based on opinion or assertions that cannot be proven.

Review Video: Supporting Details
Visit mometrix.com/academy and enter code: 396297

An example of a main idea is: *Giraffes live in the Serengeti of Africa*. A supporting detail about giraffes could be: *A giraffe in this region benefits from a long neck by reaching twigs and leaves on tall trees.* The main idea gives the general idea that the text is about giraffes. The supporting detail gives a specific fact about how the giraffes eat.

ORGANIZATION OF THE TEXT

The way a text is organized can help readers understand the author's intent and his or her conclusions. There are various ways to organize a text, and each one has a purpose and use. Usually, authors will organize information logically in a passage so the reader can follow and locate the information within the text. However, since not all passages are written with the same logical structure, you need to be familiar with several different types of passage structure.

Review Video: Organizational Methods to Structure Text
Visit mometrix.com/academy and enter code: 606263

Review Video: Sequence of Events in a Story
Visit mometrix.com/academy and enter code: 807512

CHRONOLOGICAL

When using **chronological** order, the author presents information in the order that it happened. For example, biographies are typically written in chronological order. The subject's birth and childhood are presented first, followed by their adult life, and lastly the events leading up to the person's death.

CAUSE AND EFFECT

One of the most common text structures is **cause and effect**. A **cause** is an act or event that makes something happen, and an **effect** is the thing that happens as a result of the cause. A cause-and-effect relationship is not always explicit, but there are some terms in English that signal causes, such as *since*, *because*, and *due to*. Furthermore, terms that signal effects include *consequently, therefore, this leads to*. As an example, consider the sentence *Because the sky was clear, Ron did not bring an umbrella*. The cause is the clear sky, and the effect is that Ron did not bring an umbrella. However, readers may find that sometimes the cause-and-effect relationship will not be clearly noted. For instance, the sentence *He was late and missed the meeting* does not contain any signaling words, but the sentence still contains a cause (he was late) and an effect (he missed the meeting).

Review Video: Cause and Effect
Visit mometrix.com/academy and enter code: 868099

MULTIPLE EFFECTS

Be aware of the possibility for a single cause to have **multiple effects.** (e.g., *Single cause*: Because you left your homework on the table, your dog engulfed the assignment. *Multiple effects*: As a result, you receive a failing grade, your parents do not allow you to go out with your friends, you miss out on the new movie, and one of your classmates spoils it for you before you have another chance to watch it).

MULTIPLE CAUSES

Also, there is the possibility for a single effect to have **multiple causes.** (e.g., *Single effect*: Alan has a fever. *Multiple causes*: An unexpected cold front came through the area, and Alan forgot to take his multi-vitamin to avoid getting sick.) Additionally, an effect can in turn be the cause of another effect, in what is known as a cause-and-effect chain. (e.g., As a result of her disdain for procrastination, Lynn prepared for her exam. This led to her passing her test with high marks. Hence, her resume was accepted and her application was approved.)

Cause and Effect in Persuasive Essays

Persuasive essays, in which an author tries to make a convincing argument and change the minds of readers, usually include cause-and-effect relationships. However, these relationships should not always be taken at face value. Frequently, an author will assume a cause or take an effect for granted. To read a persuasive essay effectively, readers need to judge the cause-and-effect relationships that the author is presenting. For instance, imagine an author wrote the following: *The parking deck has been unprofitable because people would prefer to ride their bikes.* The relationship is clear: the cause is that people prefer to ride their bikes, and the effect is that the parking deck has been unprofitable. However, readers should consider whether this argument is conclusive. Perhaps there are other reasons for the failure of the parking deck: a down economy, excessive fees, etc. Too often, authors present causal relationships as if they are fact rather than opinion. Readers should be on the alert for these dubious claims.

Problem-Solution

Some nonfiction texts are organized to **present a problem** followed by a solution. For this type of text, the problem is often explained before the solution is offered. In some cases, as when the problem is well known, the solution may be introduced briefly at the beginning. Other passages may focus on the solution, and the problem will be referenced only occasionally. Some texts will outline multiple solutions to a problem, leaving readers to choose among them. If the author has an interest or an allegiance to one solution, he or she may fail to mention or describe accurately some of the other solutions. Readers should be careful of the author's agenda when reading a problem-solution text. Only by understanding the author's perspective and interests can one develop a proper judgment of the proposed solution.

Compare and Contrast

Many texts follow the **compare-and-contrast** model in which the similarities and differences between two ideas or things are explored. Analysis of the similarities between ideas is called **comparison**. In an ideal comparison, the author places ideas or things in an equivalent structure, i.e., the author presents the ideas in the same way. If an author wants to show the similarities between cricket and baseball, then he or she may do so by summarizing the equipment and rules for each game. Be mindful of the similarities as they appear in the passage and take note of any differences that are mentioned. Often, these small differences will only reinforce the more general similarity.

Review Video: Compare and Contrast
Visit mometrix.com/academy and enter code: 798319

Thinking critically about ideas and conclusions can seem like a daunting task. One way to ease this task is to understand the basic elements of ideas and writing techniques. Looking at the ways different ideas relate to each other can be a good way for readers to begin their analysis. For instance, sometimes authors will write about two ideas that are in opposition to each other. Or, one author will provide his or her ideas on a topic, and another author may respond in opposition. The analysis of these opposing ideas is known as **contrast**. Contrast is often marred by the author's obvious partiality to one of the ideas. A discerning reader will be put off by an author who does not engage in a fair fight. In an analysis of opposing ideas, both ideas should be presented in clear and reasonable terms. If the author does prefer a side, you need to read carefully to determine the areas where the author shows or avoids this preference. In an analysis of opposing ideas, you should proceed through the passage by marking the major differences point by point with an eye that is looking for an explanation of each side's view. For instance, in an analysis of capitalism and communism, there is an importance in outlining each side's view on labor, markets, prices, personal responsibility, etc. Additionally, as you read through the passages, you should note whether the opposing views present each side in a similar manner.

Sequence

Readers must be able to identify a text's **sequence**, or the order in which things happen. Often, when the sequence is very important to the author, the text is indicated with signal words like *first*, *then*, *next*, and *last*. However, a sequence can be merely implied and must be noted by the reader. Consider the sentence *He walked through the garden and gave water and fertilizer to the plants*. Clearly, the man did not walk through the garden before he collected water and fertilizer for the plants. So, the implied sequence is that he first collected water, then he collected fertilizer, next he walked through the garden, and last he gave water or fertilizer as necessary to the plants. Texts do not always proceed in an orderly sequence from first to last. Sometimes they begin at the end and start over at the beginning. As a reader, you can enhance your understanding of the passage by taking brief notes to clarify the sequence.

Making Connections to Enhance Comprehension

Reading involves thinking. For good comprehension, readers make **text-to-self**, **text-to-text**, and **text-to-world connections**. Making connections helps readers understand text better and predict what might occur next based on what they already know, such as how characters in the story feel or what happened in another text. Text-to-self connections with the reader's life and experiences make literature more personally relevant and meaningful to readers. Readers can make connections before, during, and after reading—including whenever the text reminds them of something similar they have encountered in life or other texts. The genre, setting, characters, plot elements, literary structure and devices, and themes an author uses allow a reader to make connections to other works of literature or to people and events in their own lives. Venn diagrams and other graphic organizers help visualize connections. Readers can also make double-entry notes: key content, ideas, events, words, and quotations on one side, and the connections with these on the other.

Summarizing Literature to Support Comprehension

When reading literature, especially demanding works, **summarizing** helps readers identify important information and organize it in their minds. They can also identify themes, problems, and solutions, and can sequence the story. Readers can summarize before, during, and after they read. They should use their own words, as they do when describing a personal event or giving directions. Previewing a text's organization before reading by examining the book cover, table of contents, and illustrations also aids summarizing. Making notes of key words and ideas in a graphic organizer while reading can benefit readers in the same way. Graphic organizers are another useful method; readers skim the text to determine main ideas and then narrow the list with the aid of the organizer. Unimportant details should be omitted in summaries. Summaries can be organized using description, problem-solution, comparison-contrast, sequence, main ideas, or cause-and-effect.

Review Video: Summarizing Text
Visit mometrix.com/academy and enter code: 172903

Paraphrasing

Paraphrasing is another method that the reader can use to aid in comprehension. When paraphrasing, one puts what they have read into their own words by rephrasing what the author has written, or one "translates" all of what the author shared into their own words by including as many details as they can.

Chapter Quiz

1. All of the following are used for good comprehension, EXCEPT:

a. Text-to-self connections.
b. Text-to-others connections.
c. Text-to-text connections.
d. Text-to-world connections.

2. All of the following are terms in English that signal causes, EXCEPT:

a. Because.
b. Due to.
c. Since.
d. Therefore.

Chapter Quiz Answer Key

1. B: Reading involves thinking. For good comprehension, readers make text-to-self, text-to-text, and text-to-world connections. Making connections helps readers understand text better and predict what might occur next based on what they already know, such as how characters in the story feel or what happened in another text. Text-to-self connections with the reader's life and experiences make literature more personally relevant and meaningful to readers. Readers can make connections before, during, and after reading—including whenever the text reminds them of something similar they have encountered in life or other texts. The genre, setting, characters, plot elements, themes, and literary structure and devices an author uses allow a reader to make connections to other works of literature or to people and events in their own lives. Venn diagrams and other graphic organizers help visualize connections. Readers can also make double-entry notes: key content, ideas, events, words, and quotations on one side, and the connections with these on the other.

2. D: One of the most common text structures is cause and effect. A cause is an act or event that makes something happen, and an effect is the thing that happens as a result of the cause. A cause-and-effect relationship is not always explicit, but there are some terms in English that signal causes, such as *since*, *because*, and *due to*. Furthermore, terms that signal effects include *consequently, therefore,* and *this leads to*. As an example, consider the sentence, "Because the sky was clear, Ron did not bring an umbrella." The cause is the clear sky, and the effect is that Ron did not bring an umbrella. However, readers may find that sometimes the cause-and-effect relationship will not be clearly noted. For instance, the sentence, "He was late and missed the meeting," does not contain any signaling words, but the sentence still contains a cause ("he was late") and an effect ("he missed the meeting").

Making Predictions

When we read literature, **making predictions** about what will happen in the writing reinforces our purpose for reading and prepares us mentally. A **prediction** is a guess about what will happen next. Readers constantly make predictions based on what they have read and what they already know. We can make predictions before we begin reading and during our reading. Consider the following sentence: *Staring at the computer screen in shock, Kim blindly reached over for the brimming glass of water on the shelf to her side.* The sentence suggests that Kim is distracted, and that she is not looking at the glass that she is going to pick up. So, a reader might predict that Kim is going to knock over the glass. Of course, not every prediction will be accurate: perhaps Kim will pick the glass up cleanly. Nevertheless, the author has certainly created the expectation that the water might be spilled.

As we read on, we can test the accuracy of our predictions, revise them in light of additional reading, and confirm or refute our predictions. Predictions are always subject to revision as the reader acquires more information. A reader can make predictions by observing the title and illustrations; noting the structure, characters, and subject; drawing on existing knowledge relative to the subject; and asking "why" and "who" questions. Connecting reading to what we already know enables us to learn new information and construct meaning. For example, before third-graders read a book about Johnny Appleseed, they may start a KWL chart—a list of what they *Know*, what they *Want* to know or learn, and what they have *Learned* after reading. Activating existing background knowledge and thinking about the text before reading improves comprehension.

Review Video: Predictive Reading
Visit mometrix.com/academy and enter code: 437248

Test-taking tip: To respond to questions requiring future predictions, your answers should be based on evidence of past or present behavior and events.

Evaluating Predictions

When making predictions, readers should be able to explain how they developed their prediction. One way readers can defend their thought process is by citing textual evidence. Textual evidence to evaluate reader predictions about literature includes specific synopses of the work, paraphrases of the work or parts of it, and direct quotations from the work. These references to the text must support the prediction by indicating, clearly or unclearly, what will happen later in the story. A text may provide these indications through literary devices such as foreshadowing. Foreshadowing is anything in a text that gives the reader a hint about what is to come by emphasizing the likelihood of an event or development. Foreshadowing can occur through descriptions, exposition, and dialogue. Foreshadowing in dialogue usually occurs when a character gives a warning or expresses a strong feeling that a certain event will occur. Foreshadowing can also occur through irony. However, unlike other forms of foreshadowing, the events that seem the most likely are the opposite of what actually happens. Instances of foreshadowing and irony can be summarized, paraphrased, or quoted to defend a reader's prediction.

Review Video: Textual Evidence for Predictions
Visit mometrix.com/academy and enter code: 261070

Drawing Conclusions from Inferences

Inferences about literary text are logical conclusions that readers make based on their observations and previous knowledge. An inference is based on both what is found in a passage or a story and what is known from personal experience. For instance, a story may say that a character is frightened and can hear howling in the distance. Based on both what is in the text and personal knowledge, it is a logical conclusion that the character is frightened because he hears the sound of wolves. A good inference is supported by the information in a passage.

Implicit and Explicit Information

By inferring, readers construct meanings from text that are personally relevant. By combining their own schemas or concepts and their background information pertinent to the text with what they read, readers interpret it according to both what the author has conveyed and their own unique perspectives. Inferences are different from **explicit information**, which is clearly stated in a passage. Authors do not always explicitly spell out every meaning in what they write; many meanings are implicit. Through inference, readers can comprehend implied meanings in the text, and also derive personal significance from it, making the text meaningful and memorable to them. Inference is a natural process in everyday life. When readers infer, they can draw conclusions about what the author is saying, predict what may reasonably follow, amend these predictions as they continue to read, interpret the import of themes, and analyze the characters' feelings and motivations through their actions.

Example of Drawing Conclusions from Inferences

Read the excerpt and decide why Jana finally relaxed.

> Jana loved her job, but the work was very demanding. She had trouble relaxing. She called a friend, but she still thought about work. She ordered a pizza, but eating it did not help. Then, her kitten jumped on her lap and began to purr. Jana leaned back and began to hum a little tune. She felt better.

You can draw the conclusion that Jana relaxed because her kitten jumped on her lap. The kitten purred, and Jana leaned back and hummed a tune. Then she felt better. The excerpt does not explicitly say that this is the reason why she was able to relax. The text leaves the matter unclear, but the reader can infer or make a "best guess" that this is the reason she is relaxing. This is a logical conclusion based on the information in the passage. It is the best conclusion a reader can make based on the information he or she has read. Inferences are based on the information in a passage, but they are not directly stated in the passage.

Test-taking tip: While being tested on your ability to make correct inferences, you must look for **contextual clues**. An answer can be true, but not the best or most correct answer. The contextual clues will help you find the answer that is the **best answer** out of the given choices. Be careful in your reading to understand the context in which a phrase is stated. When asked for the implied meaning of a statement made in the passage, you should immediately locate the statement and read the **context** in which the statement was made. Also, look for an answer choice that has a similar phrase to the statement in question.

Review Video: Inference
Visit mometrix.com/academy and enter code: 379203

Review Video: How to Support a Conclusion
Visit mometrix.com/academy and enter code: 281653

Chapter Quiz

1. Which of the following describes logical conclusions that readers make based on their observations and previous knowledge?

a. Imperatives
b. Interrogatives
c. Inferences
d. Predictions

Chapter Quiz Answer Key

1. C: Inferences about literary text are logical conclusions that readers make based on their observations and previous knowledge. An inference is based on both what is found in a passage or a story and what is known from personal experience. For instance, a story may say that a character is frightened and can hear howling in the distance. Based on both what is in the text and personal knowledge, it is a logical conclusion that the character is frightened because they hear the sound of wolves. A good inference is supported by the information in a passage.

Purposes for Writing

In order to be an effective reader, one must pay attention to the author's **position** and **purpose**. Even those texts that seem objective and impartial, like textbooks, have a position and bias. Readers need to take these positions into account when considering the author's message. When an author uses emotional language or clearly favors one side of an argument, his or her position is clear. However, the author's position may be evident not only in what he or she writes, but also in what he or she doesn't write. In a normal setting, a reader would want to review some other texts on the same topic in order to develop a view of the author's position. If this was not possible, then you would want to at least acquire some background about the author. However, since you are in the middle of an exam and the only source of information is the text, you should look for language and argumentation that seems to indicate a particular stance on the subject.

Review Video: Author's Position
Visit mometrix.com/academy and enter code: 827954

Usually, identifying the author's **purpose** is easier than identifying his or her position. In most cases, the author has no interest in hiding his or her purpose. A text that is meant to entertain, for instance, should be written to please the reader. Most narratives, or stories, are written to entertain, though they may also inform or persuade. Informative texts are easy to identify, while the most difficult purpose of a text to identify is persuasion because the author has an interest in making this purpose hard to detect. When a reader discovers that the author is trying to persuade, he or she should be skeptical of the argument. For this reason, persuasive texts often try to establish an entertaining tone and hope to amuse the reader into agreement. On the other hand, an informative tone may be implemented to create an appearance of authority and objectivity.

An author's purpose is evident often in the organization of the text (e.g., section headings in bold font points to an informative text). However, you may not have such organization available to you in your exam. Instead, if the author makes his or her main idea clear from the beginning, then the likely purpose of the text is to inform. If the author begins by making a claim and provides various arguments to support that claim, then the purpose is probably to persuade. If the author tells a story or wants to gain the reader's attention more than to push a particular point or deliver information, then his or her purpose is most likely to entertain. As a reader, you must judge authors on how well they accomplish their purpose. In other words, you need to consider the type of passage (e.g., technical, persuasive, etc.) that the author has written and if the author has followed the requirements of the passage type.

Making Logical Conclusions about a Passage

A reader should always be drawing conclusions from the text. Sometimes conclusions are **implied** from written information, and other times the information is **stated directly** within the passage. One should always aim to draw conclusions from information stated within a passage, rather than to draw them from mere implications. At times an author may provide some information and then describe a counterargument. Readers should be alert for direct statements that are subsequently rejected or weakened by the author. Furthermore, you should always read through the entire passage before drawing conclusions. Many readers are trained to expect the author's conclusions at either the beginning or the end of the passage, but many texts do not adhere to this format.

Drawing conclusions from information implied within a passage requires confidence on the part of the reader. **Implications** are things that the author does not state directly, but readers can assume based on what the author does say. Consider the following passage: *I stepped outside and opened my umbrella. By the time I got to work, the cuffs of my pants were soaked*. The author never states that it is raining, but this fact is clearly implied. Conclusions based on implication must be well supported by the text. In order to draw a solid conclusion, readers should have **multiple pieces of evidence**. If readers have only one piece, they must be assured that there is no other possible explanation than their conclusion. A good reader will be able to draw many conclusions from information implied by the text, which will be a great help on the exam.

Drawing Conclusions

A common type of inference that a reader has to make is **drawing a conclusion**. The reader makes this conclusion based on the information provided within a text. Certain facts are included to help a reader come to a specific conclusion. For example, a story may open with a man trudging through the snow on a cold winter day, dragging a sled behind him. The reader can logically **infer** from the setting of the story that the man is wearing heavy winter clothes in order to stay warm. Information is implied based on the setting of a story, which is why **setting** is an important element of the text. If the same man in the example was trudging down a beach on a hot summer day, dragging a surf board behind him, the reader would assume that the man is not wearing heavy clothes. The reader makes inferences based on their own experiences and the information presented to them in the story.

Test-taking tip: When asked to identify a conclusion that may be drawn, look for critical "hedge" phrases, such as *likely*, *may*, *can*, and *will often*, among many others. When you are being tested on this knowledge, remember the question that writers insert into these hedge phrases to cover every possibility. Often an answer will be wrong simply because there is no room for exception. Extreme positive or negative answers (such as always or never) are usually not correct. When answering these questions, the reader **should not** use any outside knowledge that is not gathered directly or reasonably inferred from the passage. Correct answers can be derived straight from the passage.

Example

Read the following sentence from *Little Women* by Louisa May Alcott and draw a conclusion based upon the information presented:

> *You know the reason Mother proposed not having any presents this Christmas was because it is going to be a hard winter for everyone; and she thinks we ought not to spend money for pleasure, when our men are suffering so in the army.*

Based on the information in the sentence, the reader can conclude, or **infer**, that the men are away at war while the women are still at home. The pronoun *our* gives a clue to the reader that the character is speaking about men she knows. In addition, the reader can assume that the character is speaking to a brother or sister, since the term "Mother" is used by the character while speaking to another person. The reader can also come to the conclusion that the characters celebrate Christmas, since it is mentioned in the **context** of the sentence. In the sentence, the mother is presented as an unselfish character who is opinionated and thinks about the wellbeing of other people.

Comparing Two Stories

When presented with two different stories, there will be **similarities** and **differences** between the two. A reader needs to make a list, or other graphic organizer, of the points presented in each story. Once the reader has written down the main point and supporting points for each story, the two sets of ideas can be compared. The reader can then present each idea and show how it is the same or different in the other story. This is called **comparing and contrasting ideas**.

The reader can compare ideas by stating, for example: "In Story 1, the author believes that humankind will one day land on Mars, whereas in Story 2, the author believes that Mars is too far away for humans to ever step foot on." Note that the two viewpoints are different in each story that the reader is comparing. A reader may state that: "Both stories discussed the likelihood of humankind landing on Mars." This statement shows how the viewpoint presented in both stories is based on the same topic, rather than how each viewpoint is different. The reader will complete a comparison of two stories with a conclusion.

Review Video: Comparing Two Stories
Visit mometrix.com/academy and enter code: 833765

Outlining a Passage

As an aid to drawing conclusions, **outlining** the information contained in the passage should be a familiar skill to readers. An effective outline will reveal the structure of the passage and will lead to solid conclusions. An effective outline will have a title that refers to the basic subject of the text, though the title does not need to restate the main idea. In most outlines, the main idea will be the first major section. Each major idea in the passage will be established as the head of a category. For instance, the most common outline format calls for the main ideas of the passage to be indicated with Roman numerals. In an effective outline of this kind, each of the main ideas will be represented by a Roman numeral and none of the Roman numerals will designate minor details or secondary ideas. Moreover, all supporting ideas and details should be placed in the appropriate place on the outline. An outline does not need to include every detail listed in the text, but it should feature all of those that are central to the argument or message. Each of these details should be listed under the corresponding main idea.

Review Video: Outlining
Visit mometrix.com/academy and enter code: 584445

Using Graphic Organizers

Ideas from a text can also be organized using **graphic organizers**. A graphic organizer is a way to simplify information and take key points from the text. A graphic organizer such as a timeline may have an event listed for a corresponding date on the timeline, while an outline may have an event listed under a key point that occurs in the text. Each reader needs to create the type of graphic organizer that works the best for him or her in terms of being able to recall information from a story. Examples include a spider-map, which takes a main idea from the story and places it in a bubble with supporting points branching off the main idea. An outline is useful for diagramming the main and supporting points of the entire story, and a Venn diagram compares and contrasts characteristics of two or more ideas.

Review Video: Graphic Organizers
Visit mometrix.com/academy and enter code: 665513

SUMMARIZING

A helpful tool is the ability to **summarize** the information that you have read in a paragraph or passage format. This process is similar to creating an effective outline. First, a summary should accurately define the main idea of the passage, though the summary does not need to explain this main idea in exhaustive detail. The summary should continue by laying out the most important supporting details or arguments from the passage. All of the significant supporting details should be included, and none of the details included should be irrelevant or insignificant. Also, the summary should accurately report all of these details. Too often, the desire for brevity in a summary leads to the sacrifice of clarity or accuracy. Summaries are often difficult to read because they omit all of the graceful language, digressions, and asides that distinguish great writing. However, an effective summary should communicate the same overall message as the original text.

EVALUATING A PASSAGE

It is important to understand the logical conclusion of the ideas presented in an informational text. **Identifying a logical conclusion** can help you determine whether you agree with the writer or not. Coming to this conclusion is much like making an inference: the approach requires you to combine the information given by the text with what you already know and make a logical conclusion. If the author intended for the reader to draw a certain conclusion, then you can expect the author's argumentation and detail to be leading in that direction.

One way to approach the task of drawing conclusions is to make brief **notes** of all the points made by the author. When the notes are arranged on paper, they may clarify the logical conclusion. Another way to approach conclusions is to consider whether the reasoning of the author raises any pertinent questions. Sometimes you will be able to draw several conclusions from a passage. On occasion these will be conclusions that were never imagined by the author. Therefore, be aware that these conclusions must be **supported directly by the text**.

EVALUATION OF SUMMARIES

A summary of a literary passage is a condensation in the reader's own words of the passage's main points. Several guidelines can be used in evaluating a summary. The summary should be complete yet concise. It should be accurate, balanced, fair, neutral, and objective, excluding the reader's own opinions or reactions. It should reflect in similar proportion how much each point summarized was covered in the original passage. Summary writers should include tags of attribution, like "Macaulay argues that" to reference the original author whose ideas are represented in the summary. Summary writers should not overuse quotations; they should only quote central concepts or phrases they cannot precisely convey in words other than those of the original author. Another aspect of evaluating a summary is considering whether it can stand alone as a coherent, unified composition. In addition, evaluation of a summary should include whether its writer has cited the original source of the passage they have summarized so that readers can find it.

CHAPTER QUIZ

1. Which of the following is most important when drawing conclusions from a text?

a. The conclusions make sense to others.
b. The conclusions are supported directly by the text.
c. The conclusions agree with previous convictions.
d. The conclusions align with the author's purpose for writing the text.

2. All of the following are true about summaries, EXCEPT:

a. They should focus on the main point of the text rather than proportional to how much each point was covered in the passage.
b. They should be accurate, balanced, fair, neutral, and objective.
c. They should be complete and concise.
d. They should only quote central concepts or phrases that cannot be precisely conveyed in words other than those of the original author.

Chapter Quiz Answer Key

1. B: It is important to understand the logical conclusion of the ideas presented in an informational text. Identifying a logical conclusion can help readers determine whether they agree with the writer or not. Coming to this conclusion is much like making an inference: the approach requires readers to combine the information given by the text with what they already know and make a logical conclusion. If the author intended for the reader to draw a certain conclusion, then readers can expect the author's argumentation and detail to be leading in that direction. Sometimes a reader will be able to draw several conclusions from a passage. On occasion these will be conclusions that were never imagined by the author. Therefore, be aware that these conclusions must be supported directly by the text.

2. A: A summary of a literary passage is a condensation in the reader's own words of the passage's main points. Several guidelines can be used in evaluating a summary. The summary should be complete yet concise. It should be accurate, balanced, fair, neutral, and objective, excluding the reader's own opinions or reactions. It should reflect in similar proportion how much each point summarized was covered in the original passage. Summary writers should include tags of attribution, like "Macaulay argues that" to reference the original author whose ideas are represented in the summary. Summary writers should not overuse quotations, but only quote central concepts or phrases they cannot precisely convey in words other than those of the original author. Another aspect of evaluating a summary is considering whether it can stand alone as a coherent, unified composition. In addition, evaluation of a summary should include whether its writer has cited the original source of the passage they have summarized so that readers can find it.

Words in Context

Synonyms and Antonyms

When you understand how words relate to each other, you will discover more in a passage. This is explained by understanding **synonyms** (e.g., words that mean the same thing) and **antonyms** (e.g., words that mean the opposite of one another). As an example, *dry* and *arid* are synonyms, and *dry* and *wet* are antonyms.

There are many pairs of words in English that can be considered synonyms, despite having slightly different definitions. For instance, the words *friendly* and *collegial* can both be used to describe a warm interpersonal relationship, and one would be correct to call them synonyms. However, *collegial* (kin to *colleague*) is often used in reference to professional or academic relationships, and *friendly* has no such connotation.

If the difference between the two words is too great, then they should not be called synonyms. *Hot* and *warm* are not synonyms because their meanings are too distinct. A good way to determine whether two words are synonyms is to substitute one word for the other word and verify that the meaning of the sentence has not changed. Substituting *warm* for *hot* in a sentence would convey a different meaning. Although warm and hot may seem close in meaning, warm generally means that the temperature is moderate, and hot generally means that the temperature is excessively high.

Antonyms are words with opposite meanings. *Light* and *dark*, *up* and *down*, *right* and *left*, *good* and *bad*: these are all sets of antonyms. Be careful to distinguish between antonyms and pairs of words that are simply different. *Black* and *gray*, for instance, are not antonyms because gray is not the opposite of black. *Black* and *white*, on the other hand, are antonyms.

Not every word has an antonym. For instance, many nouns do not. What would be the antonym of *chair*? During your exam, the questions related to antonyms are more likely to concern adjectives. You will recall that adjectives are words that describe a noun. Some common adjectives include *purple*, *fast*, *skinny*, and *sweet*. From those four adjectives, *purple* is the item that lacks a group of obvious antonyms.

Review Video: What Are Synonyms and Antonyms?
Visit mometrix.com/academy and enter code: 105612

Affixes

Affixes in the English language are morphemes that are added to words to create related but different words. Derivational affixes form new words based on and related to the original words. For example, the affix *–ness* added to the end of the adjective *happy* forms the noun *happiness.* Inflectional affixes form different grammatical versions of words. For example, the plural affix *–s* changes the singular noun *book* to the plural noun *books*, and the past tense affix *–ed* changes the present tense verb *look* to the past tense *looked.* Prefixes are affixes placed in front of words. For example, *heat* means to make hot; *preheat* means to heat in advance. Suffixes are affixes placed at the ends of words. The *happiness* example above contains the suffix *–ness.* Circumfixes add parts both before and after words, such as how *light* becomes *enlighten* with the prefix *en-* and the suffix *–en.* Interfixes create compound words via central affixes: *speed* and *meter* become *speedometer* via the interfix *–o–*.

Review Video: Affixes
Visit mometrix.com/academy and enter code: 782422

Word Roots, Prefixes, and Suffixes to Help Determine Meanings of Words

Many English words were formed from combining multiple sources. For example, the Latin *habēre* means "to have," and the prefixes *in-* and *im-* mean a lack or prevention of something, as in *insufficient* and *imperfect.* Latin combined *in-* with *habēre* to form *inhibēre,* whose past participle was *inhibitus.* This is the origin of the English word *inhibit,* meaning to prevent from having. Hence by knowing the meanings of both the prefix and the root, one can decipher the word meaning. In Greek, the root *enkephalo-* refers to the brain. Many medical terms are based on this root, such as encephalitis and hydrocephalus. Understanding the prefix and suffix meanings (*-itis* means inflammation; *hydro-* means water) allows a person to deduce that encephalitis refers to brain inflammation and hydrocephalus refers to water (or other fluid) in the brain.

Review Video: Determining Word Meanings
Visit mometrix.com/academy and enter code: 894894

Review Video: Root Words in English
Visit mometrix.com/academy and enter code: 896380

PREFIXES

While knowing prefix meanings helps ESL and beginning readers learn new words, other readers take for granted the meanings of known words. However, prefix knowledge will also benefit them for determining meanings or definitions of unfamiliar words. For example, native English speakers and readers familiar with recipes know what *preheat* means. Knowing that *pre-* means in advance can also inform them that *presume* means to assume in advance, that *prejudice* means advance judgment, and that this understanding can be applied to many other words beginning with *pre-.* Knowing that the prefix *dis-* indicates opposition informs the meanings of words like *disbar, disagree, disestablish,* and many more. Knowing *dys-* means bad, impaired, abnormal, or difficult informs *dyslogistic, dysfunctional, dysphagia,* and *dysplasia.*

SUFFIXES

In English, certain suffixes generally indicate both that a word is a noun, and that the noun represents a state of being or quality. For example, *-ness* is commonly used to change an adjective into its noun form, as with *happy* and *happiness, nice* and *niceness,* and so on. The suffix *–tion* is commonly used to transform a verb into its noun form, as with *converse* and *conversation or move* and *motion*. Thus, if readers are unfamiliar with the second form of a word, knowing the meaning of the transforming suffix can help them determine meaning.

PREFIXES FOR NUMBERS

Prefix	Definition	Examples
bi-	two	bisect, biennial
mono-	one, single	monogamy, monologue
poly-	many	polymorphous, polygamous
semi-	half, partly	semicircle, semicolon
uni-	one	uniform, unity

PREFIXES FOR TIME, DIRECTION, AND SPACE

Prefix	Definition	Examples
a-	in, on, of, up, to	abed, afoot
ab-	from, away, off	abdicate, abjure
ad-	to, toward	advance, adventure
ante-	before, previous	antecedent, antedate
anti-	against, opposing	antipathy, antidote
cata-	down, away, thoroughly	catastrophe, cataclysm
circum-	around	circumspect, circumference
com-	with, together, very	commotion, complicate
contra-	against, opposing	contradict, contravene
de-	from	depart
dia-	through, across, apart	diameter, diagnose
dis-	away, off, down, not	dissent, disappear
epi-	upon	epilogue
ex-	out	extract, excerpt
hypo-	under, beneath	hypodermic, hypothesis
inter-	among, between	intercede, interrupt
intra-	within	intramural, intrastate
ob-	against, opposing	objection
per-	through	perceive, permit
peri-	around	periscope, perimeter
post-	after, following	postpone, postscript
pre-	before, previous	prevent, preclude
pro-	forward, in place of	propel, pronoun
retro-	back, backward	retrospect, retrograde
sub-	under, beneath	subjugate, substitute
super-	above, extra	supersede, supernumerary
trans-	across, beyond, over	transact, transport
ultra-	beyond, excessively	ultramodern, ultrasonic

NEGATIVE PREFIXES

Prefix	Definition	Examples
a-	without, lacking	atheist, agnostic
in-	not, opposing	incapable, ineligible
non-	not	nonentity, nonsense
un-	not, reverse of	unhappy, unlock

Extra Prefixes

Prefix	Definition	Examples
for-	away, off, from	forget, forswear
fore-	previous	foretell, forefathers
homo-	same, equal	homogenized, homonym
hyper-	excessive, over	hypercritical, hypertension
in-	in, into	intrude, invade
mal-	bad, poorly, not	malfunction, malpractice
mis-	bad, poorly, not	misspell, misfire
neo-	new	Neolithic, neoconservative
omni-	all, everywhere	omniscient, omnivore
ortho-	right, straight	orthogonal, orthodox
over-	above	overbearing, oversight
pan-	all, entire	panorama, pandemonium
para-	beside, beyond	parallel, paradox
re-	backward, again	revoke, recur
sym-	with, together	sympathy, symphony

Below is a list of common suffixes and their meanings:

Adjective Suffixes

Suffix	Definition	Examples
-able (-ible)	capable of being	toler*able*, ed*ible*
-esque	in the style of, like	picturesque, grotesque
-ful	filled with, marked by	thankful, zestful
-ific	make, cause	terrific, beatific
-ish	suggesting, like	churlish, childish
-less	lacking, without	hopeless, countless
-ous	marked by, given to	religious, riotous

Noun Suffixes

Suffix	Definition	Examples
-acy	state, condition	accuracy, privacy
-ance	act, condition, fact	acceptance, vigilance
-ard	one that does excessively	drunkard, sluggard
-ation	action, state, result	occupation, starvation
-dom	state, rank, condition	serfdom, wisdom
-er (-or)	office, action	teach*er*, elevat*or*, hon*or*
-ess	feminine	waitress, duchess
-hood	state, condition	manhood, statehood
-ion	action, result, state	union, fusion
-ism	act, manner, doctrine	barbarism, socialism
-ist	worker, follower	monopolist, socialist
-ity (-ty)	state, quality, condition	acid*ity*, civil*ity*, twen*ty*
-ment	result, action	Refreshment
-ness	quality, state	greatness, tallness
-ship	position	internship, statesmanship
-sion (-tion)	state, result	revi*sion*, expedi*tion*
-th	act, state, quality	warmth, width
-tude	quality, state, result	magnitude, fortitude

Verb Suffixes

Suffix	Definition	Examples
-ate	having, showing	separate, desolate
-en	cause to be, become	deepen, strengthen
-fy	make, cause to have	glorify, fortify
-ize	cause to be, treat with	sterilize, mechanize

Denotative vs. Connotative Meaning

The **denotative** meaning of a word is the literal meaning. The **connotative** meaning goes beyond the denotative meaning to include the emotional reaction that a word may invoke. The connotative meaning often takes the denotative meaning a step further due to associations the reader makes with the denotative meaning. Readers can differentiate between the denotative and connotative meanings by first recognizing how authors use each meaning. Most non-fiction, for example, is fact-based and authors do not use flowery, figurative language. The reader can assume that the writer is using the denotative meaning of words. In fiction, the author may use the connotative meaning. Readers can determine whether the author is using the denotative or connotative meaning of a word by implementing context clues.

Review Video: Connotation and Denotation
Visit mometrix.com/academy and enter code: 310092

Nuances of Word Meaning Relative to Connotation, Denotation, Diction, and Usage

A word's denotation is simply its objective dictionary definition. However, its connotation refers to the subjective associations, often emotional, that specific words evoke in listeners and readers. Two or more words can have the same dictionary meaning, but very different connotations. Writers use diction (word choice) to convey various nuances of thought and emotion by selecting synonyms for other words that best communicate the associations they want to trigger for readers. For example, a car engine is naturally greasy; in this sense, "greasy" is a neutral term. But when a person's smile, appearance, or clothing is described as "greasy," it has a negative connotation. Some words have even gained additional or different meanings over time. For example, *awful* used to be used to describe things that evoked a sense of awe. When *awful* is separated into its root word, awe, and suffix, -ful, it can be understood to mean "full of awe." However, the word is now commonly used to describe things that evoke repulsion, terror, or another intense, negative reaction.

Review Video: Word Usage in Sentences
Visit mometrix.com/academy and enter code: 197863

Context Clues

Readers of all levels will encounter words that they have either never seen or have encountered only on a limited basis. The best way to define a word in **context** is to look for nearby words that can assist in revealing the meaning of the word. For instance, unfamiliar nouns are often accompanied by examples that provide a definition. Consider the following sentence: *Dave arrived at the party in hilarious garb: a leopard-print shirt, buckskin trousers, and bright green sneakers.* If a reader was unfamiliar with the meaning of garb, he or she could read the examples (i.e., a leopard-print shirt, buckskin trousers, and high heels) and quickly determine that the word means *clothing*. Examples will not always be this obvious. Consider this sentence: *Parsley, lemon, and flowers were just a few of the items he used as garnishes.* Here, the word *garnishes* is exemplified by parsley, lemon, and flowers. Readers who have eaten in a variety of restaurants will probably be able to identify a garnish as something used to decorate a plate.

Review Video: Context Clues
Visit mometrix.com/academy and enter code: 613660

Using Contrast in Context Clues

In addition to looking at the context of a passage, readers can use contrast to define an unfamiliar word in context. In many sentences, the author will not describe the unfamiliar word directly; instead, he or she will describe the opposite of the unfamiliar word. Thus, you are provided with some information that will bring you closer to defining the word. Consider the following example: *Despite his intelligence, Hector's low brow and bad posture made him look obtuse.* The author writes that Hector's appearance does not convey intelligence. Therefore, *obtuse* must mean unintelligent. Here is another example: *Despite the horrible weather, we were beatific about our trip to Alaska*. The word *despite* indicates that the speaker's feelings were at odds with the weather. Since the weather is described as *horrible*, then *beatific* must mean something positive.

Substitution to Find Meaning

In some cases, there will be very few contextual clues to help a reader define the meaning of an unfamiliar word. When this happens, one strategy that readers may employ is **substitution**. A good reader will brainstorm some possible synonyms for the given word, and he or she will substitute these words into the sentence. If the sentence and the surrounding passage continue to make sense, then the substitution has revealed at least some information about the unfamiliar word. Consider the sentence: *Frank's admonition rang in her ears as she climbed the mountain.* A reader unfamiliar with *admonition* might come up with some substitutions like *vow, promise, advice, complaint,* or *compliment.* All of these words make general sense of the sentence, though their meanings are diverse. However, this process has suggested that an admonition is some sort of message. The substitution strategy is rarely able to pinpoint a precise definition, but this process can be effective as a last resort.

Occasionally, you will be able to define an unfamiliar word by looking at the descriptive words in the context. Consider the following sentence: *Fred dragged the recalcitrant boy kicking and screaming up the stairs.* The words *dragged*, *kicking*, and *screaming* all suggest that the boy does not want to go up the stairs. The reader may assume that *recalcitrant* means something like unwilling or protesting. In this example, an unfamiliar adjective was identified.

Additionally, using description to define an unfamiliar noun is a common practice compared to unfamiliar adjectives, as in this sentence: *Don's wrinkled frown and constantly shaking fist identified him as a curmudgeon of the first order.* Don is described as having a *wrinkled frown and constantly shaking fist*, suggesting that a *curmudgeon* must be a grumpy person. Contrasts do not always provide detailed information about the unfamiliar word, but they at least give the reader some clues.

Words with Multiple Meanings

When a word has more than one meaning, readers can have difficulty determining how the word is being used in a given sentence. For instance, the verb *cleave*, can mean either *join* or *separate*. When readers come upon this word, they will have to select the definition that makes the most sense. Consider the following sentence: *Hermione's knife cleaved the bread cleanly*. Since a knife cannot join bread together, the word must indicate separation. A slightly more difficult example would be the sentence: *The birds cleaved to one another as they flew from the oak tree.* Immediately, the presence of the words *to one another* should suggest that in this sentence *cleave* is being used to mean *join*. Discovering the intent of a word with multiple meanings requires the same tricks as defining an unknown word: look for contextual clues and evaluate the substituted words.

Context Clues to Help Determine Meanings of Words

If readers simply bypass unknown words, they can reach unclear conclusions about what they read. However, looking for the definition of every unfamiliar word in the dictionary can slow their reading progress. Moreover, the dictionary may list multiple definitions for a word, so readers must search the word's context for meaning. Hence context is important to new vocabulary regardless of reader methods. Four types of context clues are examples, definitions, descriptive words, and opposites. Authors may use a certain word, and then follow it with several different examples of what it describes. Sometimes authors actually supply a definition of a word they use, which is especially true in informational and technical texts. Authors may use descriptive words that elaborate upon a vocabulary word they just used. Authors may also use opposites with negation that help define meaning.

Examples and Definitions

An author may use a word and then give examples that illustrate its meaning. Consider this text: "Teachers who do not know how to use sign language can help students who are deaf or hard of hearing understand certain instructions by using gestures instead, like pointing their fingers to indicate which direction to look or go; holding up a hand, palm outward, to indicate stopping; holding the hands flat, palms up, curling a finger toward oneself in a beckoning motion to indicate 'come here'; or curling all fingers toward oneself repeatedly to indicate 'come on', 'more', or 'continue.'" The author of this text has used the word "gestures" and then followed it with examples, so a reader unfamiliar with the word could deduce from the examples that "gestures" means "hand motions." Readers can find examples by looking for signal words "for example," "for instance," "like," "such as," and "e.g."

While readers sometimes have to look for definitions of unfamiliar words in a dictionary or do some work to determine a word's meaning from its surrounding context, at other times an author may make it easier for readers by defining certain words. For example, an author may write, "The company did not have sufficient capital, that is, available money, to continue operations." The author defined "capital" as "available money," and heralded the definition with the phrase "that is." Another way that authors supply word definitions is with appositives. Rather than being introduced by a signal phrase like "that is," "namely," or "meaning," an appositive comes after the vocabulary word it defines and is enclosed within two commas. For example, an author may write, "The Indians introduced the Pilgrims to pemmican, cakes they made of lean meat dried and mixed with fat, which proved greatly beneficial to keep settlers from starving while trapping." In this example, the appositive phrase following "pemmican" and preceding "which" defines the word "pemmican."

Descriptions

When readers encounter a word they do not recognize in a text, the author may expand on that word to illustrate it better. While the author may do this to make the prose more picturesque and vivid, the reader can also take advantage of this description to provide context clues to the meaning of the unfamiliar word. For example, an author may write, "The man sitting next to me on the airplane was obese. His shirt stretched across his vast expanse of flesh, strained almost to bursting." The descriptive second sentence elaborates on and helps to define the previous sentence's word "obese" to mean extremely fat. A reader unfamiliar with the word "repugnant" can decipher its meaning through an author's accompanying description: "The way the child grimaced and shuddered as he swallowed the medicine showed that its taste was particularly repugnant."

Opposites

Text authors sometimes introduce a contrasting or opposing idea before or after a concept they present. They may do this to emphasize or heighten the idea they present by contrasting it with something that is the reverse. However, readers can also use these context clues to understand familiar words. For example, an author may write, "Our conversation was not cheery. We sat and talked very solemnly about his experience and a number of similar events." The reader who is not familiar with the word "solemnly" can deduce by the author's preceding use of "not cheery" that "solemn" means the opposite of cheery or happy, so it must mean serious or sad. Or if someone writes, "Don't condemn his entire project because you couldn't find anything good to say about it," readers unfamiliar with "condemn" can understand from the sentence structure that it means the opposite of saying anything good, so it must mean reject, dismiss, or disapprove. "Entire" adds another context clue, meaning total or complete rejection.

Syntax to Determine Part of Speech and Meanings of Words

Syntax refers to sentence structure and word order. Suppose that a reader encounters an unfamiliar word when reading a text. To illustrate, consider an invented word like "splunch." If this word is used in a sentence like "Please splunch that ball to me," the reader can assume from syntactic context that "splunch" is a verb. We would not use a noun, adjective, adverb, or preposition with the object "that ball," and the prepositional phrase "to me" further indicates "splunch" represents an action. However, in the sentence, "Please hand that splunch to me," the reader can assume that "splunch" is a noun. Demonstrative adjectives like "that" modify nouns. Also, we hand someone some*thing*—a thing being a noun; we do not hand someone a verb, adjective, or adverb. Some sentences contain further clues. For example, from the sentence, "The princess wore the glittering splunch on her head," the reader can deduce that it is a crown, tiara, or something similar from the syntactic context, without knowing the word.

Syntax to Indicate Different Meanings of Similar Sentences

The syntax, or structure, of a sentence affords grammatical cues that aid readers in comprehending the meanings of words, phrases, and sentences in the texts that they read. Seemingly minor differences in how the words or phrases in a sentence are ordered can make major differences in meaning. For example, two sentences can use exactly the same words but have different meanings based on the word order:

- "The man with a broken arm sat in a chair."
- "The man sat in a chair with a broken arm."

While both sentences indicate that a man sat in a chair, differing syntax indicates whether the man's or chair's arm was broken.

Determining Meaning of Phrases and Paragraphs

Like unknown words, the meanings of phrases, paragraphs, and entire works can also be difficult to discern. Each of these can be better understood with added context. However, for larger groups of words, more context is needed. Unclear phrases are similar to unclear words, and the same methods can be used to understand their meaning. However, it is also important to consider how the individual words in the phrase work together. Paragraphs are a bit more complicated. Just as words must be compared to other words in a sentence, paragraphs must be compared to other paragraphs in a composition or a section.

Determining Meaning in Various Types of Compositions

To understand the meaning of an entire composition, the type of composition must be considered. **Expository writing** is generally organized so that each paragraph focuses on explaining one idea, or part of an idea, and its relevance. **Persuasive writing** uses paragraphs for different purposes to organize the parts of the argument. **Unclear paragraphs** must be read in the context of the paragraphs around them for their meaning to be fully understood. The meaning of full texts can also be unclear at times. The purpose of composition is also important for understanding the meaning of a text. To quickly understand the broad meaning of a text, look to the introductory and concluding paragraphs. Fictional texts are different. Some fictional works have implicit meanings, but some do not. The target audience must be considered for understanding texts that do have an implicit meaning, as most children's fiction will clearly state any lessons or morals. For other fiction, the application of literary theories and criticism may be helpful for understanding the text.

Additional Resources for Determining Word Meaning and Usage

While these strategies are useful for determining the meaning of unknown words and phrases, sometimes additional resources are needed to properly use the terms in different contexts. Some words have multiple definitions, and some words are inappropriate in particular contexts or modes of writing. The following tools are helpful for understanding all meanings and proper uses for words and phrases.

- **Dictionaries** provide the meaning of a multitude of words in a language. Many dictionaries include additional information about each word, such as its etymology, its synonyms, or variations of the word.
- **Glossaries** are similar to dictionaries, as they provide the meanings of a variety of terms. However, while dictionaries typically feature an extensive list of words and comprise an entire publication, glossaries are often included at the end of a text and only include terms and definitions that are relevant to the text they follow.

- **Spell Checkers** are used to detect spelling errors in typed text. Some spell checkers may also detect the misuse of plural or singular nouns, verb tenses, or capitalization. While spell checkers are a helpful tool, they are not always reliable or attuned to the author's intent, so it is important to review the spell checker's suggestions before accepting them.
- **Style Manuals** are guidelines on the preferred punctuation, format, and grammar usage according to different fields or organizations. For example, the Associated Press Stylebook is a style guide often used for media writing. The guidelines within a style guide are not always applicable across different contexts and usages, as the guidelines often cover grammatical or formatting situations that are not objectively correct or incorrect.

Chapter Quiz

1. Which of the following affixes refers to the *-o-* in "speedometer"?

a. Prefix
b. Suffix
c. Interfix
d. Circumfix

2. Adding the suffix *-ness* to a word typically does which of the following?

a. Changes a verb to a noun
b. Changes a verb to an adjective
c. Changes an adjective to a noun
d. Changes a noun to a verb

3. Which of the following is NOT considered a common adjective suffix?

a. *-acy*
b. *-able*
c. *-ish*
d. *-less*

4. Which of the following defines the noun suffix *-ation*?

a. Act, condition, fact
b. Action, state, result
c. Quality, state, result
d. State, rank, condition

Chapter Quiz Answer Key

1. C: Prefixes are affixes placed in front of words. For example, *heat* means to make hot, while *preheat* means to heat in advance. Suffixes are affixes placed at the ends of words. The *happiness* example above contains the suffix *-ness.* Circumfixes add parts both before and after words, such as how *light* becomes *enlighten* with the prefix *en-* and the suffix *-en.* Interfixes create compound words via central affixes: *speed* and *meter* become *speedometer* via the interfix *-o-*.

2. C: In English, certain suffixes generally indicate both that a word is a noun, and that the noun represents a state of being or quality. For example, *-ness* is commonly used to change an adjective into its noun form, as with *happy* and *happiness, kind* and *kindness,* and so on.

3. A: Adjective suffixes:

Suffix	Definition	Examples
-able (-ible)	capable of being	tolerable, edible
-esque	in the style of, like	picturesque, grotesque
-ful	filled with, marked by	thankful, zestful
-ific	make, cause	terrific, beatific
-ish	suggesting, like	churlish, childish
-less	lacking, without	hopeless, countless
-ous	marked by, given to	religious, riotous

4. B: Noun suffixes:

Suffix	Definition	Examples
-acy	state, condition	accuracy, privacy
-ance	act, condition, fact	acceptance, vigilance
-ard	one that does excessively	drunkard, sluggard
-ation	action, state, result	occupation, starvation
-dom	state, rank, condition	serfdom, wisdom
-er (-or)	office, action	teacher, elevator, honor
-ess	feminine	waitress, duchess
-hood	state, condition	manhood, statehood
-ion	action, result, state	union, fusion
-ism	act, manner, doctrine	barbarism, socialism
-ist	worker, follower	monopolist, socialist
-ity (-ty)	state, quality, condition	acidity, civility, twenty
-ment	result, action	refreshment
-ness	quality, state	greatness, tallness
-ship	position	internship, statesmanship
-sion (-tion)	state, result	revision, expedition
-th	act, state, quality	warmth, width
-tude	quality, state, result	magnitude, fortitude

Literal and Figurative Meaning

When language is used **literally**, the words mean exactly what they say and nothing more. When language is used **figuratively**, the words mean something beyond their literal meaning. For example, "The weeping willow tree has long, trailing branches and leaves" is a literal description. But "The weeping willow tree looks as if it is bending over and crying" is a figurative description—specifically, a **simile** or stated comparison. Another figurative language form is **metaphor**, or an implied comparison. A good example is the metaphor of a city, state, or city-state as a ship, and its governance as sailing that ship. Ancient Greek lyrical poet Alcaeus is credited with first using this metaphor, and ancient Greek tragedian Aeschylus then used it in *Seven Against Thebes,* and then Plato used it in the *Republic.*

Figures of Speech

A **figure of speech** is a verbal expression whose meaning is figurative rather than literal. For example, the phrase "butterflies in the stomach" does not refer to actual butterflies in a person's stomach. It is a metaphor representing the fluttery feelings experienced when a person is nervous or excited—or when one "falls in love," which does not mean physically falling. "Hitting a sales target" does not mean physically hitting a target with arrows as in archery; it is a metaphor for meeting a sales quota. "Climbing the ladder of success" metaphorically likens advancing in one's career to ascending ladder rungs. Similes, such as "light as a feather" (meaning very light, not a feather's actual weight), and hyperbole, like "I'm starving/freezing/roasting," are also figures of speech. Figures of speech are often used and crafted for emphasis, freshness of expression, or clarity.

Review Video: Figures of Speech
Visit mometrix.com/academy and enter code: 111295

Figurative Language

Figurative language extends past the literal meanings of words. It offers readers new insight into the people, things, events, and subjects covered in a work of literature. Figurative language also enables readers to feel they are sharing the authors' experiences. It can stimulate the reader's senses, make comparisons that readers find intriguing or even startling, and enable readers to view the world in different ways. When looking for figurative language, it is important to consider the context of the sentence or situation. Phrases that appear out of place or make little sense when read literally are likely instances of figurative language. Once figurative language has been recognized, context is also important to determining the type of figurative language being used and its function. For example, when a comparison is being made, a metaphor or simile is likely being used. This means the comparison may emphasize or create irony through the things being compared. Seven specific types of figurative language include: alliteration, onomatopoeia, personification, imagery, similes, metaphors, and hyperbole.

Review Video: Figurative Language
Visit mometrix.com/academy and enter code: 584902

Alliteration and Onomatopoeia

Alliteration describes a series of words beginning with the same sounds. **Onomatopoeia** uses words imitating the sounds of things they name or describe. For example, in his poem "Come Down, O Maid," Alfred Tennyson writes of "The moan of doves in immemorial elms, / And murmuring of innumerable bees." The word "moan" sounds like some sounds doves make, "murmuring" represents the sounds of bees buzzing. Onomatopoeia also includes words that are simply meant to represent sounds, such as "meow," "kaboom," and "whoosh."

Review Video: Alliterations Are All Around
Visit mometrix.com/academy and enter code: 462837

Personification

Another type of figurative language is **personification**. This is describing a non-human thing, like an animal or an object, as if it were human. The general intent of personification is to describe things in a manner that will be comprehensible to readers. When an author states that a tree *groans* in the wind, he or she does not mean that the tree is emitting a low, pained sound from a mouth. Instead, the author means that the tree is making a noise similar to a human groan. Of course, this personification establishes a tone of sadness or suffering. A different tone would be established if the author said that the tree was *swaying* or *dancing*. Alfred Tennyson's poem "The Eagle" uses all of these types of figurative language: "He clasps the crag with crooked hands." Tennyson used alliteration, repeating /k/ and /kr/ sounds. These hard-sounding consonants reinforce the imagery, giving visual and tactile impressions of the eagle.

Review Video: Personification
Visit mometrix.com/academy and enter code: 260066

Similes and Metaphors

Similes are stated comparisons using "like" or "as." Similes can be used to stimulate readers' imaginations and appeal to their senses. Because a simile includes *like* or *as,* the device creates more space between the description and the thing being described than a metaphor does. If an author says that *a house was like a shoebox*, then the tone is different than the author saying that the house *was* a shoebox. Authors will choose between a metaphor and a simile depending on their intended tone.

Similes also help compare fictional characters to well-known objects or experiences, so the reader can better relate to them. William Wordsworth's poem about "Daffodils" begins, "I wandered lonely as a cloud." This simile compares his loneliness to that of a cloud. It is also personification, giving a cloud the human quality loneliness. In his novel *Lord Jim* (1900), Joseph Conrad writes in Chapter 33, "I would have given anything for the power to soothe her frail soul, tormenting itself in its invincible ignorance like a small bird beating about the cruel wires of a cage." Conrad uses the word "like" to compare the girl's soul to a small bird. His description of the bird beating at the cage shows the similar helplessness of the girl's soul to gain freedom.

Review Video: Similes
Visit mometrix.com/academy and enter code: 642949

A **metaphor** is a type of figurative language in which the writer equates something with another thing that is not particularly similar, instead of using *like* or *as*. For instance, *the bird was an arrow arcing through the sky*. In this sentence, the arrow is serving as a metaphor for the bird. The point of a metaphor is to encourage the reader to consider the item being described in a *different way*. Let's continue with this metaphor for a flying bird. You are asked to envision the bird's flight as being similar to the arc of an arrow. So, you imagine the flight to be swift and bending. Metaphors are a way for the author to describe an item *without being direct and obvious*. This literary device is a lyrical and suggestive way of providing information. Note that the reference for a metaphor will not always be mentioned explicitly by the author. Consider the following description of a forest in winter: *Swaying skeletons reached for the sky and groaned as the wind blew through them.* In this example, the author is using *skeletons* as a metaphor for leafless trees. This metaphor creates a spooky tone while inspiring the reader's imagination.

Literary Examples of Metaphor

A **metaphor** is an implied comparison, i.e., it compares something to something else without using "like", "as", or other comparative words. For example, in "The Tyger" (1794), William Blake writes, "Tyger Tyger, burning bright, / In the forests of the night." Blake compares the tiger to a flame not by saying it is like a fire, but by simply describing it as "burning." Henry Wadsworth Longfellow's poem "O Ship of State" (1850) uses an extended metaphor by referring consistently throughout the entire poem to the state, union, or republic as a seagoing vessel, referring to its keel, mast, sail, rope, anchors, and to its braving waves, rocks, gale, tempest, and "false lights on the shore." Within the extended metaphor, Wordsworth uses a specific metaphor: "the anchors of thy hope!"

Ted Hughes' Animal Metaphors

Ted Hughes frequently used animal metaphors in his poetry. In "The Thought Fox," a model of concise, structured beauty, Hughes characterizes the poet's creative process with succinct, striking imagery of an idea entering his head like a wild fox. Repeating "loneliness" in the first two stanzas emphasizes the poet's lonely work: "Something else is alive / Beside the clock's loneliness." He treats an idea's arrival as separate from himself. Three stanzas detail in vivid images a fox's approach from the outside winter forest at starless midnight—its nose, "Cold, delicately" touching twigs and leaves; "neat" paw prints in snow; "bold" body; brilliant green eyes; and self-contained, focused progress—"Till, with a sudden sharp hot stink of fox," he metaphorically depicts poetic inspiration as the fox's physical entry into "the dark hole of the head." Hughes ends by summarizing his vision of a poet as an interior, passive idea recipient, with the outside world unchanged: "The window is starless still; the clock ticks, / The page is printed."

Review Video: Metaphors in Writing
Visit mometrix.com/academy and enter code: 133295

Hyperbole

Hyperbole is excessive exaggeration used for humor or emphasis rather than for literal meaning. For example, in *To Kill a Mockingbird*, Harper Lee wrote, "People moved slowly then. There was no hurry, for there was nowhere to go, nothing to buy and no money to buy it with, nothing to see outside the boundaries of Maycomb County." This was not literally true; Lee exaggerates the scarcity of these things for emphasis. In "Old Times on the Mississippi," Mark Twain wrote, "I... could have hung my hat on my eyes, they stuck out so far." This is not literal, but makes his description vivid and funny. In his poem "As I Walked Out One Evening", W. H. Auden wrote, "I'll love you, dear, I'll love you / Till China and Africa meet, / And the river jumps over the mountain / And the salmon sing in the street." He used things not literally possible to emphasize the duration of his love.

Review Video: Hyperbole and Understatement
Visit mometrix.com/academy and enter code: 308470

Literary Irony

In literature, irony demonstrates the opposite of what is said or done. The three types of irony are **verbal irony**, **situational irony**, and **dramatic irony**. Verbal irony uses words opposite to the meaning. Sarcasm may use verbal irony. One common example is describing something that is confusing as "clear as mud." For example, in his 1986 movie *Hannah and Her Sisters*, author, director, and actor Woody Allen says to his character's date, "I had a great evening; it was like the Nuremburg Trials." Notice these employ similes. In situational irony, what happens contrasts with what was expected. O. Henry's short story *The Gift of the Magi* uses situational irony: a husband and wife each sacrifice their most prized possession to buy each other a Christmas present. The irony is that she sells her long hair to buy him a watch fob, while he sells his heirloom pocket-watch to buy her the jeweled combs for her hair she had long wanted; in the end, neither of them can use their gifts. In dramatic irony, narrative informs audiences of more than its characters know. For example, in *Romeo and Juliet*, the audience is made aware that Juliet is only asleep, while Romeo believes her to be dead, which then leads to Romeo's death.

Review Video: What is the Definition of Irony?
Visit mometrix.com/academy and enter code: 374204

Idioms

Idioms create comparisons, and often take the form of similes or metaphors. Idioms are always phrases and are understood to have a meaning that is different from its individual words' literal meaning. For example, "break a leg" is a common idiom that is used to wish someone luck or tell them to perform well. Literally, the phrase "break a leg" means to injure a person's leg, but the phrase takes on a different meaning when used as an idiom. Another example is "call it a day," which means to temporarily stop working on a task, or find a stopping point, rather than literally referring to something as "a day." Many idioms are associated with a region or group. For example, an idiom commonly used in the American South is "'til the cows come home." This phrase is often used to indicate that something will take or may last for a very long time, but not that it will literally last until the cows return to where they reside.

Chapter Quiz

1. Who is credited with first using the metaphor of a city, state, or city-state as a ship?

a. Theseus
b. Aeschylus
c. Alcaeus
d. Plato

2. How many forms of irony are there?

a. Two
b. Three
c. Four
d. Five

Chapter Quiz Answer Key

1. C: Another figurative language form is metaphor, or an implied comparison. A good example is the metaphor of a city, state, or city-state as a ship, and its governance as sailing that ship. Ancient Greek lyrical poet Alcaeus is credited with first using this metaphor, followed by ancient Greek tragedian Aeschylus using it in *Seven Against Thebes,* and then Plato using it in the *Republic*.

2. B: In literature, irony demonstrates the opposite of what is said or done. The three types of irony are verbal irony, situational irony, and dramatic irony. Verbal irony uses words opposite to the meaning. Sarcasm may use verbal irony. One common example is describing something that is confusing as "clear as mud." In his 1986 movie *Hannah and Her Sisters,* author, director, and actor Woody Allen says to his character's date, "I had a great evening; it was like the Nuremburg Trials." Notice these employ similes. In situational irony, what happens contrasts with what was expected. O. Henry's short story *The Gift of the Magi* uses situational irony: a husband and wife each sacrifice their most prized possession to buy each other a Christmas present. The irony is that she sells her long hair to buy him a watch fob, while he sells his heirloom pocket-watch to buy her the jeweled combs for her hair she had long wanted; in the end, neither of them can use their gifts. In dramatic irony, narrative informs audiences of more than its characters know. For example, in *Romeo and Juliet,* the audience is made aware that Juliet is only asleep, while Romeo believes her to be dead, which then leads to Romeo's death.

Information and Ideas

Text Features in Informational Texts

The **title of a text** gives readers some idea of its content. The **table of contents** is a list near the beginning of a text, showing the book's sections and chapters and their coinciding page numbers. This gives readers an overview of the whole text and helps them find specific chapters easily. An **appendix**, at the back of the book or document, includes important information that is not present in the main text. Also at the back, an **index** lists the book's important topics alphabetically with their page numbers to help readers find them easily. **Glossaries**, usually found at the backs of books, list technical terms alphabetically with their definitions to aid vocabulary learning and comprehension. Boldface print is used to emphasize certain words, often identifying words included in the text's glossary where readers can look up their definitions. **Headings** separate sections of text and show the topic of each. **Subheadings** divide subject headings into smaller, more specific categories to help readers organize information. **Footnotes**, at the bottom of the page, give readers more information, such as citations or links. **Bullet points** list items separately, making facts and ideas easier to see and understand. A **sidebar** is a box of information to one side of the main text giving additional information, often on a more focused or in-depth example of a topic.

Illustrations and **photographs** are pictures that visually emphasize important points in text. The captions below the illustrations explain what those images show. Charts and tables are visual forms of information that make something easier to understand quickly. Diagrams are drawings that show relationships or explain a process. Graphs visually show the relationships among multiple sets of information plotted along vertical and horizontal axes. Maps show geographical information visually to help readers understand the relative locations of places covered in the text. Timelines are visual graphics that show historical events in chronological order to help readers see their sequence.

Review Video: Informative Text
Visit mometrix.com/academy and enter code: 924964

Language Use

Literal and Figurative Language

As in fictional literature, informational text also uses both **literal language**, which means just what it says, and **figurative language**, which imparts more than literal meaning. For example, an informational text author might use a simile or direct comparison, such as writing that a racehorse "ran like the wind." Informational text authors also use metaphors or implied comparisons, such as "the cloud of the Great Depression." Imagery may also appear in informational texts to increase the reader's understanding of ideas and concepts discussed in the text.

Explicit and Implicit Information

When informational text states something explicitly, the reader is told by the author exactly what is meant, which can include the author's interpretation or perspective of events. For example, a professor writes, "I have seen students go into an absolute panic just because they weren't able to complete the exam in the time they were allotted." This explicitly tells the reader that the students were afraid, and by using the words "just because," the writer indicates their fear was exaggerated out of proportion relative to what happened. However, another professor writes, "I have had students come to me, their faces drained of all color, saying 'We weren't able to finish the exam.'" This is an example of implicit meaning: the second writer did not state explicitly that the students were panicked. Instead, he wrote a description of their faces being "drained of all color." From this description, the reader can infer that the students were so frightened that their faces paled.

Review Video: Explicit and Implicit Information
Visit mometrix.com/academy and enter code: 735771

Technical Language

Technical language is more impersonal than literary and vernacular language. Passive voice makes the tone impersonal. For example, instead of writing, "We found this a central component of protein metabolism," scientists write, "This was found a central component of protein metabolism." While science professors have traditionally instructed students to avoid active voice because it leads to first-person ("I" and "we") usage, science editors today find passive voice dull and weak. Many journal articles combine both. Tone in technical science writing should be detached, concise, and professional. While one may normally write, "This chemical has to be available for proteins to be digested," professionals write technically, "The presence of this chemical is required for the enzyme to break the covalent bonds of proteins." The use of technical language appeals to both technical and non-technical audiences by displaying the author or speaker's understanding of the subject and suggesting their credibility regarding the message they are communicating.

Technical Material for Non-Technical Readers

Writing about **technical subjects** for **non-technical readers** differs from writing for colleagues because authors place more importance on delivering a critical message than on imparting the maximum technical content possible. Technical authors also must assume that non-technical audiences do not have the expertise to comprehend extremely scientific or technical messages, concepts, and terminology. They must resist the temptation to impress audiences with their scientific knowledge and expertise and remember that their primary purpose is to communicate a message that non-technical readers will understand, feel, and respond to. Non-technical and technical styles include similarities. Both should formally cite any references or other authors' work utilized in the text. Both must follow intellectual property and copyright regulations. This includes the author's protecting his or her own rights, or a public domain statement, as he or she chooses.

Review Video: Technical Passages
Visit mometrix.com/academy and enter code: 478923

Non-Technical Audiences

Writers of technical or scientific material may need to write for many non-technical audiences. Some readers have no technical or scientific background, and those who do may not be in the same field as the authors. Government and corporate policymakers and budget managers need technical information they can understand for decision-making. Citizens affected by technology or science are a different audience. Non-governmental organizations can encompass many of the preceding groups. Elementary and secondary school programs also need non-technical language for presenting technical subject matter. Additionally, technical authors will need to use non-technical language when collecting consumer responses to surveys, presenting scientific or para-scientific material to the public, writing about the history of science, and writing about science and technology in developing countries.

Use of Everyday Language

Authors of technical information sometimes must write using non-technical language that readers outside their disciplinary fields can comprehend. They should use not only non-technical terms, but also normal, everyday language to accommodate readers whose native language is different than the language the text is written in. For example, instead of writing that "eustatic changes like thermal expansion are causing hazardous conditions in the littoral zone," an author would do better to write that "a rising sea level is threatening the coast." When technical terms cannot be avoided, authors should also define or explain them using non-technical language. Although authors must cite references and acknowledge their use of others' work, they should avoid the kinds of references or citations that they would use in scientific journals—unless they reinforce author messages. They should not use endnotes, footnotes, or any other complicated referential techniques because non-technical journal publishers usually do not accept them. Including high-resolution illustrations, photos, maps, or satellite images and incorporating multimedia into digital publications will enhance non-technical writing about technical subjects. Technical authors may publish using non-technical language in e-journals, trade journals, specialty newsletters, and daily newspapers.

Making Inferences About Informational Text

With informational text, reader comprehension depends not only on recalling important statements and details, but also on reader inferences based on examples and details. Readers add information from the text to what they already know to draw inferences about the text. These inferences help the readers to fill in the information that the text does not explicitly state, enabling them to understand the text better. When reading a nonfictional autobiography or biography, for example, the most appropriate inferences might concern the events in the book, the actions of the subject of the autobiography or biography, and the message the author means to convey. When reading a nonfictional expository (informational) text, the reader would best draw inferences about problems and their solutions, and causes and their effects. When reading a nonfictional persuasive text, the reader will want to infer ideas supporting the author's message and intent.

Structures or Organizational Patterns in Informational Texts

Informational text can be **descriptive**, appealing to the five senses and answering the questions what, who, when, where, and why. Another method of structuring informational text is sequence and order. **Chronological** texts relate events in the sequence that they occurred, from start to finish, while how-to texts organize information into a series of instructions in the sequence in which the steps should be followed. **Comparison-contrast** structures of informational text describe various ideas to their readers by pointing out how things or ideas are similar and how they are different. **Cause and effect** structures of informational text describe events that occurred and identify the causes or reasons that those events occurred. **Problem and solution** structures of informational texts introduce and describe problems and offer one or more solutions for each problem described.

Determining an Informational Author's Purpose

Informational authors' purposes are why they write texts. Readers must determine authors' motivations and goals. Readers gain greater insight into a text by considering the author's motivation. This develops critical reading skills. Readers perceive writing as a person's voice, not simply printed words. Uncovering author motivations and purposes empowers readers to know what to expect from the text, read for relevant details, evaluate authors and their work critically, and respond effectively to the motivations and persuasions of the text. The main idea of a text is what the reader is supposed to understand from reading it; the purpose of the text is why the author has written it and what the author wants readers to do with its information. Authors state some purposes clearly, while other purposes may be unstated but equally significant. When stated purposes contradict other parts of a text, the author may have a hidden agenda. Readers can better evaluate a text's effectiveness, whether they agree or disagree with it, and why they agree or disagree through identifying unstated author purposes.

Identifying Author's Point of View or Purpose

In some informational texts, readers find it easy to identify the author's point of view and purpose, such as when the author explicitly states his or her position and reason for writing. But other texts are more difficult, either because of the content or because the authors give neutral or balanced viewpoints. This is particularly true in scientific texts, in which authors may state the purpose of their research in the report, but never state their point of view except by interpreting evidence or data.

To analyze text and identify point of view or purpose, readers should ask themselves the following four questions:

1. With what main point or idea does this author want to persuade readers to agree?
2. How does this author's word choice affect the way that readers consider this subject?
3. How do this author's choices of examples and facts affect the way that readers consider this subject?
4. What is it that this author wants to accomplish by writing this text?

Review Video: Understanding the Author's Intent
Visit mometrix.com/academy and enter code: 511819

Review Video: Author's Position
Visit mometrix.com/academy and enter code: 827954

Evaluating Arguments Made by Informational Text Writers

When evaluating an informational text, the first step is to identify the argument's conclusion. Then identify the author's premises that support the conclusion. Try to paraphrase premises for clarification and make the conclusion and premises fit. List all premises first, sequentially numbered, then finish with the conclusion. Identify any premises or assumptions not stated by the author but required for the stated premises to support the conclusion. Read word assumptions sympathetically, as the author might. Evaluate whether premises reasonably support the conclusion. For inductive reasoning, the reader should ask if the premises are true, if they support the conclusion, and if so, how strongly. For deductive reasoning, the reader should ask if the argument is valid or invalid. If all premises are true, then the argument is valid unless the conclusion can be false. If it can, then the argument is invalid. An invalid argument can be made valid through alterations such as the addition of needed premises.

Use of Rhetoric in Informational Texts

There are many ways authors can support their claims, arguments, beliefs, ideas, and reasons for writing in informational texts. For example, authors can appeal to readers' sense of **logic** by communicating their reasoning through a carefully sequenced series of logical steps to help "prove" the points made. Authors can appeal to readers' **emotions** by using descriptions and words that evoke feelings of sympathy, sadness, anger, righteous indignation, hope, happiness, or any other emotion to reinforce what they express and share with their audience. Authors may appeal to the **moral** or **ethical values** of readers by using words and descriptions that can convince readers that something is right or wrong. By relating personal anecdotes, authors can supply readers with more accessible, realistic examples of points they make, as well as appealing to their emotions. They can provide supporting evidence by reporting case studies. They can also illustrate their points by making analogies to which readers can better relate.

Chapter Quiz

1. Which of the following is the first step in evaluating an informational text?

a. Read word assumptions sympathetically
b. List all premises sequentially
c. Determine if the premises are true
d. Identify the argument's conclusion

2. Which of the following is NOT considered a type of appeal for an author to use?

a. Logic
b. Ethics
c. Emotions
d. Imagination

Chapter Quiz Answer Key

1. D: When evaluating an informational text, the first step is to identify the argument's conclusion. After that comes identifying the author's premises that support the conclusion. The reader should try to paraphrase premises for clarification and make the conclusion and premises fit. List all premises first, sequentially numbered, then finish with the conclusion. Identify any premises or assumptions not stated by the author but required for the stated premises to support the conclusion. Read word assumptions sympathetically, as the author might. Evaluate whether premises reasonably support the conclusion. For inductive reasoning, the reader should ask if the premises are true, if they support the conclusion, and how strong that support is. For deductive reasoning, the reader should ask if the argument is valid or invalid. If all premises are true, then the argument is valid unless the conclusion can be false. If it can, then the argument is invalid. An invalid argument can be made valid through alterations such as the addition of needed premises.

2. D: There are many ways authors can support their claims, arguments, beliefs, ideas, and reasons for writing in informational texts. For example, authors can appeal to readers' sense of logic by communicating their reasoning through a carefully sequenced series of logical steps to support their positions. Authors can appeal to readers' emotions by using descriptions and words that evoke feelings of sympathy, sadness, anger, righteous indignation, hope, happiness, or any other emotion to reinforce what they express and share with their audience. Authors may appeal to the moral or ethical values of readers by using words and descriptions that can convince readers that something is right or wrong. By relating personal anecdotes, authors can appeal to readers' emotions and supply them with more accessible, realistic examples of points they make. They can provide supporting evidence by reporting case studies. They can also illustrate their points by making analogies to which readers can better relate.

Rhetoric

Persuasive Techniques

To **appeal using reason**, writers present logical arguments, such as using "If... then... because" statements. To **appeal to emotions**, authors may ask readers how they would feel about something or to put themselves in another's place, present their argument as one that will make the audience feel good, or tell readers how they should feel. To **appeal to character**, **morality**, or **ethics**, authors present their points to readers as the right or most moral choices. Authors cite expert opinions to show readers that someone very knowledgeable about the subject or viewpoint agrees with the author's claims. **Testimonials**, usually via anecdotes or quotations regarding the author's subject, help build the audience's trust in an author's message through positive support from ordinary people. **Bandwagon appeals** claim that everybody else agrees with the author's argument and persuade readers to conform and agree, also. Authors **appeal to greed** by presenting their choice as cheaper, free, or more valuable for less cost. They **appeal to laziness** by presenting their views as more convenient, easy, or relaxing. Authors also anticipate potential objections and argue against them before audiences think of them, thereby depicting those objections as weak.

Authors can use **comparisons** like analogies, similes, and metaphors to persuade audiences. For example, a writer might represent excessive expenses as "hemorrhaging" money, which the author's recommended solution will stop. Authors can use negative word connotations to make some choices unappealing to readers, and positive word connotations to make others more appealing. Using **humor** can relax readers and garner their agreement. However, writers must take care: ridiculing opponents can be a successful strategy for appealing to readers who already agree with the author, but can backfire by angering other readers. **Rhetorical questions** need no answer, but create effect that can force agreement, such as asking the question, "Wouldn't you rather be paid more than less?" **Generalizations** persuade readers by being impossible to disagree with. Writers can easily make generalizations that appear to support their viewpoints, like saying, "We all want peace, not war" regarding more specific political arguments. **Transfer** and **association** persuade by example: if advertisements show attractive actors enjoying their products, audiences imagine they will experience the same. **Repetition** can also sometimes effectively persuade audiences.

Review Video: Using Rhetorical Strategies for Persuasion
Visit mometrix.com/academy and enter code: 302658

Classical Author Appeals

In his *On Rhetoric,* ancient Greek philosopher Aristotle defined three basic types of appeal used in writing, which he called *pathos*, *ethos*, and *logos*. ***Pathos*** means suffering or experience and refers to appeals to the emotions (the English word *pathetic* comes from this root). Writing that is meant to entertain audiences, by making them either happy, as with comedy, or sad, as with tragedy, uses *pathos*. Aristotle's *Poetics* states that evoking the emotions of terror and pity is one of the criteria for writing tragedy. ***Ethos*** means character and connotes ideology (the English word *ethics* comes from this root). Writing that appeals to credibility, based on academic, professional, or personal merit, uses *ethos*. ***Logos*** means "I say" and refers to a plea, opinion, expectation, word or speech, account, opinion, or reason (the English word *logic* comes from this root.) Aristotle used it to mean persuasion that appeals to the audience through reasoning and logic to influence their opinions.

Critical Evaluation of Effectiveness of Persuasive Methods

First, readers should identify the author's **thesis**—what he or she argues for or against. They should consider the argument's content and the author's reason for presenting it. Does the author offer **solutions** to problems raised? If so, are they realistic? Note all central ideas and evidence supporting the author's thesis. Research any unfamiliar subjects or vocabulary. Readers should then outline or summarize the work in their own words. Identify which types of appeals the author uses. Readers should evaluate how well the author communicated meaning from the reader's perspective: Did they respond to emotional appeals with anger, concern, happiness, etc.? If so, why? Decide if the author's reasoning sufficed for changing the reader's mind. Determine whether the content and presentation were accurate, cohesive, and clear. Readers should also ask themselves whether they found the author believable or not, and why or why not.

Evaluating an Argument

Argumentative and persuasive passages take a stand on a debatable issue, seek to explore all sides of the issue, and find the best possible solution. Argumentative and persuasive passages should not be combative or abusive. The word *argument* may remind you of two or more people shouting at each other and walking away in anger. However, an argumentative or persuasive passage should be a calm and reasonable presentation of an author's ideas for others to consider. When an author writes reasonable arguments, his or her goal is not to win or have the last word. Instead, authors want to reveal current understanding of the question at hand and suggest a solution to a problem. The purpose of argument and persuasion in a free society is to reach the best solution.

Evidence

The term **text evidence** refers to information that supports a main point or minor points and can help lead the reader to a conclusion about the text's credibility. Information used as text evidence is precise, descriptive, and factual. A main point is often followed by supporting details that provide evidence to back up a claim. For example, a passage may include the claim that winter occurs during opposite months in the Northern and Southern hemispheres. Text evidence for this claim may include examples of countries where winter occurs in opposite months. Stating that the tilt of the Earth as it rotates around the sun causes winter to occur at different times in separate hemispheres is another example of text evidence. Text evidence can come from common knowledge, but it is also valuable to include text evidence from credible, relevant outside sources.

Review Video: Textual Evidence
Visit mometrix.com/academy and enter code: 486236

Evidence that supports the thesis and additional arguments needs to be provided. Most arguments must be supported by facts or statistics. A fact is something that is known with certainty, has been verified by several independent individuals, and can be proven to be true. In addition to facts, examples and illustrations can support an argument by adding an emotional component. With this component, you persuade readers in ways that facts and statistics cannot. The emotional component is effective when used alongside objective information that can be confirmed.

Credibility

The text used to support an argument can be the argument's downfall if the text is not credible. A text is **credible**, or believable, when its author is knowledgeable and objective, or unbiased. The author's motivations for writing the text play a critical role in determining the credibility of the text and must be evaluated when assessing that credibility. Reports written about the ozone layer by an environmental scientist and a hairdresser will have a different level of credibility.

Review Video: Author Credibility
Visit mometrix.com/academy and enter code: 827257

Appeal to Emotion

Sometimes, authors will appeal to the reader's emotion in an attempt to persuade or to distract the reader from the weakness of the argument. For instance, the author may try to inspire the pity of the reader by delivering a heart-rending story. An author also might use the bandwagon approach, in which he suggests that his opinion is correct because it is held by the majority. Some authors resort to name-calling, in which insults and harsh words are delivered to the opponent in an attempt to distract. In advertising, a common appeal is the celebrity testimonial, in which a famous person endorses a product. Of course, the fact that a famous person likes something should not really mean anything to the reader. These and other emotional appeals are usually evidence of poor reasoning and a weak argument.

Review Video: Emotional Language in Literature
Visit mometrix.com/academy and enter code: 759390

Counter Arguments

When authors give both sides to the argument, they build trust with their readers. As a reader, you should start with an undecided or neutral position. If an author presents only his or her side to the argument, then they are not exhibiting credibility and are weakening their argument.

Building common ground with readers can be effective for persuading neutral, skeptical, or opposed readers. Sharing values with undecided readers can allow people to switch positions without giving up what they feel is important. People who may oppose a position need to feel that they can change their minds without betraying who they are as a person. This appeal to having an open mind can be a powerful tool in arguing a position without antagonizing other views. Objections can be countered on a point-by-point basis or in a summary paragraph. Be mindful of how an author points out flaws in counter arguments. If they are unfair to the other side of the argument, then you should lose trust with the author.

Rhetorical Devices

- An **anecdote** is a brief story authors may relate to their argument, which can illustrate their points in a more real and relatable way.
- **Aphorisms** concisely state common beliefs and may rhyme. For example, Benjamin Franklin's "Early to bed and early to rise / Makes a man healthy, wealthy, and wise" is an aphorism.
- **Allusions** refer to literary or historical figures to impart symbolism to a thing or person and to create reader resonance. In John Steinbeck's *Of Mice and Men,* protagonist George's last name is Milton. This alludes to John Milton, who wrote *Paradise Lost*, and symbolizes George's eventual loss of his dream.
- **Satire** exaggerates, ridicules, or pokes fun at human flaws or ideas, as in the works of Jonathan Swift and Mark Twain.
- A **parody** is a form of satire that imitates another work to ridicule its topic or style.
- A **paradox** is a statement that is true despite appearing contradictory.
- **Hyperbole** is overstatement using exaggerated language.
- An **oxymoron** combines seeming contradictions, such as "deafening silence."
- **Analogies** compare two things that share common elements.
- **Similes** (stated comparisons using the words *like* or *as*) and **metaphors** (stated comparisons that do not use *like* or *as*) are considered forms of analogy.
- When using logic to reason with audiences, **syllogism** refers either to deductive reasoning or a deceptive, very sophisticated, or subtle argument.
- **Deductive reasoning** moves from general to specific, **inductive reasoning** from specific to general.
- **Diction** is author word choice that establishes tone and effect.
- **Understatement** achieves effects like contrast or irony by downplaying or describing something more subtly than warranted.

- **Chiasmus** uses parallel clauses, the second reversing the order of the first. Examples include T. S. Eliot's "Has the Church failed mankind, or has mankind failed the Church?" and John F. Kennedy's "Ask not what your country can do for you; ask what you can do for your country."
- **Anaphora** regularly repeats a word or phrase at the beginnings of consecutive clauses or phrases to add emphasis to an idea. A classic example of anaphora was Winston Churchill's emphasis of determination: "[W]e shall fight on the beaches, we shall fight on the landing grounds, we shall fight in the fields and in the streets, we shall fight in the hills; we shall never surrender..."

Chapter Quiz

1. Which of the following rhetorical devices exaggerates, ridicules, or pokes fun at human flaws or ideas?

a. Allusions
b. Satire
c. Parody
d. Hyperbole

2. An author arguing that his point is correct because everybody else already agrees with it is an example of which persuasive technique?

a. Appeal to laziness
b. Bandwagon appeal
c. Testimonials
d. Generalizations

Chapter Quiz Answer Key

1. B: Rhetorical devices:

- An anecdote is a brief story authors may relate to their argument, which can illustrate their points in a more real and relatable way.
- Aphorisms concisely state common beliefs and may rhyme. For example, Benjamin Franklin's "Early to bed and early to rise / Makes a man healthy, wealthy, and wise" is an aphorism.
- Allusions refer to literary or historical figures to impart symbolism to a thing or person and to create reader resonance. In John Steinbeck's *Of Mice and Men,* protagonist George's last name is Milton. This alludes to John Milton, who wrote *Paradise Lost*, and symbolizes George's eventual loss of his dream.
- Satire exaggerates, ridicules, or pokes fun at human flaws or ideas, as in the works of Jonathan Swift and Mark Twain.
- A parody is a form of satire that imitates another work to ridicule its topic or style.
- A paradox is a statement that is true despite appearing contradictory.
- Hyperbole is overstatement using exaggerated language.
- An oxymoron combines seeming contradictions, such as "deafening silence."
- Analogies compare two things that share common elements.
- Similes (stated comparisons using the words *like* or *as*) and metaphors (stated comparisons that do not use *like* or *as*) are considered forms of analogy.
- When using logic to reason with audiences, syllogism refers either to deductive reasoning or a deceptive, very sophisticated, or subtle argument.

- Deductive reasoning moves from general to specific, while inductive reasoning moves from specific to general.
- Diction is author word choice that establishes tone and effect.
- Understatement achieves effects like contrast or irony by downplaying or describing something more subtly than warranted.
- Chiasmus uses parallel clauses, with the second clause reversing the order of the first. Examples include T. S. Eliot's "Has the Church failed mankind, or has mankind failed the Church?" and John F. Kennedy's "Ask not what your country can do for you—ask what you can do for your country."
- Anaphora regularly repeats a word or phrase at the beginnings of consecutive clauses or phrases to add emphasis to an idea. A classic example of anaphora was Winston Churchill's emphasis of determination: "[W]e shall fight on the beaches, we shall fight on the landing grounds, we shall fight in the fields and in the streets, we shall fight in the hills; we shall never surrender..."

2. B: Bandwagon appeals claim that everybody else agrees with the author's argument and thus try to persuade readers to conform and agree as well.

Author's Argument in Argumentative Writing

In argumentative writing, the argument is a belief, position, or opinion that the author wants to convince readers to believe as well. For the first step, readers should identify the **issue**. Some issues are controversial, meaning people disagree about them. Gun control, foreign policy, and the death penalty are all controversial issues. The next step is to determine the **author's position** on the issue. That position or viewpoint constitutes the author's argument. Readers should then identify the **author's assumptions**: things he or she accepts, believes, or takes for granted without needing proof. Inaccurate or illogical assumptions produce flawed arguments and can mislead readers. Readers should identify what kinds of **supporting evidence** the author offers, such as research results, personal observations or experiences, case studies, facts, examples, expert testimony and opinions, and comparisons. Readers should decide how relevant this support is to the argument.

Review Video: Argumentative Writing
Visit mometrix.com/academy and enter code: 561544

Evaluating an Author's Argument

The first three reader steps to **evaluate an author's argument** are to identify the **author's assumptions**, identify the **supporting evidence**, and decide **whether the evidence is relevant**. For example, if an author is not an expert on a particular topic, then that author's personal experience or opinion might not be relevant. The fourth step is to assess the **author's objectivity**. For example, consider whether the author introduces clear, understandable supporting evidence and facts to support the argument. The fifth step is evaluating whether the author's **argument is complete**. When authors give sufficient support for their arguments and also anticipate and respond effectively to opposing arguments or objections to their points, their arguments are complete. However, some authors omit information that could detract from their arguments. If instead they stated this information and refuted it, it would strengthen their arguments. The sixth step in evaluating an author's argumentative writing is to assess whether the **argument is valid**. Providing clear, logical reasoning makes an author's argument valid. Readers should ask themselves whether the author's points follow a sequence that makes sense, and whether each point leads to the next. The seventh step is to determine whether the author's **argument is credible**, meaning that it is convincing and believable. Arguments that are not valid are not credible, so step seven depends on step six. Readers should be mindful of their own biases as they evaluate and should not expect authors to conclusively prove their arguments, but rather to provide effective support and reason.

Evaluating an Author's Method of Appeal

To evaluate the effectiveness of an appeal, it is important to consider the author's purpose for writing. Any appeals an author uses in their argument must be relevant to the argument's goal. For example, a writer that argues for the reclassification of Pluto, but primarily uses appeals to emotion, will not have an effective argument. This writer should focus on using appeals to logic and support their argument with provable facts. While most arguments should include appeals to logic, emotion, and credibility, some arguments only call for one or two of these types of appeal. Evidence can support an appeal, but the evidence must be relevant to truly strengthen the appeal's effectiveness. If the writer arguing for Pluto's reclassification uses the reasons for Jupiter's classification as evidence, their argument would be weak. This information may seem relevant because it is related to the classification of planets. However, this classification is highly dependent on the size of the celestial object, and Jupiter is significantly bigger than Pluto. This use of evidence is illogical and does not support the appeal. Even when appropriate evidence and appeals are used, appeals and arguments lose their effectiveness when they create logical fallacies.

Opinions, Facts, and Fallacies

Critical thinking skills are mastered through understanding various types of writing and the different purposes of authors can have for writing different passages. Every author writes for a purpose. When you understand their purpose and how they accomplish their goal, you will be able to analyze their writing and determine whether or not you agree with their conclusions.

Readers must always be aware of the difference between fact and opinion. A **fact** can be subjected to analysis and proven to be true. An **opinion**, on the other hand, is the author's personal thoughts or feelings and may not be altered by research or evidence. If the author writes that the distance from New York City to Boston is about two hundred miles, then he or she is stating a fact. If the author writes that New York City is too crowded, then he or she is giving an opinion because there is no objective standard for overpopulation. Opinions are often supported by facts. For instance, an author might use a comparison between the population density of New York City and that of other major American cities as evidence of an overcrowded population. An opinion supported by facts tends to be more convincing. On the other hand, when authors support their opinions with other opinions, readers should employ critical thinking and approach the argument with skepticism.

Review Video: Fact or Opinion
Visit mometrix.com/academy and enter code: 870899

Reliable Sources

When you have an argumentative passage, you need to be sure that facts are presented to the reader from **reliable sources**. An opinion is what the author thinks about a given topic. An opinion is not common knowledge or proven by expert sources, instead the information is the personal beliefs and thoughts of the author. To distinguish between fact and opinion, a reader needs to consider the type of source that is presenting information, the information that backs-up a claim, and the author's motivation to have a certain point-of-view on a given topic. For example, if a panel of scientists has conducted multiple studies on the effectiveness of taking a certain vitamin, then the results are more likely to be factual than those of a company that is selling a vitamin and simply claims that taking the vitamin can produce positive effects. The company is motivated to sell their product, and the scientists are using the scientific method to prove a theory. Remember, if you find sentences that contain phrases such as "I think...", then the statement is an opinion.

Biases

In their attempts to persuade, writers often make mistakes in their thought processes and writing choices. These processes and choices are important to understand so you can make an informed decision about the author's credibility. Every author has a point of view, but authors demonstrate a **bias** when they ignore reasonable counterarguments or distort opposing viewpoints. A bias is evident whenever the author's claims are presented in a way that is unfair or inaccurate. Bias can be intentional or unintentional, but readers should be skeptical of the author's argument in either case. Remember that a biased author may still be correct. However, the author will be correct in spite of, not because of, his or her bias.

A **stereotype** is a bias applied specifically to a group of people or a place. Stereotyping is considered to be particularly abhorrent because it promotes negative, misleading generalizations about people. Readers should be very cautious of authors who use stereotypes in their writing. These faulty assumptions typically reveal the author's ignorance and lack of curiosity.

Review Video: Bias and Stereotype
Visit mometrix.com/academy and enter code: 644829

Chapter Quiz

1. Which of the following is NOT one of the first three steps of evaluating an author's argument?

a. Identify the author's assumptions
b. Identify the supporting evidence
c. Evaluate if the author's argument is complete
d. Decide if the supporting evidence is relevant

Chapter Quiz Answer Key

1. C: The first three reader steps to evaluate an author's argument are to identify the author's assumptions, identify the supporting evidence, and decide whether the evidence is relevant. For example, if an author is not an expert on a particular topic, then that author's personal experience or opinion might not be relevant. The fourth step is to assess the author's objectivity. For example, consider whether the author introduces clear, understandable supporting evidence and facts to support the argument. The fifth step is evaluating whether the author's argument is complete. When authors give sufficient support for their arguments and also anticipate and respond effectively to opposing arguments or objections to their points, their arguments are complete. However, some authors omit information that could detract from their arguments. If instead they stated this information and refuted it, it would likely strengthen their arguments. The sixth step in evaluating an author's argumentative writing is to assess whether the argument is valid. Providing clear, logical reasoning makes an author's argument valid. Readers should ask themselves whether the author's points follow a sequence that makes sense, and whether each point leads to the next. The seventh step is to determine whether the author's argument is credible, meaning that it is convincing and believable. Arguments that are not valid are not credible, so step seven depends on step six. Readers should be mindful of their own biases as they evaluate and should not expect authors to conclusively prove their arguments, but rather to provide effective support and reason.

Writing and Language Test

Expression of Ideas

Brainstorming

Brainstorming is a technique that is used to find a creative approach to a subject. This can be accomplished by simple **free-association** with a topic. For example, with paper and pen, write every thought that you have about the topic in a word or phrase. This is done without critical thinking. You should put everything that comes to your mind about the topic on your scratch paper. Then, you need to read the list over a few times. Next, look for patterns, repetitions, and clusters of ideas. This allows a variety of fresh ideas to come as you think about the topic.

Free Writing

Free writing is a more structured form of brainstorming. The method involves taking a limited amount of time (e.g., 2 to 3 minutes) to write everything that comes to mind about the topic in complete sentences. When time expires, review everything that has been written down. Many of your sentences may make little or no sense, but the insights and observations that can come from free writing make this method a valuable approach. Usually, free writing results in a fuller expression of ideas than brainstorming because thoughts and associations are written in complete sentences. However, both techniques can be used to complement each other.

Planning

Planning is the process of organizing a piece of writing before composing a draft. Planning can include creating an outline or a graphic organizer, such as a Venn diagram, a spider-map, or a flowchart. These methods should help the writer identify their topic, main ideas, and the general organization of the composition. Preliminary research can also take place during this stage. Planning helps writers organize all of their ideas and decide if they have enough material to begin their first draft. However, writers should remember that the decisions they make during this step will likely change later in the process, so their plan does not have to be perfect.

Drafting

Writers may then use their plan, outline, or graphic organizer to compose their first draft. They may write subsequent drafts to improve their writing. Writing multiple drafts can help writers consider different ways to communicate their ideas and address errors that may be difficult to correct without rewriting a section or the whole composition. Most writers will vary in how many drafts they choose to write, as there is no "right" number of drafts. Writing drafts also takes away the pressure to write perfectly on the first try, as writers can improve with each draft they write.

Revising, Editing, and Proofreading

Once a writer completes a draft, they can move on to the revising, editing, and proofreading steps to improve their draft. These steps begin with making broad changes that may apply to large sections of a composition and then making small, specific corrections. **Revising** is the first and broadest of these steps. Revising involves ensuring that the composition addresses an appropriate audience, includes all necessary material, maintains focus throughout, and is organized logically. Revising may occur after the first draft to ensure that the following drafts improve upon errors from the first draft. Some revision should occur between each draft to avoid repeating these errors. The **editing** phase of writing is narrower than the revising phase. Editing a composition should include steps such as improving transitions between paragraphs, ensuring each paragraph is on topic, and improving the flow of the text. The editing phase may also include correcting grammatical errors that cannot be fixed without significantly altering the text. **Proofreading** involves fixing misspelled words, typos, other grammatical errors, and any remaining surface-level flaws in the composition.

RECURSIVE WRITING PROCESS

However you approach writing, you may find comfort in knowing that the revision process can occur in any order. The **recursive writing process** is not as difficult as the phrase may make it seem. Simply put, the recursive writing process means that you may need to revisit steps after completing other steps. It also implies that the steps are not required to take place in any certain order. Indeed, you may find that planning, drafting, and revising can all take place at about the same time. The writing process involves moving back and forth between planning, drafting, and revising, followed by more planning, more drafting, and more revising until the writing is satisfactory.

Review Video: Recursive Writing Process
Visit mometrix.com/academy and enter code: 951611

TECHNOLOGY IN THE WRITING PROCESS

Modern technology has yielded several tools that can be used to make the writing process more convenient and organized. Word processors and online tools, such as databases and plagiarism detectors, allow much of the writing process to be completed in one place, using one device.

TECHNOLOGY FOR PLANNING AND DRAFTING

For the planning and drafting stages of the writing process, word processors are a helpful tool. These programs also feature formatting tools, allowing users to create their own planning tools or create digital outlines that can be easily converted into sentences, paragraphs, or an entire essay draft. Online databases and references also complement the planning process by providing convenient access to information and sources for research. Word processors also allow users to keep up with their work and update it more easily than if they wrote their work by hand. Online word processors often allow users to collaborate, making group assignments more convenient. These programs also allow users to include illustrations or other supplemental media in their compositions.

TECHNOLOGY FOR REVISING, EDITING, AND PROOFREADING

Word processors also benefit the revising, editing, and proofreading stages of the writing process. Most of these programs indicate errors in spelling and grammar, allowing users to catch minor errors and correct them quickly. There are also websites designed to help writers by analyzing text for deeper errors, such as poor sentence structure, inappropriate complexity, lack of sentence variety, and style issues. These websites can help users fix errors they may not know to look for or may have simply missed. As writers finish these steps, they may benefit from checking their work for any plagiarism. There are several websites and programs that compare text to other documents and publications across the internet and detect any similarities within the text. These websites show the source of the similar information, so users know whether or not they referenced the source and unintentionally plagiarized its contents.

TECHNOLOGY FOR PUBLISHING

Technology also makes managing written work more convenient. Digitally storing documents keeps everything in one place and is easy to reference. Digital storage also makes sharing work easier, as documents can be attached to an email or stored online. This also allows writers to publish their work easily, as they can electronically submit it to other publications or freely post it to a personal blog, profile, or website.

Chapter Quiz

1. Which of the following is a more structured form of brainstorming?

a. Free writing
b. Planning
c. Drafting
d. Proofreading

Chapter Quiz Answer Key

1. A: Free writing is a more structured form of brainstorming. The method involves taking a limited amount of time (e.g., two to three minutes) to write everything that comes to mind about the topic in complete sentences. When time expires, review everything that has been written down. Many of the sentences may make little or no sense, but the insights and observations that can come from free writing make this method a valuable approach. Usually, free writing results in a fuller expression of ideas than brainstorming because thoughts and associations are written in complete sentences. However, both techniques can be used to complement each other.

Main Ideas, Supporting Details, and Outlining a Topic

A writer often begins the first paragraph of a paper by stating the **main idea** or point, also known as the **topic sentence**. The rest of the paragraph supplies particular details that develop and support the main point. One way to visualize the relationship between the main point and supporting information is by considering a table: the tabletop is the main point, and each of the table's legs is a supporting detail or group of details. Both professional authors and students can benefit from planning their writing by first making an outline of the topic. Outlines facilitate quick identification of the main point and supporting details without having to wade through the additional language that will exist in the fully developed essay, article, or paper. Outlining can also help readers to analyze a piece of existing writing for the same reason. The outline first summarizes the main idea in one sentence. Then, below that, it summarizes the supporting details in a numbered list. Writing the paper then consists of filling in the outline with detail, writing a paragraph for each supporting point, and adding an introduction and conclusion.

Introduction

The purpose of the introduction is to capture the reader's attention and announce the essay's main idea. Normally, the introduction contains 50-80 words, or 3-5 sentences. An introduction can begin with an interesting quote, a question, or a strong opinion—something that will **engage** the reader's interest and prompt them to keep reading. If you are writing your essay to a specific prompt, your introduction should include a **restatement or summarization** of the prompt so that the reader will have some context for your essay. Finally, your introduction should briefly state your **thesis or main idea**: the primary thing you hope to communicate to the reader through your essay. Don't try to include all of the details and nuances of your thesis, or all of your reasons for it, in the introduction. That's what the rest of the essay is for!

Review Video: Introduction
Visit mometrix.com/academy and enter code: 961328

Thesis Statement

The thesis is the main idea of the essay. A temporary thesis, or working thesis, should be established early in the writing process because it will serve to keep the writer focused as ideas develop. This temporary thesis is subject to change as you continue to write.

The temporary thesis has two parts: a **topic** (i.e., the focus of your essay based on the prompt) and a **comment**. The comment makes an important point about the topic. A temporary thesis should be interesting and specific. Also, you need to limit the topic to a manageable scope. These three questions are useful tools to measure the effectiveness of any temporary thesis:

- Does the focus of my essay have enough interest to hold an audience?
- Is the focus of my essay specific enough to generate interest?
- Is the focus of my essay manageable for the time limit? Too broad? Too narrow?

The thesis should be a generalization rather than a fact because the thesis prepares readers for facts and details that support the thesis. The process of bringing the thesis into sharp focus may help in outlining major sections of the work. Once the thesis and introduction are complete, you can address the body of the work.

Review Video: Thesis Statements
Visit mometrix.com/academy and enter code: 691033

Supporting the Thesis

Throughout your essay, the thesis should be **explained clearly and supported** adequately by additional arguments. The thesis sentence needs to contain a clear statement of the purpose of your essay and a comment about the thesis. With the thesis statement, you have an opportunity to state what is noteworthy of this particular treatment of the prompt. Each sentence and paragraph should build on and support the thesis.

When you respond to the prompt, use parts of the passage to support your argument or defend your position. Using supporting evidence from the passage strengths your argument because readers can see your attention to the entire passage and your response to the details and facts within the passage. You can use facts, details, statistics, and direct quotations from the passage to uphold your position. Be sure to point out which information comes from the original passage and base your argument around that evidence.

Body

In an essay's introduction, the writer establishes the thesis and may indicate how the rest of the piece will be structured. In the body of the piece, the writer **elaborates** upon, **illustrates**, and **explains** the **thesis statement**. How writers arrange supporting details and their choices of paragraph types are development techniques. Writers may give examples of the concept introduced in the thesis statement. If the subject includes a cause-and-effect relationship, the author may explain its causality. A writer will explain or analyze the main idea of the piece throughout the body, often by presenting arguments for the veracity or credibility of the thesis statement. Writers may use development to define or clarify ambiguous terms. Paragraphs within the body may be organized using natural sequences, like space and time. Writers may employ **inductive reasoning**, using multiple details to establish a generalization or causal relationship, or **deductive reasoning**, proving a generalized hypothesis or proposition through a specific example or case.

Review Video: Drafting Body Paragraphs
Visit mometrix.com/academy and enter code: 724590

Paragraphs

After the introduction of a passage, a series of body paragraphs will carry a message through to the conclusion. Each paragraph should be **unified around a main point**. Normally, a good topic sentence summarizes the paragraph's main point. A topic sentence is a general sentence that gives an introduction to the paragraph.

The sentences that follow support the topic sentence. However, though it is usually the first sentence, the topic sentence can come as the final sentence to the paragraph if the earlier sentences give a clear explanation of the paragraph's topic. This allows the topic sentence to function as a concluding sentence. Overall, the paragraphs need to stay true to the main point. This means that any unnecessary sentences that do not advance the main point should be removed.

The main point of a paragraph requires adequate development (i.e., a substantial paragraph that covers the main point). A paragraph of two or three sentences does not cover a main point. This is especially true when the main point of the paragraph gives strong support to the argument of the thesis. An occasional short paragraph is fine as a transitional device. However, a well-developed argument will have paragraphs with more than a few sentences.

Methods of Developing Paragraphs

Common methods of adding substance to paragraphs include examples, illustrations, analogies, and cause and effect.

- **Examples** are supporting details to the main idea of a paragraph or a passage. When authors write about something that their audience may not understand, they can provide an example to show their point. When authors write about something that is not easily accepted, they can give examples to prove their point.
- **Illustrations** are extended examples that require several sentences. Well-selected illustrations can be a great way for authors to develop a point that may not be familiar to their audience.
- **Analogies** make comparisons between items that appear to have nothing in common. Analogies are employed by writers to provoke fresh thoughts about a subject. These comparisons may be used to explain the unfamiliar, to clarify an abstract point, or to argue a point. Although analogies are effective literary devices, they should be used carefully in arguments. Two things may be alike in some respects but completely different in others.
- **Cause and effect** is an excellent device to explain the connection between an action or situation and a particular result. One way that authors can use cause and effect is to state the effect in the topic sentence of a paragraph and add the causes in the body of the paragraph. This method can give an author's paragraphs structure, which always strengthens writing.

Types of Paragraphs

A **paragraph of narration** tells a story or a part of a story. Normally, the sentences are arranged in chronological order (i.e., the order that the events happened). However, flashbacks (i.e., an anecdote from an earlier time) can be included.

A **descriptive paragraph** makes a verbal portrait of a person, place, or thing. When specific details are used that appeal to one or more of the senses (i.e., sight, sound, smell, taste, and touch), authors give readers a sense of being present in the moment.

A **process paragraph** is related to time order (i.e., First, you open the bottle. Second, you pour the liquid, etc.). Usually, this describes a process or teaches readers how to perform a process.

Comparing two things draws attention to their similarities and indicates a number of differences. When authors contrast, they focus only on differences. Both comparing and contrasting may be done point-by-point, noting both the similarities and differences of each point, or in sequential paragraphs, where you discuss all the similarities and then all the differences, or vice versa.

BREAKING TEXT INTO PARAGRAPHS

For most forms of writing, you will need to use multiple paragraphs. As such, determining when to start a new paragraph is very important. Reasons for starting a new paragraph include:

- To mark off the introduction and concluding paragraphs
- To signal a shift to a new idea or topic
- To indicate an important shift in time or place
- To explain a point in additional detail
- To highlight a comparison, contrast, or cause and effect relationship

PARAGRAPH LENGTH

Most readers find that their comfort level for a paragraph is between 100 and 200 words. Shorter paragraphs cause too much starting and stopping and give a choppy effect. Paragraphs that are too long often test the attention span of readers. Two notable exceptions to this rule exist. In scientific or scholarly papers, longer paragraphs suggest seriousness and depth. In journalistic writing, constraints are placed on paragraph size by the narrow columns in a newspaper format.

The first and last paragraphs of a text will usually be the introduction and conclusion. These special-purpose paragraphs are likely to be shorter than paragraphs in the body of the work. Paragraphs in the body of the essay follow the subject's outline (e.g., one paragraph per point in short essays and a group of paragraphs per point in longer works). Some ideas require more development than others, so it is good for a writer to remain flexible. A paragraph of excessive length may be divided, and shorter ones may be combined.

COHERENT PARAGRAPHS

A smooth flow of sentences and paragraphs without gaps, shifts, or bumps will lead to paragraph **coherence**. Ties between old and new information can be smoothed using several methods:

- **Linking ideas clearly**, from the topic sentence to the body of the paragraph, is essential for a smooth transition. The topic sentence states the main point, and this should be followed by specific details, examples, and illustrations that support the topic sentence. The support may be direct or indirect. In **indirect support**, the illustrations and examples may support a sentence that in turn supports the topic directly.
- The **repetition of key words** adds coherence to a paragraph. To avoid dull language, variations of the key words may be used.
- **Parallel structures** are often used within sentences to emphasize the similarity of ideas and connect sentences giving similar information.
- Maintaining a **consistent verb tense** throughout the paragraph helps. Shifting tenses affects the smooth flow of words and can disrupt the coherence of the paragraph.

Review Video: How to Write a Good Paragraph
Visit mometrix.com/academy and enter code: 682127

SEQUENCE WORDS AND PHRASES

When a paragraph opens with the topic sentence, the second sentence may begin with a phrase like *first of all*, introducing the first supporting detail or example. The writer may introduce the second supporting item with words or phrases like *also*, *in addition*, and *besides*. The writer might introduce succeeding pieces of support with wording like, *another thing, moreover, furthermore,* or *not only that, but.* The writer may introduce the last piece of support with *lastly, finally,* or *last but not least.* Writers get off the point by presenting off-target items not supporting the main point. For example, a main point *my dog is not smart* is supported by the statement, *he's six years old and still doesn't answer to his name.* But *he cries when I leave for school* is not supportive, as it does not indicate lack of intelligence. Writers stay on point by presenting only supportive statements that are directly relevant to and illustrative of their main point.

Review Video: Sequence
Visit mometrix.com/academy and enter code: 489027

TRANSITIONS

Transitions between sentences and paragraphs guide readers from idea to idea and indicate relationships between sentences and paragraphs. Writers should be judicious in their use of transitions, inserting them sparingly. They should also be selected to fit the author's purpose—transitions can indicate time, comparison, and conclusion, among other purposes. Tone is also important to consider when using transitional phrases, varying the tone for different audiences. For example, in a scholarly essay, *in summary* would be preferable to the more informal *in short.*

When working with transitional words and phrases, writers usually find a natural flow that indicates when a transition is needed. In reading a draft of the text, it should become apparent where the flow is disrupted. At this point, the writer can add transitional elements during the revision process. Revising can also afford an opportunity to delete transitional devices that seem heavy handed or unnecessary.

Review Video: Transitions in Writing
Visit mometrix.com/academy and enter code: 233246

Types of Transitional Words

Time	Afterward, immediately, earlier, meanwhile, recently, lately, now, since, soon, when, then, until, before, etc.
Sequence	too, first, second, further, moreover, also, again, and, next, still, besides, finally
Comparison	similarly, in the same way, likewise, also, again, once more
Contrasting	but, although, despite, however, instead, nevertheless, on the one hand... on the other hand, regardless, yet, in contrast.
Cause and Effect	because, consequently, thus, therefore, then, to this end, since, so, as a result, if... then, accordingly
Examples	for example, for instance, such as, to illustrate, indeed, in fact, specifically
Place	near, far, here, there, to the left/right, next to, above, below, beyond, opposite, beside
Concession	granted that, naturally, of course, it may appear, although it is true that
Repetition, Summary, or Conclusion	as mentioned earlier, as noted, in other words, in short, on the whole, to summarize, therefore, as a result, to conclude, in conclusion
Addition	and, also, furthermore, moreover
Generalization	in broad terms, broadly speaking, in general

Review Video: Transitional Words and Phrases
Visit mometrix.com/academy and enter code: 197796

Review Video: What are Transition Words?
Visit mometrix.com/academy and enter code: 707563

Review Video: How to Effectively Connect Sentences
Visit mometrix.com/academy and enter code: 948325

Conclusion

Two important principles to consider when writing a conclusion are strength and closure. A strong conclusion gives the reader a sense that the author's main points are meaningful and important, and that the supporting facts and arguments are convincing, solid, and well developed. When a conclusion achieves closure, it gives the impression that the writer has stated all necessary information and points and completed the work, rather than simply stopping after a specified length. Some things to avoid when writing concluding paragraphs include:

- Introducing a completely new idea
- Beginning with obvious or unoriginal phrases like "In conclusion" or "To summarize"
- Apologizing for one's opinions or writing
- Repeating the thesis word for word rather than rephrasing it
- Believing that the conclusion must always summarize the piece

Review Video: Drafting Conclusions
Visit mometrix.com/academy and enter code: 209408

Chapter Quiz

1. Which of the following is considered the main idea of an essay?

a. Topic
b. Body
c. Theme
d. Thesis

2. Which of the following are supporting details to the main idea of a paragraph or a passage?

a. Analogies
b. Examples
c. Cause and effect
d. Transitions

3. Which of the following is NOT a transitional word or phrase in the concession category?

a. Granted that
b. Naturally
c. Broadly speaking
d. It may appear

Chapter Quiz Answer Key

1. D: The thesis is the main idea of an essay. A temporary thesis, or working thesis, should be established early in the writing process because it will serve to keep the writer focused as ideas develop. This temporary thesis is subject to change as writing continues. The thesis should be a generalization rather than a fact because the thesis prepares readers for facts and details that support the thesis. The process of bringing the thesis into sharp focus may help in outlining major sections of the work. Once the thesis and introduction are complete, the body of the work can be addressed.

2. B: Examples are supporting details to the main idea of a paragraph or a passage. When authors write about something that their audience may not understand or that is not easily accepted, they can provide an example to show their point.

3. C: Types of transitional words

Time	Afterward, immediately, earlier, meanwhile, recently, lately, now, since, soon, when, then, until, before, etc.
Sequence	Too, first, second, further, moreover, also, again, and, next, still, besides, finally
Comparison	Similarly, in the same way, likewise, also, again, once more
Contrasting	But, although, despite, however, instead, nevertheless, on the one hand... on the other hand, regardless, yet, in contrast.
Cause and effect	Because, consequently, thus, therefore, then, to this end, since, so, as a result, if... then, accordingly
Examples	For example, for instance, such as, to illustrate, indeed, in fact, specifically
Place	Near, far, here, there, to the left/right, next to, above, below, beyond, opposite, beside
Concession	Granted that, naturally, of course, it may appear, although it is true that
Repetition, summary, or conclusion	As mentioned earlier, as noted, in other words, in short, on the whole, to summarize, therefore, as a result, to conclude, in conclusion
Addition	And, also, furthermore, moreover
Generalization	In broad terms, broadly speaking, in general

Writing Style and Linguistic Form

Linguistic form encodes the literal meanings of words and sentences. It comes from the phonological, morphological, syntactic, and semantic parts of a language. **Writing style** consists of different ways of encoding the meaning and indicating figurative and stylistic meanings. An author's writing style can also be referred to as his or her **voice**.

Writers' stylistic choices accomplish three basic effects on their audiences:

- They **communicate meanings** beyond linguistically dictated meanings,
- They communicate the **author's attitude**, such as persuasive or argumentative effects accomplished through style, and
- They communicate or **express feelings**.

Within style, component areas include:

- Narrative structure
- Viewpoint
- Focus
- Sound patterns
- Meter and rhythm
- Lexical and syntactic repetition and parallelism
- Writing genre
- Representational, realistic, and mimetic effects
- Representation of thought and speech
- Meta-representation (representing representation)
- Irony

- Metaphor and other indirect meanings
- Representation and use of historical and dialectal variations
- Gender-specific and other group-specific speech styles, both real and fictitious
- Analysis of the processes for inferring meaning from writing

Level of Formality

The relationship between writer and reader is important in choosing a **level of formality** as most writing requires some degree of formality. **Formal writing** is for addressing a superior in a school or work environment. Business letters, textbooks, and newspapers use a moderate to high level of formality. **Informal writing** is appropriate for private letters, personal emails, and business correspondence between close associates.

For your exam, you will want to be aware of informal and formal writing. One way that this can be accomplished is to watch for shifts in point of view in the essay. For example, unless writers are using a personal example, they will rarely refer to themselves (e.g., "*I* think that *my* point is very clear.") to avoid being informal when they need to be formal.

Also, be mindful of an author who addresses his or her audience **directly** in their writing (e.g., "Readers, *like you*, will understand this argument.") as this can be a sign of informal writing. Good writers understand the need to be consistent with their level of formality. Shifts in levels of formality or point of view can confuse readers and cause them to discount the message.

Clichés

Clichés are phrases that have been **overused** to the point that the phrase has no importance or has lost the original meaning. These phrases have no originality and add very little to a passage. Therefore, most writers will avoid the use of clichés. Another option is to make changes to a cliché so that it is not predictable and empty of meaning.

Examples:

> When life gives you lemons, make lemonade.
>
> Every cloud has a silver lining.

Jargon

Jargon is **specialized vocabulary** that is used among members of a certain trade or profession. Since jargon is understood by only a small audience, writers will use jargon in passages that will only be read by a specialized audience. For example, medical jargon should be used in a medical journal but not in a New York Times article. Jargon includes exaggerated language that tries to impress rather than inform. Sentences filled with jargon are not precise and are difficult to understand.

Examples:

> "He is going to *toenail* these frames for us." (Toenail is construction jargon for nailing at an angle.)
>
> "They brought in a *kip* of material today." (Kip refers to 1000 pounds in architecture and engineering.)

SLANG

Slang is an **informal** and sometimes private language that is understood by some individuals. Slang terms have some usefulness, but they can have a small audience. So, most formal writing will not include this kind of language.

Examples:

> "Yes, the event was a blast!" (In this sentence, *blast* means that the event was a great experience.)
>
> "That attempt was an epic fail." (By *epic fail*, the speaker means that his or her attempt was not a success.)

COLLOQUIALISM

A colloquialism is a word or phrase that is found in informal writing. Unlike slang, **colloquial language** will be familiar to a greater range of people. However, colloquialisms are still considered inappropriate for formal writing. Colloquial language can include some slang, but these are limited to contractions for the most part.

Examples:

> "Can *y'all* come back another time?" (Y'all is a contraction of "you all.")
>
> "Will you stop him from building this *castle in the air*?" (A "castle in the air" is an improbable or unlikely event.)

ACADEMIC LANGUAGE

In educational settings, students are often expected to use academic language in their schoolwork. Academic language is also commonly found in dissertations and theses, texts published by academic journals, and other forms of academic research. Academic language conventions may vary between fields, but general academic language is free of slang, regional terminology, and noticeable grammatical errors. Specific terms may also be used in academic language, and it is important to understand their proper usage. A writer's command of academic language impacts their ability to communicate in an academic or professional context. While it is acceptable to use colloquialisms, slang, improper grammar, or other forms of informal speech in social settings or at home, it is inappropriate to practice non-academic language in academic contexts.

TONE

Tone may be defined as the writer's **attitude** toward the topic, and to the audience. This attitude is reflected in the language used in the writing. The tone of a work should be **appropriate to the topic** and to the intended audience. While it may be fine to use slang or jargon in some pieces, other texts should not contain such terms. Tone can range from humorous to serious and any level in between. It may be more or less formal, depending on the purpose of the writing and its intended audience. All these nuances in tone can flavor the entire writing and should be kept in mind as the work evolves.

WORD SELECTION

A writer's choice of words is a signature of their style. Careful thought about the use of words can improve a piece of writing. A passage can be an exciting piece to read when attention is given to the use of vivid or specific nouns rather than general ones.

Example:

General: His kindness will never be forgotten.

Specific: His thoughtful gifts and bear hugs will never be forgotten.

Attention should also be given to the kind of verbs that are used in sentences. Active verbs (e.g., run, swim) are about an action. Whenever possible, an **active verb should replace a linking verb** to provide clear examples for arguments and to strengthen a passage overall. When using an active verb, one should be sure that the verb is used in the active voice instead of the passive voice. Verbs are in the active voice when the subject is the one doing the action. A verb is in the passive voice when the subject is the recipient of an action.

Example:

Passive: The winners were called to the stage by the judges.

Active: The judges called the winners to the stage.

Conciseness

Conciseness is writing that communicates a message in the fewest words possible. Writing concisely is valuable because short, uncluttered messages allow the reader to understand the author's message more easily and efficiently. Planning is important in writing concise messages. If you have in mind what you need to write beforehand, it will be easier to make a message short and to the point. Do not state the obvious.

Revising is also important. After the message is written, make sure you have effective, pithy sentences that efficiently get your point across. When reviewing the information, imagine a conversation taking place, and concise writing will likely result.

Appropriate Kinds of Writing for Different Tasks, Purposes, and Audiences

When preparing to write a composition, consider the audience and purpose to choose the best type of writing. Three common types of writing are persuasive, expository, and narrative. **Persuasive**, or argumentative writing, is used to convince the audience to take action or agree with the author's claims. **Expository** writing is meant to inform the audience of the author's observations or research on a topic. **Narrative** writing is used to tell the audience a story and often allows more room for creativity. While task, purpose, and audience inform a writer's mode of writing, these factors also impact elements such as tone, vocabulary, and formality.

For example, students who are writing to persuade their parents to grant them some additional privilege, such as permission for a more independent activity, should use more sophisticated vocabulary and diction that sounds more mature and serious to appeal to the parental audience. However, students who are writing for younger children should use simpler vocabulary and sentence structure, as well as choose words that are more vivid and entertaining. They should treat their topics more lightly, and include humor when appropriate. Students who are writing for their classmates may use language that is more informal, as well as age-appropriate.

Review Video: Writing Purpose and Audience
Visit mometrix.com/academy and enter code: 146627

Chapter Quiz

1. Which of the following would NOT be considered formal writing?

a. Private letters
b. Business letters
c. Textbooks
d. Newspapers

2. Which of the following sentences contains a verb in the passive voice?

a. The judges called the winners to the stage for their awards.
b. Each applicant must fill out all of the forms required.
c. He raced through the copse of trees with the grace of a deer.
d. I was told that there would be food available at the party.

Chapter Quiz Answer Key

1. A: The relationship between writer and reader is important in choosing a level of formality because most writing requires some degree of formality. Formal writing is for addressing a superior in a school or work environment. Business letters, textbooks, and newspapers use a moderate to high level of formality. Informal writing is appropriate for private letters, personal emails, and business correspondence between close associates.

2. D: Attention should also be given to the kind of verbs that are used in sentences. Active verbs (e.g., run, swim) are about an action. Whenever possible, an active verb should replace a linking verb to provide clear examples for arguments and to strengthen a passage overall. When using an active verb, one should be sure that the verb is used in the active voice instead of the passive voice. Verbs are in the active voice when the subject is the one doing the action. A verb is in the passive voice when the subject is the recipient of an action.

Essays

Essays usually focus on one topic, subject, or goal. There are several types of essays, including informative, persuasive, and narrative. An essay's structure and level of formality depend on the type of essay and its goal. While narrative essays typically do not include outside sources, other types of essays often require some research and the integration of primary and secondary sources.

The basic format of an essay typically has three major parts: the introduction, the body, and the conclusion. The body is further divided into the writer's main points. Short and simple essays may have three main points, while essays covering broader ranges and going into more depth can have almost any number of main points, depending on length.

An essay's introduction should answer three questions:

1. What is the **subject** of the essay?

   If a student writes an essay about a book, the answer would include the title and author of the book and any additional information needed—such as the subject or argument of the book.

2. How does the essay **address** the subject?

   To answer this, the writer identifies the essay's organization by briefly summarizing main points and the evidence supporting them.

3. What will the essay **prove**?

> This is the thesis statement, usually the opening paragraph's last sentence, clearly stating the writer's message.

The body elaborates on all the main points related to the thesis, introducing one main point at a time, and includes supporting evidence with each main point. Each body paragraph should state the point in a topic sentence, which is usually the first sentence in the paragraph. The paragraph should then explain the point's meaning, support it with quotations or other evidence, and then explain how this point and the evidence are related to the thesis. The writer should then repeat this procedure in a new paragraph for each additional main point.

The conclusion reiterates the content of the introduction, including the thesis, to remind the reader of the essay's main argument or subject. The essay writer may also summarize the highlights of the argument or description contained in the body of the essay, following the same sequence originally used in the body. For example, a conclusion might look like: Point 1 + Point 2 + Point 3 = Thesis, or Point 1 → Point 2 → Point 3 → Thesis Proof. Good organization makes essays easier for writers to compose and provides a guide for readers to follow. Well-organized essays hold attention better and are more likely to get readers to accept their theses as valid.

INFORMATIVE VS. PERSUASIVE WRITING

Informative writing, also called explanatory or expository writing, begins with the basis that something is true or factual, while **persuasive** writing strives to prove something that may or may not be true or factual. Whereas argumentative text is written to **persuade** readers to agree with the author's position, informative text merely **provides information and insight** to readers. Informative writing concentrates on **informing** readers about why or how something is as it is. This can include offering new information, explaining how a process works, and developing a concept for readers. To accomplish these objectives, the essay may name and distinguish various things within a category, provide definitions, provide details about the parts of something, explain a particular function or behavior, and give readers explanations for why a fact, object, event, or process exists or occurs.

NARRATIVE WRITING

Put simply, **narrative** writing tells a story. The most common examples of literary narratives are novels. Non-fictional biographies, autobiographies, memoirs, and histories are also narratives. Narratives should tell stories in such a way that the readers learn something or gain insight or understanding. Students can write more interesting narratives by describing events or experiences that were meaningful to them. Narratives should start with the story's actions or events, rather than long descriptions or introductions. Students should ensure that there is a point to each story by describing what they learned from the experience they narrate. To write an effective description, students should include sensory details, asking themselves what they saw, heard, felt or touched, smelled, and tasted during the experiences they describe. In narrative writing, the details should be **concrete** rather than **abstract**. Using concrete details enables readers to imagine everything that the writer describes.

Review Video: Narratives
Visit mometrix.com/academy and enter code: 280100

SENSORY DETAILS

Students need to use vivid descriptions when writing descriptive essays. Narratives should also include descriptions of characters, things, and events. Students should remember to describe not only the visual detail of what someone or something looks like, but details from other senses, as well. For example, they can contrast the feeling of a sea breeze to that of a mountain breeze, describe how they think something inedible would taste, and compare sounds they hear in the same location at different times of day and night. Readers have trouble visualizing images or imagining sensory impressions and feelings from abstract descriptions, so concrete descriptions make these more real.

Concrete vs. Abstract Descriptions in Narrative

Concrete language provides information that readers can grasp and may empathize with, while **abstract language**, which is more general, can leave readers feeling disconnected, empty, or even confused. "It was a lovely day" is abstract, but "The sun shone brightly, the sky was blue, the air felt warm, and a gentle breeze wafted across my skin" is concrete. "Ms. Couch was a good teacher" uses abstract language, giving only a general idea of the writer's opinion. But "Ms. Couch is excellent at helping us take our ideas and turn them into good essays and stories" uses concrete language, giving more specific examples of what makes Ms. Couch a good teacher. "I like writing poems but not essays" gives readers a general idea that the student prefers one genre over another, but not why. But when reading, "I like writing short poems with rhythm and rhyme, but I hate writing five-page essays that go on and on about the same ideas," readers understand that the student prefers the brevity, rhyme, and meter of short poetry over the length and redundancy of longer prose.

Autobiographical Narratives

Autobiographical narratives are narratives written by an author about an event or period in their life. Autobiographical narratives are written from one person's perspective, in first person, and often include the author's thoughts and feelings alongside their description of the event or period. Structure, style, or theme varies between different autobiographical narratives, since each narrative is personal and specific to its author and his or her experience.

Reflective Essay

A less common type of essay is the reflective essay. **Reflective essays** allow the author to reflect, or think back, on an experience and analyze what they recall. They should consider what they learned from the experience, what they could have done differently, what would have helped them during the experience, or anything else that they have realized from looking back on the experience. Reflection essays incorporate both objective reflection on one's own actions and subjective explanation of thoughts and feelings. These essays can be written for a number of experiences in a formal or informal context.

Journals and Diaries

A **journal** is a personal account of events, experiences, feelings, and thoughts. Many people write journals to express their feelings and thoughts or to help them process experiences they have had. Since journals are **private documents** not meant to be shared with others, writers may not be concerned with grammar, spelling, or other mechanics. However, authors may write journals that they expect or hope to publish someday; in this case, they not only express their thoughts and feelings and process their experiences, but they also attend to their craft in writing them. Some authors compose journals to record a particular time period or a series of related events, such as a cancer diagnosis, treatment, surviving the disease, and how these experiences have changed or affected them. Other experiences someone might include in a journal are recovering from addiction, journeys of spiritual exploration and discovery, time spent in another country, or anything else someone wants to personally document. Journaling can also be therapeutic, as some people use journals to work through feelings of grief over loss or to wrestle with big decisions.

Examples of Diaries in Literature

The Diary of a Young Girl by Dutch Jew Anne Frank (1947) contains her life-affirming, nonfictional diary entries from 1942-1944 while her family hid in an attic from World War II's genocidal Nazis. *Go Ask Alice* (1971) by Beatrice Sparks is a cautionary, fictional novel in the form of diary entries by Alice, an unhappy, rebellious teen who takes LSD, runs away from home and lives with hippies, and eventually returns home. Frank's writing reveals an intelligent, sensitive, insightful girl, raised by intellectual European parents—a girl who believes in the goodness of human nature despite surrounding atrocities. Alice, influenced by early 1970s counterculture, becomes less optimistic. However, similarities can be found between them: Frank dies in a Nazi concentration camp while the fictitious Alice dies from a drug overdose. Both young women are also unable to escape their surroundings. Additionally, adolescent searches for personal identity are evident in both books.

Review Video: Journals, Diaries, Letters, and Blogs
Visit mometrix.com/academy and enter code: 432845

Letters

Letters are messages written to other people. In addition to letters written between individuals, some writers compose letters to the editors of newspapers, magazines, and other publications, while some write "Open Letters" to be published and read by the general public. Open letters, while intended for everyone to read, may also identify a group of people or a single person whom the letter directly addresses. In everyday use, the most-used forms are business letters and personal or friendly letters. Both kinds share common elements: business or personal letterhead stationery; the writer's return address at the top; the addressee's address next; a salutation, such as "Dear [name]" or some similar opening greeting, followed by a colon in business letters or a comma in personal letters; the body of the letter, with paragraphs as indicated; and a closing, like "Sincerely/Cordially/Best regards/etc." or "Love," in intimate personal letters.

Early Letters

The Greek word for "letter" is *epistolē*, which became the English word "epistle." The earliest letters were called epistles, including the New Testament's epistles from the apostles to the Christians. In ancient Egypt, the writing curriculum in scribal schools included the epistolary genre. Epistolary novels frame a story in the form of letters. Examples of noteworthy epistolary novels include:

- *Pamela* (1740), by 18th-century English novelist Samuel Richardson
- *Shamela* (1741), Henry Fielding's satire of *Pamela* that mocked epistolary writing.
- *Lettres persanes* (1721) by French author Montesquieu
- *The Sorrows of Young Werther* (1774) by German author Johann Wolfgang von Goethe
- *The History of Emily Montague* (1769), the first Canadian novel, by Frances Brooke
- *Dracula* (1897) by Bram Stoker
- *Frankenstein* (1818) by Mary Shelley
- *The Color Purple* (1982) by Alice Walker

Blogs

The word "blog" is derived from "weblog" and refers to writing done exclusively on the internet. Readers of reputable newspapers expect quality content and layouts that enable easy reading. These expectations also apply to blogs. For example, readers can easily move visually from line to line when columns are narrow, while overly wide columns cause readers to lose their places. Blogs must also be posted with layouts enabling online readers to follow them easily. However, because the way people read on computer, tablet, and smartphone screens differs from how they read print on paper, formatting and writing blog content is more complex than writing newspaper articles. Two major principles are the bases for blog-writing rules: The first is while readers of print articles skim to estimate their length, online they must scroll down to scan; therefore, blog layouts need more subheadings, graphics, and other indications of what information follows. The second is onscreen reading can be harder on the eyes than reading printed paper, so legibility is crucial in blogs.

Rules and Rationales for Writing Blogs

1. Format all posts for smooth page layout and easy scanning.
2. Column width should not be too wide, as larger lines of text can be difficult to read
3. Headings and subheadings separate text visually, enable scanning or skimming, and encourage continued reading.
4. Bullet-pointed or numbered lists enable quick information location and scanning.
5. Punctuation is critical, so beginners should use shorter sentences until confident in their knowledge of punctuation rules.
6. Blog paragraphs should be far shorter—two to six sentences each—than paragraphs written on paper to enable "chunking" because reading onscreen is more difficult.
7. Sans-serif fonts are usually clearer than serif fonts, and larger font sizes are better.
8. Highlight important material and draw attention with **boldface**, but avoid overuse. Avoid hard-to-read *italics* and ALL CAPITALS.
9. Include enough blank spaces: overly busy blogs tire eyes and brains. Images not only break up text but also emphasize and enhance text and can attract initial reader attention.
10. Use background colors judiciously to avoid distracting the eye or making it difficult to read.
11. Be consistent throughout posts, since people read them in different orders.
12. Tell a story with a beginning, middle, and end.

Specialized Modes of Writing

Editorials

Editorials are articles in newspapers, magazines, and other serial publications. Editorials express an opinion or belief belonging to the majority of the publication's leadership. This opinion or belief generally refers to a specific issue, topic, or event. These articles are authored by a member, or a small number of members, of the publication's leadership and are often written to affect their readers, such as persuading them to adopt a stance or take a particular action.

Resumes

Resumes are brief, but formal, documents that outline an individual's experience in a certain area. Resumes are most often used for job applications. Such resumes will list the applicant's work experience, certification, and achievements or qualifications related to the position. Resumes should only include the most pertinent information. They should also use strategic formatting to highlight the applicant's most impressive experiences and achievements, to ensure the document can be read quickly and easily, and to eliminate both visual clutter and excessive negative space.

Reports

Reports summarize the results of research, new methodology, or other developments in an academic or professional context. Reports often include details about methodology and outside influences and factors. However, a report should focus primarily on the results of the research or development. Reports are objective and deliver information efficiently, sacrificing style for clear and effective communication.

Memoranda

A memorandum, also called a memo, is a formal method of communication used in professional settings. Memoranda are printed documents that include a heading listing the sender and their job title, the recipient and their job title, the date, and a specific subject line. Memoranda often include an introductory section explaining the reason and context for the memorandum. Next, a memorandum includes a section with details relevant to the topic. Finally, the memorandum will conclude with a paragraph that politely and clearly defines the sender's expectations of the recipient.

Chapter Quiz

1. The Greek word *epistolē* means:

a. Pistol.
b. Epistaxis.
c. Essay.
d. Letter.

2. What are the two major principles used to create an orderly blog?

a. The content must be interesting with various fonts and color combinations, and it should take less than 10 minutes to read in its entirety.
b. Blog layouts need more subheadings, graphics, and other indications of what information follows, and the content must be interesting with various fonts and color combinations.
c. Legibility is crucial because onscreen reading is hard on the eyes, and it should take less than 10 minutes to read in its entirety.
d. Blog layouts need more subheadings, graphics, and other indications of what information follows, and legibility is crucial because onscreen reading is hard on the eyes.

Chapter Quiz Answer Key

1. D: The Greek word for "letter" is *epistolē*, which became the English word "epistle." The earliest letters were called epistles, including the New Testament's epistles from the apostles to the Christians. In ancient Egypt, the writing curriculum in scribal schools included the epistolary genre. Epistolary novels frame a story in the form of letters.

2. D: There are two major principles that form the basis for blog-writing rules. The first is that while readers of print can skim articles to estimate their length, they must scroll down to scan something published online, meaning that blog layouts need more subheadings, graphics, and other indications of what information follows. The second principle is that onscreen reading can be harder on the eyes than reading printed paper, so legibility is crucial in blogs.

Standard English Conventions

The Eight Parts of Speech

Nouns

When you talk about a person, place, thing, or idea, you are talking about a **noun**. The two main types of nouns are **common** and **proper** nouns. Also, nouns can be abstract (i.e., general) or concrete (i.e., specific).

Common Nouns

Common nouns are generic names for people, places, and things. Common nouns are not usually capitalized.

Examples of common nouns:

People: boy, girl, worker, manager

Places: school, bank, library, home

Things: dog, cat, truck, car

Review Video: What is a Noun?
Visit mometrix.com/academy and enter code: 344028

Proper Nouns

Proper nouns name specific people, places, or things. All proper nouns are capitalized.

Examples of proper nouns:

People: Abraham Lincoln, George Washington, Martin Luther King, Jr.

Places: Los Angeles, California; New York; Asia

Things: Statue of Liberty, Earth, Lincoln Memorial

Note: When referring to the planet that we live on, capitalize *Earth*. When referring to the dirt, rocks, or land, lowercase *earth*.

General and Specific Nouns

General nouns are the names of conditions or ideas. **Specific nouns** name people, places, and things that are understood by using your senses.

General nouns:

Condition: beauty, strength

Idea: truth, peace

Specific nouns:

People: baby, friend, father

Places: town, park, city hall

Things: rainbow, cough, apple, silk, gasoline

Collective Nouns

Collective nouns are the names for a group of people, places, or things that may act as a whole. The following are examples of collective nouns: *class, company, dozen, group, herd, team,* and *public*. Collective nouns usually require an article, which denotes the noun as being a single unit. For instance, a choir is a group of singers. Even though there are many singers in a choir, the word choir is grammatically treated as a single unit. If we refer to the members of the group, and not the group itself, it is no longer a collective noun.

Incorrect: The *choir are* going to compete nationally this year.

Correct: The *choir is* going to compete nationally this year.

Incorrect: The *members* of the choir *is* competing nationally this year.

Correct: The *members* of the choir *are* competing nationally this year.

PRONOUNS

Pronouns are words that are used to stand in for nouns. A pronoun may be classified as personal, intensive, relative, interrogative, demonstrative, indefinite, and reciprocal.

Personal: *Nominative* is the case for nouns and pronouns that are the subject of a sentence. *Objective* is the case for nouns and pronouns that are an object in a sentence. *Possessive* is the case for nouns and pronouns that show possession or ownership.

Singular

	Nominative	Objective	Possessive
First Person	I	me	my, mine
Second Person	you	you	your, yours
Third Person	he, she, it	him, her, it	his, her, hers, its

Plural

	Nominative	Objective	Possessive
First Person	we	us	our, ours
Second Person	you	you	your, yours
Third Person	they	them	their, theirs

Intensive: I myself, you yourself, he himself, she herself, the (thing) itself, we ourselves, you yourselves, they themselves

Relative: which, who, whom, whose

Interrogative: what, which, who, whom, whose

Demonstrative: this, that, these, those

Indefinite: all, any, each, everyone, either/neither, one, some, several

Reciprocal: each other, one another

Review Video: Nouns and Pronouns
Visit mometrix.com/academy and enter code: 312073

VERBS

If you want to write a sentence, then you need a verb. Without a verb, you have no sentence. The verb of a sentence indicates action or being. In other words, the verb shows something's action or state of being or the action that has been done to something.

Transitive and Intransitive Verbs

A **transitive verb** is a verb whose action (e.g., drive, run, jump) indicates a receiver (e.g., car, dog, kangaroo). **Intransitive verbs** do not indicate a receiver of an action. In other words, the action of the verb does not point to a subject or object.

> **Transitive**: He plays the piano. | The piano was played by him.
>
> **Intransitive**: He plays. | John plays well.

A dictionary will tell you whether a verb is transitive or intransitive. Some verbs can be transitive and intransitive.

Action Verbs and Linking Verbs

Action verbs show what the subject is doing. In other words, an action verb shows action. Unlike most types of words, a single action verb, in the right context, can be an entire sentence. **Linking verbs** link the subject of a sentence to a noun or pronoun, or they link a subject with an adjective. You always need a verb if you want a complete sentence. However, linking verbs on their own cannot be a complete sentence.

Common linking verbs include *appear, be, become, feel, grow, look, seem, smell, sound,* and *taste*. However, any verb that shows a condition and connects to a noun, pronoun, or adjective that describes the subject of a sentence is a linking verb.

Action: He sings. | Run! | Go! | I talk with him every day. | She reads.

Linking:

> Incorrect: I am.
>
> Correct: I am John. | The roses smell lovely. | I feel tired.

Note: Some verbs are followed by words that look like prepositions, but they are a part of the verb and a part of the verb's meaning. These are known as phrasal verbs, and examples include *call off*, *look up*, and *drop off*.

> **Review Video: Action Verbs and Linking Verbs**
> Visit mometrix.com/academy and enter code: 743142

Voice

Transitive verbs come in active or passive **voice**. If something does an action or is acted upon, then you will know whether a verb is active or passive. When the subject of the sentence is doing the action, the verb is in **active voice**. When the subject is acted upon, the verb is in **passive voice**.

> **Active**: Jon drew the picture. (The subject *Jon* is doing the action of *drawing a picture*.)
>
> **Passive**: The picture is drawn by Jon. (The subject *picture* is receiving the action from Jon.)

Verb Tenses

A verb **tense** shows the different form of a verb to point to the time of an action. The present and past tense are indicated by the verb's form. An action in the present, *I talk,* can change form for the past: *I talked*. However, for the other tenses, an auxiliary (i.e., helping) verb is needed to show the change in form. These helping verbs include *am, are, is* | *have, has, had* | *was, were, will* (or *shall*).

Present: I talk	Present perfect: I have talked
Past: I talked	Past perfect: I had talked
Future: I will talk	Future perfect: I will have talked

Present: The action happens at the current time.

Example: He *walks* to the store every morning.

To show that something is happening right now, use the progressive present tense: I *am walking*.

Past: The action happened in the past.

Example: He *walked* to the store an hour ago.

Future: The action is going to happen later.

Example: I *will walk* to the store tomorrow.

Present perfect: The action started in the past and continues into the present or took place previously at an unspecified time.

Example: I *have walked* to the store three times today.

Past perfect: The second action happened in the past. The first action came before the second.

Example: Before I walked to the store (Action 2), I *had walked* to the library (Action 1).

Future perfect: An action that uses the past and the future. In other words, the action is complete before a future moment.

Example: When she comes for the supplies (future moment), I *will have walked* to the store (action completed before the future moment).

Review Video: Present Perfect, Past Perfect, and Future Perfect Verb Tenses
Visit mometrix.com/academy and enter code: 269472

Conjugating Verbs

When you need to change the form of a verb, you are **conjugating** a verb. The key forms of a verb are singular, present tense (dream); singular, past tense (dreamed); and the past participle (have dreamed). Note: the past participle needs a helping verb to make a verb tense. For example, I *have dreamed* of this day. The following tables demonstrate some of the different ways to conjugate a verb:

Singular

Tense	First Person	Second Person	Third Person
Present	I dream	You dream	He, she, it dreams
Past	I dreamed	You dreamed	He, she, it dreamed
Past Participle	I have dreamed	You have dreamed	He, she, it has dreamed

Plural

Tense	First Person	Second Person	Third Person
Present	We dream	You dream	They dream
Past	We dreamed	You dreamed	They dreamed
Past Participle	We have dreamed	You have dreamed	They have dreamed

Mood

There are three **moods** in English: the indicative, the imperative, and the subjunctive.

The **indicative mood** is used for facts, opinions, and questions.

Fact: You can do this.

Opinion: I think that you can do this.

Question: Do you know that you can do this?

The **imperative** is used for orders or requests.

Order: You are going to do this!

Request: Will you do this for me?

The **subjunctive mood** is for wishes and statements that go against fact.

Wish: I wish that I were famous.

Statement against fact: If I were you, I would do this. (This goes against fact because I am not you. You have the chance to do this, and I do not have the chance.)

Adjectives

An **adjective** is a word that is used to modify a noun or pronoun. An adjective answers a question: *Which one? What kind?* or *How many?* Usually, adjectives come before the words that they modify, but they may also come after a linking verb.

Which one? The *third* suit is my favorite.

What kind? This suit is *navy blue.*

How many? I am going to buy *four* pairs of socks to match the suit.

Review Video: Descriptive Text
Visit mometrix.com/academy and enter code: 174903

ARTICLES

Articles are adjectives that are used to distinguish nouns as definite or indefinite. **Definite** nouns are preceded by the article *the* and indicate a specific person, place, thing, or idea. **Indefinite** nouns are preceded by *a* or *an* and do not indicate a specific person, place, thing, or idea. *A*, *an*, and *the* are the only articles. Note: *An* comes before words that start with a vowel sound. For example, "Are you going to get an **u**mbrella?"

> **Definite**: I lost *the* bottle that belongs to me.
>
> **Indefinite**: Does anyone have *a* bottle to share?

Review Video: Function of Articles
Visit mometrix.com/academy and enter code: 449383

COMPARISON WITH ADJECTIVES

Some adjectives are relative and other adjectives are absolute. Adjectives that are **relative** can show the comparison between things. **Absolute** adjectives can also show comparison, but they do so in a different way. Let's say that you are reading two books. You think that one book is perfect, and the other book is not exactly perfect. It is not possible for one book to be more perfect than the other. Either you think that the book is perfect, or you think that the book is imperfect. In this case, perfect and imperfect are absolute adjectives.

Relative adjectives will show the different **degrees** of something or someone to something else or someone else. The three degrees of adjectives include positive, comparative, and superlative.

The **positive** degree is the normal form of an adjective.

> Example: This work is *difficult*. | She is *smart*.

The **comparative** degree compares one person or thing to another person or thing.

> Example: This work is *more difficult* than your work. | She is *smarter* than me.

The **superlative** degree compares more than two people or things.

> Example: This is the *most difficult* work of my life. | She is the *smartest* lady in school.

Review Video: What is an Adjective?
Visit mometrix.com/academy and enter code: 470154

ADVERBS

An **adverb** is a word that is used to **modify** a verb, adjective, or another adverb. Usually, adverbs answer one of these questions: *When? Where? How?* and *Why?* The negatives *not* and *never* are considered adverbs. Adverbs that modify adjectives or other adverbs **strengthen** or **weaken** the words that they modify.

Examples:

> He walks *quickly* through the crowd.
>
> The water flows *smoothly* on the rocks.

Note: Adverbs are usually indicated by the morpheme *-ly*, which has been added to the root word. For instance, *quick* can be made into an adverb by adding *-ly* to construct *quickly*. Some words that end in *-ly* do not follow this rule and can behave as other parts of speech. Examples of adjectives ending in *-ly* include: *early, friendly, holy, lonely, silly*, and *ugly*. To know if a word that ends in *-ly* is an adjective or adverb, check your dictionary. Also, while many adverbs end in *-ly*, you need to remember that not all adverbs end in *-ly*.

Examples:

He is *never* angry.

You are *too* irresponsible to travel alone.

Review Video: What is an Adverb?
Visit mometrix.com/academy and enter code: 713951

Review Video: Adverbs that Modify Adjectives
Visit mometrix.com/academy and enter code: 122570

COMPARISON WITH ADVERBS

The rules for comparing adverbs are the same as the rules for adjectives.

The **positive** degree is the standard form of an adverb.

Example: He arrives *soon.* | She speaks *softly* to her friends.

The **comparative** degree compares one person or thing to another person or thing.

Example: He arrives *sooner* than Sarah. | She speaks *more softly* than him.

The **superlative** degree compares more than two people or things.

Example: He arrives *soonest* of the group. | She speaks the *most softly* of any of her friends.

PREPOSITIONS

A **preposition** is a word placed before a noun or pronoun that shows the relationship between an object and another word in the sentence.

Common prepositions:

about	before	during	on	under
after	beneath	for	over	until
against	between	from	past	up
among	beyond	in	through	with
around	by	of	to	within
at	down	off	toward	without

Examples:

The napkin is *in* the drawer.

The Earth rotates *around* the Sun.

The needle is *beneath* the haystack.

Can you find "me" *among* the words?

Review Video: Prepositions
Visit mometrix.com/academy and enter code: 946763

Conjunctions

Conjunctions join words, phrases, or clauses and they show the connection between the joined pieces. **Coordinating conjunctions** connect equal parts of sentences. **Correlative conjunctions** show the connection between pairs. **Subordinating conjunctions** join subordinate (i.e., dependent) clauses with independent clauses.

Coordinating Conjunctions

The **coordinating conjunctions** include: *and, but, yet, or, nor, for,* and *so*

Examples:

The rock was small, *but* it was heavy.

She drove in the night, *and* he drove in the day.

Correlative Conjunctions

The **correlative conjunctions** are: *either...or* | *neither...nor* | *not only...but also*

Examples:

Either you are coming *or* you are staying.

He *not only* ran three miles *but also* swam 200 yards.

Review Video: Coordinating and Correlative Conjunctions
Visit mometrix.com/academy and enter code: 390329

Review Video: Adverb Equal Comparisons
Visit mometrix.com/academy and enter code: 231291

Subordinating Conjunctions

Common **subordinating conjunctions** include:

after	since	whenever
although	so that	where
because	unless	wherever
before	until	whether
in order that	when	while

Examples:

I am hungry *because* I did not eat breakfast.

He went home *when* everyone left.

Review Video: Subordinating Conjunctions
Visit mometrix.com/academy and enter code: 958913

Interjections

Interjections are words of exclamation (i.e., audible expression of great feeling) that are used alone or as a part of a sentence. Often, they are used at the beginning of a sentence for an introduction. Sometimes, they can be used in the middle of a sentence to show a change in thought or attitude.

Common Interjections: Hey! | Oh, | Ouch! | Please! | Wow!

Chapter Quiz

1. Which of the following is NOT considered a type of mood?

a. Indicative
b. Imperative
c. Subjunctive
d. Conjunctive

2. How many different degrees of relative adjectives are there?

a. Two
b. Three
c. Four
d. Five

3. In general, adverbs may modify all of the following, EXCEPT:

a. Another adverb.
b. Adjectives.
c. Proper nouns.
d. Verbs.

Chapter Quiz Answer Key

1. D: There are three moods in English: the indicative, the imperative, and the subjunctive.

2. B: Relative adjectives will show the different degrees of something or someone to something else or someone else. The three degrees of adjectives include positive, comparative, and superlative.

3. C: An adverb is a word that is used to modify a verb, adjective, or another adverb. Usually, adverbs answer one of the questions: *When? Where? How?* and *Why?* The negatives *not* and *never* are considered adverbs. Adverbs that modify adjectives or other adverbs strengthen or weaken the words that they modify.

Subjects and Predicates

Subjects

The **subject** of a sentence names who or what the sentence is about. The subject may be directly stated in a sentence, or the subject may be the implied *you*. The **complete subject** includes the simple subject and all of its modifiers. To find the complete subject, ask *Who* or *What* and insert the verb to complete the question. The answer, including any modifiers (adjectives, prepositional phrases, etc.), is the complete subject. To find the **simple subject**, remove all of the modifiers in the complete subject. Being able to locate the subject of a sentence helps with many problems, such as those involving sentence fragments and subject-verb agreement.

Examples:

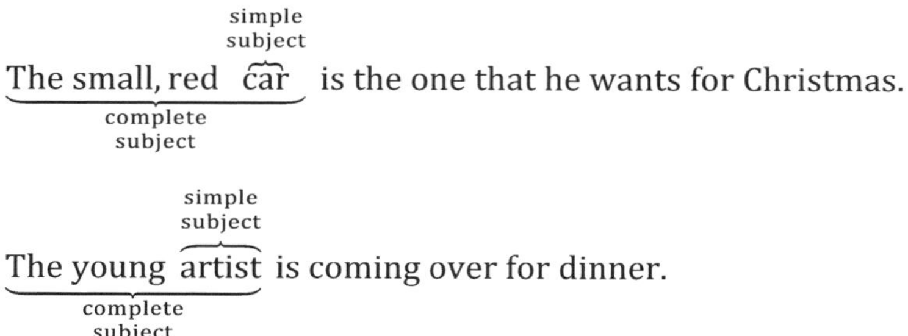

Review Video: Subjects in English
Visit mometrix.com/academy and enter code: 444771

In **imperative** sentences, the verb's subject is understood (e.g., [You] Run to the store), but is not actually present in the sentence. Normally, the subject comes before the verb. However, the subject comes after the verb in sentences that begin with *There are* or *There was.*

Direct:

John knows the way to the park.	Who knows the way to the park?	John
The cookies need ten more minutes.	What needs ten minutes?	The cookies
By five o'clock, Bill will need to leave.	Who needs to leave?	Bill
There are five letters on the table for him.	What is on the table?	Five letters
There were coffee and doughnuts in the house.	What was in the house?	Coffee and doughnuts

Implied:

Go to the post office for me.	Who is going to the post office?	You
Come and sit with me, please?	Who needs to come and sit?	You

PREDICATES

In a sentence, you always have a predicate and a subject. The subject tells what the sentence is about, and the **predicate** explains or describes the subject.

Think about the sentence *He sings*. In this sentence, we have a subject (He) and a predicate (sings). This is all that is needed for a sentence to be complete. Most sentences contain more information, but if this is all the information that you are given, then you have a complete sentence.

Now, let's look at another sentence: *John and Jane sing on Tuesday nights at the dance hall.*

subject: John and Jane | predicate: sing on Tuesday nights at the dance hall.

John and Jane sing on Tuesday nights at the dance hall.

Subject-Verb Agreement

Verbs **agree** with their subjects in number. In other words, singular subjects need singular verbs. Plural subjects need plural verbs. **Singular** is for **one** person, place, or thing. **Plural** is for **more than one** person, place, or thing. Subjects and verbs must also share the same point of view, as in first, second, or third person. The present tense ending *-s* is used on a verb if its subject is third person singular; otherwise, the verb's ending is not modified.

Review Video: Subject-Verb Agreement
Visit mometrix.com/academy and enter code: 479190

Number Agreement Examples:

Single Subject and Verb: Dan (singular subject) calls (singular verb) home.

Dan is one person. So, the singular verb *calls* is needed.

Plural Subject and Verb: Dan and Bob (plural subject) call (plural verb) home.

More than one person needs the plural verb *call.*

Person Agreement Examples:

First Person: I *am* walking.

Second Person: You *are* walking.

Third Person: He *is* walking.

Complications with Subject-Verb Agreement

Words Between Subject and Verb

Words that come between the simple subject and the verb have no bearing on subject-verb agreement.

Examples:

The joy (singular subject) of my life returns (singular verb) home tonight.

The phrase *of my life* does not influence the verb *returns.*

The question (singular subject) that still remains unanswered is (singular verb) "Who are you?"

Don't let the phrase "*that still remains…*" trouble you. The subject *question* goes with *is.*

Compound Subjects

A compound subject is formed when two or more nouns joined by *and*, *or*, or *nor* jointly act as the subject of the sentence.

Joined by And

When a compound subject is joined by *and*, it is treated as a plural subject and requires a plural verb.

Examples:

You and Jon (plural subject) are (plural verb) invited to come to my house.

The pencil and paper (plural subject) belong (plural verb) to me.

Joined by Or/Nor

For a compound subject joined by *or* or *nor*, the verb must agree in number with the part of the subject that is closest to the verb (italicized in the examples below).

Examples:

Today or tomorrow (subject) is (verb) the day.

Stan or Phil (subject) wants (verb) to read the book.

Neither the pen nor the book (subject) is (verb) on the desk.

Either the blanket or pillows (subject) arrive (verb) this afternoon.

Indefinite Pronouns as Subject

An indefinite pronoun is a pronoun that does not refer to a specific noun. Different indefinite pronouns may only function as a singular noun, only function as a plural noun, or change depending on how they are used.

Always Singular

Pronouns such as *each*, *either*, *everybody*, *anybody*, *somebody*, and *nobody* are always singular.

Examples:

Each (singular subject) of the runners has (singular verb) a different bib number.

Is (singular verb) either (singular subject) of you ready for the game?

Note: The words *each* and *either* can also be used as adjectives (e.g., *each* person is unique). When one of these adjectives modifies the subject of a sentence, it is always a singular subject.

> $\overbrace{\text{Everybody}}^{\text{singular subject}}$ $\overbrace{\text{grows}}^{\text{singular verb}}$ a day older every day.

> $\overbrace{\text{Anybody}}^{\text{singular subject}}$ $\overbrace{\text{is}}^{\text{singular verb}}$ welcome to bring a tent.

ALWAYS PLURAL

Pronouns such as *both*, *several*, and *many* are always plural.

Examples:

> $\overbrace{\text{Both}}^{\text{plural subject}}$ of the siblings $\overbrace{\text{were}}^{\text{plural verb}}$ too tired to argue.

> $\overbrace{\text{Many}}^{\text{plural subject}}$ $\overbrace{\text{have tried}}^{\text{plural verb}}$, but none have succeeded.

DEPEND ON CONTEXT

Pronouns such as *some*, *any*, *all*, *none*, *more*, and *most* can be either singular or plural depending on what they are representing in the context of the sentence.

Examples:

> $\overbrace{\text{All}}^{\text{singular subject}}$ of my dog's food $\overbrace{\text{was}}^{\text{singular verb}}$ still there in his bowl.

> By the end of the night, $\overbrace{\text{all}}^{\text{plural subject}}$ of my guests $\overbrace{\text{were}}^{\text{plural verb}}$ already excited about coming to my next party.

OTHER CASES INVOLVING PLURAL OR IRREGULAR FORM

Some nouns are **singular in meaning but plural in form**: news, mathematics, physics, and economics.

> The *news is* coming on now.

> *Mathematics is* my favorite class.

Some nouns are plural in form and meaning, and have **no singular equivalent**: scissors and pants.

> Do these *pants come* with a shirt?

> The *scissors are* for my project.

Mathematical operations are **irregular** in their construction, but are normally considered to be **singular in meaning**.

One plus one is two.

Three times three is nine.

Note: Look to your **dictionary** for help when you aren't sure whether a noun with a plural form has a singular or plural meaning.

Complements

A complement is a noun, pronoun, or adjective that is used to give more information about the subject or verb in the sentence.

Direct Objects

A direct object is a noun or pronoun that takes or receives the **action** of a verb. (Remember: a complete sentence does not need a direct object, so not all sentences will have them. A sentence needs only a subject and a verb.) When you are looking for a direct object, find the verb and ask *who* or *what.*

Examples:

I took *the blanket.*

Jane read *books.*

Indirect Objects

An indirect object is a word or group of words that show how an action had an **influence** on someone or something. If there is an indirect object in a sentence, then you always have a direct object in the sentence. When you are looking for the indirect object, find the verb and ask *to/for whom or what.*

Examples:

We taught the old dog (indirect object) a new trick (direct object).

I gave them (indirect object) a math lesson (direct object).

Review Video: Direct and Indirect Objects
Visit mometrix.com/academy and enter code: 817385

Predicate Nominatives and Predicate Adjectives

As we looked at previously, verbs may be classified as either action verbs or linking verbs. A linking verb is so named because it links the subject to words in the predicate that describe or define the subject. These words are called predicate nominatives (if nouns or pronouns) or predicate adjectives (if adjectives).

Examples:

My father (subject) is a lawyer (predicate nominative).

Your mother (subject) is patient (predicate adjective).

PRONOUN USAGE

The **antecedent** is the noun that has been replaced by a pronoun. A pronoun and its antecedent **agree** when they have the same number (singular or plural) and gender (male, female, or neutral).

Examples:

Singular agreement: John (antecedent) came into town, and he (pronoun) played for us.

Plural agreement: John and Rick (antecedent) came into town, and they (pronoun) played for us.

To determine which is the correct pronoun to use in a compound subject or object, try each pronoun **alone** in place of the compound in the sentence. Your knowledge of pronouns will tell you which one is correct.

Example:

Bob and (I, me) will be going.

Test: (1) *I will be going* or (2) *Me will be going*. The second choice cannot be correct because *me* cannot be used as the subject of a sentence. Instead, *me* is used as an object.

Answer: Bob and I will be going.

When a pronoun is used with a noun immediately following (as in "we boys"), try the sentence **without the added noun**.

Example:

(We/Us) boys played football last year.

Test: (1) *We played football last ye*ar or (2) *Us played football last year*. Again, the second choice cannot be correct because *us* cannot be used as a subject of a sentence. Instead, *us* is used as an object.

Answer: We boys played football last year.

Review Video: Pronoun Usage
Visit mometrix.com/academy and enter code: 666500

Review Video: What is Pronoun-Antecedent Agreement?
Visit mometrix.com/academy and enter code: 919704

A pronoun should point clearly to the **antecedent**. Here is how a pronoun reference can be unhelpful if it is puzzling or not directly stated.

> antecedent pronoun
> **Unhelpful**: Ron and Jim went to the store, and he bought soda.
>
> Who bought soda? Ron or Jim?
>
> antecedent pronoun
> **Helpful**: Jim went to the store, and he bought soda.
>
> The sentence is clear. Jim bought the soda.

Some pronouns change their form by their placement in a sentence. A pronoun that is a **subject** in a sentence comes in the **subjective case**. Pronouns that serve as **objects** appear in the **objective case**. Finally, the pronouns that are used as **possessives** appear in the **possessive case**.

Examples:

> **Subjective case**: *He* is coming to the show.
>
> The pronoun *He* is the subject of the sentence.
>
> **Objective case**: Josh drove *him* to the airport.
>
> The pronoun *him* is the object of the sentence.
>
> **Possessive case**: The flowers are *mine*.
>
> The pronoun *mine* shows ownership of the flowers.

The word *who* is a subjective-case pronoun that can be used as a **subject**. The word *whom* is an objective-case pronoun that can be used as an **object**. The words *who* and *whom* are common in subordinate clauses or in questions.

Examples:

> subject verb
> He knows who wants to come.
>
> object verb
> He knows the man whom we want at the party.

CLAUSES

A clause is a group of words that contains both a subject and a predicate (verb). There are two types of clauses: independent and dependent. An **independent clause** contains a complete thought, while a **dependent (or subordinate) clause** does not. A dependent clause includes a subject and a verb, and may also contain objects or complements, but it cannot stand as a complete thought without being joined to an independent clause. Dependent clauses function within sentences as adjectives, adverbs, or nouns.

Example:

independent clause: I am running | dependent clause: because I want to stay in shape.

The clause *I am running* is an independent clause: it has a subject and a verb, and it gives a complete thought. The clause *because I want to stay in shape* is a dependent clause: it has a subject and a verb, but it does not express a complete thought. It adds detail to the independent clause to which it is attached.

Review Video: What is a Clause?
Visit mometrix.com/academy and enter code: 940170

Review Video: Independent and Dependent Clauses
Visit mometrix.com/academy and enter code: 556903

Types of Dependent Clauses

Adjective Clauses

An **adjective clause** is a dependent clause that modifies a noun or a pronoun. Adjective clauses begin with a relative pronoun (*who, whose, whom, which,* and *that*) or a relative adverb (*where, when,* and *why*).

Also, adjective clauses come after the noun that the clause needs to explain or rename. This is done to have a clear connection to the independent clause.

Examples:

independent clause: I learned the reason | adjective clause: why I won the award.

independent clause: This is the place | adjective clause: where I started my first job.

An adjective clause can be an essential or nonessential clause. An essential clause is very important to the sentence. **Essential clauses** explain or define a person or thing. **Nonessential clauses** give more information about a person or thing but are not necessary to define them. Nonessential clauses are set off with commas while essential clauses are not.

Examples:

A person | essential clause: who works hard at first | can often rest later in life.

Neil Armstrong, | nonessential clause: who walked on the moon, | is my hero.

Review Video: Adjective Clauses and Phrases
Visit mometrix.com/academy and enter code: 520888

Adverb Clauses

An **adverb clause** is a dependent clause that modifies a verb, adjective, or adverb. In sentences with multiple dependent clauses, adverb clauses are usually placed immediately before or after the independent clause. An adverb clause is introduced with words such as *after, although, as, before, because, if, since, so, unless, when, where*, and *while.*

Examples:

> [When you walked outside,]adverb clause I called the manager.
>
> I will go with you [unless you want to stay.]adverb clause

Noun Clauses

A **noun clause** is a dependent clause that can be used as a subject, object, or complement. Noun clauses begin with words such as *how, that, what, whether, which, who,* and *why.* These words can also come with an adjective clause. Unless the noun clause is being used as the subject of the sentence, it should come after the verb of the independent clause.

Examples:

> The real mystery is [how you avoided serious injury.]noun clause
>
> [What you learn from each other]noun clause depends on your honesty with others.

Subordination

When two related ideas are not of equal importance, the ideal way to combine them is to make the more important idea an independent clause and the less important idea a dependent or subordinate clause. This is called **subordination**.

Example:

> **Separate ideas**: The team had a perfect regular season. The team lost the championship.
>
> **Subordinated**: Despite having a perfect regular season, *the team lost the championship.*

Phrases

A phrase is a group of words that functions as a single part of speech, usually a noun, adjective, or adverb. A **phrase** is not a complete thought, but it adds detail or explanation to a sentence, or renames something within the sentence.

Prepositional Phrases

One of the most common types of phrases is the prepositional phrase. A **prepositional phrase** begins with a preposition and ends with a noun or pronoun that is the object of the preposition. Normally, the prepositional phrase functions as an **adjective** or an **adverb** within the sentence.

Examples:

The picnic is on the blanket. (prepositional phrase: on the blanket)

I am sick with a fever today. (prepositional phrase: with a fever)

Among the many flowers, John found a four-leaf clover. (prepositional phrase: Among the many flowers)

Verbal Phrases

A **verbal** is a word or phrase that is formed from a verb but does not function as a verb. Depending on its particular form, it may be used as a noun, adjective, or adverb. A verbal does **not** replace a verb in a sentence.

Examples:

Correct: Walk a mile daily. (verb: Walk)

This is a complete sentence with the implied subject *you*.

Incorrect: To walk a mile. (verbal: To walk)

This is not a sentence since there is no functional verb.

There are three types of verbal: **participles**, **gerunds**, and **infinitives**. Each type of verbal has a corresponding **phrase** that consists of the verbal itself along with any complements or modifiers.

Participles

A **participle** is a type of verbal that always functions as an adjective. The present participle always ends with *-ing*. Past participles end with *-d, -ed, -n,* or *-t*.

Examples: dance (verb) | dancing (present participle) | danced (past participle)

Participial phrases most often come right before or right after the noun or pronoun that they modify.

Examples:

participial phrase

Shipwrecked on an island, the boys started to fish for food.

participial phrase

Having been seated for five hours, we got out of the car to stretch our legs.

participial phrase

Praised for their work, the group accepted the first-place trophy.

Gerunds

A **gerund** is a type of verbal that always functions as a **noun**. Like present participles, gerunds always end with *-ing*, but they can be easily distinguished from one another by the part of speech they represent (participles always function as adjectives). Since a gerund or gerund phrase always functions as a noun, it can be used as the subject of a sentence, the predicate nominative, or the object of a verb or preposition.

Examples:

gerund

We want to be known for teaching the poor.

object of preposition

gerund

Coaching this team is the best job of my life.

subject

gerund

We like practicing our songs in the basement.

object of verb

Infinitives

An **infinitive** is a type of verbal that can function as a noun, an adjective, or an adverb. An infinitive is made of the word *to* and the basic form of the verb. As with all other types of verbal phrases, an infinitive phrase includes the verbal itself and all of its complements or modifiers.

Examples:

> infinitive: To join; noun: To join the team
>
> To join the team is my goal in life.

> infinitive: to eat; adjective: to eat for the night
>
> The animals have enough food to eat for the night.

> infinitive: to exercise; adverb: to exercise their muscles
>
> People lift weights to exercise their muscles.

Review Video: <u>Gerunds, Infinitives, and Participles</u>
Visit mometrix.com/academy and enter code: 634263

Appositive Phrases

An **appositive** is a word or phrase that is used to explain or rename nouns or pronouns. Noun phrases, gerund phrases, and infinitive phrases can all be used as appositives.

Examples:

> appositive: hunters at heart
>
> Terriers, hunters at heart, have been dressed up to look like lap dogs.
>
> The noun phrase *hunters at heart* renames the noun *terriers*.

> appositive: to save and invest his money
>
> His plan, to save and invest his money, was proven as a safe approach.
>
> The infinitive phrase explains what the plan is.

Appositive phrases can be **essential** or **nonessential**. An appositive phrase is essential if the person, place, or thing being described or renamed is too general for its meaning to be understood without the appositive.

Examples:

> essential: George Washington and Thomas Jefferson
>
> Two of America's Founding Fathers, George Washington and Thomas Jefferson, served as presidents.

> nonessential: two Founding Fathers
>
> George Washington and Thomas Jefferson, two Founding Fathers, served as presidents.

Absolute Phrases

An absolute phrase is a phrase that consists of **a noun followed by a participle**. An absolute phrase provides **context** to what is being described in the sentence, but it does not modify or explain any particular word; it is essentially independent.

Examples:

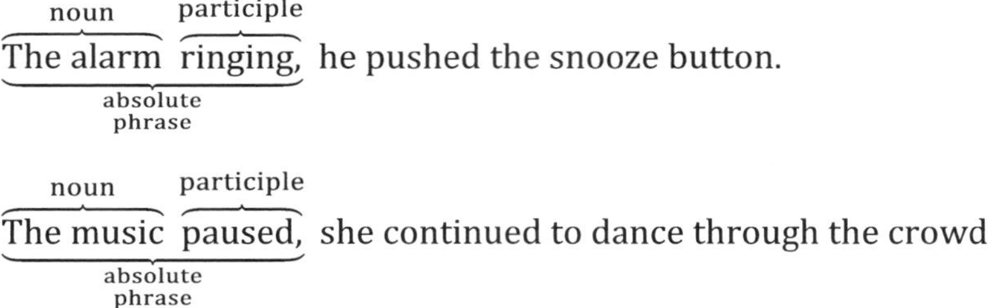

Parallelism

When multiple items or ideas are presented in a sentence in series, such as in a list, the items or ideas must be stated in grammatically equivalent ways. In other words, if one idea is stated in gerund form, the second cannot be stated in infinitive form. For example, to write, *I enjoy reading and to study* would be incorrect. An infinitive and a gerund are not equivalent. Instead, you should write *I enjoy reading and studying*. In lists of more than two, all items must be parallel.

Example:

> **Incorrect**: He stopped at the office, grocery store, and the pharmacy before heading home.
>
> The first and third items in the list of places include the article *the*, so the second item needs it as well.
>
> **Correct**: He stopped at the office, *the* grocery store, and the pharmacy before heading home.

Example:

> **Incorrect**: While vacationing in Europe, she went biking, skiing, and climbed mountains.
>
> The first and second items in the list are gerunds, so the third item must be as well.
>
> **Correct**: While vacationing in Europe, she went biking, skiing, and *mountain climbing*.

Review Video: Parallel Sentence Construction
Visit mometrix.com/academy and enter code: 831988

Sentence Purpose

There are four types of sentences: declarative, imperative, interrogative, and exclamatory.

A **declarative** sentence states a fact and ends with a period.

> *The football game starts at seven o'clock.*

An **imperative** sentence tells someone to do something and generally ends with a period. An urgent command might end with an exclamation point instead.

> *Don't forget to buy your ticket.*

An **interrogative** sentence asks a question and ends with a question mark.

> *Are you going to the game on Friday?*

An **exclamatory** sentence shows strong emotion and ends with an exclamation point.

I can't believe we won the game!

Review Video: Functions of a Sentence
Visit mometrix.com/academy and enter code: 475974

SENTENCE STRUCTURE

Sentences are classified by structure based on the type and number of clauses present. The four classifications of sentence structure are the following:

Simple: A simple sentence has one independent clause with no dependent clauses. A simple sentence may have **compound elements** (i.e., compound subject or verb).

Examples:

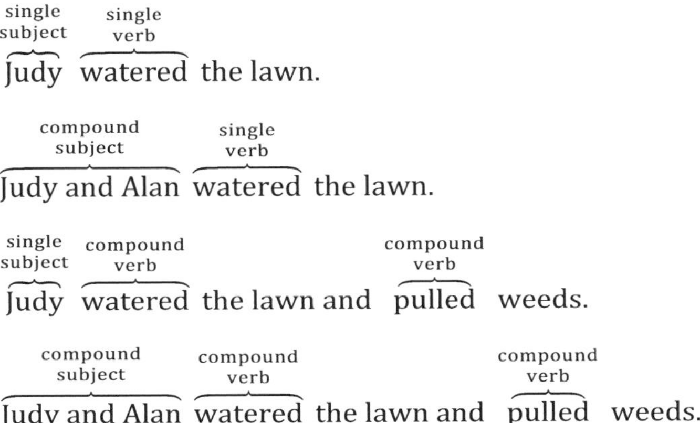

Compound: A compound sentence has two or more independent clauses with no dependent clauses. Usually, the independent clauses are joined with a comma and a coordinating conjunction or with a semicolon.

Examples:

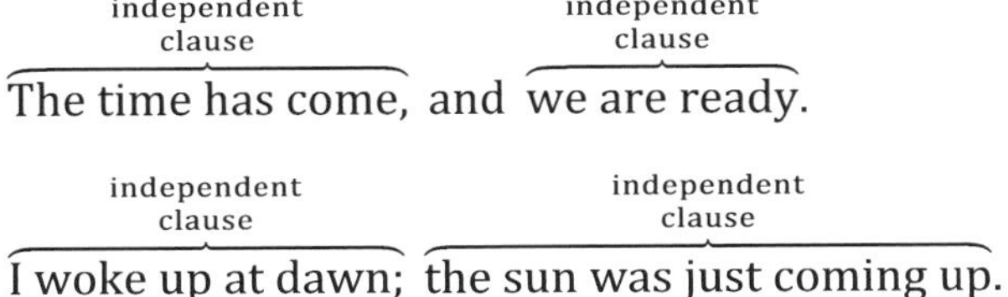

Complex: A complex sentence has one independent clause and at least one dependent clause.

Examples:

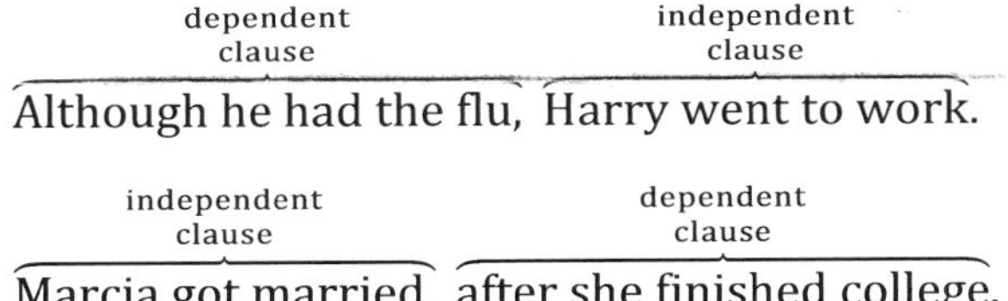

Compound-Complex: A compound-complex sentence has at least two independent clauses and at least one dependent clause.

Examples:

John is my friend (independent clause) who went to India, (dependent clause) and he brought back souvenirs. (independent clause)

You may not realize this, (independent clause) but we heard the music (independent clause) that you played last night. (dependent clause)

Review Video: Sentence Structure
Visit mometrix.com/academy and enter code: 700478

Sentence variety is important to consider when writing an essay or speech. A variety of sentence lengths and types creates rhythm, makes a passage more engaging, and gives writers an opportunity to demonstrate their writing style. Writing that uses the same length or type of sentence without variation can be boring or difficult to read. To evaluate a passage for effective sentence variety, it is helpful to note whether the passage contains diverse sentence structures and lengths. It is also important to pay attention to the way each sentence starts and avoid beginning with the same words or phrases.

Sentence Fragments

Recall that a group of words must contain at least one **independent clause** in order to be considered a sentence. If it doesn't contain even one independent clause, it is called a **sentence fragment**.

The appropriate process for **repairing** a sentence fragment depends on what type of fragment it is. If the fragment is a dependent clause, it can sometimes be as simple as removing a subordinating word (e.g., when, because, if) from the beginning of the fragment. Alternatively, a dependent clause can be incorporated into a closely related neighboring sentence. If the fragment is missing some required part, like a subject or a verb, the fix might be as simple as adding the missing part.

Examples:

Fragment: Because he wanted to sail the Mediterranean.

Removed subordinating word: He wanted to sail the Mediterranean.

Combined with another sentence: Because he wanted to sail the Mediterranean, he booked a Greek island cruise.

Run-on Sentences

Run-on sentences consist of multiple independent clauses that have not been joined together properly. Run-on sentences can be corrected in several different ways:

Join clauses properly: This can be done with a comma and coordinating conjunction, with a semicolon, or with a colon or dash if the second clause is explaining something in the first.

Example:

Incorrect: I went on the trip, we visited lots of castles.

Corrected: I went on the trip, and we visited lots of castles.

Split into separate sentences: This correction is most effective when the independent clauses are very long or when they are not closely related.

Example:

Incorrect: The drive to New York takes ten hours, my uncle lives in Boston.

Corrected: The drive to New York takes ten hours. My uncle lives in Boston.

Make one clause dependent: This is the easiest way to make the sentence correct and more interesting at the same time. It's often as simple as adding a subordinating word between the two clauses or before the first clause.

Example:

Incorrect: I finally made it to the store and I bought some eggs.

Corrected: When I finally made it to the store, I bought some eggs.

Reduce to one clause with a compound verb: If both clauses have the same subject, remove the subject from the second clause, and you now have just one clause with a compound verb.

Example:

Incorrect: The drive to New York takes ten hours, it makes me very tired.

Corrected: The drive to New York takes ten hours and makes me very tired.

Note: While these are the simplest ways to correct a run-on sentence, often the best way is to completely reorganize the thoughts in the sentence and rewrite it.

Review Video: Fragments and Run-on Sentences
Visit mometrix.com/academy and enter code: 541989

DANGLING AND MISPLACED MODIFIERS

DANGLING MODIFIERS

A dangling modifier is a dependent clause or verbal phrase that does not have a clear logical connection to a word in the sentence.

Example:

dangling modifier

Incorrect: Reading each magazine article, the stories caught my attention.

The word *stories* cannot be modified by *Reading each magazine article*. People can read, but stories cannot read. Therefore, the subject of the sentence must be a person.

dependent clause

Corrected: Reading each magazine article, I was entertained by the stories.

Example:

dangling modifier

Incorrect: Ever since childhood, my grandparents have visited me for Christmas.

The speaker in this sentence can't have been visited by her grandparents when *they* were children, since she wouldn't have been born yet. Either the modifier should be clarified or the sentence should be rearranged to specify whose childhood is being referenced.

dependent clause

Clarified: Ever since I was a child, my grandparents have visited for Christmas.

dependent clause

Rearranged: I have enjoyed my grandparents visiting for Christmas, ever since childhood.

MISPLACED MODIFIERS

Because modifiers are grammatically versatile, they can be put in many different places within the structure of a sentence. The danger of this versatility is that a modifier can accidentally be placed where it is modifying the wrong word or where it is not clear which word it is modifying.

Example:

modifier

Incorrect: She read the book to a crowd that was filled with beautiful pictures.

The book was filled with beautiful pictures, not the crowd.

modifier

Corrected: She read the book that was filled with beautiful pictures to a crowd.

Example:

modifier

Ambiguous: Derek saw a bus nearly hit a man on his way to work.

Was Derek on his way to work or was the other man?

modifier

Derek: On his way to work, Derek saw a bus nearly hit a man.

modifier

The other man: Derek saw a bus nearly hit a man who was on his way to work.

Split Infinitives

A split infinitive occurs when a modifying word comes between the word *to* and the verb that pairs with *to*.

Example: To *clearly* explain vs. *To explain* clearly | To *softly* sing vs. *To sing* softly

Though considered improper by some, split infinitives may provide better clarity and simplicity in some cases than the alternatives. As such, avoiding them should not be considered a universal rule.

Double Negatives

Standard English allows **two negatives** only when a **positive** meaning is intended. For example, *The team was not displeased with their performance*. Double negatives to emphasize negation are not used in standard English.

Negative modifiers (e.g., never, no, and not) should not be paired with other negative modifiers or negative words (e.g., none, nobody, nothing, or neither). The modifiers *hardly, barely*, and *scarcely* are also considered negatives in standard English, so they should not be used with other negatives.

Chapter Quiz

1. Which of the following is an imperative statement?

a. John knows the way to the park.
b. There are five letters on the table for him.
c. Go to the post office for me.
d. The cookies need to cook for a few more minutes.

2. Which of the following is NOT a word used to combine nouns to make a compound subject?

a. Or
b. Nor
c. And
d. Also

3. Which of the following is always singular?

a. Each
b. Both
c. Several
d. Many

4. Identify the indirect object of the following sentence: "We taught the old dog a new trick."

a. We
b. Taught
c. The old dog
d. A new trick

5. Identify the infinitive of the following sentence: "The animals have enough food to eat for the night."

a. The animals
b. Have enough food

c. To eat
d. For the night

6. How many types of sentences are there?

a. Three
b. Four
c. Five
d. Six

7. Which of the following sentences correctly expresses the idea of parallelism?

a. He stopped at the office, grocery store, and the pharmacy before heading home.
b. While vacationing in Europe, she went biking, skiing, and climbed mountains.
c. The crowd jumped and cheered, roared and hollered, and whistled as the game concluded.
d. The flurry of blows left him staggered, discombobulated, and overwhelmed before falling.

8. Identify the phrase, "The music paused," in the following sample sentence:

"The music paused, she continued to dance through the crowd."

a. Subordinate phrase
b. Essential appositive
c. Nonessential appositive
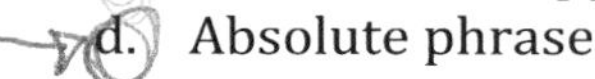
d. Absolute phrase

CHAPTER QUIZ ANSWER KEY

1. C: In an imperative sentence, the verb's subject is understood without actually appearing or being named in the sentence itself. For example, in the imperative sentence, "Run to the store," the subject is the person being told to run.

2. D: A compound subject is formed when two or more nouns joined by *and*, *or*, or *nor* jointly act as the subject of the sentence.

3. A: Pronouns such as *each*, *either*, *everybody*, *anybody*, *somebody*, and *nobody* are always singular.

4. C: An indirect object is a word or group of words that show how an action had an influence on someone or something. If there is an indirect object in a sentence, then there will always be a direct object in the sentence. When looking for the indirect object, find the verb and ask *to, for whom*, or *what*.

We taught the old dog (indirect object) a new trick (direct object).

5. C: An infinitive is a type of verbal that can function as a noun, an adjective, or an adverb. An infinitive is made of the word *to* and the basic form of the verb. As with all other types of verbal phrases, an infinitive phrase includes the verbal itself and all of its complements or modifiers.

The animals have enough food to eat (infinitive) for the night. [to eat for the night: adjective]

6. B: There are four types of sentences: declarative, imperative, interrogative, and exclamatory.

7. D: When multiple items or ideas are presented in a sentence in series, such as in a list, the items or ideas must be stated in grammatically equivalent ways. In other words, if one idea is stated in gerund form, the second cannot be stated in infinitive form. For example, writing "I enjoy *reading* and *to study*" would be incorrect. An infinitive and a gerund are not equivalent. Instead, the sentence should be, "I enjoy *reading* and *studying*." In lists of more than two, all items must be parallel.

Example:

Incorrect: He stopped at the office, grocery store, and the pharmacy before heading home.

(The first and third items in the list of places include the article *the*, so the second item needs it as well.)

Correct: He stopped at the office, *the* grocery store, and the pharmacy before heading home.

8. D: An absolute phrase is a phrase that consists of a noun followed by a participle. An absolute phrase provides context to what is being described in the sentence, but it does not modify or explain any particular word; it is essentially independent.

The music (noun) paused (participle), she continued to dance through the crowd. [The music paused: absolute phrase]

End Punctuation

Periods

Use a period to end all sentences except direct questions and exclamations. Periods are also used for abbreviations.

Examples: 3 p.m. | 2 a.m. | Mr. Jones | Mrs. Stevens | Dr. Smith | Bill, Jr. | Pennsylvania Ave.

Note: An abbreviation is a shortened form of a word or phrase.

Question Marks

Question marks should be used following a **direct question**. A polite request can be followed by a period instead of a question mark.

> **Direct Question**: What is for lunch today? | How are you? | Why is that the answer?
>
> **Polite Requests**: Can you please send me the item tomorrow. | Will you please walk with me on the track.

Review Video: Question Marks
Visit mometrix.com/academy and enter code: 118471

Exclamation Marks

Exclamation marks are used after a word group or sentence that shows much feeling or has special importance. Exclamation marks should not be overused. They are saved for proper **exclamatory interjections**.

> Example: We're going to the finals! | You have a beautiful car! | "That's crazy!" she yelled.

Review Video: Exclamation Points
Visit mometrix.com/academy and enter code: 199367

Commas

The comma is a punctuation mark that can help you understand connections in a sentence. Not every sentence needs a comma. However, if a sentence needs a comma, you need to put it in the right place. A comma in the wrong place (or an absent comma) will make a sentence's meaning unclear. These are some of the rules for commas:

Use Case	Example
Before a **coordinating conjunction** joining independent clauses	Bob caught three fish, and I caught two fish.
After an **introductory phrase**	After the final out, we went to a restaurant to celebrate.
After an **adverbial clause**	Studying the stars, I was awed by the beauty of the sky.
Between **items in a series**	I will bring the turkey, the pie, and the coffee.
For **interjections**	Wow, you know how to play this game.
After ***yes* and *no* responses**	No, I cannot come tomorrow.
Separate **nonessential modifiers**	John Frank, who coaches the team, was promoted today.
Separate **nonessential appositives**	Thomas Edison, an American inventor, was born in Ohio.
Separate **nouns of direct address**	You, John, are my only hope in this moment.
Separate **interrogative tags**	This is the last time, correct?
Separate **contrasts**	You are my friend, not my enemy.
Writing **dates**	July 4, 1776, is an important date to remember.
Writing **addresses**	He is meeting me at 456 Delaware Avenue, Washington, D.C., tomorrow morning.
Writing **geographical names**	Paris, France, is my favorite city.
Writing **titles**	John Smith, PhD, will be visiting your class today.
Separate **expressions like *he said***	"You can start," she said, "with an apology."

Also, you can use a comma **between coordinate adjectives** not joined with *and*. However, not all adjectives are coordinate (i.e., equal or parallel).

Incorrect: The kind, brown dog followed me home.

Correct: The kind, loyal dog followed me home.

There are two simple ways to know if your adjectives are coordinate. One, you can join the adjectives with *and*: *The kind and loyal dog*. Two, you can change the order of the adjectives: *The loyal, kind dog*.

Review Video: When to Use a Comma
Visit mometrix.com/academy and enter code: 786797

Semicolons

The semicolon is used to connect major sentence pieces of equal value. Some rules for semicolons include:

Use Case	Example
Between closely connected independent clauses **not connected with a coordinating conjunction**	You are right; we should go with your plan.
Between independent clauses **linked with a transitional word**	I think that we can agree on this; however, I am not sure about my friends.
Between items in a **series that has internal punctuation**	I have visited New York, New York; Augusta, Maine; and Baltimore, Maryland.

Review Video: How to Use Semicolons
Visit mometrix.com/academy and enter code: 370605

Colons

The colon is used to call attention to the words that follow it. A colon must come after a **complete independent clause**. The rules for colons are as follows:

Use Case	Example
After an independent clause to **make a list**	I want to learn many languages: Spanish, German, and Italian.
For **explanations**	There is one thing that stands out on your resume: responsibility.
To give a **quote**	He started with an idea: "We are able to do more than we imagine."
After the **greeting in a formal letter**	To Whom It May Concern:
Show **hours and minutes**	It is 3:14 p.m.
Separate a **title and subtitle**	The essay is titled "America: A Short Introduction to a Modern Country."

Review Video: Colons
Visit mometrix.com/academy and enter code: 868673

PARENTHESES

Parentheses are used for additional information. Also, they can be used to put labels for letters or numbers in a series. Parentheses should be not be used very often. If they are overused, parentheses can be a distraction instead of a help.

Examples:

Extra Information: The rattlesnake (see Image 2) is a dangerous snake of North and South America.

Series: Include in the email (1) your name, (2) your address, and (3) your question for the author.

Review Video: Parentheses
Visit mometrix.com/academy and enter code: 947743

QUOTATION MARKS

Use quotation marks to close off **direct quotations** of a person's spoken or written words. Do not use quotation marks around indirect quotations. An indirect quotation gives someone's message without using the person's exact words. Use **single quotation marks** to close off a quotation inside a quotation.

Direct Quote: Nancy said, "I am waiting for Henry to arrive."

Indirect Quote: Henry said that he is going to be late to the meeting.

Quote inside a Quote: The teacher asked, "Has everyone read 'The Gift of the Magi'?"

Quotation marks should be used around the titles of **short works**: newspaper and magazine articles, poems, short stories, songs, television episodes, radio programs, and subdivisions of books or websites.

Examples:

"Rip Van Winkle" (short story by Washington Irving)

"O Captain! My Captain!" (poem by Walt Whitman)

Although it is not standard usage, quotation marks are sometimes used to highlight **irony** or the use of words to mean something other than their dictionary definition. This type of usage should be employed sparingly, if at all.

Examples:

The boss warned Frank that he was walking on "thin ice."	Frank is not walking on real ice. Instead, he is being warned to avoid mistakes.
The teacher thanked the young man for his "honesty."	The quotation marks around *honesty* show that the teacher does not believe the young man's explanation.

Review Video: Quotation Marks
Visit mometrix.com/academy and enter code: 884918

Periods and commas are put **inside** quotation marks. Colons and semicolons are put **outside** the quotation marks. Question marks and exclamation points are placed inside quotation marks when they are part of a quote. When the question or exclamation mark goes with the whole sentence, the mark is left outside of the quotation marks.

Examples:

Period and comma	We read "The Gift of the Magi," "The Skylight Room," and "The Cactus."
Semicolon	They watched "The Nutcracker"; then, they went home.
Exclamation mark that is a part of a quote	The crowd cheered, "Victory!"
Question mark that goes with the whole sentence	Is your favorite short story "The Tell-Tale Heart"?

Apostrophes

An apostrophe is used to show **possession** or the **deletion of letters in contractions**. An apostrophe is not needed with the possessive pronouns *his, hers, its, ours, theirs, whose*, and *yours*.

Singular Nouns: David's car | a book's theme | my brother's board game

Plural Nouns that end with -*s*: the scissors' handle | boys' basketball

Plural Nouns that end without -*s*: Men's department | the people's adventure

Review Video: When to Use an Apostrophe
Visit mometrix.com/academy and enter code: 213068

Review Video: Punctuation Errors in Possessive Pronouns
Visit mometrix.com/academy and enter code: 221438

Hyphens

Hyphens are used to **separate compound words**. Use hyphens in the following cases:

Use Case	Example
Compound numbers from 21 to 99 when written out in words	This team needs twenty-five points to win the game.
Written-out fractions that are used as adjectives	The recipe says that we need a three-fourths cup of butter.
Compound adjectives that come before a noun	The well-fed dog took a nap.
Unusual compound words that would be hard to read or easily confused with other words	This is the best anti-itch cream on the market.

Note: This is not a complete set of the rules for hyphens. A dictionary is the best tool for knowing if a compound word needs a hyphen.

Review Video: Hyphens
Visit mometrix.com/academy and enter code: 981632

Dashes

Dashes are used to show a **break** or a **change in thought** in a sentence or to act as parentheses in a sentence. When typing, use two hyphens to make a dash. Do not put a space before or after the dash. The following are the functions of dashes:

Use Case	Example
Set off parenthetical statements or an **appositive with internal punctuation**	The three trees—oak, pine, and magnolia—are coming on a truck tomorrow.
Show a **break or change in tone or thought**	The first question—how silly of me—does not have a correct answer.

Ellipsis Marks

The ellipsis mark has **three** periods (…) to show when **words have been removed** from a quotation. If a **full sentence or more** is removed from a quoted passage, you need to use **four** periods to show the removed text and the end punctuation mark. The ellipsis mark should not be used at the beginning of a quotation. The ellipsis mark should also not be used at the end of a quotation unless some words have been deleted from the end of the final sentence.

Example:

> "Then he picked up the groceries…paid for them…later he went home."

Brackets

There are two main reasons to use brackets:

Use Case	Example
Placing **parentheses inside of parentheses**	The hero of this story, Paul Revere (a silversmith and industrialist [see Ch. 4]), rode through towns of Massachusetts to warn of advancing British troops.
Adding **clarification or detail to a quotation** that is not part of the quotation	The father explained, "My children are planning to attend my alma mater [State University]."

Review Video: Brackets
Visit mometrix.com/academy and enter code: 727546

Chapter Quiz

1. Which of the following correctly implements the use of parentheses?

a. The rattlesnake (see Image 2) is a dangerous snake of North and South America.
b. The rattlesnake see (Image 2) is a dangerous snake of North and South America.
c. The rattlesnake see Image (2) is a dangerous snake of North and South America.
d. The rattlesnake (see Image) (2) is a dangerous snake of North and South America.

2. Which of the following correctly describes the placement of punctuation in reference to quotations?

a. Periods and commas are put outside quotation marks; colons and semicolons go inside.
b. Periods and colons are put outside quotation marks; commas and semicolons go inside.
c. Periods and commas are put inside quotation marks; colons and semicolons go outside.
d. Periods and colons are put inside quotation marks; commas and semicolons go outside.

3. Which of the following correctly implements the use of commas?

a. He is meeting me at, 456 Delaware Avenue, Washington, D.C., tomorrow morning.
b. He is meeting me at 456 Delaware Avenue, Washington, D.C., tomorrow morning.
c. He is meeting me at 456 Delaware Avenue Washington, D.C. tomorrow morning.
d. He is meeting me at 456 Delaware Avenue, Washington, D.C. tomorrow morning.

Chapter Quiz Answer Key

1. A: Parentheses are used for additional information. Also, they can be used to put labels for letters or numbers in a series. Parentheses should be not be used very often because their overuse can become a distraction.

2. C: Periods and commas are put inside quotation marks, while colons and semicolons are put outside quotation marks. Question marks and exclamation points are placed inside quotation marks when they are part of a quote. When the question mark or exclamation point is not part of a quoted section but instead part of an entire sentence, then it is left outside of the quotation marks.

3. B: These are some of the rules for commas:

Use Case	Example
Before a **coordinating conjunction** joining independent clauses	Bob caught three fish, and I caught two fish.
After an **introductory phrase**	After the final out, we went to a restaurant to celebrate.
After an **adverbial clause**	Studying the stars, I was awed by the beauty of the sky.
Between **items in a series**	I will bring the turkey, the pie, and the coffee.
For **interjections**	Wow, you know how to play this game.
After ***yes*** **and** ***no*** **responses**	No, I cannot come tomorrow.
Separate **nonessential modifiers**	John Frank, who coaches the team, was promoted today.
Separate **nonessential appositives**	Thomas Edison, an American inventor, was born in Ohio.
Separate **nouns of direct address**	You, John, are my only hope in this moment.
Separate **interrogative tags**	This is the last time, correct?
Separate **contrasts**	You are my friend, not my enemy.
Writing **dates**	July 4, 1776, is an important date to remember.
Writing **addresses**	He is meeting me at 456 Delaware Avenue, Washington, D.C., tomorrow morning.
Writing **geographical names**	Paris, France, is my favorite city.
Writing **titles**	John Smith, PhD, will be visiting your class today.
Separate **expressions like "he said"**	"You can start," she said, "with an apology."

Word Confusion

Which, That, and Who

The words *which*, *that*, and *who* can act as **relative pronouns** to help clarify or describe a noun.

Which is used for things only.

Example: Andrew's car, *which is old and rusty*, broke down last week.

That is used for people or things. *That* is usually informal when used to describe people.

Example: Is this the only book *that Louis L'Amour wrote?*

Example: Is Louis L'Amour the author *that wrote Western novels?*

Who is used for people or for animals that have an identity or personality.

Example: Mozart was the composer *who wrote those operas.*

Example: John's dog, *who is called Max*, is large and fierce.

Homophones

Homophones are words that sound alike (or similar) but have different **spellings** and **definitions**. A homophone is a type of **homonym**, which is a pair or group of words that are pronounced or spelled the same, but do not mean the same thing.

To, Too, and Two

To can be an adverb or a preposition for showing direction, purpose, and relationship. See your dictionary for the many other ways to use *to* in a sentence.

Examples: I went to the store. | I want to go with you.

Too is an adverb that means *also, as well, very,* or *in excess*.

Examples: I can walk a mile too. | You have eaten too much.

Two is a number.

Example: You have two minutes left.

There, Their, and They're

There can be an adjective, adverb, or pronoun. Often, *there* is used to show a place or to start a sentence.

Examples: I went there yesterday. | There is something in his pocket.

Their is a pronoun that is used to show ownership.

Examples: He is their father. | This is their fourth apology this week.

They're is a contraction of *they are*.

Example: Did you know that they're in town?

Knew and New

Knew is the past tense of *know.*

Example: I knew the answer.

New is an adjective that means something is current, has not been used, or is modern.

Example: This is my new phone.

Then and Than

Then is an adverb that indicates sequence or order:

Example: I'm going to run to the library and then come home.

Than is special-purpose word used only for comparisons:

Example: Susie likes chips more than candy.

Its and It's

Its is a pronoun that shows ownership.

Example: The guitar is in its case.

It's is a contraction of *it is.*

Example: It's an honor and a privilege to meet you.

Note: The *h* in honor is silent, so *honor* starts with the vowel sound *o*, which must have the article *an*.

Your and You're

Your is a pronoun that shows ownership.

Example: This is your moment to shine.

You're is a contraction of *you are.*

Example: Yes, you're correct.

Saw and Seen

Saw is the past-tense form of *see.*

Example: I saw a turtle on my walk this morning.

Seen is the past participle of *see.*

Example: I have seen this movie before.

Affect and Effect

There are two main reasons that *affect* and *effect* are so often confused: 1) both words can be used as either a noun or a verb, and 2) unlike most homophones, their usage and meanings are closely related to each other. Here is a quick rundown of the four usage options:

Affect (n): feeling, emotion, or mood that is displayed

Example: The patient had a flat *affect*. (i.e., his face showed little or no emotion)

Affect (v): to alter, to change, to influence

Example: The sunshine *affects* the plant's growth.

Effect (n): a result, a consequence

Example: What *effect* will this weather have on our schedule?

Effect (v): to bring about, to cause to be

Example: These new rules will *effect* order in the office.

The noun form of *affect* is rarely used outside of technical medical descriptions, so if a noun form is needed on the test, you can safely select *effect*. The verb form of *effect* is not as rare as the noun form of *affect*, but it's still not all that likely to show up on your test. If you need a verb and you can't decide which to use based on the definitions, choosing *affect* is your best bet.

Homographs

Homographs are words that share the same spelling, but have different meanings and sometimes different pronunciations. To figure out which meaning is being used, you should be looking for context clues. The context clues give hints to the meaning of the word. For example, the word *spot* has many meanings. It can mean "a place" or "a stain or blot." In the sentence "After my lunch, I saw a spot on my shirt," the word *spot* means "a stain or blot." The context clues of "After my lunch" and "on my shirt" guide you to this decision. A homograph is another type of homonym.

Bank

(noun): an establishment where money is held for savings or lending

(verb): to collect or pile up

Content

(noun): the topics that will be addressed within a book

(adjective): pleased or satisfied

(verb): to make someone pleased or satisfied

Fine

(noun): an amount of money that acts a penalty for an offense

(adjective): very small or thin

(adverb): in an acceptable way

(verb): to make someone pay money as a punishment

Incense

(noun): a material that is burned in religious settings and makes a pleasant aroma

(verb): to frustrate or anger

Lead

(noun): the first or highest position

(noun): a heavy metallic element

(verb): to direct a person or group of followers

(adjective): containing lead

Object

(noun): a lifeless item that can be held and observed

(verb): to disagree

Produce

(noun): fruits and vegetables

(verb): to make or create something

Refuse

(noun): garbage or debris that has been thrown away

(verb): to not allow

Subject

(noun): an area of study

(verb): to force or subdue

Tear

(noun): a fluid secreted by the eyes

(verb): to separate or pull apart

Chapter Quiz

1. Which of the following correctly implements the word "affect"?

a. These new rules will affect order in the office.
b. What affect will this weather have on our schedule?
c. The patient had a flat affect during her examination.
d. His narcissism had a detrimental affect on everyone around him.

2. "Affect" and "effect" would be considered which of the following?

a. Homographs
b. Synonyms
c. Antonyms
d. Homophones

Chapter Quiz Answer Key

1. C: There are two main reasons that *affect* and *effect* are so often confused: 1) both words can be used as either a noun or a verb; and 2) unlike most homophones, their usage and meanings are closely related to each other. Here is a quick rundown of the four usage options:

Affect (n): feeling, emotion, or mood that is displayed

Example: The patient had a flat *affect* (i.e., his face showed little or no emotion).

Affect (v): to alter, to change, to influence

Example: The sunshine *affects* the plant's growth.

Effect (n): a result, a consequence

Example: What *effect* will this weather have on our schedule?

Effect (v): to bring about, to cause to be

Example: These new rules will *effect* order in the office.

The noun form of *affect* is rarely used outside of technical medical descriptions, so if a noun form is needed on the test, *effect* is a safe selection. The verb form of *effect* is not as rare as the noun form of *affect*, but it's still not likely to show up on a test. If a verb is needed and the definitions aren't enough of an indicator for which one to use, choosing *affect* is the safest option.

2. D: Homophones are words that sound alike (or similar) but have different spellings and definitions. A homophone is a type of homonym, which is a pair or group of words that are pronounced or spelled the same, but do not mean the same thing.

Mathematics Test

Foundational Math Concepts

Classifications of Numbers

Numbers are the basic building blocks of mathematics. Specific features of numbers are identified by the following terms:

Integer – any positive or negative whole number, including zero. Integers do not include fractions $\left(\frac{1}{3}\right)$, decimals (0.56), or mixed numbers $\left(7\frac{3}{4}\right)$.

Prime number – any whole number greater than 1 that has only two factors, itself and 1; that is, a number that can be divided evenly only by 1 and itself.

Composite number – any whole number greater than 1 that has more than two different factors; in other words, any whole number that is not a prime number. For example: The composite number 8 has the factors of 1, 2, 4, and 8.

Even number – any integer that can be divided by 2 without leaving a remainder. For example: 2, 4, 6, 8, and so on.

Odd number – any integer that cannot be divided evenly by 2. For example: 3, 5, 7, 9, and so on.

Decimal number – any number that uses a decimal point to show the part of the number that is less than one. Example: 1.234.

Decimal point – a symbol used to separate the ones place from the tenths place in decimals or dollars from cents in currency.

Decimal place – the position of a number to the right of the decimal point. In the decimal 0.123, the 1 is in the first place to the right of the decimal point, indicating tenths; the 2 is in the second place, indicating hundredths; and the 3 is in the third place, indicating thousandths.

The **decimal**, or base 10, system is a number system that uses ten different digits (0, 1, 2, 3, 4, 5, 6, 7, 8, 9). An example of a number system that uses something other than ten digits is the **binary**, or base 2, number system, used by computers, which uses only the numbers 0 and 1. It is thought that the decimal system originated because people had only their 10 fingers for counting.

Rational numbers include all integers, decimals, and fractions. Any terminating or repeating decimal number is a rational number.

Irrational numbers cannot be written as fractions or decimals because the number of decimal places is infinite and there is no recurring pattern of digits within the number. For example, pi (π) begins with 3.141592 and continues without terminating or repeating, so pi is an irrational number.

Real numbers are the set of all rational and irrational numbers.

> **Review Video: Classification of Numbers**
> Visit mometrix.com/academy and enter code: 461071
>
> **Review Video: Prime and Composite Numbers**
> Visit mometrix.com/academy and enter code: 565581

Numbers in Word Form and Place Value

When writing numbers out in word form or translating word form to numbers, it is essential to understand how a place value system works. In the decimal or base-10 system, each digit of a number represents how many of the corresponding place value—a specific factor of 10—are contained in the number being represented. To make reading numbers easier, every three digits to the left of the decimal place is preceded by a comma. The following table demonstrates some of the place values:

Power of 10	10^3	10^2	10^1	10^0	10^{-1}	10^{-2}	10^{-3}
Value	1,000	100	10	1	0.1	0.01	0.001
Place	thousands	hundreds	tens	ones	tenths	hundredths	thousandths

For example, consider the number 4,546.09, which can be separated into each place value like this:

4: thousands
5: hundreds
4: tens
6: ones
0: tenths
9: hundredths

This number in word form would be *four thousand five hundred forty-six and nine hundredths.*

> **Review Video: Place Value**
> Visit mometrix.com/academy and enter code: 205433

Rational Numbers

The term **rational** means that the number can be expressed as a ratio or fraction. That is, a number, r, is rational if and only if it can be represented by a fraction $\frac{a}{b}$ where a and b are integers and b does not equal 0. The set of rational numbers includes integers and decimals. If there is no finite way to represent a value with a fraction of integers, then the number is **irrational**. Common examples of irrational numbers include: $\sqrt{5}$, $(1+\sqrt{2})$, and π.

> **Review Video: Rational and Irrational Numbers**
> Visit mometrix.com/academy and enter code: 280645

The Number Line

A number line is a graph to see the distance between numbers. Basically, this graph shows the relationship between numbers. So a number line may have a point for zero and may show negative numbers on the left side of the line. Any positive numbers are placed on the right side of the line. For example, consider the points labeled on the following number line:

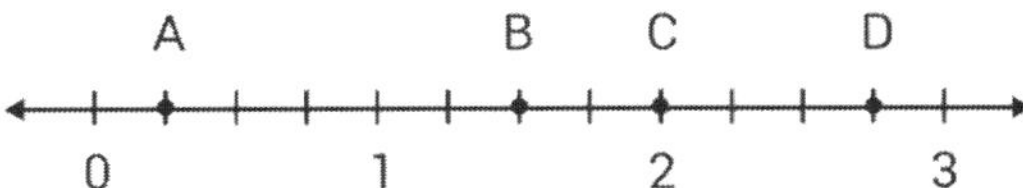

We can use the dashed lines on the number line to identify each point. Each dashed line between two whole numbers is $\frac{1}{4}$. The line halfway between two numbers is $\frac{1}{2}$.

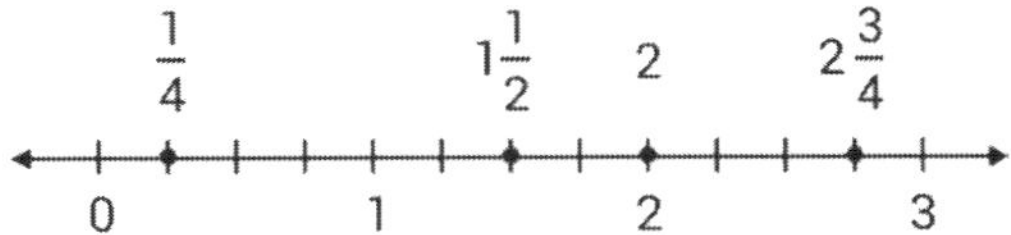

Review Video: The Number Line
Visit mometrix.com/academy and enter code: 816439

Absolute Value

A precursor to working with negative numbers is understanding what **absolute values** are. A number's absolute value is simply the distance away from zero a number is on the number line. The absolute value of a number is always positive and is written $|x|$. For example, the absolute value of 3, written as $|3|$, is 3 because the distance between 0 and 3 on a number line is three units. Likewise, the absolute value of –3, written as $|-3|$, is 3 because the distance between 0 and –3 on a number line is three units. So $|3| = |-3|$.

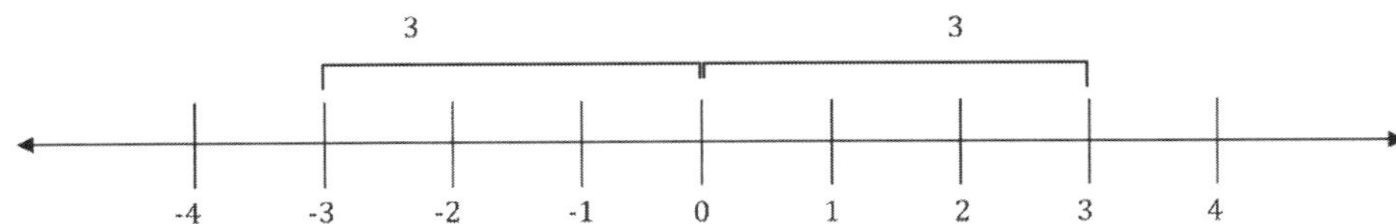

Review Video: Absolute Value
Visit mometrix.com/academy and enter code: 314669

Operations

An **operation** is simply a mathematical process that takes some value(s) as input(s) and produces an output. Elementary operations are often written in the following form: *value operation value*. For instance, in the expression $1 + 2$ the values are 1 and 2 and the operation is addition. Performing the operation gives the output of 3. In this way we can say that $1 + 2$ and 3 are equal, or $1 + 2 = 3$.

Addition

Addition increases the value of one quantity by the value of another quantity (both called **addends**). Example: $2 + 4 = 6$ or $8 + 9 = 17$. The result is called the **sum**. With addition, the order does not matter, $4 + 2 = 2 + 4$.

When adding signed numbers, if the signs are the same simply add the absolute values of the addends and apply the original sign to the sum. For example, $(+4) + (+8) = +12$ and $(-4) + (-8) = -12$. When the original signs are different, take the absolute values of the addends and subtract the smaller value from the larger value, then apply the original sign of the larger value to the difference. Example: $(+4) + (-8) = -4$ and $(-4) + (+8) = +4$.

SUBTRACTION

Subtraction is the opposite operation to addition; it decreases the value of one quantity (the **minuend**) by the value of another quantity (the **subtrahend**). For example, $6 - 4 = 2$ or $17 - 8 = 9$. The result is called the **difference**. Note that with subtraction, the order does matter, $6 - 4 \neq 4 - 6$.

For subtracting signed numbers, change the sign of the subtrahend and then follow the same rules used for addition. Example: $(+4) - (+8) = (+4) + (-8) = -4$

MULTIPLICATION

Multiplication can be thought of as repeated addition. One number (the **multiplier**) indicates how many times to add the other number (the **multiplicand**) to itself. Example: $3 \times 2 = 2 + 2 + 2 = 6$. With multiplication, the order does not matter, $2 \times 3 = 3 \times 2$ or $3 + 3 = 2 + 2 + 2$, either way the result (the **product**) is the same.

If the signs are the same, the product is positive when multiplying signed numbers. Example: $(+4) \times (+8) = +32$ and $(-4) \times (-8) = +32$. If the signs are opposite, the product is negative. Example: $(+4) \times (-8) = -32$ and $(-4) \times (+8) = -32$. When more than two factors are multiplied together, the sign of the product is determined by how many negative factors are present. If there are an odd number of negative factors then the product is negative, whereas an even number of negative factors indicates a positive product. Example: $(+4) \times (-8) \times (-2) = +64$ and $(-4) \times (-8) \times (-2) = -64$.

DIVISION

Division is the opposite operation to multiplication; one number (the **divisor**) tells us how many parts to divide the other number (the **dividend**) into. The result of division is called the **quotient**. Example: $20 \div 4 = 5$. If 20 is split into 4 equal parts, each part is 5. With division, the order of the numbers does matter, $20 \div 4 \neq 4 \div 20$.

The rules for dividing signed numbers are similar to multiplying signed numbers. If the dividend and divisor have the same sign, the quotient is positive. If the dividend and divisor have opposite signs, the quotient is negative. Example: $(-4) \div (+8) = -0.5$.

Review Video: Mathematical Operations
Visit mometrix.com/academy and enter code: 208095

PARENTHESES

Parentheses are used to designate which operations should be done first when there are multiple operations. Example: $4 - (2 + 1) = 1$; the parentheses tell us that we must add 2 and 1, and then subtract the sum from 4, rather than subtracting 2 from 4 and then adding 1 (this would give us an answer of 3).

Review Video: Mathematical Parentheses
Visit mometrix.com/academy and enter code: 978600

Exponents

An **exponent** is a superscript number placed next to another number at the top right. It indicates how many times the base number is to be multiplied by itself. Exponents provide a shorthand way to write what would be a longer mathematical expression, Example: $2^4 = 2 \times 2 \times 2 \times 2$. A number with an exponent of 2 is said to be "squared," while a number with an exponent of 3 is said to be "cubed." The value of a number raised to an exponent is called its power. So 8^4 is read as "8 to the 4th power," or "8 raised to the power of 4."

Review Video: Introduction to Exponents
Visit mometrix.com/academy and enter code: 600998

Roots

A **root**, such as a square root, is another way of writing a fractional exponent. Instead of using a superscript, roots use the radical symbol ($\sqrt{\ }$) to indicate the operation. A radical will have a number underneath the bar, and may sometimes have a number in the upper left: $\sqrt[n]{a}$, read as "the nth root of a." The relationship between radical notation and exponent notation can be described by this equation:

$$\sqrt[n]{a} = a^{\frac{1}{n}}$$

The two special cases of $n = 2$ and $n = 3$ are called square roots and cube roots. If there is no number to the upper left, the radical is understood to be a square root ($n = 2$). Nearly all of the roots you encounter will be square roots. A square root is the same as a number raised to the one-half power. When we say that a is the square root of b ($a = \sqrt{b}$), we mean that a multiplied by itself equals b: ($a \times a = b$).

A **perfect square** is a number that has an integer for its square root. There are 10 perfect squares from 1 to 100: 1, 4, 9, 16, 25, 36, 49, 64, 81, 100 (the squares of integers 1 through 10).

Review Video: Roots
Visit mometrix.com/academy and enter code: 795655

Review Video: Square Root and Perfect Squares
Visit mometrix.com/academy and enter code: 648063

Word Problems and Mathematical Symbols

When working on word problems, you must be able to translate verbal expressions or "math words" into math symbols. This chart contains several "math words" and their appropriate symbols:

Phrase	Symbol
equal, is, was, will be, has, costs, gets to, is the same as, becomes	$=$
times, of, multiplied by, product of, twice, doubles, halves, triples	$\times$
divided by, per, ratio of/to, out of	$\div$
plus, added to, sum, combined, and, more than, totals of	$+$
subtracted from, less than, decreased by, minus, difference between	$-$
what, how much, original value, how many, a number, a variable	x, n, etc.

Examples of Translated Mathematical Phrases

- The phrase four more than twice a number can be written algebraically as $2x + 4$.

- The phrase half a number decreased by six can be written algebraically as $\frac{1}{2}x - 6$.
- The phrase the sum of a number and the product of five and that number can be written algebraically as $x + 5x$.
- You may see a test question that says, "Olivia is constructing a bookcase from seven boards. Two of them are for vertical supports and five are for shelves. The height of the bookcase is twice the width of the bookcase. If the seven boards total 36 feet in length, what will be the height of Olivia's bookcase?" You would need to make a sketch and then create the equation to determine the width of the shelves. The height can be represented as double the width. (If x represents the width of the shelves in feet, then the height of the bookcase is $2x$. Since the seven boards total 36 feet, $2x + 2x + x + x + x + x + x = 36$ or $9x = 36$; $x = 4$. The height is twice the width, or 8 feet.)

Subtraction with Regrouping

A great way to make use of some of the features built into the decimal system would be regrouping when attempting longform subtraction operations. When subtracting within a place value, sometimes the minuend is smaller than the subtrahend, **regrouping** enables you to 'borrow' a unit from a place value to the left in order to get a positive difference. For example, consider subtracting 189 from 525 with regrouping.

First, set up the subtraction problem in vertical form:

$$\begin{array}{r} 525 \\ -\ 189 \\ \hline \end{array}$$

Notice that the numbers in the ones and tens columns of 525 are smaller than the numbers in the ones and tens columns of 189. This means you will need to use regrouping to perform subtraction:

$$\begin{array}{cccc} & 5 & 2 & 5 \\ - & 1 & 8 & 9 \\ \hline \end{array}$$

To subtract 9 from 5 in the ones column you will need to borrow from the 2 in the tens columns:

$$\begin{array}{cccc} & 5 & 1 & 15 \\ - & 1 & 8 & 9 \\ \hline & & & 6 \end{array}$$

Next, to subtract 8 from 1 in the tens column you will need to borrow from the 5 in the hundreds column:

$$\begin{array}{cccc} & 4 & 11 & 15 \\ - & 1 & 8 & 9 \\ \hline & & 3 & 6 \end{array}$$

Last, subtract the 1 from the 4 in the hundreds column:

$$\begin{array}{cccc} & 4 & 11 & 15 \\ - & 1 & 8 & 9 \\ \hline & 3 & 3 & 6 \end{array}$$

Review Video: Subtracting Large Numbers
Visit mometrix.com/academy and enter code: 603350

ORDER OF OPERATIONS

The **order of operations** is a set of rules that dictates the order in which we must perform each operation in an expression so that we will evaluate it accurately. If we have an expression that includes multiple different operations, the order of operations tells us which operations to do first. The most common mnemonic for the order of operations is **PEMDAS**, or "Please Excuse My Dear Aunt Sally." PEMDAS stands for parentheses, exponents, multiplication, division, addition, and subtraction. It is important to understand that multiplication and division have equal precedence, as do addition and subtraction, so those pairs of operations are simply worked from left to right in order.

For example, evaluating the expression $5 + 20 \div 4 \times (2 + 3)^2 - 6$ using the correct order of operations would be done like this:

- **P:** Perform the operations inside the parentheses: $(2 + 3) = 5$
- **E:** Simplify the exponents: $(5)^2 = 5 \times 5 = 25$
    - The expression now looks like this: $5 + 20 \div 4 \times 25 - 6$
- **MD:** Perform multiplication and division from left to right: $20 \div 4 = 5$; then $5 \times 25 = 125$
    - The expression now looks like this: $5 + 125 - 6$
- **AS:** Perform addition and subtraction from left to right: $5 + 125 = 130$; then $130 - 6 = 124$

Review Video: Order of Operations
Visit mometrix.com/academy and enter code: 259675

The properties of exponents are as follows:

Property	Description
$a^1 = a$	Any number to the power of 1 is equal to itself
$1^n = 1$	The number 1 raised to any power is equal to 1
$a^0 = 1$	Any number raised to the power of 0 is equal to 1
$a^n \times a^m = a^{n+m}$	Add exponents to multiply powers of the same base number
$a^n \div a^m = a^{n-m}$	Subtract exponents to divide powers of the same base number
$(a^n)^m = a^{n \times m}$	When a power is raised to a power, the exponents are multiplied
$(a \times b)^n = a^n \times b^n$ $(a \div b)^n = a^n \div b^n$	Multiplication and division operations inside parentheses can be raised to a power. This is the same as each term being raised to that power.
$a^{-n} = \frac{1}{a^n}$	A negative exponent is the same as the reciprocal of a positive exponent

Note that exponents do not have to be integers. Fractional or decimal exponents follow all the rules above as well. Example: $5^{\frac{1}{4}} \times 5^{\frac{3}{4}} = 5^{\frac{1}{4}+\frac{3}{4}} = 5^1 = 5$.

Review Video: Properties of Exponents
Visit mometrix.com/academy and enter code: 532558

Factors and Greatest Common Factor

Factors are numbers that are multiplied together to obtain a **product**. For example, in the equation $2 \times 3 = 6$, the numbers 2 and 3 are factors. A **prime number** has only two factors (1 and itself), but other numbers can have many factors.

A **common factor** is a number that divides exactly into two or more other numbers. For example, the factors of 12 are 1, 2, 3, 4, 6, and 12, while the factors of 15 are 1, 3, 5, and 15. The common factors of 12 and 15 are 1 and 3.

A **prime factor** is also a prime number. Therefore, the prime factors of 12 are 2 and 3. For 15, the prime factors are 3 and 5.

The **greatest common factor** (**GCF**) is the largest number that is a factor of two or more numbers. For example, the factors of 15 are 1, 3, 5, and 15; the factors of 35 are 1, 5, 7, and 35. Therefore, the greatest common factor of 15 and 35 is 5.

Review Video: Factors
Visit mometrix.com/academy and enter code: 920086

Review Video: Prime Numbers and Factorization
Visit mometrix.com/academy and enter code: 760669

Review Video: Greatest Common Factor and Least Common Multiple
Visit mometrix.com/academy and enter code: 838699

Multiples and Least Common Multiple

Often listed out in multiplication tables, **multiples** are integer increments of a given factor. In other words, dividing a multiple by the factor will result in an integer. For example, the multiples of 7 include: $1 \times 7 = 7$, $2 \times 7 = 14$, $3 \times 7 = 21$, $4 \times 7 = 28$, $5 \times 7 = 35$. Dividing 7, 14, 21, 28, or 35 by 7 will result in the integers 1, 2, 3, 4, and 5, respectively.

The least common multiple (**LCM**) is the smallest number that is a multiple of two or more numbers. For example, the multiples of 3 include 3, 6, 9, 12, 15, etc.; the multiples of 5 include 5, 10, 15, 20, etc. Therefore, the least common multiple of 3 and 5 is 15.

Review Video: Multiples
Visit mometrix.com/academy and enter code: 626738

FRACTIONS

A **fraction** is a number that is expressed as one integer written above another integer, with a dividing line between them $\left(\frac{x}{y}\right)$. It represents the **quotient** of the two numbers "x divided by y." It can also be thought of as x out of y equal parts.

The top number of a fraction is called the **numerator**, and it represents the number of parts under consideration. The 1 in $\frac{1}{4}$ means that 1 part out of the whole is being considered in the calculation. The bottom number of a fraction is called the **denominator**, and it represents the total number of equal parts. The 4 in $\frac{1}{4}$ means that the whole consists of 4 equal parts. A fraction cannot have a denominator of zero; this is referred to as "*undefined*."

Fractions can be manipulated, without changing the value of the fraction, by multiplying or dividing (but not adding or subtracting) both the numerator and denominator by the same number. If you divide both numbers by a common factor, you are **reducing** or simplifying the fraction. Two fractions that have the same value but are expressed differently are known as **equivalent fractions**. For example, $\frac{2}{10}, \frac{3}{15}, \frac{4}{20}$, and $\frac{5}{25}$ are all equivalent fractions. They can also all be reduced or simplified to $\frac{1}{5}$.

When two fractions are manipulated so that they have the same denominator, this is known as finding a **common denominator**. The number chosen to be that common denominator should be the least common multiple of the two original denominators. Example: $\frac{3}{4}$ and $\frac{5}{6}$; the least common multiple of 4 and 6 is 12. Manipulating to achieve the common denominator: $\frac{3}{4} = \frac{9}{12}; \frac{5}{6} = \frac{10}{12}$.

Review Video: Overview of Fractions
Visit mometrix.com/academy and enter code: 262335

PROPER FRACTIONS AND MIXED NUMBERS

A fraction whose denominator is greater than its numerator is known as a **proper fraction**, while a fraction whose numerator is greater than its denominator is known as an **improper fraction**. Proper fractions have values *less than one* and improper fractions have values *greater than one*.

A **mixed number** is a number that contains both an integer and a fraction. Any improper fraction can be rewritten as a mixed number. Example: $\frac{8}{3} = \frac{6}{3} + \frac{2}{3} = 2 + \frac{2}{3} = 2\frac{2}{3}$. Similarly, any mixed number can be rewritten as an improper fraction. Example: $1\frac{3}{5} = 1 + \frac{3}{5} = \frac{5}{5} + \frac{3}{5} = \frac{8}{5}$.

Review Video: Improper Fractions and Mixed Numbers
Visit mometrix.com/academy and enter code: 211077

ADDING AND SUBTRACTING FRACTIONS

If two fractions have a common denominator, they can be added or subtracted simply by adding or subtracting the two numerators and retaining the same denominator. If the two fractions do not already have the same denominator, one or both of them must be manipulated to achieve a common denominator before they can be added or subtracted. Example: $\frac{1}{2}+\frac{1}{4}=\frac{2}{4}+\frac{1}{4}=\frac{3}{4}$.

Review Video: Adding and Subtracting Fractions
Visit mometrix.com/academy and enter code: 378080

Multiplying Fractions

Two fractions can be multiplied by multiplying the two numerators to find the new numerator and the two denominators to find the new denominator. Example: $\frac{1}{3}\times\frac{2}{3}=\frac{1\times 2}{3\times 3}=\frac{2}{9}$.

Dividing Fractions

Two fractions can be divided by flipping the numerator and denominator of the second fraction and then proceeding as though it were a multiplication problem. Example: $\frac{2}{3}\div\frac{3}{4}=\frac{2}{3}\times\frac{4}{3}=\frac{8}{9}$.

Review Video: Multiplying and Dividing Fractions
Visit mometrix.com/academy and enter code: 473632

Multiplying a Mixed Number by a Whole Number or a Decimal

When multiplying a mixed number by something, it is usually best to convert it to an improper fraction first. Additionally, if the multiplicand is a decimal, it is most often simplest to convert it to a fraction. For instance, to multiply $4\frac{3}{8}$ by 3.5, begin by rewriting each quantity as a whole number plus a proper fraction. Remember, a mixed number is a fraction added to a whole number and a decimal is a representation of the sum of fractions, specifically tenths, hundredths, thousandths, and so on:

$$4\frac{3}{8}\times 3.5=\left(4+\frac{3}{8}\right)\times\left(3+\frac{1}{2}\right)$$

Next, the quantities being added need to be expressed with the same denominator. This is achieved by multiplying and dividing the whole number by the denominator of the fraction. Recall that a whole number is equivalent to that number divided by 1:

$$=\left(\frac{4}{1}\times\frac{8}{8}+\frac{3}{8}\right)\times\left(\frac{3}{1}\times\frac{2}{2}+\frac{1}{2}\right)$$

When multiplying fractions, remember to multiply the numerators and denominators separately:

$$=\left(\frac{4\times 8}{1\times 8}+\frac{3}{8}\right)\times\left(\frac{3\times 2}{1\times 2}+\frac{1}{2}\right)$$
$$=\left(\frac{32}{8}+\frac{3}{8}\right)\times\left(\frac{6}{2}+\frac{1}{2}\right)$$

Now that the fractions have the same denominators, they can be added:

$$=\frac{35}{8}\times\frac{7}{2}$$

Finally, perform the last multiplication and then simplify:

$$= \frac{35 \times 7}{8 \times 2} = \frac{245}{16} = \frac{240}{16} + \frac{5}{16} = 15\frac{5}{16}$$

Decimals

Decimals are one way to represent parts of a whole. Using the place value system, each digit to the right of a decimal point denotes the number of units of a corresponding *negative* power of ten. For example, consider the decimal 0.24. We can use a model to represent the decimal. Since a dime is worth one-tenth of a dollar and a penny is worth one-hundredth of a dollar, one possible model to represent this fraction is to have 2 dimes representing the 2 in the tenths place and 4 pennies representing the 4 in the hundredths place:

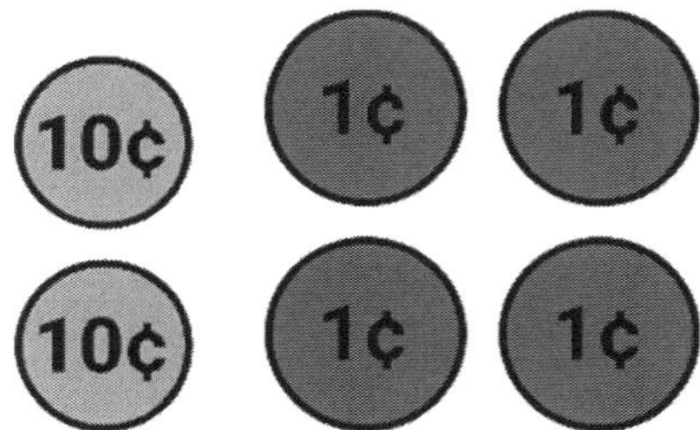

To write the decimal as a fraction, put the decimal in the numerator with 1 in the denominator. Multiply the numerator and denominator by tens until there are no more decimal places. Then simplify the fraction to lowest terms. For example, converting 0.24 to a fraction:

$$0.24 = \frac{0.24}{1} = \frac{0.24 \times 100}{1 \times 100} = \frac{24}{100} = \frac{6}{25}$$

Review Video: Decimals
Visit mometrix.com/academy and enter code: 837268

Operations with Decimals

Adding and Subtracting Decimals

When adding and subtracting decimals, the decimal points must always be aligned. Adding decimals is just like adding regular whole numbers. Example: $4.5 + 2.0 = 6.5$.

If the problem-solver does not properly align the decimal points, an incorrect answer of 4.7 may result. An easy way to add decimals is to align all of the decimal points in a vertical column visually. This will allow you to see exactly where the decimal should be placed in the final answer. Begin adding from right to left. Add each column in turn, making sure to carry the number to the left if a column adds up to more than 9. The same rules apply to the subtraction of decimals.

Review Video: Adding and Subtracting Decimals
Visit mometrix.com/academy and enter code: 381101

Multiplying Decimals

A simple multiplication problem has two components: a **multiplicand** and a **multiplier**. When multiplying decimals, work as though the numbers were whole rather than decimals. Once the final product is calculated, count the number of places to the right of the decimal in both the multiplicand and the multiplier. Then, count that number of places from the right of the product and place the decimal in that position.

For example, 12.3×2.56 has a total of three places to the right of the respective decimals. Multiply 123×256 to get 31,488. Now, beginning on the right, count three places to the left and insert the decimal. The final product will be 31.488.

Review Video: How to Multiply Decimals
Visit mometrix.com/academy and enter code: 731574

DIVIDING DECIMALS

Every division problem has a **divisor** and a **dividend**. The dividend is the number that is being divided. In the problem $14 \div 7$, 14 is the dividend and 7 is the divisor. In a division problem with decimals, the divisor must be converted into a whole number. Begin by moving the decimal in the divisor to the right until a whole number is created. Next, move the decimal in the dividend the same number of spaces to the right. For example, 4.9 into 24.5 would become 49 into 245. The decimal was moved one space to the right to create a whole number in the divisor, and then the same was done for the dividend. Once the whole numbers are created, the problem is carried out normally: $245 \div 49 = 5$.

Review Video: How to Divide Decimals
Visit mometrix.com/academy and enter code: 560690

Review Video: Dividing Decimals by Whole Numbers
Visit mometrix.com/academy and enter code: 535669

PERCENTAGES

Percentages can be thought of as fractions that are based on a whole of 100; that is, one whole is equal to 100%. The word **percent** means "per hundred." Percentage problems are often presented in three main ways:

- Find what percentage of some number another number is.
  - Example: What percentage of 40 is 8?
- Find what number is some percentage of a given number.
  - Example: What number is 20% of 40?
- Find what number another number is a given percentage of.
  - Example: What number is 8 20% of?

There are three components in each of these cases: a **whole** (W), a **part** (P), and a **percentage** (%). These are related by the equation: $P = W \times \%$. This can easily be rearranged into other forms that may suit different questions better: $\% = \frac{P}{W}$ and $W = \frac{P}{\%}$. Percentage problems are often also word problems. As such, a large part of solving them is figuring out which quantities are what. For example, consider the following word problem:

In a school cafeteria, 7 students choose pizza, 9 choose hamburgers, and 4 choose tacos. What percentage of student choose tacos?

To find the whole, you must first add all of the parts: $7 + 9 + 4 = 20$. The percentage can then be found by dividing the part by the whole $\left(\% = \frac{P}{W}\right)$: $\frac{4}{20} = \frac{20}{100} = 20\%$.

Review Video: Computation with Percentages
Visit mometrix.com/academy and enter code: 693099

Converting Between Percentages, Fractions, and Decimals

Converting decimals to percentages and percentages to decimals is as simple as moving the decimal point. To *convert from a decimal to a percentage*, move the decimal point **two places to the right**. To *convert from a percentage to a decimal*, move it **two places to the left**. It may be helpful to remember that the percentage number will always be larger than the equivalent decimal number. Example:

$$0.23 = 23\% \qquad 5.34 = 534\% \qquad 0.007 = 0.7\%$$
$$700\% = 7.00 \qquad 86\% = 0.86 \qquad 0.15\% = 0.0015$$

To convert a fraction to a decimal, simply divide the numerator by the denominator in the fraction. To convert a decimal to a fraction, put the decimal in the numerator with 1 in the denominator. Multiply the numerator and denominator by tens until there are no more decimal places. Then simplify the fraction to lowest terms. For example, converting 0.24 to a fraction:

$$0.24 = \frac{0.24}{1} = \frac{0.24 \times 100}{1 \times 100} = \frac{24}{100} = \frac{6}{25}$$

Fractions can be converted to a percentage by finding equivalent fractions with a denominator of 100. Example:

$$\frac{7}{10} = \frac{70}{100} = 70\% \quad \frac{1}{4} = \frac{25}{100} = 25\%$$

To convert a percentage to a fraction, divide the percentage number by 100 and reduce the fraction to its simplest possible terms. Example:

$$60\% = \frac{60}{100} = \frac{3}{5} \quad 96\% = \frac{96}{100} = \frac{24}{25}$$

Review Video: Converting Fractions to Percentages and Decimals
Visit mometrix.com/academy and enter code: 306233

Review Video: Converting Percentages to Decimals and Fractions
Visit mometrix.com/academy and enter code: 287297

Review Video: Converting Decimals to Fractions and Percentages
Visit mometrix.com/academy and enter code: 986765

Review Video: Converting Decimals, Improper Fractions, and Mixed Numbers
Visit mometrix.com/academy and enter code: 696924

Heart of Algebra

Heart of Algebra Overview

The questions in this section will cover a range of topics in algebra. Students will be tested on their ability to analyze and solve linear equations and systems of equations. They will also need to be able to create these equations to represent a relationship between two or more quantities and solve problems. Along with linear equations, students will need to be able to create and solve linear inequalities. Some questions will also require the student to interpret formulas and rearrange them to solve the problem.

Question Types in Heart of Algebra

The **heart of algebra** section will test your knowledge of the following:

- Create, solve, or interpret a **linear expression or equation in one variable** that represents a context.
  - The expression or equation will have rational coefficients, and multiple steps may be required to simplify the expression, simplify the equation, or solve for the variable in the equation.
- Create, solve, or interpret **linear inequalities in one variable** that represent a context.
  - The inequality will have rational coefficients, and multiple steps may be required to simplify or solve for the variable.
- Build a linear function that models a linear relationship between two quantities.
  - The student will describe a linear relationship that models a context using either an equation in two variables or function notation.
  - The equation or function will have rational coefficients, and multiple steps may be required to build and simplify the equation or function.
- Create, solve, and interpret **systems of linear inequalities** in two variables.
  - The student will analyze one or more constraints that exist between two variables by creating, solving, or interpreting an inequality in two variables or a system of inequalities in two variables to represent a context.
  - Multiple steps may be required to create the inequality or system of inequalities or to determine whether a given point is in the solution set.
- Create, solve, and interpret **systems of two linear equations** in two variables.
  - The student will analyze one or more constraints that exist between two variables by creating, solving, or analyzing a system of linear equations to represent a context.
  - The equations will have rational coefficients, and multiple steps may be required to simplify or solve the system.
- Algebraically solve linear equations (or inequalities) in one variable.
  - The equation (or inequality) will have rational coefficients and may require multiple steps to solve for the variable; the equation may yield no solution, one solution, or infinitely many solutions.
  - The student may also be asked to determine the value of a constant or coefficient for an equation with no solution or infinitely many solutions.

- Algebraically solve systems of two linear equations in two variables.
    - The equations will have rational coefficients, and the system may yield no solution, one solution, or infinitely many solutions.
    - The student may also be asked to determine the value of a constant or coefficient of an equation in which the system has no solution, one solution, or infinitely many solutions.
- Interpret the variables and constants in expressions for linear functions within the context presented.
    - The student will make connections between a context and the linear equation that models the context and will identify or describe the real-life meaning of a constant term, a variable, or a feature of the given equation.
- Understand connections between algebraic and graphical representations.
    - The student will select a graph described by a given linear equation, select a linear equation that describes a given graph, determine the equation of a line given a verbal description of its graph, determine key features of the graph of a linear function from its equation, or determine how a graph may be affected by a change in its equation.

Other Necessary Skills

Translating Verbal Expressions into Mathematical Language

You must be able to translate **verbal expressions** into mathematical language. These may be simple or complex algebraic expressions (linear, quadratic, or exponential); you must be able to simplify these expressions using order of operations. You may be asked to determine an algebraic model involving costs or interest and then use that model to perform a calculation. You may be given a geometric situation involving area or perimeter, in which you have to write and simplify an expression. These problems may be complex and require sketches in order to choose or produce a correct answer.

Modeling Scenarios with Linear Equations

You should expect to be given a real-world scenario and the linear function associated with that scenario. You may be asked to identify variable terms or constant terms from the given function as well as interpret their meanings in the given real-world situation. You may see a test question like "The school van begins a field trip with 14 gallons of gasoline. After traveling 120 miles, the van has 8 gallons of gasoline. If this relationship is modeled by the linear function $f(x) = -20x + 280$, what does the x represent?" Or you might be asked what -20 and 280 represent in the given function.

Systems of Three Equations

This test typically has one problem with a system of three equations. Usually, the graphs as well as the equations are given. The key point is that the only solutions to this graph are the points at which all three graphs coincide or intersect. For example, the graph might include a circle, a parabola, and a line. There are no solutions to the given system if all three graphs do not intersect at one or more points. If the three graphs intersect at one point, then there is one solution to the given system, and that solution is the point of intersection. If the line intersects the circle at two points, and the line also intersects the parabola at the same exact two points, there are two solutions to the given system, and those solutions are the points of intersection. This system has at most two solutions.

Terms and Coefficients

Mathematical expressions consist of a combination of one or more values arranged in terms that are added together. As such, an expression could be just a single number, including zero. A **variable term** is the product of a real number, also called a **coefficient**, and one or more variables, each of which may be raised to an exponent. Expressions may also include numbers without a variable, called **constants** or **constant terms**. The expression $6s^2$, for example, is a single term where the coefficient is the real number 6 and the variable term is s^2. Note that if a term is written as simply a variable to some exponent, like t^2, then the coefficient is 1, because $t^2 = 1t^2$.

LINEAR EXPRESSIONS

A **single variable linear expression** is the sum of a single variable term, where the variable has no exponent, and a constant, which may be zero. For instance, the expression $2w + 7$ has $2w$ as the variable term and 7 as the constant term. It is important to realize that terms are separated by addition or subtraction. Since an expression is a sum of terms, expressions such as $5x - 3$ can be written as $5x + (-3)$ to emphasize that the constant term is negative. A real-world example of a single variable linear expression is the perimeter of a square, four times the side length, often expressed: $4s$.

In general, a **linear expression** is the sum of any number of variable terms so long as none of the variables have an exponent. For example, $3m + 8n - \frac{1}{4}p + 5.5q - 1$ is a linear expression, but $3y^3$ is not. In the same way, the expression for the perimeter of a general triangle, the sum of the side lengths $(a + b + c)$ is considered to be linear, but the expression for the area of a square, the side length squared $(s^2)$is not.

LINEAR EQUATIONS

Equations that can be written as $ax + b = 0$, where $a \neq 0$, are referred to as **one variable linear equations**. A solution to such an equation is called a **root**. In the case where we have the equation $5x + 10 = 0$, if we solve for x we get a solution of $x = -2$. In other words, the root of the equation is –2. This is found by first subtracting 10 from both sides, which gives $5x = -10$. Next, simply divide both sides by the coefficient of the variable, in this case 5, to get $x = -2$. This can be checked by plugging –2 back into the original equation $(5)(-2) + 10 = -10 + 10 = 0$.

The **solution set** is the set of all solutions of an equation. In our example, the solution set would simply be –2. If there were more solutions (there usually are in multivariable equations) then they would also be included in the solution set. When an equation has no true solutions, it is referred to as an **empty set**. Equations with identical solution sets are **equivalent equations**. An **identity** is a term whose value or determinant is equal to 1.

Linear equations can be written many ways. Below is a list of some forms linear equations can take:

- **Standard Form**: $Ax + By = C$; the slope is $\frac{-A}{B}$ and the y-intercept is $\frac{C}{B}$
- **Slope Intercept Form**: $y = mx + b$, where m is the slope and b is the y-intercept
- **Point-Slope Form**: $y - y_1 = m(x - x_1)$, where m is the slope and (x_1, y_1) is a point on the line
- **Two-Point Form**: $\frac{y-y_1}{x-x_1} = \frac{y_2-y_1}{x_2-x_1}$, where (x_1, y_1) and (x_2, y_2) are two points on the given line

- **Intercept Form**: $\frac{x}{x_1} + \frac{y}{y_1} = 1$, where $(x_1, 0)$ is the point at which a line intersects the x-axis, and $(0, y_1)$ is the point at which the same line intersects the y-axis

Review Video: Slope-Intercept and Point-Slope Forms
Visit mometrix.com/academy and enter code: 113216

Review Video: Linear Equations Basics
Visit mometrix.com/academy and enter code: 793005

Solving One-Variable Linear Equations

Multiply all terms by the lowest common denominator to eliminate any fractions. Look for addition or subtraction to undo so you can isolate the variable on one side of the equal sign. Divide both sides by the coefficient of the variable. When you have a value for the variable, substitute this value into the original equation to make sure you have a true equation. Consider the following example:

Kim's savings are represented by the table below. Represent her savings, using an equation.

X (Months)	Y (Total Savings)
2	$1,300
5	$2,050
9	$3,050
11	$3,550
16	$4,800

The table shows a function with a constant rate of change, or slope, of 250. Given the points on the table, the slopes can be calculated as $\frac{(2{,}050-1300)}{(5-2)}$, $\frac{(3{,}050-2{,}050)}{(9-5)}$, $\frac{(3{,}550-3{,}050)}{(11-9)}$, and $\frac{(4{,}800-3{,}550)}{(16-11)}$, each of which equals 250. Thus, the table shows a constant rate of change, indicating a linear function. The slope-intercept form of a linear equation is written as $y = mx + b$, where m represents the slope and b represents the y-intercept. Substituting the slope into this form gives $y = 250x + b$. Substituting corresponding x- and y-values from any point into this equation will give the y-intercept, or b. Using the point, $(2, 1{,}300)$, gives $1{,}300 = 250(2) + b$, which simplifies as $b = 800$. Thus, her savings may be represented by the equation, $y = 250x + 800$.

Rules for Manipulating Equations

Like Terms

Like terms are terms in an equation that have the same variable, regardless of whether or not they also have the same coefficient. This includes terms that *lack* a variable; all constants (i.e., numbers without variables) are considered like terms. If the equation involves terms with a variable raised to different powers, the like terms are those that have the variable raised to the same power.

For example, consider the equation $x^2 + 3x + 2 = 2x^2 + x - 7 + 2x$. In this equation, 2 and -7 are like terms; they are both constants. $3x$, x, and $2x$ are like terms, they all include the variable x raised to the first power. x^2 and $2x^2$ are like terms, they both include the variable x, raised to the second power. $2x$ and $2x^2$ are not like terms; although they both involve the variable x, the variable is not raised to the same power in both terms. The fact that they have the same coefficient, 2, is not relevant.

> **Review Video: Rules for Manipulating Equations**
> Visit mometrix.com/academy and enter code: 838871

Carrying Out the Same Operation on Both Sides of an Equation

When solving an equation, the general procedure is to carry out a series of operations on both sides of an equation, choosing operations that will tend to simplify the equation when doing so. The reason why the same operation must be carried out on both sides of the equation is because that leaves the meaning of the equation unchanged, and yields a result that is equivalent to the original equation. This would not be the case if we carried out an operation on one side of an equation and not the other. Consider what an equation means: it is a statement that two values or expressions are equal. If we carry out the same operation on both sides of the equation—add 3 to both sides, for example—then the two sides of the equation are changed in the same way, and so remain equal. If we do that to only one side of the equation—add 3 to one side but not the other—then that wouldn't be true; if we change one side of the equation but not the other then the two sides are no longer equal.

Advantage of Combining Like Terms

Combining like terms refers to adding or subtracting like terms—terms with the same variable—and therefore reducing sets of like terms to a single term. The main advantage of doing this is that it simplifies the equation. Often, combining like terms can be done as the first step in solving an equation, though it can also be done later, such as after distributing terms in a product.

For example, consider the equation $2(x+3)+3(2+\ x+3)=-4$. The 2 and the 3 in the second set of parentheses are like terms, and we can combine them, yielding $2(x+3)+3(x+5)=-4$. Now we can carry out the multiplications implied by the parentheses, distributing the outer 2 and 3 accordingly: $2x+6+3x+15=-4$. The $2x$ and the $3x$ are like terms, and we can add them together: $5x+6+15=-4$. Now, the constants 6, 15, and -4 are also like terms, and we can combine them as well: subtracting 6 and 15 from both sides of the equation, we get $5x=-4-6-15$, or $5x=-25$, which simplifies further to $x=-5$.

> **Review Video: Solving Equations by Combining Like Terms**
> Visit mometrix.com/academy and enter code: 668506

Canceling Terms on Opposite Sides of an Equation

Two terms on opposite sides of an equation can be canceled if and only if they *exactly* match each other. They must have the same variable raised to the same power and the same coefficient. For example, in the equation $3x+2x^2+6=2x^2-6$, $2x^2$ appears on both sides of the equation and can be canceled, leaving $3x+6=-6$. The 6 on each side of the equation *cannot* be canceled, because it is added on one side of the equation and subtracted on the other. While they cannot be canceled, however, the 6 and -6 are like terms and can be combined, yielding $3x=-12$, which simplifies further to $x=-4$.

It's also important to note that the terms to be canceled must be independent terms and cannot be part of a larger term. For example, consider the equation $2(x+6)=3(x+4)+1$. We cannot cancel the x's, because even though they match each other they are part of the larger terms $2(x+6)$ and $3(x+4)$. We must first distribute the 2 and 3, yielding $2x+12=3x+12+1$. Now we see that the terms with the x's do not match, but the 12s do, and can be canceled, leaving $2x = 3x + 1$, which simplifies to $x = -1$.

Process for Manipulating Equations

Isolating Variables

To **isolate a variable** means to manipulate the equation so that the variable appears by itself on one side of the equation, and does not appear at all on the other side. Generally, an equation or inequality is considered to be solved once the variable is isolated and the other side of the equation or inequality is simplified as much as possible. In the case of a two-variable equation or inequality, only one variable needs to be isolated; it will not usually be possible to simultaneously isolate both variables.

For a linear equation—an equation in which the variable only appears raised to the first power—isolating a variable can be done by first moving all the terms with the variable to one side of the equation and all other terms to the other side. (*Moving* a term really means adding the inverse of the term to both sides; when a term is *moved* to the other side of the equation its sign is flipped.) Then combine like terms on each side. Finally, divide both sides by the coefficient of the variable, if applicable. The steps need not necessarily be done in this order, but this order will always work.

> **Review Video: Solving One-Step Equations**
> Visit mometrix.com/academy and enter code: 777004

Equations with More Than One Solution

Some types of non-linear equations, such as equations involving squares of variables, may have more than one solution. For example, the equation $x^2 = 4$ has two solutions: 2 and –2. Equations with absolute values can also have multiple solutions: $|x| = 1$ has the solutions $x = 1$ and $x = -1$.

It is also possible for a linear equation to have more than one solution, but only if the equation is true regardless of the value of the variable. In this case, the equation is considered to have infinitely many solutions, because any possible value of the variable is a solution. We know a linear equation has infinitely many solutions if when we combine like terms the variables cancel, leaving a true statement. For example, consider the equation $2(3x + 5) = x + 5(x + 2)$. Distributing, we get $6x + 10 = x + 5x + 10$; combining like terms gives $6x + 10 = 6x + 10$, and the $6x$-terms cancel to leave $10 = 10$. This is clearly true, so the original equation is true for any value of x. We could also have canceled the 10s leaving $0 = 0$, but again this is clearly true—in general if both sides of the equation match exactly, it has infinitely many solutions.

Equations with No Solution

Some types of non-linear equations, such as equations involving squares of variables, may have no solution. For example, the equation $x^2 = -2$ has no solutions in the real numbers, because the square of any real number must be positive. Similarly, $|x| = -1$ has no solution, because the absolute value of a number is always positive.

It is also possible for an equation to have no solution even if does not involve any powers greater than one, absolute values, or other special functions. For example, the equation $2(x + 3) + x = 3x$ has no solution. We can see that if we try to solve it: first we distribute, leaving $2x + 6 + x = 3x$. But now if we try to combine all the terms with the variable, we find that they cancel: we have $3x$ on the left and $3x$ on the right, canceling to leave us with $6 = 0$. This is clearly false. In general, whenever the variable terms in an equation cancel leaving different constants on both sides, it means that the equation has no solution. (If we are left with the *same* constant on both sides, the equation has infinitely many solutions instead.)

Features of Equations That Require Special Treatment

Linear Equations

A linear equation is an equation in which variables only appear by themselves: not multiplied together, not with exponents other than one, and not inside absolute value signs or any other functions. For example, the equation $x + 1 - 3x = 5 - x$ is a linear equation; while x appears multiple times, it never appears with an exponent other than one, or inside any function. The two-variable equation $2x - 3y = 5 + 2x$ is also a linear equation. In contrast, the equation $x^2 - 5 = 3x$ is *not* a linear equation, because it involves the term x^2. $\sqrt{x} = 5$ is not a linear equation, because it involves a square root. $(x - 1)^2 = 4$ is not a linear equation because even though there's no exponent on the x directly, it appears as part of an expression that is squared. The two-variable equation $x + xy - y = 5$ is not a linear equation because it includes the term xy, where two variables are multiplied together.

Linear equations can always be solved (or shown to have no solution) by combining like terms and performing simple operations on both sides of the equation. Some non-linear equations can be solved by similar methods, but others may require more advanced methods of solution, if they can be solved analytically at all.

Solving Equations Involving Roots

In an equation involving roots, the first step is to isolate the term with the root, if possible, and then raise both sides of the equation to the appropriate power to eliminate it. Consider an example equation, $2\sqrt{x + 1} - 1 = 3$. In this case, begin by adding 1 to both sides, yielding $2\sqrt{x + 1} = 4$, and then dividing both sides by 2, yielding $\sqrt{x + 1} = 2$. Now square both sides, yielding $x + 1 = 4$. Finally, subtracting 1 from both sides yields $x = 3$.

Squaring both sides of an equation may, however, yield a spurious solution—a solution to the squared equation that is *not* a solution of the original equation. It's therefore necessary to plug the solution back into the original equation to make sure it works. In this case, it does: $2\sqrt{3 + 1} - 1 = 2\sqrt{4} - 1 = 2(2) - 1 = 4 - 1 = 3$.

The same procedure applies for other roots as well. For example, given the equation $3 + \sqrt[3]{2x} = 5$, we can first subtract 3 from both sides, yielding $\sqrt[3]{2x} = 2$ and isolating the root. Raising both sides to the third power yields $2x = 2^3$; i.e., $2x = 8$. We can now divide both sides by 2 to get $x = 4$.

Review Video: Solving Equations Involving Roots
Visit mometrix.com/academy and enter code: 297670

Solving Equations with Exponents

To solve an equation involving an exponent, the first step is to isolate the variable with the exponent. We can then take the appropriate root of both sides to eliminate the exponent. For instance, for the equation $2x^3 + 17 = 5x^3 - 7$, we can subtract $5x^3$ from both sides to get $-3x^3 + 17 = -7$, and then subtract 17 from both sides to get $-3x^3 = -24$. Finally, we can divide both sides by –3 to get $x^3 = 8$. Finally, we can take the cube root of both sides to get $x = \sqrt[3]{8} = 2$.

One important but often overlooked point is that equations with an exponent greater than 1 may have more than one answer. The solution to $x^2 = 9$ isn't simply $x = 3$; it's $x = \pm 3$ (that is, $x = 3$ or

$x = -3$). For a slightly more complicated example, consider the equation $(x-1)^2 - 1 = 3$. Adding 1 to both sides yields $(x-1)^2 = 4$; taking the square root of both sides yields $x - 1 = 2$. We can then add 1 to both sides to get $x = 3$. However, there's a second solution. We also have the possibility that $x - 1 = -2$, in which case $x = -1$. Both $x = 3$ and $x = -1$ are valid solutions, as can be verified by substituting them both into the original equation.

Review Video: Solving Equations with Exponents
Visit mometrix.com/academy and enter code: 514557

Solving Equations with Absolute Values

When solving an equation with an absolute value, the first step is to isolate the absolute value term. We then consider two possibilities: when the expression inside the absolute value is positive or when it is negative. In the former case, the expression in the absolute value equals the expression on the other side of the equation; in the latter, it equals the additive inverse of that expression—the expression times negative one. We consider each case separately and finally check for spurious solutions.

For instance, consider solving $|2x - 1| + x = 5$ for x. We can first isolate the absolute value by moving the x to the other side: $|2x - 1| = -x + 5$. Now, we have two possibilities. First, that $2x - 1$ is positive, and hence $2x - 1 = -x + 5$. Rearranging and combining like terms yields $3x = 6$, and hence $x = 2$. The other possibility is that $2x - 1$ is negative, and hence $2x - 1 = -(-x + 5) = x - 5$. In this case, rearranging and combining like terms yields $x = -4$. Substituting $x = 2$ and $x = -4$ back into the original equation, we see that they are both valid solutions.

Note that the absolute value of a sum or difference applies to the sum or difference as a whole, not to the individual terms; in general, $|2x - 1|$ is not equal to $|2x + 1|$ or to $|2x| - 1$.

Spurious Solutions

A **spurious solution** may arise when we square both sides of an equation as a step in solving it or under certain other operations on the equation. It is a solution to the squared or otherwise modified equation that is *not* a solution of the original equation. To identify a spurious solution, it's useful when you solve an equation involving roots or absolute values to plug the solution back into the original equation to make sure it's valid.

Choosing Which Variable to Isolate in Two-Variable Equations

Similar to methods for a one-variable equation, solving a two-variable equation involves isolating a variable: manipulating the equation so that a variable appears by itself on one side of the equation, and not at all on the other side. However, in a two-variable equation, you will usually only be able to isolate one of the variables; the other variable may appear on the other side along with constant terms, or with exponents or other functions.

Often one variable will be much more easily isolated than the other, and therefore that's the variable you should choose. If one variable appears with various exponents, and the other is only raised to the first power, the latter variable is the one to isolate: given the equation $a^2 + 2b = a^3 + b + 3$, the b only appears to the first power, whereas a appears squared and cubed, so b is the variable that can be solved for: combining like terms and isolating the b on the left side of the equation, we get $b = a^3 - a^2 + 3$. If both variables are equally easy to isolate, then it's best to isolate the independent variable, if one is defined; if the two variables are x and y, the convention is that y is the independent variable.

Graphical Solutions to Equations and Inequalities

When equations are shown graphically, they are usually shown on a **Cartesian coordinate plane**. The Cartesian coordinate plane consists of two number lines placed perpendicular to each other and intersecting at the zero point, also known as the origin. The horizontal number line is known as the x-axis, with positive values to the right of the origin, and negative values to the left of the origin. The vertical number line is known as the y-axis, with positive values above the origin, and negative values below the origin. Any point on the plane can be identified by an ordered pair in the form (x, y), called coordinates. The x-value of the coordinate is called the abscissa, and the y-value of the coordinate is called the ordinate. The two number lines divide the plane into **four quadrants**: I, II, III, and IV.

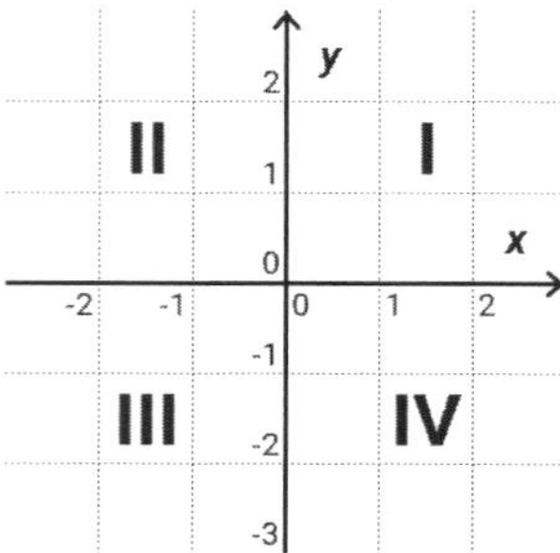

Note that in quadrant I $x > 0$ and $y > 0$, in quadrant II $x < 0$ and $y > 0$, in quadrant III $x < 0$ and $y < 0$, and in quadrant IV $x > 0$ and $y < 0$.

Recall that if the value of the slope of a line is positive, the line slopes upward from left to right. If the value of the slope is negative, the line slopes downward from left to right. If the y-coordinates are the same for two points on a line, the slope is 0 and the line is a **horizontal line**. If the x-coordinates are the same for two points on a line, there is no slope and the line is a **vertical line**. Two or more lines that have equivalent slopes are **parallel lines**. **Perpendicular lines** have slopes that are negative reciprocals of each other, such as $\frac{a}{b}$ and $\frac{-b}{a}$.

Review Video: Cartesian Coordinate Plane and Graphing
Visit mometrix.com/academy and enter code: 115173

Graphing Equations in Two Variables

One way of graphing an equation in two variables is to plot enough points to get an idea for its shape and then draw the appropriate curve through those points. A point can be plotted by substituting in a value for one variable and solving for the other. If the equation is linear, we only need two points and can then draw a straight line between them.

For example, consider the equation $y = 2x - 1$. This is a linear equation—both variables only appear raised to the first power—so we only need two points. When $x = 0$, $y = 2(0) - 1 = -1$.

When $x = 2$, $y = 2(2) - 1 = 3$. We can therefore choose the points $(0, -1)$ and $(2, 3)$, and draw a line between them:

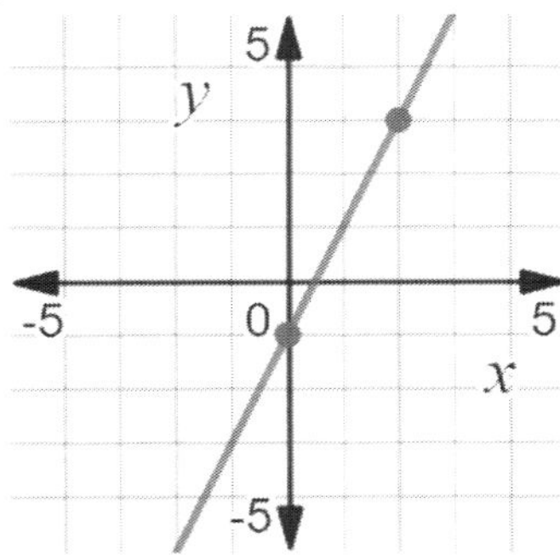

Working with Inequalities

Commonly in algebra and other upper-level fields of math you find yourself working with mathematical expressions that do not equal each other. The statement comparing such expressions with symbols such as $<$ (less than) or $>$ (greater than) is called an *inequality*. An example of an inequality is $7x > 5$. To solve for x, simply divide both sides by 7 and the solution is shown to be $x > \frac{5}{7}$. Graphs of the solution set of inequalities are represented on a number line. Open circles are used to show that an expression approaches a number but is never quite equal to that number.

> **Review Video: Solving Multi-Step Inequalities**
> Visit mometrix.com/academy and enter code: 347842
>
> **Review Video: Solving Inequalities Using All 4 Basic Operations**
> Visit mometrix.com/academy and enter code: 401111

Conditional inequalities are those with certain values for the variable that will make the condition true and other values for the variable where the condition will be false. **Absolute inequalities** can have any real number as the value for the variable to make the condition true, while there is no real number value for the variable that will make the condition false. Solving inequalities is done by following the same rules for solving equations with the exception that when multiplying or dividing by a negative number the direction of the inequality sign must be flipped or reversed. **Double inequalities** are situations where two inequality statements apply to the same variable expression. Example: $-c < ax + b < c$.

> **Review Video: Conditional and Absolute Inequalities**
> Visit mometrix.com/academy and enter code: 980164

Determining Solutions to Inequalities

To determine whether a coordinate is a solution of an inequality, you can substitute the values of the coordinate into the inequality, simplify, and check whether the resulting statement holds true. For instance, to determine whether $(-2,4)$ is a solution of the inequality $y \geq -2x + 3$, substitute the values into the inequality, $4 \geq -2(-2) + 3$. Simplify the right side of the inequality and the result is $4 \geq 7$, which is a false statement. Therefore, the coordinate is not a solution of the inequality. You can also use this method to determine which part of the graph of an inequality is shaded. The graph of $y \geq -2x + 3$ includes the solid line $y = -2x + 3$ and, since it excludes the point $(-2,4)$ to the left of the line, it is shaded to the right of the line.

Review Video: Graphing Linear Inequalities
Visit mometrix.com/academy and enter code: 439421

Flipping Inequality Signs

When given an inequality, we can always turn the entire inequality around, swapping the two sides of the inequality and changing the inequality sign. For instance, $x + 2 > 2x - 3$ is equivalent to $2x - 3 < x + 2$. Aside from that, normally the inequality does not change if we carry out the same operation on both sides of the inequality. There is, however, one principal exception: if we *multiply* or *divide* both sides of the inequality by a *negative number*, the inequality is flipped. For example, if we take the inequality $-2x < 6$ and divide both sides by -2, the inequality flips and we are left with $x > -3$. This *only* applies to multiplication and division, and only with negative numbers. Multiplying or dividing both sides by a positive number, or adding or subtracting any number regardless of sign, does not flip the inequality. Another special case that flips the inequality sign is when reciprocals are used. For instance, $3 > 2$ but the relation of the reciprocals is $\frac{1}{2} < \frac{1}{3}$.

Compound Inequalities

A **compound inequality** is an equality that consists of two inequalities combined with *and* or *or*. The two components of a proper compound inequality must be of opposite type: that is, one must be greater than (or greater than or equal to), the other less than (or less than or equal to). For instance, "$x + 1 < 2$ or $x + 1 > 3$" is a compound inequality, as is "$2x \geq 4$ and $2x \leq 6$." An *and* inequality can be written more compactly by having one inequality on each side of the common part: "$2x \geq 1$ and $2x \leq 6$," can also be written as $1 \leq 2x \leq 6$.

In order for the compound inequality to be meaningful, the two parts of an *and* inequality must overlap; otherwise, no numbers satisfy the inequality. On the other hand, if the two parts of an *or* inequality overlap, then *all* numbers satisfy the inequality and as such the inequality is usually not meaningful.

Solving a compound inequality requires solving each part separately. For example, given the compound inequality "$x + 1 < 2$ or $x + 1 > 3$," the first inequality, $x + 1 < 2$, reduces to $x < 1$, and the second part, $x + 1 > 3$, reduces to $x > 2$, so the whole compound inequality can be written as "$x < 1$ or $x > 2$." Similarly, $1 \leq 2x \leq 6$ can be solved by dividing each term by 2, yielding $\frac{1}{2} \leq x \leq 3$.

Review Video: Compound Inequalities
Visit mometrix.com/academy and enter code: 786318

Solving Inequalities Involving Absolute Values

To solve an inequality involving an absolute value, first isolate the term with the absolute value. Then proceed to treat the two cases separately as with an absolute value equation, but flipping the inequality in the case where the expression in the absolute value is negative (since that essentially involves multiplying both sides by -1.) The two cases are then combined into a compound inequality; if the absolute value is on the greater side of the inequality, then it is an *or* compound inequality, if on the lesser side, then it's an *and*.

Consider the inequality $2 + |x - 1| \geq 3$. We can isolate the absolute value term by subtracting 2 from both sides: $|x - 1| \geq 1$. Now, we're left with the two cases $x - 1 \geq 1$ or $x - 1 \leq -1$: note that in the latter, negative case, the inequality is flipped. $x - 1 \geq 1$ reduces to $x \geq 2$, and $x - 1 \leq -1$

reduces to $x \leq 0$. Since in the inequality $|x - 1| \geq 1$ the absolute value is on the greater side, the two cases combine into an *or* compound inequality, so the final, solved inequality is "$x \leq 0$ or $x \geq 2$."

Review Video: Solving Absolute Value Inequalities
Visit mometrix.com/academy and enter code: 997008

Solving Inequalities Involving Square Roots

Solving an inequality with a square root involves two parts. First, we solve the inequality as if it were an equation, isolating the square root and then squaring both sides of the equation. Second, we restrict the solution to the set of values of x for which the value inside the square root sign is non-negative.

For example, in the inequality, $\sqrt{x - 2} + 1 < 5$, we can isolate the square root by subtracting 1 from both sides, yielding $\sqrt{x - 2} < 4$. Squaring both sides of the inequality yields $x - 2 < 16$, so $x < 18$. Since we can't take the square root of a negative number, we also require the part inside the square root to be non-negative. In this case, that means $x - 2 \geq 0$. Adding 2 to both sides of the inequality yields $x \geq 2$. Our final answer is a compound inequality combining the two simple inequalities: $x \geq 2$ and $x < 18$, or $2 \leq x < 18$.

Note that we only get a compound inequality if the two simple inequalities are in opposite directions; otherwise, we take the one that is more restrictive.

The same technique can be used for other even roots, such as fourth roots. It is *not*, however, used for cube roots or other odd roots—negative numbers *do* have cube roots, so the condition that the quantity inside the root sign cannot be negative does not apply.

Review Video: Solving Inequalities Involving Square Roots
Visit mometrix.com/academy and enter code: 800288

Special Circumstances

Sometimes an inequality involving an absolute value or an even exponent is true for all values of x, and we don't need to do any further work to solve it. This is true if the inequality, once the absolute value or exponent term is isolated, says that term is greater than a negative number (or greater than or equal to zero). Since an absolute value or a number raised to an even exponent is *always* non-negative, this inequality is always true.

Graphical Solutions to Inequalities

Graphing Simple Inequalities

To graph a simple inequality, we first mark on the number line the value that signifies the end point of the inequality. If the inequality is strict (involves a less than or greater than), we use a hollow circle; if it is not strict (less than or equal to or greater than or equal to), we use a solid circle. We then fill in the part of the number line that satisfies the inequality: to the left of the marked point for less than (or less than or equal to), to the right for greater than (or greater than or equal to).

For example, we would graph the inequality $x < 5$ by putting a hollow circle at 5 and filling in the part of the line to the left:

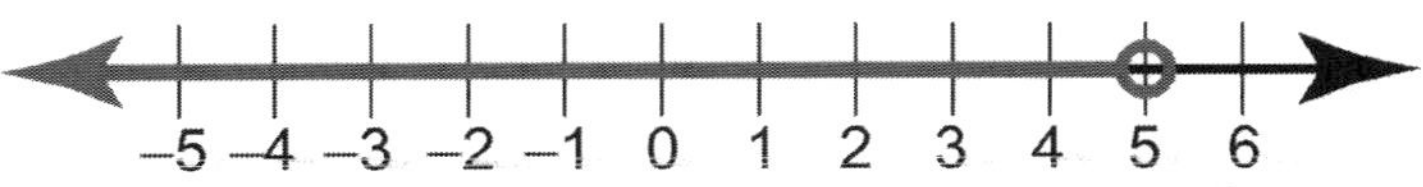

Graphing Compound Inequalities

To graph a compound inequality, we fill in both parts of the inequality for an *or* inequality, or the overlap between them for an *and* inequality. More specifically, we start by plotting the endpoints of each inequality on the number line. For an *or* inequality, we then fill in the appropriate side of the line for each inequality. Typically, the two component inequalities do not overlap, which means the shaded part is *outside* the two points. For an *and* inequality, we instead fill in the part of the line that meets both inequalities.

For the inequality "$x \leq -3$ or $x > 4$," we first put a solid circle at –3 and a hollow circle at 4. We then fill the parts of the line *outside* these circles:

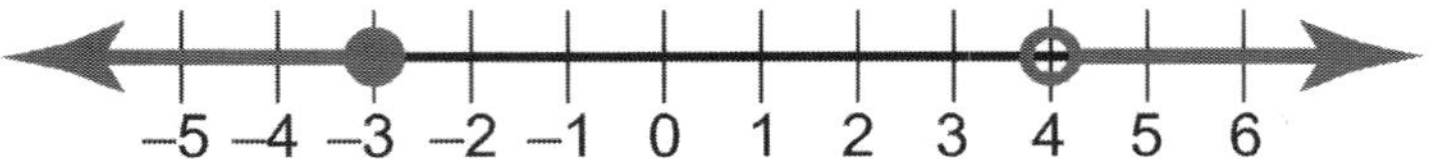

Graphing Inequalities Including Absolute Values

An inequality with an absolute value can be converted to a compound inequality. To graph the inequality, first convert it to a compound inequality, and then graph that normally. If the absolute value is on the greater side of the inequality, we end up with an *or* inequality; we plot the endpoints of the inequality on the number line and fill in the part of the line *outside* those points. If the absolute value is on the smaller side of the inequality, we end up with an *and* inequality; we plot the endpoints of the inequality on the number line and fill in the part of the line *between* those points.

For example, the inequality $|x + 1| \geq 4$ can be rewritten as $x \geq 3$ or $x \leq -5$. We place solid circles at the points 3 and –5 and fill in the part of the line *outside* them:

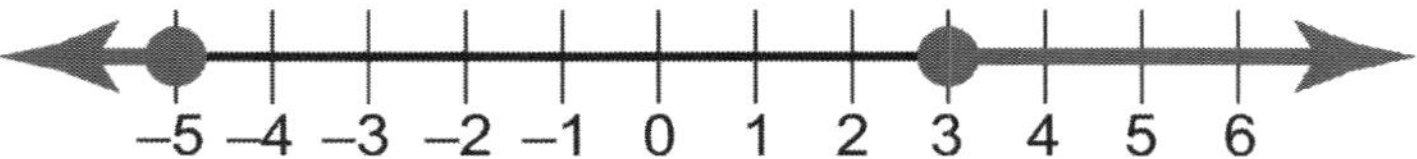

Graphing Inequalities in Two Variables

To graph an inequality in two variables, we first graph the border of the inequality. This means graphing the equation that we get if we replace the inequality sign with an equals sign. If the inequality is strict ($>$ or $<$), we graph the border with a dashed or dotted line; if it is not strict ($\geq$ or $\leq$), we use a solid line. We can then test any point not on the border to see if it satisfies the inequality. If it does, we shade in that side of the border; if not, we shade in the other side. As an example, consider $y > 2x + 2$. To graph this inequality, we first graph the border, $y = 2x + 2$. Since it is a strict inequality, we use a dashed line. Then, we choose a test point. This can be any point not on the border; in this case, we will choose the origin, $(0,0)$. (This makes the calculation easy and is generally a good choice unless the border passes through the origin.) Putting this into the original inequality, we get $0 > 2(0) + 2$, i.e., $0 > 2$. This is *not* true, so we shade in the side of the border that does *not* include the point (0,0):

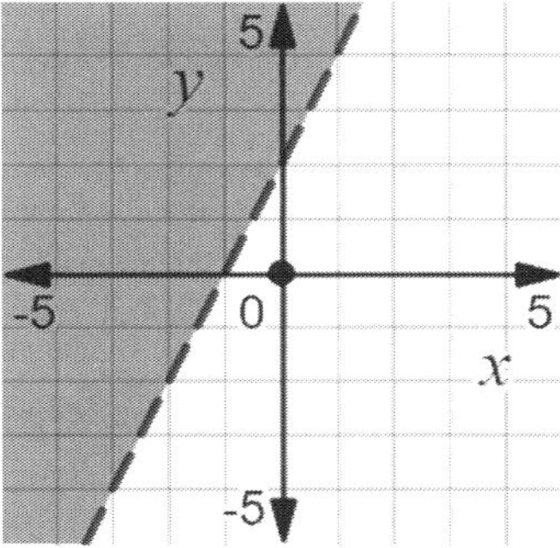

GRAPHING COMPOUND INEQUALITIES IN TWO VARIABLES

One way to graph a compound inequality in two variables is to first graph each of the component inequalities. For an *and* inequality, we then shade in only the parts where the two graphs overlap; for an *or* inequality, we shade in any region that pertains to either of the individual inequalities.

Consider the graph of "$y \geq x - 1$ and $y \leq -x$":

We first shade in the individual inequalities:

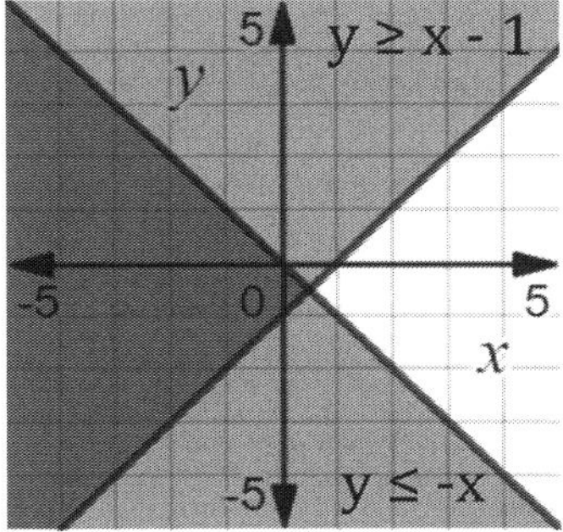

Now, since the compound inequality has an *and*, we only leave shaded the overlap—the part that pertains to *both* inequalities:

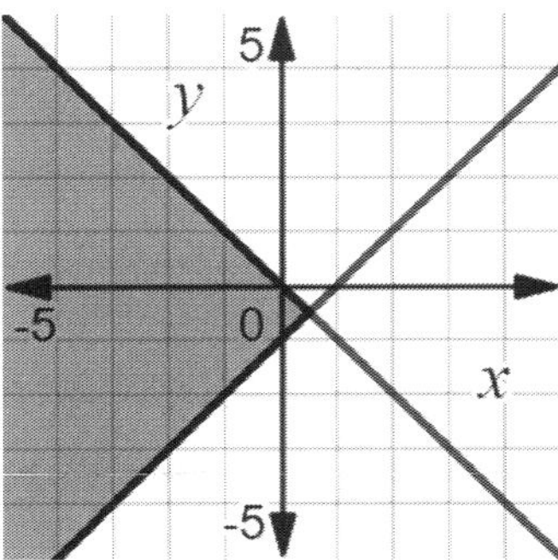

If instead the inequality had been "$y \geq x - 1$ or $y \leq -x$," our final graph would involve the *total* shaded area:

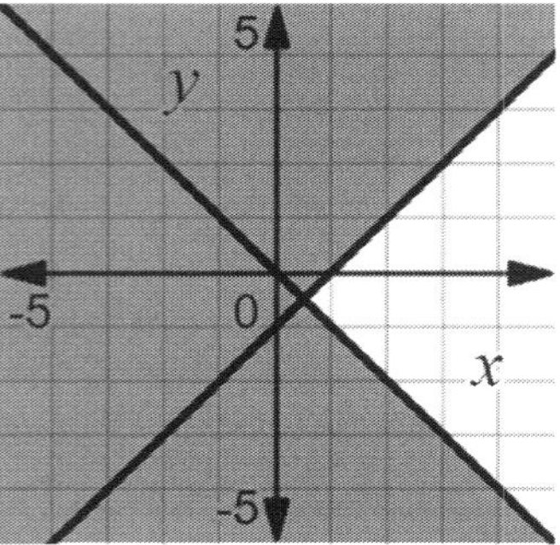

Review Video: Graphing Solutions to Inequalities
Visit mometrix.com/academy and enter code: 391281

SOLVING SYSTEMS OF EQUATIONS

A **system of equations** is a set of simultaneous equations that all use the same variables. A solution to a system of equations must be true for each equation in the system. **Consistent systems** are those with at least one solution. **Inconsistent systems** are systems of equations that have no solution.

Review Video: Solving Systems and Linear Equations
Visit mometrix.com/academy and enter code: 746745

SUBSTITUTION

To solve a system of linear equations by **substitution**, start with the easier equation and solve for one of the variables. Express this variable in terms of the other variable. Substitute this expression in the other equation and solve for the other variable. The solution should be expressed in the form (x, y). Substitute the values into both of the original equations to check your answer. Consider the following system of equations:

$$x + 6y = 15$$
$$3x - 12y = 18$$

Solving the first equation for x: $x = 15 - 6y$

Substitute this value in place of x in the second equation, and solve for y:

$$3(15 - 6y) - 12y = 18$$
$$45 - 18y - 12y = 18$$
$$30y = 27$$
$$y = \frac{27}{30} = \frac{9}{10} = 0.9$$

Plug this value for y back into the first equation to solve for x:

$$x = 15 - 6(0.9) = 15 - 5.4 = 9.6$$

Check both equations if you have time:

$$\begin{aligned} 9.6 + 6(0.9) &= 15 \\ 9.6 + 5.4 &= 15 \\ 15 &= 15 \end{aligned} \qquad \begin{aligned} 3(9.6) - 12(0.9) &= 18 \\ 28.8 - 10.8 &= 18 \\ 18 &= 18 \end{aligned}$$

Therefore, the solution is (9.6,0.9).

Review Video: The Substitution Method
Visit mometrix.com/academy and enter code: 565151

ELIMINATION

To solve a system of equations using **elimination**, begin by rewriting both equations in standard form $Ax + By = C$. Check to see if the coefficients of one pair of like variables add to zero. If not, multiply one or both of the equations by a non-zero number to make one set of like variables add to zero. Add the two equations to solve for one of the variables. Substitute this value into one of the original equations to solve for the other variable. Check your work by substituting into the other equation. Now, let's look at solving the following system using the elimination method:

$$\begin{aligned} 5x + 6y &= 4 \\ x + 2y &= 4 \end{aligned}$$

If we multiply the second equation by -3, we can eliminate the y-terms:

$$\begin{aligned} 5x + 6y &= 4 \\ -3x - 6y &= -12 \end{aligned}$$

Add the equations together and solve for x:

$$\begin{aligned} 2x &= -8 \\ x &= \frac{-8}{2} = -4 \end{aligned}$$

Plug the value for x back in to either of the original equations and solve for y:

$$\begin{aligned} -4 + 2y &= 4 \\ y &= \frac{4 + 4}{2} = 4 \end{aligned}$$

Check both equations if you have time:

$$\begin{aligned} 5(-4) + 6(4) &= 4 \\ -20 + 24 &= 4 \\ 4 &= 4 \end{aligned} \qquad \begin{aligned} -4 + 2(4) &= 4 \\ -4 + 8 &= 4 \\ 4 &= 4 \end{aligned}$$

Therefore, the solution is $(-4,4)$.

Review Video: The Elimination Method
Visit mometrix.com/academy and enter code: 449121

Graphically

To solve a system of linear equations **graphically**, plot both equations on the same graph. The solution of the equations is the point where both lines cross. If the lines do not cross (are parallel), then there is **no solution**.

For example, consider the following system of equations:

$$y = 2x + 7$$
$$y = -x + 1$$

Since these equations are given in slope-intercept form, they are easy to graph; the y-intercepts of the lines are $(0,7)$ and $(0,1)$. The respective slopes are 2 and –1, thus the graphs look like this:

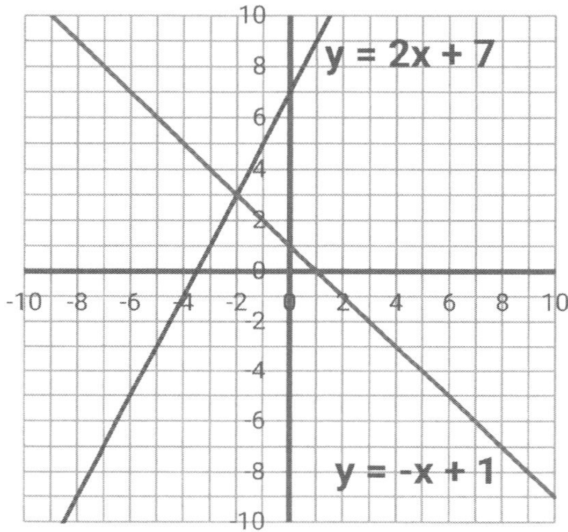

The two lines intersect at the point $(-2,3)$, thus this is the solution to the system of equations.

Solving a system graphically is generally only practical if both coordinates of the solution are integers; otherwise the intersection will lie between gridlines on the graph and the coordinates will be difficult or impossible to determine exactly. It also helps if, as in this example, the equations are in slope-intercept form or some other form that makes them easy to graph. Otherwise, another method of solution (by substitution or elimination) is likely to be more useful.

Review Video: Solving Systems by Graphing
Visit mometrix.com/academy and enter code: 634812

Solving Systems of Equations Using the Trace Feature

Using the trace feature on a calculator requires that you rewrite each equation, isolating the y-variable on one side of the equal sign. Enter both equations in the graphing calculator and plot the graphs simultaneously. Use the trace cursor to find where the two lines cross. Use the zoom feature if necessary to obtain more accurate results. Always check your answer by substituting into the original equations. The trace method is likely to be less accurate than other methods due to the resolution of graphing calculators but is a useful tool to provide an approximate answer.

Calculations Using Points

Sometimes you need to perform calculations using only points on a graph as input data. Using points, you can determine what the **midpoint** and **distance** are. If you know the equation for a line, you can calculate the distance between the line and the point.

To find the **midpoint** of two points (x_1, y_1) and (x_2, y_2), average the x-coordinates to get the x-coordinate of the midpoint, and average the y-coordinates to get the y-coordinate of the midpoint. The formula is: $\left(\frac{x_1+x_2}{2}, \frac{y_1+y_2}{2}\right)$.

The **distance** between two points is the same as the length of the hypotenuse of a right triangle with the two given points as endpoints, and the two sides of the right triangle parallel to the x-axis and y-axis, respectively. The length of the segment parallel to the x-axis is the difference between the x-coordinates of the two points. The length of the segment parallel to the y-axis is the difference between the y-coordinates of the two points. Use the Pythagorean theorem $a^2 + b^2 = c^2$ or $c = \sqrt{a^2 + b^2}$ to find the distance. The formula is $d = \sqrt{(x_2 - x_1)^2 + (y_2 - y_1)^2}$.

When a line is in the format $Ax + By + C = 0$, where A, B, and C are coefficients, you can use a point (x_1, y_1) not on the line and apply the formula $d = \frac{|Ax_1+By_1+C|}{\sqrt{A^2+B^2}}$ to find the distance between the line and the point (x_1, y_1).

Review Video: Calculations Using Points on a Graph
Visit mometrix.com/academy and enter code: 883228

Problem Solving and Data Analysis

Problem Solving and Data Analysis Overview

The questions in this section will require students to create and analyze relationships. They will solve single-step and multistep problems using ratios, rates, proportions, and percentages. Some questions will also require students to describe relationships that are presented graphically. In addition, students should be able to analyze and summarize both qualitative and quantitative data.

Question Types in Problem Solving and Data Analysis

The problem solving and data analysis section will test your knowledge of the following:

- Use ratios, rates, proportional relationships, and scale drawings to solve single- and multistep problems.
    - The student will use a proportional relationship between two variables to solve a multistep problem to determine a ratio or rate; calculate a ratio or rate and then solve a multistep problem; or take a given ratio or rate and solve a multistep problem.

- Solve single- and multistep problems involving **percentages**.
  - The student will solve a multistep problem to determine a percentage; calculate a percentage and then solve a multistep problem; or take a given percentage and solve a multistep problem.
- Solve single- and multistep problems involving **measurement quantities, units,** and **unit conversion.**
  - The student will solve a multistep problem to determine a unit rate;
  - calculate a unit rate and then solve a multistep problem;
  - solve a multistep problem to complete a unit conversion;
  - solve a multistep problem to calculate density;
  - or use the concept of density to solve a multistep problem.
- Given a scatterplot, use **linear**, **quadratic**, or **exponential models** to describe how the variables are related.
  - The student will, given a scatterplot, select the equation of a line or curve of best fit;
  - interpret the line in the context of the situation;
  - or use the line or curve of best fit to make a prediction.
- Use the relationship between two variables to investigate **key features of the graph**.
  - The student will make connections between the graphical representation of a relationship and properties of the graph by selecting the graph that represents the properties described, or using the graph to identify a value or set of values.
- Compare linear growth with exponential growth.
  - The student will infer the connection between two variables given a context in order to determine what type of model fits best.
- Use two-way tables to summarize categorical data and relative frequencies, and calculate conditional probability.
  - The student will summarize categorical data or use categorical data to calculate conditional frequencies, conditional probabilities, association of variables, or independence of events.
- Make inferences about **population parameters** based on **sample data**.
  - The student will estimate a population parameter given the results from a random sample of the population.
  - The sample statistics may mention confidence intervals and measurement error that the student should understand and make use of, but need not calculate.
- Use statistics to investigate **measures of center of data** and analyze **shape**, **center**, and **spread**.
  - The student will calculate measures of center and/or spread for a given set of data or use given statistics to compare two separate sets of data.
  - The measures of center that may be calculated include mean, median, and mode, and the measures of spread that may be calculated include range.
  - When comparing two data sets, the student may investigate mean, median, mode, range, and/or standard deviation.
- Evaluate reports to **make inferences**, justify **conclusions**, and determine appropriateness of **data collection methods**.
  - The reports may consist of tables, graphs, or text summaries.

PROPORTIONS

A proportion is a relationship between two quantities that dictates how one changes when the other changes. A **direct proportion** describes a relationship in which a quantity increases by a set amount for every increase in the other quantity, or decreases by that same amount for every decrease in the other quantity. Example: Assuming a constant driving speed, the time required for a car trip increases as the distance of the trip increases. The distance to be traveled and the time required to travel are directly proportional.

An **inverse proportion** is a relationship in which an increase in one quantity is accompanied by a decrease in the other, or vice versa. Example: the time required for a car trip decreases as the speed increases and increases as the speed decreases, so the time required is inversely proportional to the speed of the car.

Review Video: Proportions
Visit mometrix.com/academy and enter code: 505355

RATIOS

A **ratio** is a comparison of two quantities in a particular order. Example: If there are 14 computers in a lab, and the class has 20 students, there is a student to computer ratio of 20 to 14, commonly written as $20:14$. Ratios are normally reduced to their smallest whole number representation, so $20:14$ would be reduced to $10:7$ by dividing both sides by 2.

Review Video: Ratios
Visit mometrix.com/academy and enter code: 996914

CONSTANT OF PROPORTIONALITY

When two quantities have a proportional relationship, there exists a **constant of proportionality** between the quantities. The product of this constant and one of the quantities is equal to the other quantity. For example, if one lemon costs $0.25, two lemons cost $0.50, and three lemons cost $0.75, there is a proportional relationship between the total cost of lemons and the number of lemons purchased. The constant of proportionality is the **unit price**, namely $0.25/lemon. Notice that the total price of lemons, t, can be found by multiplying the unit price of lemons, p, and the number of lemons, n: $t = pn$.

WORK/UNIT RATE

Unit rate expresses a quantity of one thing in terms of one unit of another. For example, if you travel 30 miles every two hours, a unit rate expresses this comparison in terms of one hour: in one hour you travel 15 miles, so your unit rate is 15 miles per hour. Other examples are how much one ounce of food costs (price per ounce) or figuring out how much one egg costs out of the dozen (price per 1 egg, instead of price per 12 eggs). The denominator of a unit rate is always 1. Unit rates are used to compare different situations to solve problems. For example, to make sure you get the best deal when deciding which kind of soda to buy, you can find the unit rate of each. If soda #1 costs $1.50 for a 1-liter bottle, and soda #2 costs $2.75 for a 2-liter bottle, it would be a better deal to buy soda #2, because its unit rate is only $1.375 per 1-liter, which is cheaper than soda #1. Unit rates can also help determine the length of time a given event will take. For example, if you can paint 2 rooms in 4.5 hours, you can determine how long it will take you to paint 5 rooms by solving for the unit rate per room and then multiplying that by 5.

Review Video: Rates and Unit Rates
Visit mometrix.com/academy and enter code: 185363

SLOPE

On a graph with two points, (x_1, y_1) and (x_2, y_2), the **slope** is found with the formula $m = \frac{y_2 - y_1}{x_2 - x_1}$; where $x_1 \neq x_2$ and m stands for slope. If the value of the slope is **positive**, the line has an *upward direction* from left to right. If the value of the slope is **negative**, the line has a *downward direction* from left to right. Consider the following example:

A new book goes on sale in bookstores and online stores. In the first month, 5,000 copies of the book are sold. Over time, the book continues to grow in popularity. The data for the number of copies sold is in the table below.

# of Months on Sale	1	2	3	4	5
# of Copies Sold (In Thousands)	5	10	15	20	25

So, the number of copies that are sold and the time that the book is on sale is a proportional relationship. In this example, an equation can be used to show the data: $y = 5x$, where x is the number of months that the book is on sale. Also, y is the number of copies sold. So, the slope of the corresponding line is $\frac{\text{rise}}{\text{run}} = \frac{5}{1} = 5$.

Review Video: Finding the Slope of a Line
Visit mometrix.com/academy and enter code: 766664

FINDING AN UNKNOWN IN EQUIVALENT EXPRESSIONS

It is often necessary to apply information given about a rate or proportion to a new scenario. For example, if you know that Jedha can run a marathon (26.2 miles) in 3 hours, how long would it take her to run 10 miles at the same pace? Start by setting up equivalent expressions:

$$\frac{26.2 \text{ mi}}{3 \text{ hr}} = \frac{10 \text{ mi}}{x \text{ hr}}$$

Now, cross multiply and solve for x:

$$26.2x = 30$$
$$x = \frac{30}{26.2} = \frac{15}{13.1}$$
$$x \approx 1.15 \text{ hrs } or \text{ 1 hr 9 min}$$

So, at this pace, Jedha could run 10 miles in about 1.15 hours or about 1 hour and 9 minutes.

Review Video: Cross Multiply Fractions
Visit mometrix.com/academy and enter code: 893904

METRIC MEASUREMENT PREFIXES

Giga-	One billion	1 *giga*watt is one billion watts
Mega-	One million	1 *mega*hertz is one million hertz
Kilo-	One thousand	1 *kilo*gram is one thousand grams
Deci-	One-tenth	1 *deci*meter is one-tenth of a meter
Centi-	One-hundredth	1 *centi*meter is one-hundredth of a meter
Milli-	One-thousandth	1 *milli*liter is one-thousandth of a liter
Micro-	One-millionth	1 *micro*gram is one-millionth of a gram

Review Video: Metric System Conversion - How the Metric System Works
Visit mometrix.com/academy and enter code: 163709

MEASUREMENT CONVERSION

When converting between units, the goal is to maintain the same meaning but change the way it is displayed. In order to go from a larger unit to a smaller unit, multiply the number of the known amount by the equivalent amount. When going from a smaller unit to a larger unit, divide the number of the known amount by the equivalent amount.

For complicated conversions, it may be helpful to set up conversion fractions. In these fractions, one fraction is the **conversion factor**. The other fraction has the unknown amount in the numerator. So, the known value is placed in the denominator. Sometimes, the second fraction has the known value from the problem in the numerator and the unknown in the denominator. Multiply the two fractions to get the converted measurement. Note that since the numerator and the denominator of the factor are equivalent, the value of the fraction is 1. That is why we can say that the result in the new units is equal to the result in the old units even though they have different numbers.

It can often be necessary to chain known conversion factors together. As an example, consider converting 512 square inches to square meters. We know that there are 2.54 centimeters in an inch and 100 centimeters in a meter, and we know we will need to square each of these factors to achieve the conversion we are looking for.

$$\frac{512\text{ in}^2}{1} \times \left(\frac{2.54\text{ cm}}{1\text{ in}}\right)^2 \times \left(\frac{1\text{ m}}{100\text{ cm}}\right)^2 = \frac{512\,\cancel{\text{in}^2}}{1} \times \left(\frac{6.4516\,\cancel{\text{cm}^2}}{1\,\cancel{\text{in}^2}}\right) \times \left(\frac{1\text{ m}^2}{10{,}000\,\cancel{\text{cm}^2}}\right) = 0.330\text{ m}^2$$

Review Video: Measurement Conversions
Visit mometrix.com/academy and enter code: 316703

Common Units and Equivalents

Metric Equivalents

1000 μg (microgram)	1 mg
1000 mg (milligram)	1 g
1000 g (gram)	1 kg
1000 kg (kilogram)	1 metric ton
1000 mL (milliliter)	1 L
1000 μm (micrometer)	1 mm
1000 mm (millimeter)	1 m
100 cm (centimeter)	1 m
1000 m (meter)	1 km

Distance and Area Measurement

Unit	Abbreviation	US equivalent	Metric equivalent
Inch	in	1 inch	2.54 centimeters
Foot	ft	12 inches	0.305 meters
Yard	yd	3 feet	0.914 meters
Mile	mi	5280 feet	1.609 kilometers
Acre	ac	4840 square yards	0.405 hectares
Square Mile	sq. mi. or $mi.^2$	640 acres	2.590 square kilometers

Capacity Measurements

Unit	Abbreviation	US equivalent	Metric equivalent
Fluid Ounce	fl oz	8 fluid drams	29.573 milliliters
Cup	c	8 fluid ounces	0.237 liter
Pint	pt.	16 fluid ounces	0.473 liter
Quart	qt.	2 pints	0.946 liter
Gallon	gal.	4 quarts	3.785 liters
Teaspoon	t or tsp.	1 fluid dram	5 milliliters
Tablespoon	T or tbsp.	4 fluid drams	15 or 16 milliliters
Cubic Centimeter	cc or cm^3	0.271 drams	1 milliliter

Weight Measurements

Unit	Abbreviation	US equivalent	Metric equivalent
Ounce	oz	16 drams	28.35 grams
Pound	lb	16 ounces	453.6 grams
Ton	tn.	2,000 pounds	907.2 kilograms

Volume and Weight Measurement Clarifications

Always be careful when using ounces and fluid ounces. They are not equivalent.

1 pint = 16 fluid ounces	1 fluid ounce $\neq$ 1 ounce
1 pound = 16 ounces	1 pint $\neq$ 1 pound

Having one pint of something does not mean you have one pound of it. In the same way, just because something weighs one pound does not mean that its volume is one pint.

In the United States, the word "ton" by itself refers to a short ton or a net ton. Do not confuse this with a long ton (also called a gross ton) or a metric ton (also spelled *tonne*), which have different measurement equivalents.

$$1 \text{ US ton} = 2000 \text{ pounds} \quad \neq \quad 1 \text{ metric ton} = 1000 \text{ kilograms}$$

Probability

Probability is the likelihood of a certain outcome occurring for a given event. An **event** is any situation that produces a result. It could be something as simple as flipping a coin or as complex as launching a rocket. Determining the probability of an outcome for an event can be equally simple or complex. As such, there are specific terms used in the study of probability that need to be understood:

- **Compound event**—an event that involves two or more independent events (rolling a pair of dice and taking the sum)
- **Desired outcome** (or success)—an outcome that meets a particular set of criteria (a roll of 1 or 2 if we are looking for numbers less than 3)
- **Independent events**—two or more events whose outcomes do not affect one another (two coins tossed at the same time)
- **Dependent events**—two or more events whose outcomes affect one another (two cards drawn consecutively from the same deck)
- **Certain outcome**—probability of outcome is 100% or 1
- **Impossible outcome**—probability of outcome is 0% or 0
- **Mutually exclusive outcomes**—two or more outcomes whose criteria cannot all be satisfied in a single event (a coin coming up heads and tails on the same toss)
- **Random variable**—refers to all possible outcomes of a single event which may be discrete or continuous.

Review Video: Intro to Probability
Visit mometrix.com/academy and enter code: 212374

Sample Space

The total set of all possible results of a test or experiment is called a **sample space**, or sometimes a universal sample space. The sample space, represented by one of the variables S, Ω, or U (for universal sample space) has individual elements called outcomes. Other terms for outcome that may be used interchangeably include elementary outcome, simple event, or sample point. The number of outcomes in a given sample space could be infinite or finite, and some tests may yield multiple unique sample sets. For example, tests conducted by drawing playing cards from a standard deck would have one sample space of the card values, another sample space of the card suits, and a third sample space of suit-denomination combinations. For most tests, the sample spaces considered will be finite.

An **event**, represented by the variable E, is a portion of a sample space. It may be one outcome or a group of outcomes from the same sample space. If an event occurs, then the test or experiment will generate an outcome that satisfies the requirement of that event. For example, given a standard deck of 52 playing cards as the sample space, and defining the event as the collection of face cards, then the event will occur if the card drawn is a J, Q, or K. If any other card is drawn, the event is said to have not occurred.

For every sample space, each possible outcome has a specific likelihood, or probability, that it will occur. The probability measure, also called the **distribution**, is a function that assigns a real number probability, from zero to one, to each outcome. For a probability measure to be accurate, every outcome must have a real number probability measure that is greater than or equal to zero and less than or equal to one. Also, the probability measure of the sample space must equal one, and the probability measure of the union of multiple outcomes must equal the sum of the individual probability measures.

Probabilities of events are expressed as real numbers from zero to one. They give a numerical value to the chance that a particular event will occur. The probability of an event occurring is the sum of the probabilities of the individual elements of that event. For example, in a standard deck of 52 playing cards as the sample space and the collection of face cards as the event, the probability of drawing a specific face card is $\frac{1}{52} = 0.019$, but the probability of drawing any one of the twelve face cards is $12(0.019) = 0.228$. Note that rounding of numbers can generate different results. If you multiplied 12 by the fraction $\frac{1}{52}$ before converting to a decimal, you would get the answer $\frac{12}{52} = 0.231$.

Theoretical and Experimental Probability

Theoretical probability can usually be determined without actually performing the event. The likelihood of an outcome occurring, or the probability of an outcome occurring, is given by the formula:

$$P(A) = \frac{\text{Number of acceptable outcomes}}{\text{Number of possible outcomes}}$$

Note that $P(A)$ is the probability of an outcome A occurring, and each outcome is just as likely to occur as any other outcome. If each outcome has the same probability of occurring as every other possible outcome, the outcomes are said to be equally likely to occur. The total number of acceptable outcomes must be less than or equal to the total number of possible outcomes. If the two are equal, then the outcome is certain to occur and the probability is 1. If the number of acceptable outcomes is zero, then the outcome is impossible and the probability is 0. For example, if there are 20 marbles in a bag and 5 are red, then the theoretical probability of randomly selecting a red marble is 5 out of 20, $\left(\frac{5}{20} = \frac{1}{4}, 0.25, \text{or } 25\%\right)$.

If the theoretical probability is unknown or too complicated to calculate, it can be estimated by an experimental probability. **Experimental probability**, also called empirical probability, is an estimate of the likelihood of a certain outcome based on repeated experiments or collected data. In other words, while theoretical probability is based on what *should* happen, experimental probability is based on what *has* happened. Experimental probability is calculated in the same way as theoretical probability, except that actual outcomes are used instead of possible outcomes. The more experiments performed or datapoints gathered, the better the estimate should be.

Theoretical and experimental probability do not always line up with one another. Theoretical probability says that out of 20 coin-tosses, 10 should be heads. However, if we were actually to toss 20 coins, we might record just 5 heads. This doesn't mean that our theoretical probability is incorrect; it just means that this particular experiment had results that were different from what was predicted. A practical application of empirical probability is the insurance industry. There are no set functions that define lifespan, health, or safety. Insurance companies look at factors from hundreds of thousands of individuals to find patterns that they then use to set the formulas for insurance premiums.

Review Video: Empirical Probability
Visit mometrix.com/academy and enter code: 513468

Objective and Subjective Probability

Objective probability is based on mathematical formulas and documented evidence. Examples of objective probability include raffles or lottery drawings where there is a pre-determined number of possible outcomes and a predetermined number of outcomes that correspond to an event. Other cases of objective probability include probabilities of rolling dice, flipping coins, or drawing cards. Most gambling games are based on objective probability.

In contrast, **subjective probability** is based on personal or professional feelings and judgments. Often, there is a lot of guesswork following extensive research. Areas where subjective probability is applicable include sales trends and business expenses. Attractions set admission prices based on subjective probabilities of attendance based on varying admission rates in an effort to maximize their profit.

Complement of an Event

Sometimes it may be easier to calculate the possibility of something not happening, or the **complement of an event**. Represented by the symbol $\bar{A}$, the complement of A is the probability that event A does not happen. When you know the probability of event A occurring, you can use the formula $P(\bar{A}) = 1 - P(A)$, where $P(\bar{A})$ is the probability of event A not occurring, and $P(A)$ is the probability of event A occurring.

Addition Rule

The **addition rule** for probability is used for finding the probability of a compound event. Use the formula $P(A \cup B) = P(A) + P(B) - P(A \cap B)$, where $P(A \cap B)$ is the probability of both events occurring to find the probability of a compound event. The probability of both events occurring at the same time must be subtracted to eliminate any overlap in the first two probabilities.

Conditional Probability

Given two events A and B, the **conditional probability** $P(A|B)$ is the probability that event A will occur, given that event B has occurred. The conditional probability cannot be calculated simply from $P(A)$ and $P(B)$; these probabilities alone do not give sufficient information to determine the conditional probability. It can, however, be determined if you are also given the probability of the intersection of events A and B, $P(A \cap B)$, the probability that events A and B both occur. Specifically, $P(A|B) = \frac{P(A \cap B)}{P(B)}$. For instance, suppose you have a jar containing two red marbles and two blue marbles, and you draw two marbles at random. Consider event A being the event that the first marble drawn is red, and event B being the event that the second marble drawn is blue. If we want to find the probability that B occurs given that A occurred, $P(B|A)$, then we can compute it using the fact that $P(A)$ is $\frac{1}{2}$, and $P(A \cap B)$ is $\frac{1}{3}$. (The latter may not be obvious, but may be determined by finding the product of $\frac{1}{2}$ and $\frac{2}{3}$). Therefore $P(B|A) = \frac{P(A \cap B)}{P(A)} = \frac{1/3}{1/2} = \frac{2}{3}$.

Conditional Probability in Everyday Situations

Conditional probability often arises in everyday situations in, for example, estimating the risk or benefit of certain activities. The conditional probability of having a heart attack given that you exercise daily may be smaller than the overall probability of having a heart attack. The conditional probability of having lung cancer given that you are a smoker is larger than the overall probability of having lung cancer. Note that changing the order of the conditional probability changes the meaning: the conditional probability of having lung cancer given that you are a smoker is a very different thing from the probability of being a smoker given that you have lung cancer. In an extreme case, suppose that a certain rare disease is caused only by eating a certain food, but even then, it is unlikely. Then the conditional probability of having that disease given that you eat the dangerous food is nonzero but low, but the conditional probability of having eaten that food given that you have the disease is 100%!

Review Video: Conditional Probability
Visit mometrix.com/academy and enter code: 397924

Independence

The conditional probability $P(A|B)$ is the probability that event A will occur given that event B occurs. If the two events are independent, we do not expect that whether or not event B occurs should have any effect on whether or not event A occurs. In other words, we expect $P(A|B) = P(A)$.

This can be proven using the usual equations for conditional probability and the joint probability of independent events. The conditional probability $P(A|B) = \frac{P(A \cap B)}{P(B)}$. If A and B are independent, then $P(A \cap B) = P(A)P(B)$. So $P(A|B) = \frac{P(A)P(B)}{P(B)} = P(A)$. By similar reasoning, if A and B are independent then $P(B|A) = P(B)$.

Multiplication Rule

The **multiplication rule** can be used to find the probability of two independent events occurring using the formula $P(A \cap B) = P(A) \times P(B)$, where $P(A \cap B)$ is the probability of two independent events occurring, $P(A)$ is the probability of the first event occurring, and $P(B)$ is the probability of the second event occurring.

The multiplication rule can also be used to find the probability of two dependent events occurring using the formula $P(A \cap B) = P(A) \times P(B|A)$, where $P(A \cap B)$ is the probability of two dependent events occurring and $P(B|A)$ is the probability of the second event occurring after the first event has already occurred.

Use a **combination of the multiplication** rule and the rule of complements to find the probability that at least one outcome of the element will occur. This is given by the general formula $P(\text{at least one event occurring}) = 1 - P(\text{no outcomes occurring})$. For example, to find the probability that at least one even number will show when a pair of dice is rolled, find the probability that two odd numbers will be rolled (no even numbers) and subtract from one. You can always use a tree diagram or make a chart to list the possible outcomes when the sample space is small, such as in the dice-rolling example, but in most cases it will be much faster to use the multiplication and complement formulas.

Review Video: Multiplication Rule
Visit mometrix.com/academy and enter code: 782598

Union and Intersection of Two Sets of Outcomes

If A and B are each a set of elements or outcomes from an experiment, then the **union** (symbol $\cup$) of the two sets is the set of elements found in set A or set B. For example, if $A = \{2, 3, 4\}$ and $B = \{3, 4, 5\}$, $A \cup B = \{2, 3, 4, 5\}$. Note that the outcomes 3 and 4 appear only once in the union. For statistical events, the union is equivalent to "or"; $P(A \cup B)$ is the same thing as $P(A \text{ or } B)$. The **intersection** (symbol $\cap$) of two sets is the set of outcomes common to both sets. For the above sets A and B, $A \cap B = \{3, 4\}$. For statistical events, the intersection is equivalent to "and"; $P(A \cap B)$ is the same thing as $P(A \text{ and } B)$. It is important to note that union and intersection operations commute. That is:

$$A \cup B = B \cup A \text{ and } A \cap B = B \cap A$$

Permutations and Combinations

When trying to calculate the probability of an event using the $\frac{\text{desired outcomes}}{\text{total outcomes}}$ formula, you may frequently find that there are too many outcomes to individually count them. **Permutation** and **combination formulas** offer a shortcut to counting outcomes. A permutation is an arrangement of a specific number of a set of objects in a specific order. The number of **permutations** of r items given a set of n items can be calculated as ${}_nP_r = \frac{n!}{(n-r)!}$. Combinations are similar to permutations, except there are no restrictions regarding the order of the elements. While ABC is considered a different permutation than BCA, ABC and BCA are considered the same combination. The number of **combinations** of r items given a set of n items can be calculated as ${}_nC_r = \frac{n!}{r!(n-r)!}$ or ${}_nC_r = \frac{{}_nP_r}{r!}$.

Suppose you want to calculate how many different 5-card hands can be drawn from a deck of 52 cards. This is a combination since the order of the cards in a hand does not matter. There are 52 cards available, and 5 to be selected. Thus, the number of different hands is ${}_{52}C_5 = \frac{52!}{5! \times 47!} = 2{,}598{,}960$.

Review Video: Probability - Permutation and Combination
Visit mometrix.com/academy and enter code: 907664

Tree Diagram

For a simple sample space, possible outcomes may be determined by using a **tree diagram** or an organized chart. In either case, you can easily draw or list out the possible outcomes. For example, to determine all the possible ways three objects can be ordered, you can draw a tree diagram:

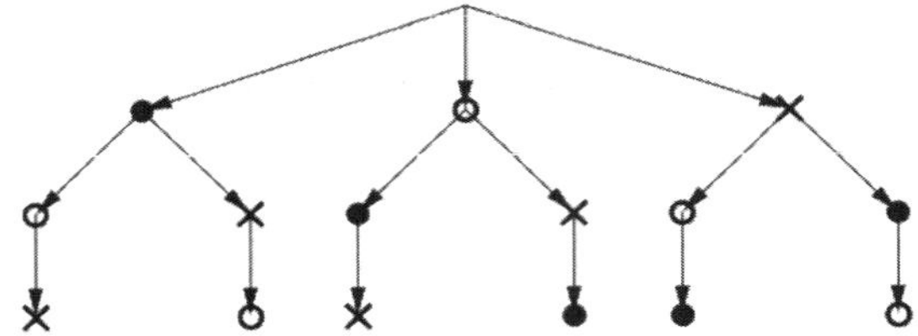

Review Video: Tree Diagrams
Visit mometrix.com/academy and enter code: 829158

You can also make a chart to list all the possibilities:

First object	Second object	Third object
●	x	o
●	o	x
O	●	x
o	x	●
x	●	o
x	o	●

Either way, you can easily see there are six possible ways the three objects can be ordered.

If two events have no outcomes in common, they are said to be **mutually exclusive**. For example, in a standard deck of 52 playing cards, the event of all card suits is mutually exclusive to the event of all card values. If two events have no bearing on each other so that one event occurring has no influence on the probability of another event occurring, the two events are said to be independent. For example, rolling a standard six-sided die multiple times does not change that probability that a particular number will be rolled from one roll to the next. If the outcome of one event does affect the probability of the second event, the two events are said to be dependent. For example, if cards are drawn from a deck, the probability of drawing an ace after an ace has been drawn is different than the probability of drawing an ace if no ace (or no other card, for that matter) has been drawn.

In probability, the **odds in favor of an event** are the number of times the event will occur compared to the number of times the event will not occur. To calculate the odds in favor of an event, use the formula $\frac{P(A)}{1-P(A)}$, where $P(A)$ is the probability that the event will occur. Many times, odds in favor is given as a ratio in the form $\frac{a}{b}$ or $a{:}\,b$, where a is the probability of the event occurring and b is the complement of the event, the probability of the event not occurring. If the odds in favor are given as 2:5, that means that you can expect the event to occur two times for every 5 times that it does not occur. In other words, the probability that the event will occur is $\frac{2}{2+5} = \frac{2}{7}$.

In probability, the **odds against an event** are the number of times the event will not occur compared to the number of times the event will occur. To calculate the odds against an event, use the formula $\frac{1-P(A)}{P(A)}$, where $P(A)$ is the probability that the event will occur. Many times, odds against is given as a ratio in the form $\frac{b}{a}$ or $b{:}\,a$, where b is the probability the event will not occur (the complement of the event) and a is the probability the event will occur. If the odds against an event are given as 3:1, that means that you can expect the event to not occur 3 times for every one time it does occur. In other words, 3 out of every 4 trials will fail.

TWO-WAY FREQUENCY TABLES

If we have a two-way frequency table, it is generally a straightforward matter to read off the probabilities of any two events A and B, as well as the joint probability of both events occurring, $P(A \cap B)$. We can then find the conditional probability $P(A|B)$ by calculating $P(A|B) = \frac{P(A \cap B)}{P(B)}$. We could also check whether or not events are independent by verifying whether $P(A)P(B) = P(A \cap B)$.

For example, a certain store's recent T-shirt sales:

	Small	Medium	Large	Total
Blue	25	40	35	100
White	27	25	22	74
Black	8	23	15	46
Total	60	88	72	220

Suppose we want to find the conditional probability that a customer buys a black shirt (event A), given that the shirt he buys is size small (event B). From the table, the probability $P(B)$ that a customer buys a small shirt is $\frac{60}{220} = \frac{3}{11}$. The probability $P(A \cap B)$ that he buys a small, black shirt is $\frac{8}{220} = \frac{2}{55}$. The conditional probability $P(A|B)$ that he buys a black shirt, given that he buys a small shirt, is therefore $P(A|B) = \frac{2/55}{3/11} = \frac{2}{15}$.

Similarly, if we want to check whether the event a customer buys a blue shirt, A, is independent of the event that a customer buys a medium shirt, B. From the table, $P(A) = \frac{100}{220} = \frac{5}{11}$ and $P(B) = \frac{88}{220} = \frac{4}{10}$. Also, $P(A \cap B) = \frac{40}{220} = \frac{2}{11}$. Since $\left(\frac{5}{11}\right)\left(\frac{4}{10}\right) = \frac{20}{110} = \frac{2}{11}$, $P(A)P(B) = P(A \cap B)$ and these two events are indeed independent.

EXPECTED VALUE

Expected value is a method of determining the expected outcome in a random situation. It is a sum of the weighted probabilities of the possible outcomes. Multiply the probability of an event occurring by the weight assigned to that probability (such as the amount of money won or lost). A practical application of the expected value is to determine whether a game of chance is really fair. If the sum of the weighted probabilities is equal to zero, the game is generally considered fair because the player has a fair chance to at least break even. If the expected value is less than zero, then players are expected to lose more than they win. For example, a lottery drawing might allow the player to choose any three-digit number, 000–999. The probability of choosing the winning number is 1:1000. If it costs $1 to play, and a winning number receives $500, the expected value is $\left(-\$1 \times \frac{999}{1{,}000}\right) + \left(\$499 \times \frac{1}{1{,}000}\right) = -\$0.50$. You can expect to lose on average 50 cents for every dollar you spend.

Review Video: Expected Value
Visit mometrix.com/academy and enter code: 643554

EXPECTED VALUE AND SIMULATORS

A die roll simulator will show the results of n rolls of a die. The result of each die roll may be recorded. For example, suppose a die is rolled 100 times. All results may be recorded. The numbers of 1s, 2s, 3s, 4s, 5s, and 6s, may be counted. The experimental probability of rolling each number will equal the ratio of the frequency of the rolled number to the total number of rolls. As the number of rolls increases, or approaches infinity, the experimental probability will approach the theoretical probability of $\frac{1}{6}$. Thus, the expected value for the roll of a die is shown to be $\left(1 \times \frac{1}{6}\right) + \left(2 \times \frac{1}{6}\right) + \left(3 \times \frac{1}{6}\right) + \left(4 \times \frac{1}{6}\right) + \left(5 \times \frac{1}{6}\right) + \left(6 \times \frac{1}{6}\right)$, or 3.5.

STATISTICS

Statistics is the branch of mathematics that deals with collecting, recording, interpreting, illustrating, and analyzing large amounts of **data**. The following terms are often used in the discussion of data and **statistics**:

- **Data** – the collective name for pieces of information (singular is datum)
- **Quantitative data** – measurements (such as length, mass, and speed) that provide information about quantities in numbers
- **Qualitative data** – information (such as colors, scents, tastes, and shapes) that cannot be measured using numbers
- **Discrete data** – information that can be expressed only by a specific value, such as whole or half numbers. (e.g., since people can be counted only in whole numbers, a population count would be discrete data.)
- **Continuous data** – information (such as time and temperature) that can be expressed by any value within a given range
- **Primary data** – information that has been collected directly from a survey, investigation, or experiment, such as a questionnaire or the recording of daily temperatures. (Primary data that has not yet been organized or analyzed is called **raw data**.)
- **Secondary data** – information that has been collected, sorted, and processed by the researcher
- **Ordinal data** – information that can be placed in numerical order, such as age or weight
- **Nominal data** – information that *cannot* be placed in numerical order, such as names or places

DATA COLLECTION

POPULATION

In statistics, the **population** is the entire collection of people, plants, etc., that data can be collected from. For example, a study to determine how well students in local schools perform on a standardized test would have a population of all the students enrolled in those schools, although a study may include just a small sample of students from each school. A **parameter** is a numerical value that gives information about the population, such as the mean, median, mode, or standard deviation. Remember that the symbol for the mean of a population is μ and the symbol for the standard deviation of a population is σ.

SAMPLE

A **sample** is a portion of the entire population. Whereas a parameter helped describe the population, a **statistic** is a numerical value that gives information about the sample, such as mean, median, mode, or standard deviation. Keep in mind that the symbols for mean and standard deviation are different when they are referring to a sample rather than the entire population. For a sample, the symbol for mean is $\bar{x}$ and the symbol for standard deviation is s. The mean and standard deviation of a sample may or may not be identical to that of the entire population due to a sample only being a subset of the population. However, if the sample is random and large enough, statistically significant values can be attained. Samples are generally used when the population is too large to justify including every element or when acquiring data for the entire population is impossible.

INFERENTIAL STATISTICS

Inferential statistics is the branch of statistics that uses samples to make predictions about an entire population. This type of statistic is often seen in political polls, where a sample of the population is questioned about a particular topic or politician to gain an understanding of the attitudes of the entire population of the country. Often, exit polls are conducted on election days using this method. Inferential statistics can have a large margin of error if you do not have a valid sample.

SAMPLING DISTRIBUTION

Statistical values calculated from various samples of the same size make up the **sampling distribution**. For example, if several samples of identical size are randomly selected from a large population and then the mean of each sample is calculated, the distribution of values of the means would be a sampling distribution.

The **sampling distribution of the mean** is the distribution of the sample mean, $\bar{x}$, derived from random samples of a given size. It has three important characteristics. First, the mean of the sampling distribution of the mean is equal to the mean of the population that was sampled. Second, assuming the standard deviation is non-zero, the standard deviation of the sampling distribution of the mean equals the standard deviation of the sampled population divided by the square root of the sample size. This is sometimes called the standard error. Finally, as the sample size gets larger, the sampling distribution of the mean gets closer to a normal distribution via the central limit theorem.

SURVEY STUDY

A **survey study** is a method of gathering information from a small group in an attempt to gain enough information to make accurate general assumptions about the population. Once a survey study is completed, the results are then put into a summary report.

Survey studies are generally in the format of surveys, interviews, or questionnaires as part of an effort to find opinions of a particular group or to find facts about a group.

It is important to note that the findings from a survey study are only as accurate as the sample chosen from the population.

CORRELATIONAL STUDIES

Correlational studies seek to determine how much one variable is affected by changes in a second variable. For example, correlational studies may look for a relationship between the amount of time a student spends studying for a test and the grade that student earned on the test or between student scores on college admissions tests and student grades in college.

It is important to note that correlational studies cannot show a cause and effect, but rather can show only that two variables are or are not potentially correlated.

Experimental Studies

Experimental studies take correlational studies one step farther, in that they attempt to prove or disprove a cause-and-effect relationship. These studies are performed by conducting a series of experiments to test the hypothesis. For a study to be scientifically accurate, it must have both an experimental group that receives the specified treatment and a control group that does not get the treatment. This is the type of study pharmaceutical companies do as part of drug trials for new medications. Experimental studies are only valid when the proper scientific method has been followed. In other words, the experiment must be well-planned and executed without bias in the testing process, all subjects must be selected at random, and the process of determining which subject is in which of the two groups must also be completely random.

Observational Studies

Observational studies are the opposite of experimental studies. In observational studies, the tester cannot change or in any way control all of the variables in the test. For example, a study to determine which gender does better in math classes in school is strictly observational. You cannot change a person's gender, and you cannot change the subject being studied. The big downfall of observational studies is that you have no way of proving a cause-and-effect relationship because you cannot control outside influences. Events outside of school can influence a student's performance in school, and observational studies cannot take that into consideration.

Random Samples

For most studies, a **random sample** is necessary to produce valid results. Random samples should not have any particular influence to cause sampled subjects to behave one way or another. The goal is for the random sample to be a **representative sample**, or a sample whose characteristics give an accurate picture of the characteristics of the entire population. To accomplish this, you must make sure you have a proper **sample size**, or an appropriate number of elements in the sample.

Biases

In statistical studies, biases must be avoided. **Bias** is an error that causes the study to favor one set of results over another. For example, if a survey to determine how the country views the president's job performance only speaks to registered voters in the president's party, the results will be skewed because a disproportionately large number of responders would tend to show approval, while a disproportionately large number of people in the opposite party would tend to express disapproval. **Extraneous variables** are, as the name implies, outside influences that can affect the outcome of a study. They are not always avoidable but could trigger bias in the result.

Dispersion

A **measure of dispersion** is a single value that helps to "interpret" the measure of central tendency by providing more information about how the data values in the set are distributed about the measure of central tendency. The measure of dispersion helps to eliminate or reduce the disadvantages of using the mean, median, or mode as a single measure of central tendency, and give a more accurate picture of the dataset as a whole. To have a measure of dispersion, you must know or calculate the range, standard deviation, or variance of the data set.

Range

The **range** of a set of data is the difference between the greatest and lowest values of the data in the set. To calculate the range, you must first make sure the units for all data values are the same, and then identify the greatest and lowest values. If there are multiple data values that are equal for the highest or lowest, just use one of the values in the formula. Write the answer with the same units as the data values you used to do the calculations.

Review Video: Statistical Range
Visit mometrix.com/academy and enter code: 778541

Sample Standard Deviation

Standard deviation is a measure of dispersion that compares all the data values in the set to the mean of the set to give a more accurate picture. To find the **standard deviation of a sample**, use the formula

$$s = \sqrt{\frac{\sum_{i=1}^{n}(x_i - \bar{x})^2}{n - 1}}$$

Note that s is the standard deviation of a sample, x_i represents the individual values in the data set, $\bar{x}$ is the mean of the data values in the set, and n is the number of data values in the set. The higher the value of the standard deviation is, the greater the variance of the data values from the mean. The units associated with the standard deviation are the same as the units of the data values.

Review Video: Standard Deviation
Visit mometrix.com/academy and enter code: 419469

Sample Variance

The **variance of a sample** is the square of the sample standard deviation (denoted s^2). While the mean of a set of data gives the average of the set and gives information about where a specific data value lies in relation to the average, the variance of the sample gives information about the degree to which the data values are spread out and tells you how close an individual value is to the average compared to the other values. The units associated with variance are the same as the units of the data values squared.

Percentile

Percentiles and quartiles are other methods of describing data within a set. **Percentiles** tell what percentage of the data in the set fall below a specific point. For example, achievement test scores are often given in percentiles. A score at the 80th percentile is one which is equal to or higher than 80 percent of the scores in the set. In other words, 80 percent of the scores were lower than that score.

Quartiles are percentile groups that make up quarter sections of the data set. The first quartile is the 25th percentile. The second quartile is the 50th percentile; this is also the median of the dataset. The third quartile is the 75th percentile.

Skewness

Skewness is a way to describe the symmetry or asymmetry of the distribution of values in a dataset. If the distribution of values is symmetrical, there is no skew. In general the closer the mean of a data set is to the median of the data set, the less skew there is. Generally, if the mean is to the right of the median, the data set is *positively skewed*, or right-skewed, and if the mean is to the left of the median, the data set is *negatively skewed*, or left-skewed. However, this rule of thumb is not infallible. When the data values are graphed on a curve, a set with no skew will be a perfect bell curve.

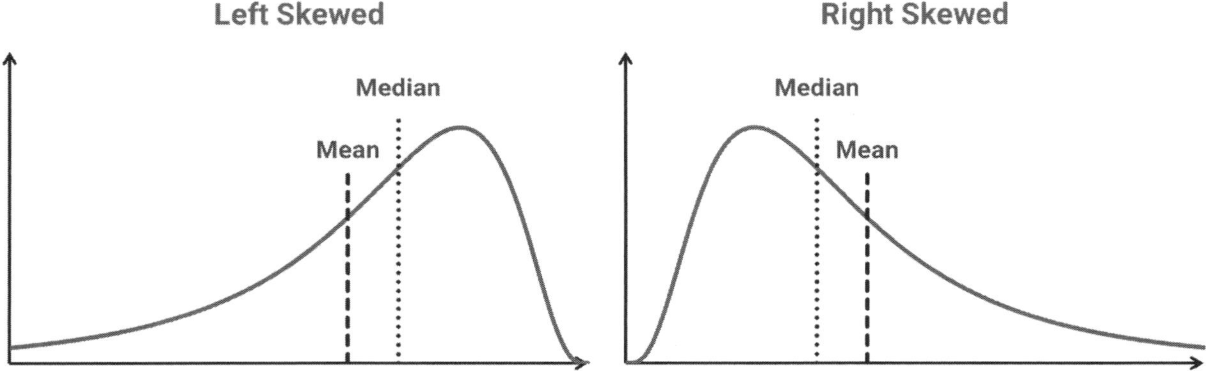

To estimate skew, use the formula:

$$\text{skew} = \frac{\sqrt{n(n-1)}}{n-2}\left(\frac{\frac{1}{n}\sum_{i=1}^{n}(x_i - \bar{x})^3}{\left(\frac{1}{n}\sum_{i=1}^{n}(x_i - \bar{x})^2\right)^{\frac{3}{2}}}\right)$$

Note that n is the datapoints in the set, x_i is the ith value in the set, and $\bar{x}$ is the mean of the set.

Review Video: Skew
Visit mometrix.com/academy and enter code: 661486

Unimodal vs. Bimodal

If a distribution has a single peak, it would be considered **unimodal**. If it has two discernible peaks it would be considered **bimodal**. Bimodal distributions may be an indication that the set of data being considered is actually the combination of two sets of data with significant differences. A **uniform distribution** is a distribution in which there is *no distinct peak or variation* in the data. No values or ranges are particularly more common than any other values or ranges.

Outlier

An outlier is an extremely high or extremely low value in the data set. It may be the result of measurement error, in which case, the outlier is not a valid member of the data set. However, it may also be a valid member of the distribution. Unless a measurement error is identified, the experimenter cannot know for certain if an outlier is or is not a member of the distribution. There are arbitrary methods that can be employed to designate an extreme value as an outlier. One method designates an outlier (or possible outlier) to be any value less than $Q_1 - 1.5(IQR)$ or any value greater than $Q_3 + 1.5(IQR)$.

Data Analysis

Simple Regression

In statistics, **simple regression** is using an equation to represent a relation between independent and dependent variables. The independent variable is also referred to as the explanatory variable or the predictor and is generally represented by the variable x in the equation. The dependent variable, usually represented by the variable y, is also referred to as the response variable. The equation may be any type of function – linear, quadratic, exponential, etc. The best way to handle this task is to use the regression feature of your graphing calculator. This will easily give you the curve of best fit and provide you with the coefficients and other information you need to derive an equation.

Line of Best Fit

In a scatter plot, the **line of best fit** is the line that best shows the trends of the data. The line of best fit is given by the equation $\hat{y} = ax + b$, where a and b are the regression coefficients. The regression coefficient a is also the slope of the line of best fit, and b is also the y-coordinate of the point at which the line of best fit crosses the y-axis. Not every point on the scatter plot will be on the line of best fit. The differences between the y-values of the points in the scatter plot and the corresponding y-values according to the equation of the line of best fit are the residuals. The line of best fit is also called the least-squares regression line because it is also the line that has the lowest sum of the squares of the residuals.

Correlation Coefficient

The **correlation coefficient** is the numerical value that indicates how strong the relationship is between the two variables of a linear regression equation. A correlation coefficient of –1 is a perfect negative correlation. A correlation coefficient of +1 is a perfect positive correlation. Correlation coefficients close to –1 or +1 are very strong correlations. A correlation coefficient equal to zero indicates there is no correlation between the two variables. This test is a good indicator of whether or not the equation for the line of best fit is accurate. The formula for the correlation coefficient is

$$r = \frac{\sum_{i=1}^{n}(x_i - \bar{x})(y_i - \bar{y})}{\sqrt{\sum_{i=1}^{n}(x_i - \bar{x})^2}\sqrt{\sum_{i=1}^{n}(y_i - \bar{y})^2}}$$

where r is the correlation coefficient, n is the number of data values in the set, (x_i, y_i) is a point in the set, and $\bar{x}$ and $\bar{y}$ are the means.

Z-Score

A **z-score** is an indication of how many standard deviations a given value falls from the sample mean. To calculate a z-score, use the formula:

$$\frac{x - \bar{x}}{\sigma}$$

In this formula x is the data value, $\bar{x}$ is the mean of the sample data, and σ is the standard deviation of the population. If the z-score is positive, the data value lies above the mean. If the z-score is negative, the data value falls below the mean. These scores are useful in interpreting data such as standardized test scores, where every piece of data in the set has been counted, rather than just a small random sample. In cases where standard deviations are calculated from a random sample of the set, the z-scores will not be as accurate.

Central Limit Theorem

According to the **central limit theorem**, regardless of what the original distribution of a sample is, the distribution of the means tends to get closer and closer to a normal distribution as the sample size gets larger and larger (this is necessary because the sample is becoming more all-encompassing of the elements of the population). As the sample size gets larger, the distribution of the sample mean will approach a normal distribution with a mean of the population mean and a variance of the population variance divided by the sample size.

MEASURES OF CENTRAL TENDENCY

A **measure of central tendency** is a statistical value that gives a reasonable estimate for the center of a group of data. There are several different ways of describing the measure of central tendency. Each one has a unique way it is calculated, and each one gives a slightly different perspective on the data set. Whenever you give a measure of central tendency, always make sure the units are the same. If the data has different units, such as hours, minutes, and seconds, convert all the data to the same unit, and use the same unit in the measure of central tendency. If no units are given in the data, do not give units for the measure of central tendency.

MEAN

The **statistical mean** of a group of data is the same as the arithmetic average of that group. To find the mean of a set of data, first convert each value to the same units, if necessary. Then find the sum of all the values, and count the total number of data values, making sure you take into consideration each individual value. If a value appears more than once, count it more than once. Divide the sum of the values by the total number of values and apply the units, if any. Note that the mean does not have to be one of the data values in the set, and may not divide evenly.

$$\text{mean} = \frac{\text{sum of the data values}}{\text{quantity of data values}}$$

For instance, the mean of the data set {88, 72, 61, 90, 97, 68, 88, 79, 86, 93, 97, 71, 80, 84, 89} would be the sum of the fifteen numbers divided by 15:

$$\frac{88 + 72 + 61 + 90 + 97 + 68 + 88 + 79 + 86 + 93 + 97 + 71 + 80 + 84 + 88}{15} = \frac{1242}{15} = 82.8$$

While the mean is relatively easy to calculate and averages are understood by most people, the mean can be very misleading if it is used as the sole measure of central tendency. If the data set has outliers (data values that are unusually high or unusually low compared to the rest of the data values), the mean can be very distorted, especially if the data set has a small number of values. If unusually high values are countered with unusually low values, the mean is not affected as much. For example, if five of twenty students in a class get a 100 on a test, but the other 15 students have an average of 60 on the same test, the class average would appear as 70. Whenever the mean is skewed by outliers, it is always a good idea to include the median as an alternate measure of central tendency.

A **weighted mean**, or weighted average, is a mean that uses "weighted" values. The formula is weighted mean $= \frac{w_1x_1+w_2x_2+w_3x_3...+w_nx_n}{w_1+w_2+w_3+\cdots+w_n}$. Weighted values, such as $w_1, w_2, w_3, ... w_n$ are assigned to each member of the set $x_1, x_2, x_3, ... x_n$. When calculating the weighted mean, make sure a weight value for each member of the set is used.

Review Video: All About Averages
Visit mometrix.com/academy and enter code: 176521

MEDIAN

The **statistical median** is the value in the middle of the set of data. To find the median, list all data values in order from smallest to largest or from largest to smallest. Any value that is repeated in the set must be listed the number of times it appears. If there are an odd number of data values, the median is the value in the middle of the list. If there is an even number of data values, the median is the arithmetic mean of the two middle values.

For example, the median of the data set {88, 72, 61, 90, 97, 68, 88, 79, 86, 93, 97, 71, 80, 84, 88} is 86 since the ordered set is {61, 68, 71, 72, 79, 80, 84, **86**, 88, 88, 88, 90, 93, 97, 97}.

The big disadvantage of using the median as a measure of central tendency is that is relies solely on a value's relative size as compared to the other values in the set. When the individual values in a set of data are evenly dispersed, the median can be an accurate tool. However, if there is a group of rather large values or a group of rather small values that are not offset by a different group of values, the information that can be inferred from the median may not be accurate because the distribution of values is skewed.

MODE

The **statistical mode** is the data value that occurs the greatest number of times in the data set. It is possible to have exactly one mode, more than one mode, or no mode. To find the mode of a set of data, arrange the data like you do to find the median (all values in order, listing all multiples of data values). Count the number of times each value appears in the data set. If all values appear an equal number of times, there is no mode. If one value appears more than any other value, that value is the mode. If two or more values appear the same number of times, but there are other values that appear fewer times and no values that appear more times, all of those values are the modes.

For example, the mode of the data set {**88**, 72, 61, 90, 97, 68, **88**, 79, 86, 93, 97, 71, 80, 84, **88**} is 88.

The main disadvantage of the mode is that the values of the other data in the set have no bearing on the mode. The mode may be the largest value, the smallest value, or a value anywhere in between in the set. The mode only tells which value or values, if any, occurred the greatest number of times. It does not give any suggestions about the remaining values in the set.

Review Video: Mean, Median, and Mode
Visit mometrix.com/academy and enter code: 286207

FREQUENCY TABLES

Frequency tables show how frequently each unique value appears in a set. A **relative frequency table** is one that shows the proportions of each unique value compared to the entire set. Relative frequencies are given as percentages; however, the total percent for a relative frequency table will not necessarily equal 100 percent due to rounding. An example of a frequency table with relative frequencies is below.

Favorite Color	Frequency	Relative Frequency
Blue	4	13%
Red	7	22%
Green	3	9%
Purple	6	19%
Cyan	12	38%

Review Video: Data Interpretation of Graphs
Visit mometrix.com/academy and enter code: 200439

CIRCLE GRAPHS

Circle graphs, also known as *pie charts*, provide a visual depiction of the relationship of each type of data compared to the whole set of data. The circle graph is divided into sections by drawing radii to create central angles whose percentage of the circle is equal to the individual data's percentage of the whole set. Each 1% of data is equal to 3.6° in the circle graph. Therefore, data represented by a 90° section of the circle graph makes up 25% of the whole. When complete, a circle graph often looks like a pie cut into uneven wedges. The pie chart below shows the data from the frequency table referenced earlier where people were asked their favorite color.

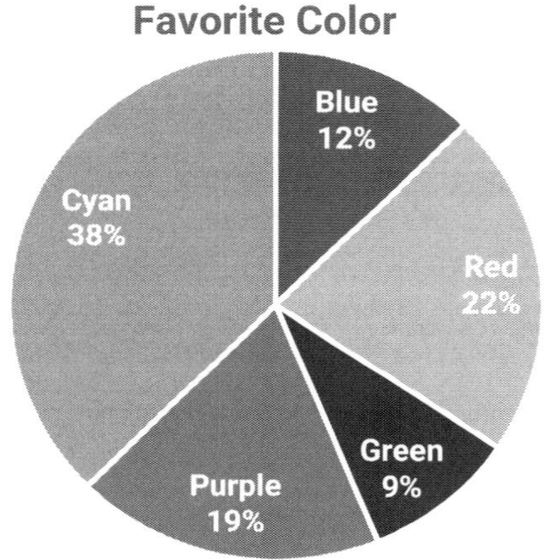

PICTOGRAPHS

A **pictograph** is a graph, generally in the horizontal orientation, that uses pictures or symbols to represent the data. Each pictograph must have a key that defines the picture or symbol and gives the quantity each picture or symbol represents. Pictures or symbols on a pictograph are not always shown as whole elements. In this case, the fraction of the picture or symbol shown represents the same fraction of the quantity a whole picture or symbol stands for. For example, a row with $3\frac{1}{2}$ ears of corn, where each ear of corn represents 100 stalks of corn in a field, would equal $3\frac{1}{2} \times 100 = 350$ stalks of corn in the field.

Review Video: Pictographs
Visit mometrix.com/academy and enter code: 147860

LINE GRAPHS

Line graphs have one or more lines of varying styles (solid or broken) to show the different values for a set of data. The individual data are represented as ordered pairs, much like on a Cartesian plane. In this case, the x- and y-axes are defined in terms of their units, such as dollars or time. The individual plotted points are joined by line segments to show whether the value of the data is increasing (line sloping upward), decreasing (line sloping downward), or staying the same (horizontal line). Multiple sets of data can be graphed on the same line graph to give an easy visual comparison. An example of this would be graphing achievement test scores for different groups of students over the same time period to see which group had the greatest increase or decrease in performance from year to year (as shown below).

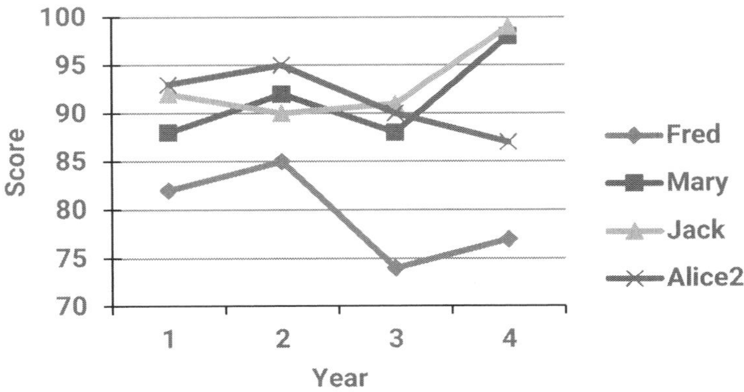

Review Video: How to Create a Line Graph
Visit mometrix.com/academy and enter code: 480147

LINE PLOTS

A **line plot**, also known as a *dot plot*, has plotted points that are not connected by line segments. In this graph, the horizontal axis lists the different possible values for the data, and the vertical axis lists the number of times the individual value occurs. A single dot is graphed for each value to show the number of times it occurs. This graph is more closely related to a bar graph than a line graph. Do not connect the dots in a line plot or it will misrepresent the data.

Review Video: Line Plot
Visit mometrix.com/academy and enter code: 754610

STEM AND LEAF PLOTS

A **stem and leaf plot** is useful for depicting groups of data that fall into a range of values. Each piece of data is separated into two parts: the first, or left, part is called the stem; the second, or right, part is called the leaf. Each stem is listed in a column from smallest to largest. Each leaf that has the common stem is listed in that stem's row from smallest to largest. For example, in a set of two-digit numbers, the digit in the tens place is the stem, and the digit in the ones place is the leaf. With a stem and leaf plot, you can easily see which subset of numbers (10s, 20s, 30s, etc.) is the largest. This information is also readily available by looking at a histogram, but a stem and leaf plot also allows you to look closer and see exactly which values fall in that range. Using a sample set of test scores (82, 88, 92, 93, 85, 90, 92, 95, 74, 88, 90, 91, 78, 87, 98, 99), we can assemble a stem and leaf plot like the one below.

Test Scores

7	4	8							
8	2	5	7	8	8				
9	0	0	1	2	2	3	5	8	9

Review Video: Stem and Leaf Plots
Visit mometrix.com/academy and enter code: 302339

Bar Graphs

A **bar graph** is one of the few graphs that can be drawn correctly in two different configurations – both horizontally and vertically. A bar graph is similar to a line plot in the way the data is organized on the graph. Both axes must have their categories defined for the graph to be useful. Rather than placing a single dot to mark the point of the data's value, a bar, or thick line, is drawn from zero to the exact value of the data, whether it is a number, percentage, or other numerical value. Longer bar lengths correspond to greater data values. To read a bar graph, read the labels for the axes to find the units being reported. Then, look where the bars end in relation to the scale given on the corresponding axis and determine the associated value.

The bar chart below represents the responses from our favorite-color survey.

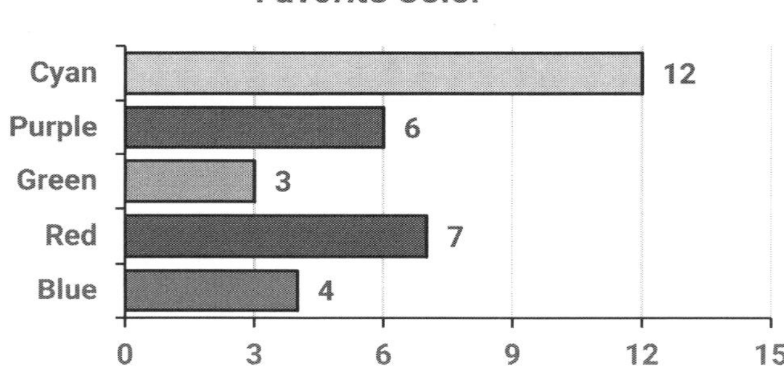

Histograms

At first glance, a **histogram** looks like a vertical bar graph. The difference is that a bar graph has a separate bar for each piece of data and a histogram has one continuous bar for each *range* of data. For example, a histogram may have one bar for the range 0–9, one bar for 10–19, etc. While a bar graph has numerical values on one axis, a histogram has numerical values on both axes. Each range is of equal size, and they are ordered left to right from lowest to highest. The height of each column on a histogram represents the number of data values within that range. Like a stem and leaf plot, a histogram makes it easy to glance at the graph and quickly determine which range has the greatest quantity of values. A simple example of a histogram is below.

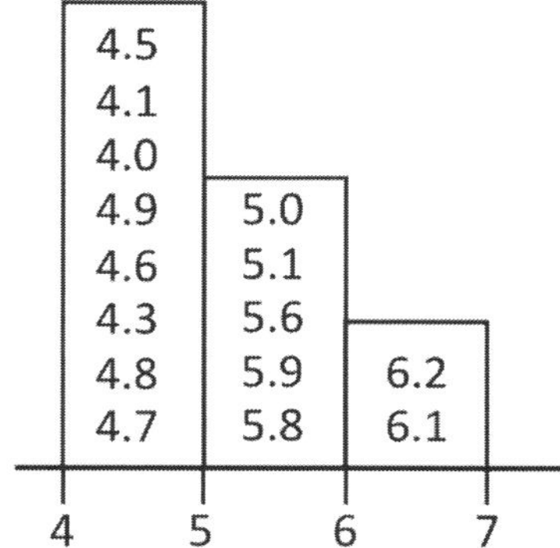

5-Number Summary

The **5-number summary** of a set of data gives a very informative picture of the set. The five numbers in the summary include the minimum value, maximum value, and the three quartiles. This information gives the reader the range and median of the set, as well as an indication of how the data is spread about the median.

Box and Whisker Plots

A **box-and-whiskers plot** is a graphical representation of the 5-number summary. To draw a box-and-whiskers plot, plot the points of the 5-number summary on a number line. Draw a box whose ends are through the points for the first and third quartiles. Draw a vertical line in the box through the median to divide the box in half. Draw a line segment from the first quartile point to the minimum value, and from the third quartile point to the maximum value.

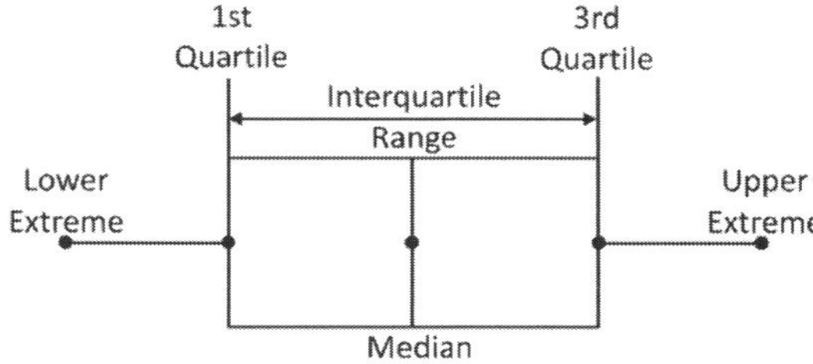

Review Video: Box and Whisker Plots
Visit mometrix.com/academy and enter code: 810817

Example

Given the following data (32, 28, 29, 26, 35, 27, 30, 31, 27, 32), we first sort it into numerical order: 26, 27, 27, 28, 29, 30, 31, 32, 32, 35. We can then find the median. Since there are ten values, we take the average of the 5th and 6th values to get 29.5. We find the lower quartile by taking the median of the data smaller than the median. Since there are five values, we take the 3rd value, which is 27. We find the upper quartile by taking the median of the data larger than the overall median, which is 32. Finally, we note our minimum and maximum, which are simply the smallest and largest values in the set: 26 and 35, respectively. Now we can create our box plot:

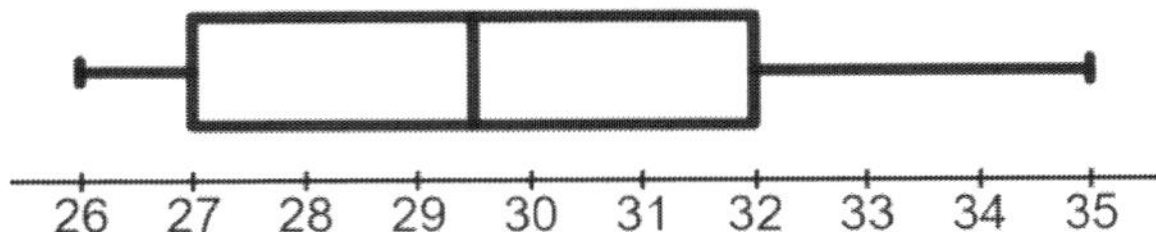

This plot is fairly "long" on the right whisker, showing one or more unusually high values (but not quite outliers). The other quartiles are similar in length, showing a fairly even distribution of data.

INTERQUARTILE RANGE

The **interquartile range, or IQR**, is the difference between the upper and lower quartiles. It measures how the data is dispersed: a high IQR means that the data is more spread out, while a low IQR means that the data is clustered more tightly around the median. To find the IQR, subtract the lower quartile value (Q_1) from the upper quartile value (Q_3).

EXAMPLE

To find the upper and lower quartiles, we first find the median and then take the median of all values above it and all values below it. In the following data set (16, 18, 13, 24, 16, 51, 32, 21, 27, 39), we first rearrange the values in numerical order: 13, 16, 16, 18, 21, 24, 27, 32, 39, 51. There are 10 values, so the median is the average of the 5th and 6th: $\frac{21+24}{2} = \frac{45}{2} = 22.5$. We do not actually need this value to find the upper and lower quartiles. We look at the set of numbers below the median: 13, 16, 16, 18, 21. There are five values, so the 3rd is the median (16), or the value of the lower quartile (Q_1). Then we look at the numbers above the median: 24, 27, 32, 39, 51. Again there are five values, so the 3rd is the median (32), or the value of the upper quartile (Q_3). We find the IQR by subtracting Q_1 from Q_3: $32 - 16 = 16$.

68-95-99.7 RULE

The **68–95–99.7 rule** describes how a normal distribution of data should appear when compared to the mean. This is also a description of a normal bell curve. According to this rule, 68 percent of the data values in a normally distributed set should fall within one standard deviation of the mean (34 percent above and 34 percent below the mean), 95 percent of the data values should fall within two standard deviations of the mean (47.5 percent above and 47.5 percent below the mean), and 99.7 percent of the data values should fall within three standard deviations of the mean, again, equally distributed on either side of the mean. This means that only 0.3 percent of all data values should fall more than three standard deviations from the mean. On the graph below, the normal curve is centered on the y-axis. The x-axis labels are how many standard deviations away from the center you are. Therefore, it is easy to see how the 68-95-99.7 rule can apply.

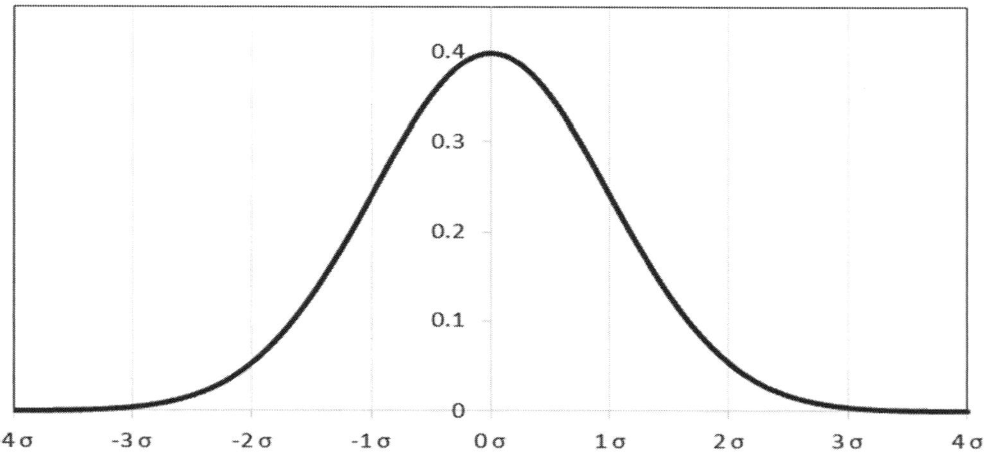

Bivariate Data

Bivariate data is simply data from two different variables. (The prefix *bi-* means *two.*) In a *scatter plot*, each value in the set of data is plotted on a grid similar to a Cartesian plane, where each axis represents one of the two variables. By looking at the pattern formed by the points on the grid, you can often determine whether or not there is a relationship between the two variables, and what that relationship is, if it exists. The variables may be directly proportionate, inversely proportionate, or show no proportion at all. It may also be possible to determine if the data is linear, and if so, to find an equation to relate the two variables. The following scatter plot shows the relationship between preference for brand "A" and the age of the consumers surveyed.

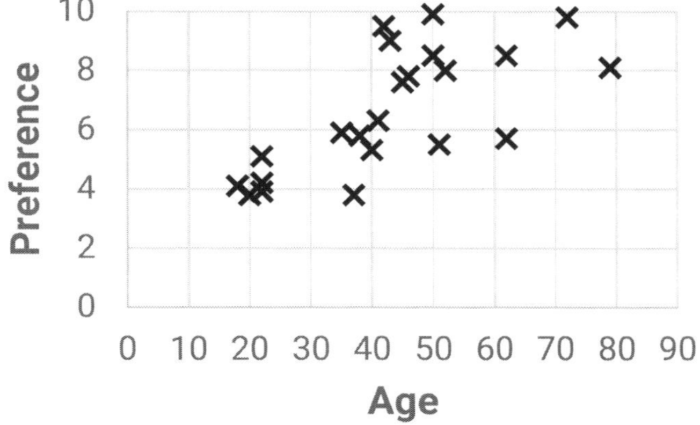

Scatter Plots

Scatter plots are also useful in determining the type of function represented by the data and finding the simple regression. Linear scatter plots may be positive or negative. Nonlinear scatter plots are generally exponential or quadratic. Below are some common types of scatter plots:

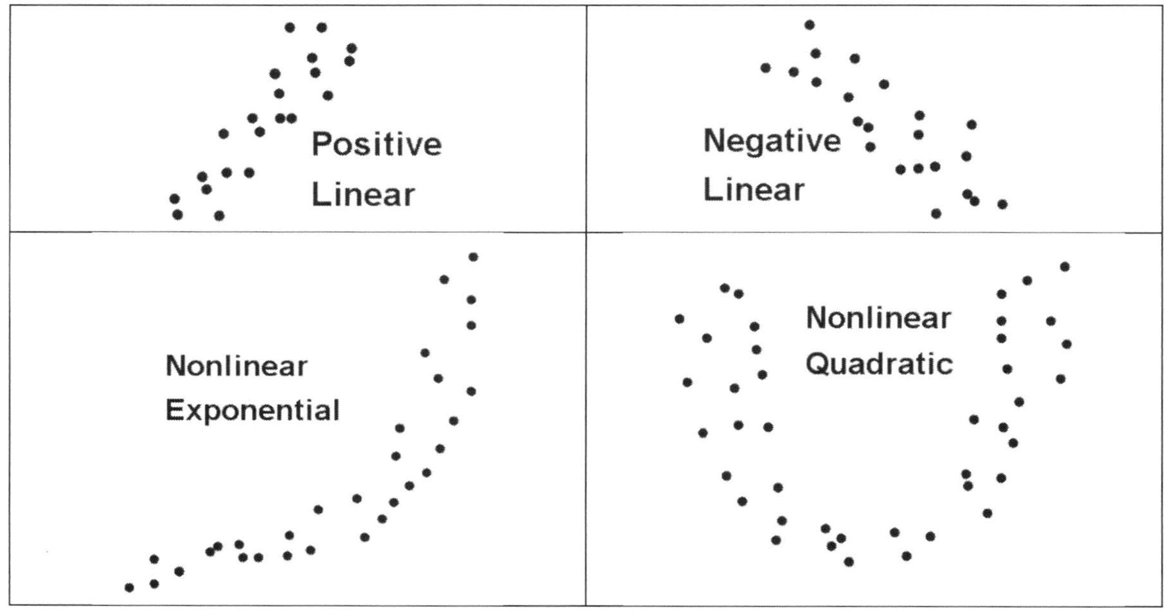

Review Video: What is a Scatter Plot?
Visit mometrix.com/academy and enter code: 596526

Passport to Advanced Math

Passport to Advanced Math Overview

In this section, the questions will deal with more advanced equations and expressions. Students need to be able to create quadratic and exponential equations that model a context. They also need to be able to solve these equations. Students should also be able to create equivalent expressions that involve radicals and rational exponents. Like the Heart of Algebra section, this section will test systems of equations. These systems, however, will involve one linear and one quadratic equation in two variables. Finally, students should be able to perform operations such as addition, subtraction, and multiplication on polynomials.

Question Types in Passport to Advanced Math

The passport to advanced math section will test your knowledge of the following:

- Create a **quadratic** or **exponential function** or equation that models a context.
  - The equation will have rational coefficients and may require multiple steps to simplify or solve the equation.
- Determine the most suitable form of an expression or equation to **reveal a particular trait**, given a context.

- Create **equivalent expressions** involving **rational exponents** and **radicals**, including simplifying or rewriting in other forms.
- Create an **equivalent form** of an algebraic expression by using structure and fluency with operations.
- Solve a quadratic equation having **rational coefficients**.
    - The equation can be presented in a wide range of forms to reward attending to algebraic structure and can require manipulation in order to solve.
- Add, subtract, and multiply **polynomial expressions** and simplify the result.
    - The expressions will have rational coefficients.
- Solve an equation in one variable that contains **radicals** or contains the **variable in the denominator** of a fraction.
    - The equation will have rational coefficients, and the student may be required to identify when a resulting solution is extraneous.
- Solve a system of one linear equation and one quadratic equation.
    - The equations will have rational coefficients.
- Rewrite simple rational expressions.
    - Students will add, subtract, multiply, or divide two rational expressions or divide two polynomial expressions and simplify the result.
    - The expressions will have rational coefficients.
- Interpret parts of **nonlinear expressions** in terms of their context.
    - Students will make connections between a context and the nonlinear equation that models the context to identify or describe the real-life meaning of a constant term, a variable, or a feature of the given equation.
- Understand the **relationship between zeros** and **factors of polynomials**, and use that knowledge to sketch graphs.
    - Students will use properties of factorable polynomials to solve conceptual problems relating to zeros, such as determining whether an expression is a factor of a polynomial based on other information provided.
- Understand a **nonlinear relationship** between two variables by making connections between their **algebraic** and **graphical representations**.
    - The student will select a graph corresponding to a given nonlinear equation; interpret graphs in the context of solving systems of equations; select a nonlinear equation corresponding to a given graph; determine the equation of a curve given a verbal description of a graph; determine key features of the graph of a linear function from its equation; or determine the impact on a graph of a change in the defining equation.
- Use **function notation**, and interpret statements using function notation.
    - The student will use function notation to solve conceptual problems related to transformations and compositions of functions.
- Use structure to **isolate or identify a quantity of interest** in an expression or isolate a quantity of interest in an equation.
    - The student will rearrange an equation or formula to isolate a single variable or a quantity of interest.

Solving a System of Equations Consisting of a Linear Equation and a Quadratic Equation

Algebraically

Generally, the simplest way to solve a system of equations consisting of a linear equation and a quadratic equation algebraically is through the method of substitution. One possible strategy is to solve the linear equation for y and then substitute that expression into the quadratic equation. After expansion and combining like terms, this will result in a new quadratic equation for x, which, like all quadratic equations, may have zero, one, or two solutions. Plugging each solution for x back into one of the original equations will then produce the corresponding value of y.

For example, consider the following system of equations:

$$x + y = 1$$
$$y = (x + 3)^2 - 2$$

We can solve the linear equation for y to yield $y = -x + 1$. Substituting this expression into the quadratic equation produces $-x + 1 = (x + 3)^2 - 2$. We can simplify this equation:

$$\begin{aligned} -x + 1 &= (x + 3)^2 - 2 \\ -x + 1 &= x^2 + 6x + 9 - 2 \\ -x + 1 &= x^2 + 6x + 7 \\ 0 &= x^2 + 7x + 6 \end{aligned}$$

This quadratic equation can be factored as $(x + 1)(x + 6) = 0$. It therefore has two solutions: $x_1 = -1$ and $x_2 = -6$. Plugging each of these back into the original linear equation yields $y_1 = -x_1 + 1 = -(-1) + 1 = 2$ and $y_2 = -x_2 + 1 = -(-6) + 1 = 7$. Thus, this system of equations has two solutions, $(-1,2)$ and $(-6,7)$.

It may help to check your work by putting each x- and y-value back into the original equations and verifying that they do provide a solution.

Graphically

To solve a system of equations consisting of a linear equation and a quadratic equation graphically, plot both equations on the same graph. The linear equation will, of course, produce a straight line, while the quadratic equation will produce a parabola. These two graphs will intersect at zero, one, or two points; each point of intersection is a solution of the system.

For example, consider the following system of equations:

$$y = -2x + 2$$
$$y = -2x^2 + 4x + 2$$

The linear equation describes a line with a y-intercept of $(0,2)$ and a slope of -2.

To graph the quadratic equation, we can first find the vertex of the parabola: the x-coordinate of the vertex is $h = -\frac{b}{2a} = -\frac{4}{2(-2)} = 1$, and the y-coordinate is $k = -2(1)^2 + 4(1) + 2 = 4$. Thus, the vertex lies at $(1,4)$. To get a feel for the rest of the parabola, we can plug in a few more values of x to find more points; by putting in $x = 2$ and $x = 3$ in the quadratic equation, we find that the points

$(2,2)$ and $(3,-4)$ lie on the parabola; by symmetry, so must $(0,2)$ and $(-1,-4)$. We can now plot both equations:

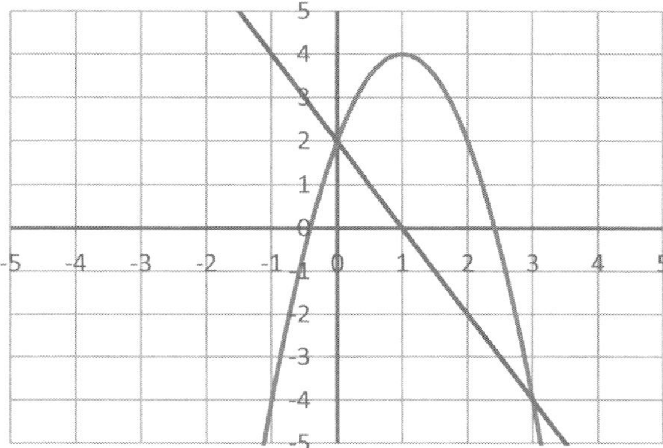

These two curves intersect at the points $(0,2)$ and $(3,-4)$, thus these are the solutions of the equation.

Review Video: Solving a System of Equations Consisting of a Linear Equation and Quadratic Equations
Visit mometrix.com/academy and enter code: 194870

Monomials and Polynomials

A **monomial** is a single constant, variable, or product of constants and variables, such as 7, x, $2x$, or x^3y. There will never be addition or subtraction symbols in a monomial. Like monomials have like variables, but they may have different coefficients. **Polynomials** are algebraic expressions that use addition and subtraction to combine two or more monomials. Two terms make a **binomial**, three terms make a **trinomial**, etc. The **degree of a monomial** is the sum of the exponents of the variables. The **degree of a polynomial** is the highest degree of any individual term.

Review Video: Polynomials
Visit mometrix.com/academy and enter code: 305005

Simplifying Polynomials

Simplifying polynomials requires combining like terms. The like terms in a polynomial expression are those that have the same variable raised to the same power. It is often helpful to connect the like terms with arrows or lines in order to separate them from the other monomials. Once you have determined the like terms, you can rearrange the polynomial by placing them together. Remember to include the sign that is in front of each term. Once the like terms are placed together, you can apply each operation and simplify. When adding and subtracting polynomials, only add and subtract the **coefficient**, or the number part; the variable and exponent stay the same.

Review Video: Adding and Subtracting Polynomials
Visit mometrix.com/academy and enter code: 124088

THE FOIL METHOD

In general, multiplying polynomials is done by multiplying each term in one polynomial by each term in the other and adding the results. In the specific case for multiplying binomials, there is a useful acronym, FOIL, that can help you make sure to cover each combination of terms. The **FOIL method** for $(Ax + By)(Cx + Dy)$ would be:

F	Multiply the *first* terms of each binomial	$(\overbrace{Ax}^{first} + By)(\overbrace{Cx}^{first} + Dy)$	ACx^2
O	Multiply the *outer* terms	$(\overbrace{Ax}^{outer} + By)(Cx + \overbrace{Dy}^{outer})$	$ADxy$
I	Multiply the *inner* terms	$(Ax + \overbrace{By}^{inner})(\overbrace{Cx}^{inner} + Dy)$	$BCxy$
L	Multiply the *last* terms of each binomial	$(Ax + \overbrace{By}^{last})(Cx + \overbrace{Dy}^{last})$	BDy^2

Then, add up the result of each and combine like terms: $ACx^2 + (AD + BC)xy + BDy^2$.

For example, using the FOIL method on binomials $(x + 2)$ and $(x - 3)$:

$$\begin{aligned}
&\text{First:} && (\boxed{x} + 2)(\boxed{x} + (-3)) && \rightarrow && (x)(x) && = x^2 \\
&\text{Outer:} && (\boxed{x} + 2)(x + \boxed{(-3)}) && \rightarrow && (x)(-3) && = -3x \\
&\text{Inner:} && (x + \boxed{2})(\boxed{x} + (-3)) && \rightarrow && (2)(x) && = 2x \\
&\text{Last:} && (x + \boxed{2})(x + \boxed{(-3)}) && \rightarrow && (2)(-3) && = -6
\end{aligned}$$

This results in: $(x^2) + (-3x) + (2x) + (-6)$

Combine like terms: $x^2 + (-3 + 2)x + (-6) = x^2 - x - 6$

Review Video: Multiplying Terms Using the FOIL Method
Visit mometrix.com/academy and enter code: 854792

DIVIDING POLYNOMIALS

Use long division to divide a polynomial by either a monomial or another polynomial of equal or lesser degree.

When **dividing by a monomial**, divide each term of the polynomial by the monomial.

When **dividing by a polynomial**, begin by arranging the terms of each polynomial in order of one variable. You may arrange in ascending or descending order, but be consistent with both polynomials. To get the first term of the quotient, divide the first term of the dividend by the first term of the divisor. Multiply the first term of the quotient by the entire divisor and subtract that product from the dividend. Repeat for the second and successive terms until you either get a remainder of zero or a remainder whose degree is less than the degree of the divisor. If the quotient has a remainder, write the answer as a mixed expression in the form:

$$\text{quotient} + \frac{\text{remainder}}{\text{divisor}}$$

For example, we can evaluate the following expression in the same way as long division:

$$\frac{x^3 - 3x^2 - 2x + 5}{x - 5}$$

$$\begin{array}{r l}
 & \quad x^2 \;\; + 2x \;\; + 8 \\
x - 5 \,\big) & x^3 \;\; - 3x^2 - 2x \;\; + 5 \\
 & -(x^3 - 5x^2) \\
 & \qquad 2x^2 \;\; - 2x \\
 & \qquad -(2x^2 - 10x) \\
 & \qquad\qquad 8x \;\; + 5 \\
 & \qquad\qquad -(8x - 40) \\
 & \qquad\qquad\qquad 45
\end{array}$$

$$\frac{x^3 - 3x^2 - 2x + 5}{x - 5} = x^2 + 2x + 8 + \frac{45}{x - 5}$$

When **factoring** a polynomial, first check for a common monomial factor, that is, look to see if each coefficient has a common factor or if each term has an x in it. If the factor is a trinomial but not a perfect trinomial square, look for a factorable form, such as one of these:

$$x^2 + (a + b)x + ab = (x + a)(x + b)$$
$$(ac)x^2 + (ad + bc)x + bd = (ax + b)(cx + d)$$

For factors with four terms, look for groups to factor. Once you have found the factors, write the original polynomial as the product of all the factors. Make sure all of the polynomial factors are prime. Monomial factors may be *prime* or *composite*. Check your work by multiplying the factors to make sure you get the original polynomial.

Below are patterns of some special products to remember to help make factoring easier:

- Perfect trinomial squares: $x^2 + 2xy + y^2 = (x + y)^2$ or $x^2 - 2xy + y^2 = (x - y)^2$
- Difference between two squares: $x^2 - y^2 = (x + y)(x - y)$
- Sum of two cubes: $x^3 + y^3 = (x + y)(x^2 - xy + y^2)$
    - Note: the second factor is *not* the same as a perfect trinomial square, so do not try to factor it further.
- Difference between two cubes: $x^3 - y^3 = (x - y)(x^2 + xy + y^2)$
    - Again, the second factor is *not* the same as a perfect trinomial square.
- Perfect cubes: $x^3 + 3x^2y + 3xy^2 + y^3 = (x + y)^3$ and $x^3 - 3x^2y + 3xy^2 - y^3 = (x - y)^3$

RATIONAL EXPRESSIONS

Rational expressions are fractions with polynomials in both the numerator and the denominator; the value of the polynomial in the denominator cannot be equal to zero. Be sure to keep track of values that make the denominator of the original expression zero as the final result inherits the same restrictions. For example, a denominator of $x - 3$ indicates that the expression is not defined when $x = 3$ and, as such, regardless of any operations done to the expression, it remains undefined there.

To **add or subtract** rational expressions, first find the common denominator, then rewrite each fraction as an equivalent fraction with the common denominator. Finally, add or subtract the numerators to get the numerator of the answer, and keep the common denominator as the denominator of the answer.

When **multiplying** rational expressions, factor each polynomial and cancel like factors (a factor which appears in both the numerator and the denominator). Then, multiply all remaining factors in the numerator to get the numerator of the product, and multiply the remaining factors in the denominator to get the denominator of the product. Remember: cancel entire factors, not individual terms.

To **divide** rational expressions, take the reciprocal of the divisor (the rational expression you are dividing by) and multiply by the dividend.

Review Video: Rational Expressions
Visit mometrix.com/academy and enter code: 415183

Simplifying Rational Expressions

To simplify a rational expression, factor the numerator and denominator completely. Factors that are the same and appear in the numerator and denominator have a ratio of 1. For example, look at the following expression:

$$\frac{x-1}{1-x^2}$$

The denominator, $(1 - x^2)$, is a difference of squares. It can be factored as $(1 - x)(1 + x)$. The factor $1 - x$ and the numerator $x - 1$ are opposites and have a ratio of –1. Rewrite the numerator as $-1(1 - x)$. So, the rational expression can be simplified as follows:

$$\frac{x-1}{1-x^2} = \frac{-1(1-x)}{(1-x)(1+x)} = \frac{-1}{1+x}$$

Note that since the original expression is only defined for $x \neq \{-1, 1\}$, the simplified expression has the same restrictions.

Review Video: Reducing Rational Expressions
Visit mometrix.com/academy and enter code: 788868

Algebraic Theorems

According to the **fundamental theorem of algebra**, every non-constant, single-variable polynomial has exactly as many roots as the polynomial's highest exponent. For example, if x^4 is the largest exponent of a term, the polynomial will have exactly 4 roots. However, some of these roots may have multiplicity or be complex numbers. For instance, in the polynomial function $f(x) = x^4 - 4x + 3$, the only real root is 1, though it has multiplicity of 2 – that is, it occurs twice. The other two roots, $(-1 - i\sqrt{2})$ and $(-1 + i\sqrt{2})$, are complex, consisting of both real and non-real components.

The **remainder theorem** is useful for determining the remainder when a polynomial is divided by a binomial. The remainder theorem states that if a polynomial function $f(x)$ is divided by a binomial $x - a$, where a is a real number, the remainder of the division will be the value of $f(a)$. If $f(a) = 0$, then a is a root of the polynomial.

The **factor theorem** is related to the remainder theorem and states that if $f(a) = 0$ then $(x - a)$ is a factor of the function.

According to the **rational root theorem,** any rational root of a polynomial function $f(x) = a_n x^n + a_{n-1}x^{n-1} + \cdots + a_1 x + a_0$ with integer coefficients will, when reduced to its lowest terms, be a positive or negative fraction such that the numerator is a factor of a_0 and the denominator is a factor of a_n. For instance, if the polynomial function $f(x) = x^3 + 3x^2 - 4$ has any rational roots, the numerators of those roots can only be factors of 4 (1, 2, 4), and the denominators can only be factors of 1 (1). The function in this example has roots of 1 (or $\frac{1}{1}$) and –2 (or $\frac{-2}{1}$).

Solving Quadratic Equations

Quadratic equations are a special set of trinomials of the form $y = ax^2 + bx + c$ that occur commonly in math and real-world applications. The **roots** of a quadratic equation are the solutions that satisfy the equation when $y = 0$; in other words, where the graph touches the x-axis. There are several ways to determine these solutions including using the quadratic formula, factoring, completing the square, and graphing the function.

Review Video: Quadratic Equations Overview
Visit mometrix.com/academy and enter code: 476276

Review Video: Solutions of a Quadratic Equation on a Graph
Visit mometrix.com/academy and enter code: 328231

Quadratic Formula

The **quadratic formula** is used to solve quadratic equations when other methods are more difficult. To use the quadratic formula to solve a quadratic equation, begin by rewriting the equation in standard form $ax^2 + bx + c = 0$, where a, b, and c are coefficients. Once you have identified the values of the coefficients, substitute those values into the quadratic formula

$$x = \frac{-b \pm \sqrt{b^2 - 4ac}}{2a}$$

Evaluate the equation and simplify the expression. Again, check each root by substituting into the original equation. In the quadratic formula, the portion of the formula under the radical $(b^2 - 4ac)$ is called the **discriminant**. If the discriminant is zero, there is only one root: $-\frac{b}{2a}$. If the discriminant is positive, there are two different real roots. If the discriminant is negative, there are no real roots; you will instead find complex roots. Often these solutions don't make sense in context and are ignored.

Review Video: Using the Quadratic Formula
Visit mometrix.com/academy and enter code: 163102

Factoring

To solve a quadratic equation by factoring, begin by rewriting the equation in standard form, $x^2 + bx + c = 0$. Remember that the goal of factoring is to find numbers f and g such that

$(x + f)(x + g) = x^2 + (f + g)x + fg$, in other words $(f + g) = b$ and $fg = c$. This can be a really useful method when b and c are integers. Determine the factors of c and look for pairs that could sum to b.

For example, consider finding the roots of $x^2 + 6x - 16 = 0$. The factors of -16 include, -4 and 4, -8 and 2, -2 and 8, -1 and 16, and 1 and -16. The factors that sum to 6 are -2 and 8. Write these factors as the product of two binomials, $0 = (x - 2)(x + 8)$. Finally, since these binomials multiply together to equal zero, set them each equal to zero and solve each for x. This results in $x - 2 = 0$, which simplifies to $x = 2$ and $x + 8 = 0$, which simplifies to $x = -8$. Therefore, the roots of the equation are 2 and -8.

Review Video: Factoring Quadratic Equations
Visit mometrix.com/academy and enter code: 336566

Completing the Square

One way to find the roots of a quadratic equation is to find a way to manipulate it such that it follows the form of a perfect square $(x^2 + 2px + p^2)$ by adding and subtracting a constant. This process is called **completing the square**. In other words, if you are given a quadratic that is not a perfect square, $x^2 + bx + c = 0$, you can find a constant d that could be added in to make it a perfect square:

$$x^2 + bx + c + (d - d) = 0; \{\text{Let } b = 2p \text{ and } c + d = p^2\}$$

then:

$$x^2 + 2px + p^2 - d = 0 \text{ and } d = \frac{b^2}{4} - c$$

Once you have completed the square you can find the roots of the resulting equation:

$$\begin{aligned} x^2 + 2px + p^2 - d &= 0 \\ (x + p)^2 &= d \\ x + p &= \pm\sqrt{d} \\ x &= -p \pm \sqrt{d} \end{aligned}$$

It is worth noting that substituting the original expressions into this solution gives the same result as the quadratic formula where $a = 1$:

$$x = -p \pm \sqrt{d} = -\frac{b}{2} \pm \sqrt{\frac{b^2}{4} - c} = -\frac{b}{2} \pm \frac{\sqrt{b^2 - 4c}}{2} = \frac{-b \pm \sqrt{b^2 - 4c}}{2}$$

Completing the square can be seen as arranging block representations of each of the terms to be as close to a square as possible and then filling in the gaps. For example, consider the quadratic expression $x^2 + 6x + 2$:

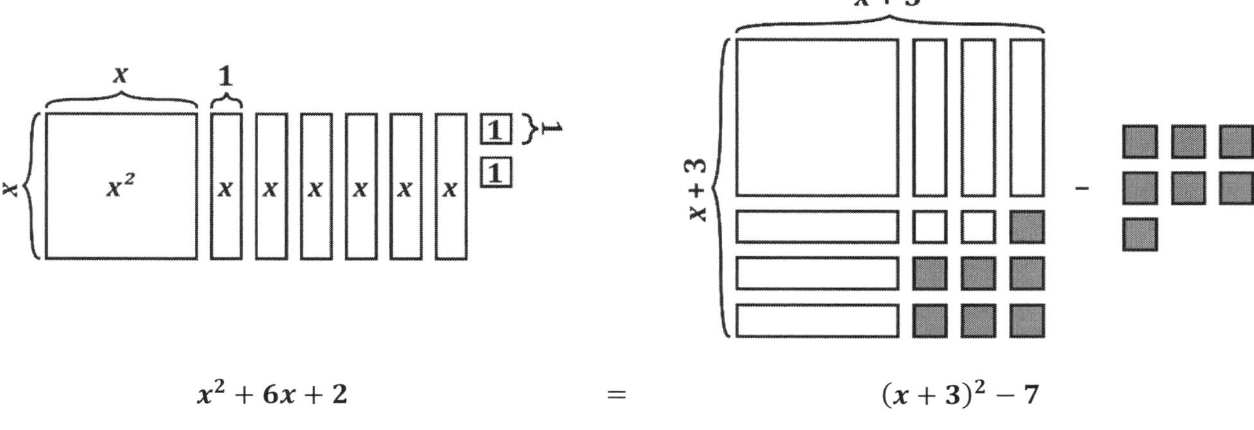

$$x^2 + 6x + 2 = (x + 3)^2 - 7$$

Review Video: Completing the Square
Visit mometrix.com/academy and enter code: 982479

Using Given Roots to Find Quadratic Equation

One way to find the roots of a quadratic equation is to factor the equation and use the **zero product property**, setting each factor of the equation equal to zero to find the corresponding root. We can use this technique in reverse to find an equation given its roots. Each root corresponds to a linear equation which in turn corresponds to a factor of the quadratic equation.

For example, we can find a quadratic equation whose roots are $x = 2$ and $x = -1$. The root $x = 2$ corresponds to the equation $x - 2 = 0$, and the root $x = -1$ corresponds to the equation $x + 1 = 0$.

These two equations correspond to the factors $(x - 2)$ and $(x + 1)$, from which we can derive the equation $(x - 2)(x + 1) = 0$, or $x^2 - x - 2 = 0$.

Any integer multiple of this entire equation will also yield the same roots, as the integer will simply cancel out when the equation is factored. For example, $2x^2 - 2x - 4 = 0$ factors as $2(x - 2)(x + 1) = 0$.

Function and Relation

When expressing functional relationships, the **variables** x and y are typically used. These values are often written as the **coordinates** (x, y). The x-value is the independent variable and the y-value is the dependent variable. A **relation** is a set of data in which there is not a unique y-value for each x-value in the dataset. This means that there can be two of the same x-values assigned to different y-values. A relation is simply a relationship between the x- and y-values in each coordinate but does not apply to the relationship between the values of x and y in the data set. A **function** is a relation where one quantity depends on the other. For example, the amount of money that you make depends on the number of hours that you work. In a function, each x-value in the data set has one unique y-value because the y-value depends on the x-value.

FUNCTIONS

A function has exactly one value of **output variable** (dependent variable) for each value of the **input variable** (independent variable). The set of all values for the input variable (here assumed to be x) is the domain of the function, and the set of all corresponding values of the output variable (here assumed to be y) is the range of the function. When looking at a graph of an equation, the easiest way to determine if the equation is a function or not is to conduct the vertical line test. If a vertical line drawn through any value of x crosses the graph in more than one place, the equation is not a function.

DETERMINING A FUNCTION

You can determine whether an equation is a **function** by substituting different values into the equation for x. You can display and organize these numbers in a data table. A **data table** contains the values for x and y, which you can also list as coordinates. In order for a function to exist, the table cannot contain any repeating x-values that correspond with different y-values. If each x-coordinate has a unique y-coordinate, the table contains a function. However, there can be repeating y-values that correspond with different x-values. An example of this is when the function contains an exponent. Example: if $x^2 = y$, $2^2 = 4$, and $(-2)^2 = 4$.

Review Video: Definition of a Function
Visit mometrix.com/academy and enter code: 784611

FINDING THE DOMAIN AND RANGE OF A FUNCTION

The **domain** of a function $f(x)$ is the set of all input values for which the function is defined. The **range** of a function $f(x)$ is the set of all possible output values of the function—that is, of every possible value of $f(x)$, for any value of x in the function's domain. For a function expressed in a table, every input-output pair is given explicitly. To find the domain, we just list all the x-values and to find the range, we just list all the values of $f(x)$. Consider the following example:

x	–1	4	2	1	0	3	8	6
$f(x)$	3	0	3	–1	–1	2	4	6

In this case, the domain would be $\{-1, 4, 2, 1, 0, 3, 8, 6\}$ or, putting them in ascending order, $\{-1, 0, 1, 2, 3, 4, 6, 8\}$. (Putting the values in ascending order isn't strictly necessary, but generally makes the set easier to read.) The range would be $\{3, 0, 3, -1, -1, 2, 4, 6\}$. Note that some of these values appear more than once. This is entirely permissible for a function; while each value of x must be matched to a unique value of $f(x)$, the converse is not true. We don't need to list each value more than once, so eliminating duplicates, the range is $\{3, 0, -1, 2, 4, 6\}$, or, putting them in ascending order, $\{-1, 0, 2, 3, 4, 6\}$.

Note that by definition of a function, no input value can be matched to more than one output value. It is good to double-check to make sure that the data given follows this and is therefore actually a function.

Review Video: Domain and Range
Visit mometrix.com/academy and enter code: 778133

Review Video: Domain and Range of Quadratic Functions
Visit mometrix.com/academy and enter code: 331768

Writing a Function Rule Using a Table

If given a set of data, place the corresponding x- and y-values into a table and analyze the relationship between them. Consider what you can do to each x-value to obtain the corresponding y-value. Try adding or subtracting different numbers to and from x and then try multiplying or dividing different numbers to and from x. If none of these **operations** give you the y-value, try combining the operations. Once you find a rule that works for one pair, make sure to try it with each additional set of ordered pairs in the table. If the same operation or combination of operations satisfies each set of coordinates, then the table contains a function. The rule is then used to write the equation of the function in "$y = f(x)$" form.

Direct and Inverse Variations of Variables

Variables that vary directly are those that either both increase at the same rate or both decrease at the same rate. For example, in the functions $y = kx$ or $y = kx^n$, where k and n are positive, the value of y increases as the value of x increases and decreases as the value of x decreases.

Variables that vary inversely are those where one increases while the other decreases. For example, in the functions $y = \frac{k}{x}$ or $y = \frac{k}{x^n}$ where k and n are positive, the value of y increases as the value of x decreases and decreases as the value of x increases.

In both cases, k is the constant of variation.

Properties of Functions

There are many different ways to classify functions based on their structure or behavior. Important features of functions include:

- **End behavior**: the behavior of the function at extreme values ($f(x)$ as $x \to \pm\infty$)
- **y-intercept**: the value of the function at $f(0)$
- **Roots**: the values of x where the function equals zero ($f(x) = 0$)
- **Extrema**: minimum or maximum values of the function or where the function changes direction ($f(x) \geq k$ or $f(x) \leq k$)

Classification of Functions

An **invertible function** is defined as a function, $f(x)$, for which there is another function, $f^{-1}(x)$, such that $f^{-1}\big(f(x)\big) = x$. For example, if $f(x) = 3x - 2$ the inverse function, $f^{-1}(x)$, can be found:

$$x = 3\big(f^{-1}(x)\big) - 2$$
$$\frac{x+2}{3} = f^{-1}(x)$$

$$f^{-1}\big(f(x)\big) = \frac{3x - 2 + 2}{3} = \frac{3x}{3} = x$$

Note that $f^{-1}(x)$ is a valid function over all values of x.

In a **one-to-one function**, each value of x has exactly one value for y on the coordinate plane (this is the definition of a function) and each value of y has exactly one value for x. While the vertical line test will determine if a graph is that of a function, the horizontal line test will determine if a function is a one-to-one function. If a horizontal line drawn at any value of y intersects the graph in more than one place, the graph is not that of a one-to-one function. Do not make the mistake of using the horizontal line test exclusively in determining if a graph is that of a one-to-one function. A one-to-one function must pass both the vertical line test and the horizontal line test. As such, one-to-one functions are invertible functions.

A **many-to-one function** is a function whereby the relation is a function, but the inverse of the function is not a function. In other words, each element in the domain is mapped to one and only one element in the range. However, one or more elements in the range may be mapped to the same element in the domain. A graph of a many-to-one function would pass the vertical line test, but not the horizontal line test. This is why many-to-one functions are not invertible.

A **monotone function** is a function whose graph either constantly increases or constantly decreases. Examples include the functions $f(x) = x$, $f(x) = -x$, or $f(x) = x^3$.

An **even function** has a graph that is symmetric with respect to the y-axis and satisfies the equation $f(x) = f(-x)$. Examples include the functions $f(x) = x^2$ and $f(x) = ax^n$, where a is any real number and n is a positive even integer.

An **odd function** has a graph that is symmetric with respect to the origin and satisfies the equation $f(x) = -f(-x)$. Examples include the functions $f(x) = x^3$ and $f(x) = ax^n$, where a is any real number and n is a positive odd integer.

Review Video: Even and Odd Functions
Visit mometrix.com/academy and enter code: 278985

Constant functions are given by the equation $f(x) = b$, where b is a real number. There is no independent variable present in the equation, so the function has a constant value for all x. The graph of a constant function is a horizontal line of slope 0 that is positioned b units from the x-axis. If b is positive, the line is above the x-axis; if b is negative, the line is below the x-axis.

Identity functions are identified by the equation $f(x) = x$, where every value of the function is equal to its corresponding value of x. The only zero is the point (0,0). The graph is a line with a slope of 1.

In **linear functions**, the value of the function changes in direct proportion to x. The rate of change, represented by the slope on its graph, is constant throughout. The standard form of a linear equation is $ax + cy = d$, where a, c, and d are real numbers. As a function, this equation is commonly in the form $y = mx + b$ or $f(x) = mx + b$ where $m = -\frac{a}{c}$ and $b = \frac{d}{c}$. This is known as the slope-intercept form, because the coefficients give the slope of the graphed function (m) and its y-intercept (b). Solve the equation $mx + b = 0$ for x to get $x = -\frac{b}{m}$, which is the only zero of the function. The domain and range are both the set of all real numbers.

Review Video: Linear Functions
Visit mometrix.com/academy and enter code: 699478

Algebraic functions are those that exclusively use polynomials and roots. These would include polynomial functions, rational functions, square root functions, and all combinations of these functions, such as polynomials as the radicand. These combinations may be joined by addition, subtraction, multiplication, or division, but may not include variables as exponents.

Review Video: Common Functions
Visit mometrix.com/academy and enter code: 629798

ABSOLUTE VALUE FUNCTIONS

An **absolute value function** is in the format $f(x) = |ax + b|$. Like other functions, the domain is the set of all real numbers. However, because absolute value indicates positive numbers, the range is limited to positive real numbers. To find the zero of an absolute value function, set the portion inside the absolute value sign equal to zero and solve for x. An absolute value function is also known as a piecewise function because it must be solved in pieces—one for if the value inside the absolute value sign is positive, and one for if the value is negative. The function can be expressed as:

$$f(x) = \begin{cases} ax + b \text{ if } ax + b \geq 0 \\ -(ax + b) \text{ if } ax + b < 0 \end{cases}$$

This will allow for an accurate statement of the range. The graph of an example absolute value function, $f(x) = |2x - 1|$, is below:

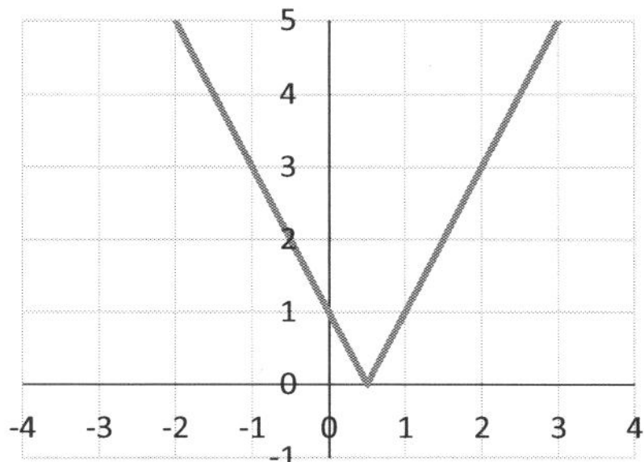

PIECEWISE FUNCTIONS

A **piecewise function** is a function that has different definitions on two or more different intervals. The following, for instance, is one example of a piecewise-defined function:

$$f(x) = \begin{cases} x^2, & x < 0 \\ x, & 0 \leq x \leq 2 \\ (x-2)^2, & x > 2 \end{cases}$$

To graph this function, you would simply graph each part separately in the appropriate domain. The final graph would look like this:

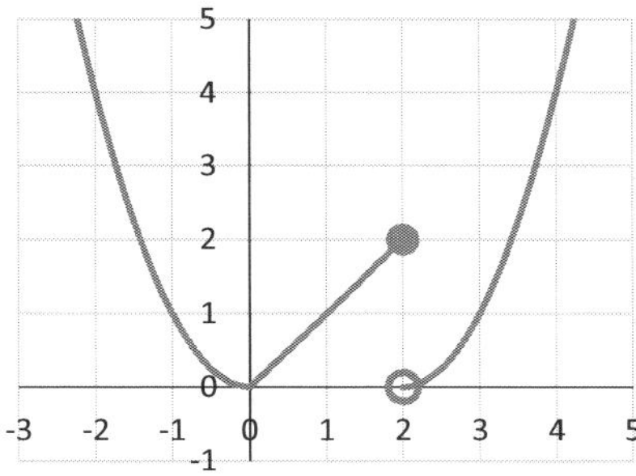

Note the filled and hollow dots at the discontinuity at $x = 2$. This is important to show which side of the graph that point corresponds to. Because $f(x) = x$ on the closed interval $0 \leq x \leq 2$, $f(2) = 2$. The point $(2, 2)$ is therefore marked with a filled circle, and the point (2,0), which is the endpoint of the rightmost $(x - 2)^2$ part of the graph but *not actually part of the function*, is marked with a hollow dot to indicate this.

Review Video: Piecewise Functions
Visit mometrix.com/academy and enter code: 707921

Quadratic Functions

A **quadratic function** is a function in the form $y = ax^2 + bx + c$, where a does not equal 0. While a linear function forms a line, a quadratic function forms a **parabola**, which is a u-shaped figure that either opens upward or downward. A parabola that opens upward is said to be a **positive quadratic function,** and a parabola that opens downward is said to be a **negative quadratic function**. The shape of a parabola can differ, depending on the values of a, b, and c. All parabolas contain a **vertex**, which is the highest possible point, the **maximum**, or the lowest possible point, the **minimum**. This is the point where the graph begins moving in the opposite direction. A quadratic function can have zero, one, or two solutions, and therefore zero, one, or two x-intercepts. Recall that the x-intercepts are referred to as the zeros, or roots, of a function. A quadratic function will have only one y-intercept. Understanding the basic components of a quadratic function can give you an idea of the shape of its graph.

Example graph of a positive quadratic function, $x^2 + 2x - 3$:

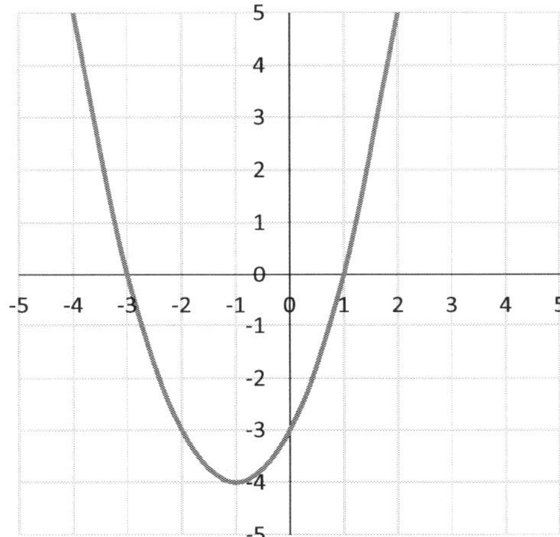

Polynomial Functions

A **polynomial function** is a function with multiple terms and multiple powers of x, such as:

$$f(x) = a_n x^n + a_{n-1} x^{n-1} + a_{n-2} x^{n-2} + \cdots + a_1 x + a_0$$

where n is a non-negative integer that is the highest exponent in the polynomial and $a_n \neq 0$. The domain of a polynomial function is the set of all real numbers. If the greatest exponent in the polynomial is even, the polynomial is said to be of even degree and the range is the set of real numbers that satisfy the function. If the greatest exponent in the polynomial is odd, the polynomial is said to be odd and the range, like the domain, is the set of all real numbers.

Rational Functions

A **rational function** is a function that can be constructed as a ratio of two polynomial expressions: $f(x) = \frac{p(x)}{q(x)}$, where $p(x)$ and $q(x)$ are both polynomial expressions and $q(x) \neq 0$. The domain is the set of all real numbers, except any values for which $q(x) = 0$. The range is the set of real numbers that satisfies the function when the domain is applied. When you graph a rational function, you will have vertical asymptotes wherever $q(x) = 0$. If the polynomial in the numerator is of lesser degree than the polynomial in the denominator, the x-axis will also be a horizontal asymptote. If the numerator and denominator have equal degrees, there will be a horizontal asymptote not on the x-axis. If the degree of the numerator is exactly one greater than the degree of the denominator, the graph will have an oblique, or diagonal, asymptote. The asymptote will be along the line $y = \frac{p_n}{q_{n-1}}x + \frac{p_{n-1}}{q_{n-1}}$, where p_n and q_{n-1} are the coefficients of the highest degree terms in their respective polynomials.

Square Root Functions

A **square root function** is a function that contains a radical and is in the format $f(x) = \sqrt{ax + b}$. The domain is the set of all real numbers that yields a positive radicand or a radicand equal to zero. Because square root values are assumed to be positive unless otherwise identified, the range is all real numbers from zero to infinity. To find the zero of a square root function, set the radicand equal to zero and solve for x. The graph of a square root function is always to the right of the zero and always above the x-axis.

Example graph of a square root function, $f(x) = \sqrt{2x + 1}$:

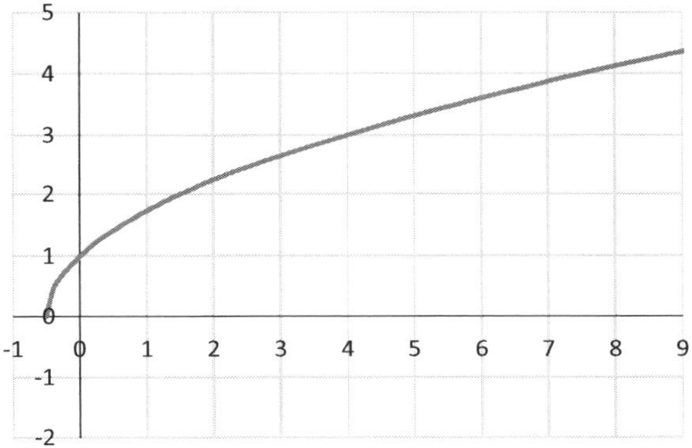

Manipulation of Functions

Translation occurs when values are added to or subtracted from the x- or y-values. If a constant is added to the y-portion of each point, the graph shifts up. If a constant is subtracted from the y-portion of each point, the graph shifts down. This is represented by the expression $f(x) \pm k$, where k is a constant. If a constant is added to the x-portion of each point, the graph shifts left. If a constant is subtracted from the x-portion of each point, the graph shifts right. This is represented by the expression $f(x \pm k)$, where k is a constant.

Stretching, compression, and reflection occur when different parts of a function are multiplied by different groups of constants. If the function as a whole is multiplied by a real number constant greater than 1, $(k \times f(x))$, the graph is stretched vertically. If k in the previous equation is greater than zero but less than 1, the graph is compressed vertically. If k is less than zero, the graph is reflected about the x-axis, in addition to being either stretched or compressed vertically if k is less than or greater than -1, respectively. If instead, just the x-term is multiplied by a constant greater than 1 $(f(k \times x))$, the graph is compressed horizontally. If k in the previous equation is greater than zero but less than 1, the graph is stretched horizontally. If k is less than zero, the graph is reflected about the y-axis, in addition to being either stretched or compressed horizontally if k is greater than or less than –1, respectively.

Review Video: Manipulation of Functions
Visit mometrix.com/academy and enter code: 669117

Applying the Basic Operations to Functions

For each of the basic operations, we will use these functions as examples: $f(x) = x^2$ and $g(x) = x$.

To find the sum of two functions f and g, assuming the domains are compatible, simply add the two functions together: $(f + g)(x) = f(x) + g(x) = x^2 + x$.

To find the difference of two functions f and g, assuming the domains are compatible, simply subtract the second function from the first: $(f - g)(x) = f(x) - g(x) = x^2 - x$.

To find the product of two functions f and g, assuming the domains are compatible, multiply the two functions together: $(f \times g)(x) = f(x) \times g(x) = x^2 \times x = x^3$.

To find the quotient of two functions f and g, assuming the domains are compatible, divide the first function by the second: $\frac{f}{g}(x) = \frac{f(x)}{g(x)} = \frac{x^2}{x} = x\,; x \neq 0$.

The example given in each case is fairly simple, but on a given problem, if you are looking only for the value of the sum, difference, product, or quotient of two functions at a particular x-value, it may be simpler to solve the functions individually and then perform the given operation using those values.

The composite of two functions f and g, written as $(f \circ g)(x)$ simply means that the output of the second function is used as the input of the first. This can also be written as $f\big(g(x)\big)$. In general, this can be solved by substituting $g(x)$ for all instances of x in $f(x)$ and simplifying. Using the example functions $f(x) = x^2 - x + 2$ and $g(x) = x + 1$, we can find that $(f \circ g)(x)$ or $f\big(g(x)\big)$ is equal to $f(x + 1) = (x + 1)^2 - (x + 1) + 2$, which simplifies to $x^2 + x + 2$.

It is important to note that $(f \circ g)(x)$ is not necessarily the same as $(g \circ f)(x)$. The process is not always commutative like addition or multiplication expressions. It *can* be commutative, but most often this is not the case.

Step Functions

The double brackets indicate a step function. For a step function, the value inside the double brackets is rounded down to the nearest integer. The graph of the function $f_0(x) = [\![x]\!]$ appears on the left graph. In comparison $f(x) = 2\left[\!\left[\frac{1}{3}(x - 1)\right]\!\right]$ is on the right graph. The coefficient of 2 shows that it's stretched vertically by a factor of 2 (so there's a vertical distance of 2 units between successive "steps"). The coefficient of $\frac{1}{3}$ in front of the x shows that it's stretched horizontally by a factor of 3 (so each "step" is three units long), and the $x - 1$ shows that it's displaced one unit to the right.

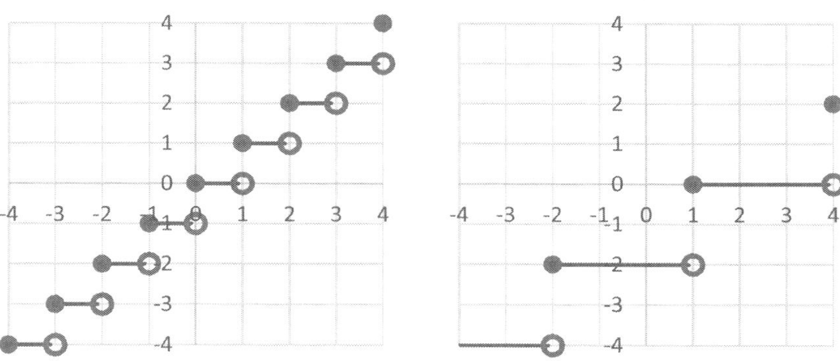

Transcendental Functions

Transcendental functions are all functions that are non-algebraic. Any function that includes logarithms, trigonometric functions, variables as exponents, or any combination that includes any of these is not algebraic in nature, even if the function includes polynomials or roots.

Exponential Functions

Exponential functions are equations that have the format $y = b^x$, where base $b > 0$ and $b \neq 1$. The exponential function can also be written $f(x) = b^x$. Recall the properties of exponents, like the product of terms with the same base is equal to the base raised to the sum of the exponents ($a^x \times a^y = a^{x+y}$) and a term with an exponent that is raised to an exponent is equal to the base of the original term raised to the product of the exponents: ($(a^x)^y = a^{xy}$). The graph of an example exponential function, $f(x) = 2^x$, is below:

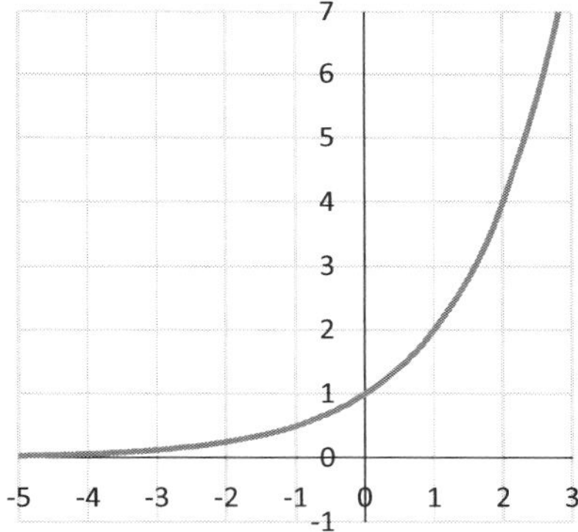

Note in the graph that the y-value approaches zero to the left and infinity to the right. One of the key features of an exponential function is that there will be one end that goes off to infinity and another that asymptotically approaches a lower bound. Common forms of exponential functions include:

Geometric sequences: $a_n = a_1 \times r^{n-1}$, where a_n is the value of the nth term, a_1 is the initial value, r is the common ratio, and n is the number of terms. Note that $a_1 \times r^{1-1} = a_1 \times r^0 = a_1 \times 1 = a_1$.

Population growth: $f(t) = ae^{rt}$, where $f(t)$ is the population at time $t \geq 0$, a is the initial population, e is the mathematical constant known as Euler's number, and r is the growth rate.

Review Video: Population Growth
Visit mometrix.com/academy and enter code: 109278

Compound interest: $f(t) = P\left(1 + \frac{r}{n}\right)^{nt}$, where $f(t)$ is the account value at a certain number of time periods $t \geq 0$, P is the initial principal balance, r is the interest rate, and n is the number of times the interest is applied per time period.

Review Video: Interest Functions
Visit mometrix.com/academy and enter code: 559176

General exponential growth or decay: $f(t) = a(1 + r)^t$, where $f(t)$ is the future count, a is the current or initial count, r is the growth or decay rate, and t is the time.

For example, suppose the initial population of a town was 1,200 people. The annual population growth is 5%. The current population is 2,400. To find out how much time has passed since the town was founded, we can use the following function:

$$2{,}400 = 1{,}200e^{0.05t}.$$

The general form for population growth may be represented as $f(t) = ae^{rt}$, where $f(t)$ represents the current population, a represents the initial population, r represents the growth rate, and t represents the time. Thus, substituting the initial population, current population, and rate into this form gives the equation above.

The number of years that have passed were found by first dividing both sides of the equation by 1,200. Doing so gives $2 = e^{0.05t}$. Taking the natural logarithm of both sides gives $\ln(2) = ln(e^{0.05t})$. Applying the power property of logarithms, the equation may be rewritten as $\ln(2) = 0.05t \times \ln(e)$, which simplifies as $\ln(2) = 0.05t$. Dividing both sides of this equation by 0.05 gives $t \approx 13.86$. Thus, approximately 13.86 years passed.

Logarithmic Functions

Logarithmic functions are equations that have the format $y = \log_b x$ or $f(x) = \log_b x$. The base b may be any number except one; however, the most common bases for logarithms are base 10 and base e. The log base e is the natural logarithm, or ln, expressed by the function $f(x) = \ln x$.

Any logarithm that does not have an assigned value of b is assumed to be base 10: $\log x = \log_{10} x$. Exponential functions and logarithmic functions are related in that one is the inverse of the other. If $f(x) = b^x$, then $f^{-1}(x) = \log_b x$. This can perhaps be expressed more clearly by the two equations: $y = b^x$ and $x = \log_b y$.

The following properties apply to logarithmic expressions:

Property	Description
$\log_b 1 = 0$	The log of 1 is equal to 0 for any base
$\log_b b = 1$	The log of the base is equal to 1
$\log_b b^p = p$	The log of the base raised to a power is equal to that power
$\log_b MN = \log_b M + \log_b N$	The log of a product is the sum of the log of each factor
$\log_b \frac{M}{N} = \log_b M - \log_b N$	The log of a quotient is equal to the log of the dividend minus the log of the divisor
$\log_b M^p = p \log_b M$	The log of a value raised to a power is equal to the power times the log of the value

The graph of an example logarithmic function, $f(x) = \log_2(x + 2)$, is below:

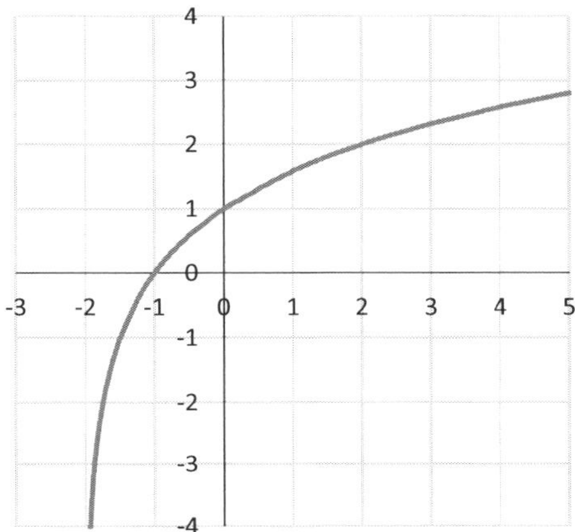

Review Video: Logarithmic Function
Visit mometrix.com/academy and enter code: 658985

Trigonometric Functions

Trigonometric functions are periodic, meaning that they repeat the same form over and over. The basic trigonometric functions are sine (abbreviated 'sin'), cosine (abbreviated 'cos'), and tangent (abbreviated 'tan'). The simplest way to think of them is as describing the ratio of the side lengths of a right triangle in relation to the angles of the triangle.

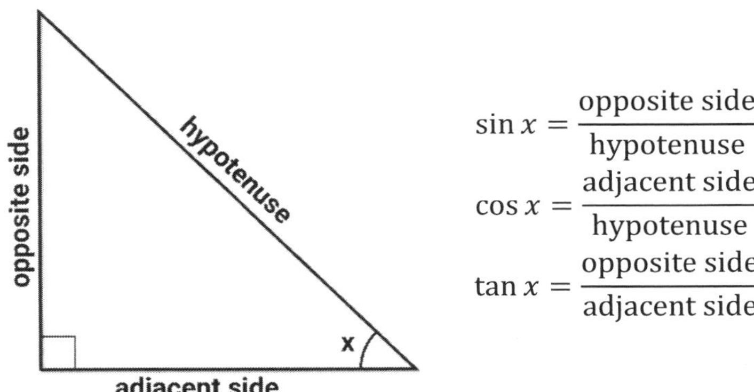

$$\sin x = \frac{\text{opposite side}}{\text{hypotenuse}}$$
$$\cos x = \frac{\text{adjacent side}}{\text{hypotenuse}}$$
$$\tan x = \frac{\text{opposite side}}{\text{adjacent side}}$$

Using sine as an example, trigonometric functions take the form $f(x) = A\sin(Bx + C) + D$, where the **amplitude** is simply equal to A. The **period** is the distance between successive peaks or troughs, essentially the length of the repeated pattern. In this form, the period is equal to $\frac{2\pi}{B}$. As for C, this is the **phase shift** or the horizontal shift of the function. The last term, D, is the vertical shift and determines the **midline** as $y = D$.

For instance, consider the function $f(x) = 2 + \frac{3}{2}\sin\left(\pi x + \frac{\pi}{2}\right)$. Here, $A = \frac{3}{2}$, $B = \pi$, $C = \frac{\pi}{2}$, and $D = 2$, so the midline is at $y = 2$, the amplitude is $\frac{3}{2}$, and the period is $\frac{2\pi}{\pi} = 2$. To graph this function, we center the sine wave on the midline and extend it to a height above and below the midline equal to the amplitude—so this graph would have a minimum value of $2 - \frac{3}{2} = \frac{1}{2}$ and a maximum of $2 + \frac{3}{2} = \frac{7}{2}$. So, the function would be graphed as follows:

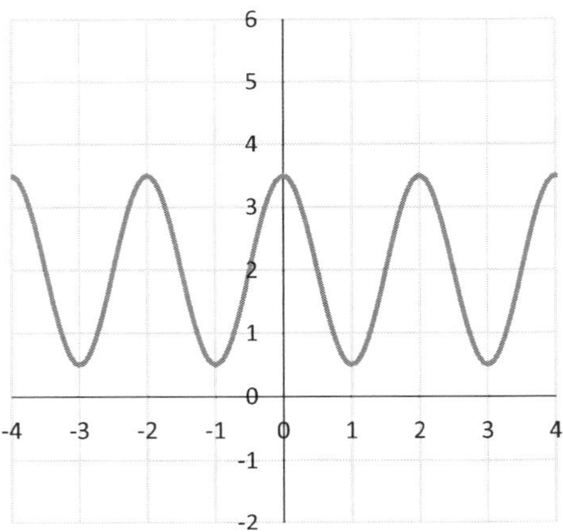

Additional Topics in Math

Additional Topics in Math Overview

Questions in this section will test geometric and trigonometric concepts and the Pythagorean theorem. The student should be familiar with geometric concepts such as volume, radius, diameter, chord length, angle, arc, and sector area. The questions will give certain information about a figure and require the student to solve for some missing information. Any required volume formulas will be provided on the test. The trigonometry questions will require students to use trigonometric ratios and the Pythagorean theorem to solve problems dealing with right triangles. The student should be able to use these ratios and the Pythagorean theorem to solve for missing lengths and angle measures in right triangles.

Question Types in Additional Topics in Math

The additional topics in math section will test your knowledge of the following:

- Solve problems using **volume formulas**.
    - The student will use given information about figures, such as length of a side, area of a face, or volume of a solid, to calculate missing information.

  - Any required volume formulas will be provided to students either on the formula sheet or within the question.
- Use **trigonometric ratios** and the **Pythagorean theorem** to solve applied problems involving right triangles.
  - The student will use information about triangle side lengths or angles presented in a context to calculate missing information using the Pythagorean theorem and/or trigonometric ratios.
- Add, subtract, multiply, divide, and simplify **complex numbers**.
- Convert between **degrees** and **radians** and use radians to determine **arc lengths**; use trigonometric functions of radian measure.
  - The student will convert between angle measures in degrees and radians in order to calculate arc lengths by recognizing the relationship between an angle measured in radians and an arc length, evaluating trigonometric functions of angles in radians.
- Apply **theorems about circles** to find arc lengths, angle measures, chord lengths, and areas of sectors.
  - The student will use given information about circles and lines to calculate missing values for radius, diameter, chord length, angle, arc, and sector area.
- Use concepts and theorems about **congruence and similarity** to solve problems about lines, angles, and triangles.
  - The student will use theorems about triangles and intersecting lines to determine missing lengths and angle measures of triangles.
  - The student may also be asked to provide a missing length or angle to satisfy a given theorem.
- Use the relationship between **similarity**, **right triangles**, and **trigonometric ratios**; use the relationship between sine and cosine of **complementary angles**.
  - The student will use trigonometry and theorems about triangles and intersecting lines to determine missing lengths and angle measures of right triangles.
  - The student may also be asked to provide a missing length or angle that would satisfy a given theorem.
- Create or use an equation in two variables to solve a problem about a **circle in the coordinate plane**.
  - The student will create an equation or use properties of an equation of a circle to demonstrate or determine a property of the circle's graph.

Basic Trigonometric Functions

Sine

The **sine** (sin) function has a period of 360° or 2π radians. This means that its graph makes one complete cycle every 360° or 2π. Because $\sin 0 = 0$, the graph of $y = \sin x$ begins at the origin, with the x-axis representing the angle measure, and the y-axis representing the sine of the angle. The graph of the sine function is a smooth curve that begins at the origin, peaks at the point $\left(\frac{\pi}{2}, 1\right)$, crosses the x-axis at $(\pi, 0)$, has its lowest point at $\left(\frac{3\pi}{2}, -1\right)$, and returns to the x-axis to complete one cycle at $(2\pi, 0)$.

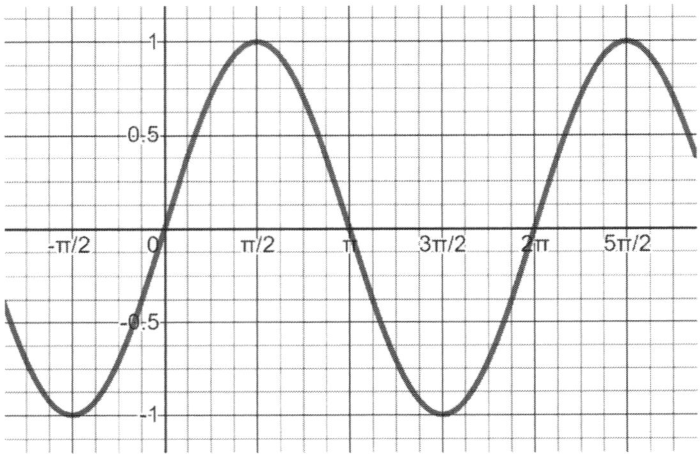

Review Video: Sine
Visit mometrix.com/academy and enter code: 193339

Cosine

The **cosine** (cos) function also has a period of 360° or 2π radians, which means that its graph also makes one complete cycle every 360° or 2π. Because $\cos 0° = 1$, the graph of $y = \cos x$ begins at the point $(0, 1)$, with the x-axis representing the angle measure, and the y-axis representing the cosine of the angle. The graph of the cosine function is a smooth curve that begins at the point $(0,1)$, crosses the x-axis at the point $\left(\frac{\pi}{2}, 0\right)$, has its lowest point at $(\pi, -1)$, crosses the x-axis again at the point $\left(\frac{3\pi}{2}, 0\right)$, and returns to a peak at the point $(2\pi, 1)$ to complete one cycle.

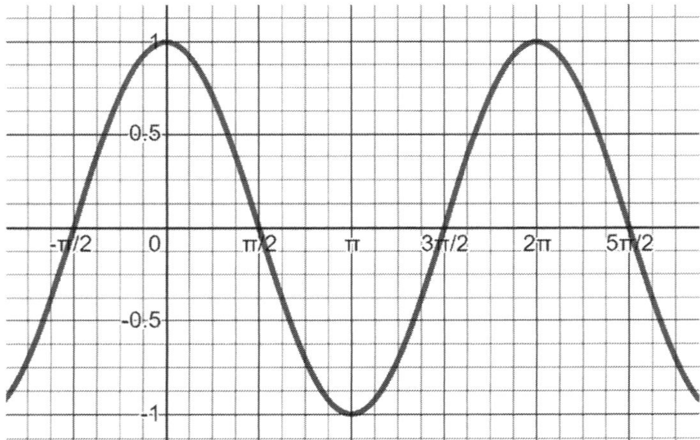

Review Video: Cosine
Visit mometrix.com/academy and enter code: 361120

Tangent

The **tangent** (tan) function has a period of 180° or π radians, which means that its graph makes one complete cycle every 180° or π radians. The x-axis represents the angle measure, and the y-axis represents the tangent of the angle. The graph of the tangent function is a series of smooth curves that cross the x-axis at every 180° or π radians and have an asymptote every $k \times 90°$ or $\frac{k\pi}{2}$ radians, where k is an odd integer. This can be explained by the fact that the tangent is calculated by dividing the sine by the cosine, since the cosine equals zero at those asymptote points.

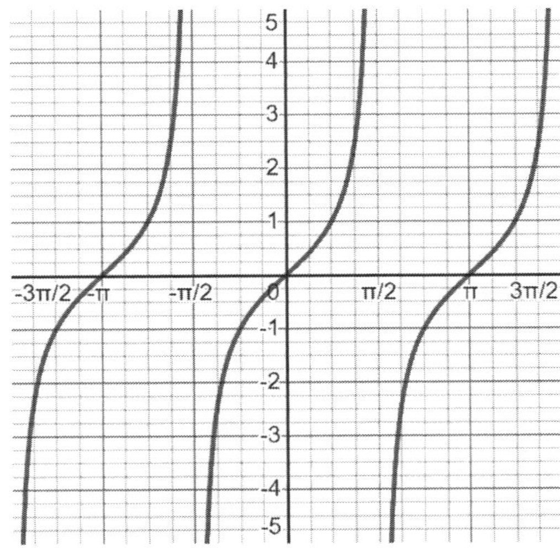

Review Video: Tangent
Visit mometrix.com/academy and enter code: 947639

Complex Numbers

Complex numbers consist of a real component and an imaginary component. Complex numbers are expressed in the form $a + bi$ with real component a and imaginary component bi. The imaginary unit i is equal to $\sqrt{-1}$. That means $i^2 = -1$. The imaginary unit provides a way to find the square root of a negative number. For example, $\sqrt{-25}$ is $5i$. You should expect questions asking you to add, subtract, multiply, divide, and simplify complex numbers. You may see a question that says, "Add $3 + 2i$ and $5 - 7i$" or "Subtract $4 + i\sqrt{5}$ from $2 + i\sqrt{5}$." Or you may see a question that says, "Multiply $6 + 2i$ by $8 - 4i$" or "Divide $1 - 3i$ by $9 - 7i$."

Operations on Complex Numbers

Operations with complex numbers resemble operations with variables in algebra. When adding or subtracting complex numbers, you can only combine like terms—real terms with real terms and imaginary terms with imaginary terms. For example, if you are asked to simplify the expression $-2 + 4i - (-3 + 7i) - 5i$, you should first remove the parentheses to yield $-2 + 4i + 3 - 7i - 5i$. Combining like terms yields $1 - 8i$. One interesting aspect of imaginary numbers is that if i has an exponent greater than 1, it can be simplified. Example: $i^2 = -1$, $i^3 = -i$, and $i^4 = 1$. When multiplying complex numbers, remember to simplify each i with an exponent greater than 1. For example, you might see a question that says, "Simplify $(2 - i)(3 + 2i)$." You need to distribute and multiply to get $6 + 4i - 3i - 2i^2$. This is further simplified to $6 + i - 2(-1)$, or $8 + i$.

Simplifying Expressions with Complex Denominators

If an expression contains an i in the denominator, it must be simplified. Remember, roots cannot be left in the denominator of a fraction. Since i is equivalent to $\sqrt{-1}$, i cannot be left in the denominator of a fraction. You must rationalize the denominator of a fraction that contains a complex denominator by multiplying the numerator and denominator by the conjugate of the denominator. The conjugate of the complex number $a + bi$ is $a - bi$. You can simplify $\frac{2}{5i}$ by simply multiplying $\frac{2}{5i} \times \frac{i}{i}$, which yields $-\frac{2}{5}i$. And you can simplify $\frac{5+3i}{2-4i}$ by multiplying $\frac{5+3i}{2-4i} \times \frac{2+4i}{2+4i}$. This yields $\frac{10+20i+6i-12}{4-8i+8i+16}$ which simplifies to $\frac{-2+26i}{20}$ or $\frac{-1+13i}{10}$, which can also be written as $-\frac{1}{10} + \frac{13}{10}i$.

Points and Lines

A **point** is a fixed location in space, has no size or dimensions, and is commonly represented by a dot. A **line** is a set of points that extends infinitely in two opposite directions. It has length, but no width or depth. A line can be defined by any two distinct points that it contains. A **line segment** is a portion of a line that has definite endpoints. A **ray** is a portion of a line that extends from a single point on that line in one direction along the line. It has a definite beginning, but no ending.

Interactions between Lines

Intersecting lines are lines that have exactly one point in common. **Concurrent lines** are multiple lines that intersect at a single point. **Perpendicular lines** are lines that intersect at right angles. They are represented by the symbol $\perp$. The shortest distance from a line to a point not on the line is a perpendicular segment from the point to the line. **Parallel lines** are lines in the same plane that have no points in common and never meet. It is possible for lines to be in different planes, have no points in common, and never meet, but they are not parallel because they are in different planes.

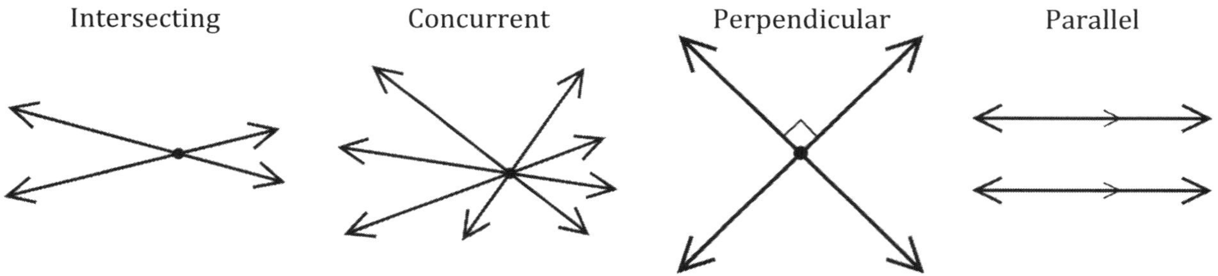

Review Video: Parallel and Perpendicular Lines
Visit mometrix.com/academy and enter code: 815923

A **transversal** is a line that intersects at least two other lines, which may or may not be parallel to one another. A transversal that intersects parallel lines is a common occurrence in geometry. A **bisector** is a line or line segment that divides another line segment into two equal lengths. A

perpendicular bisector of a line segment is composed of points that are equidistant from the endpoints of the segment it is dividing.

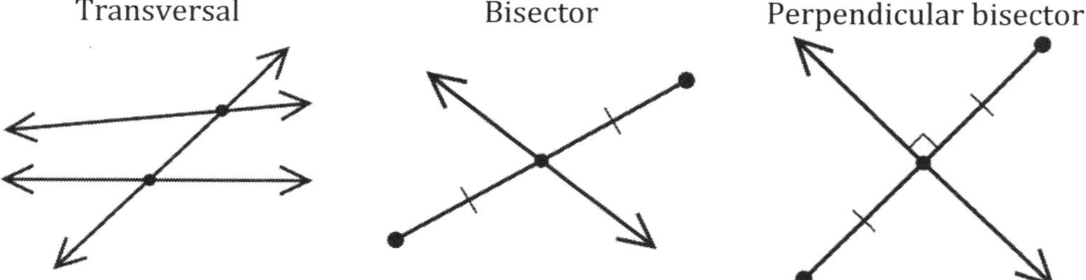

The **projection of a point on a line** is the point at which a perpendicular line drawn from the given point to the given line intersects the line. This is also the shortest distance from the given point to the line. The **projection of a segment on a line** is a segment whose endpoints are the points formed when perpendicular lines are drawn from the endpoints of the given segment to the given line. This is similar to the length a diagonal line appears to be when viewed from above.

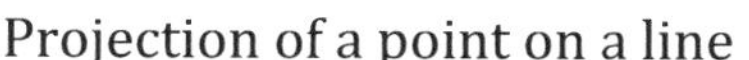

Projection of a segment on a line

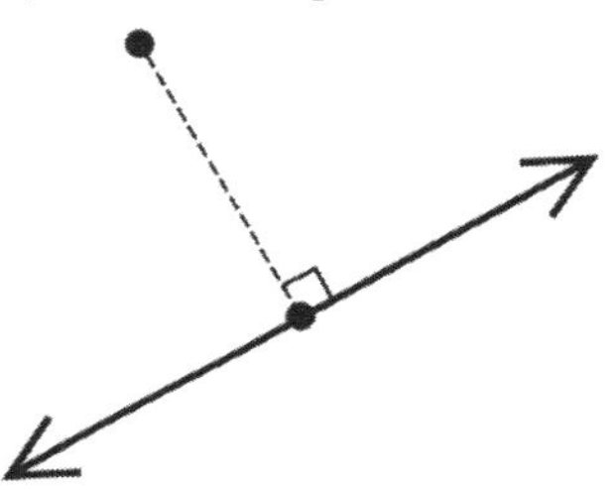

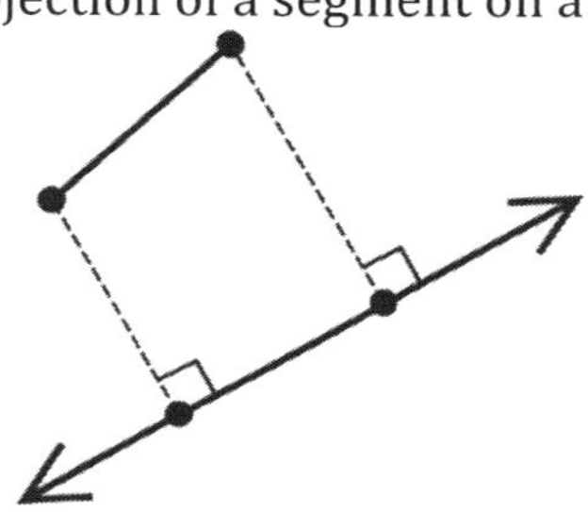

PLANES

A **plane** is a two-dimensional flat surface defined by three non-collinear points. A plane extends an infinite distance in all directions in those two dimensions. It contains an infinite number of points, parallel lines and segments, intersecting lines and segments, as well as parallel or intersecting rays. A plane will never contain a three-dimensional figure or skew lines, which are lines that don't intersect and are not parallel. Two given planes are either parallel or they intersect at a line. A plane may intersect a circular conic surface to form **conic sections**, such as a parabola, hyperbola, circle or ellipse.

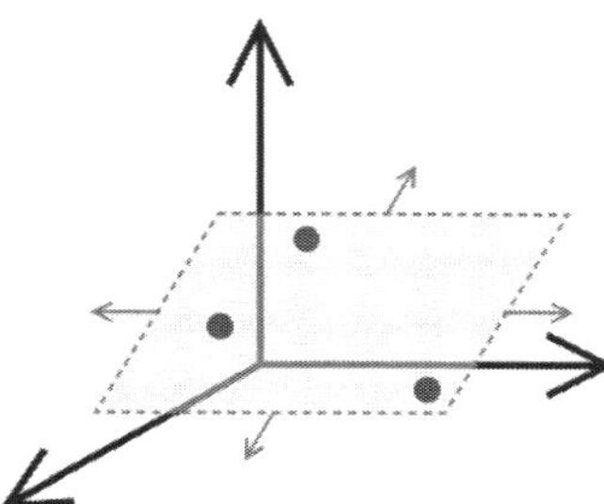

Review Video: Lines and Planes
Visit mometrix.com/academy and enter code: 554267

ANGLES AND VERTICES

An **angle** is formed when two lines or line segments meet at a common point. It may be a common starting point for a pair of segments or rays, or it may be the intersection of lines. Angles are represented by the symbol ∠.

The **vertex** is the point at which two segments or rays meet to form an angle. If the angle is formed by intersecting rays, lines, and/or line segments, the vertex is the point at which four angles are formed. The pairs of angles opposite one another are called vertical angles, and their measures are equal.

- An **acute** angle is an angle with a degree measure less than 90°.
- A **right** angle is an angle with a degree measure of exactly 90°.
- An **obtuse** angle is an angle with a degree measure greater than 90° but less than 180°.
- A **straight angle** is an angle with a degree measure of exactly 180°. This is also a semicircle.
- A **reflex angle** is an angle with a degree measure greater than 180° but less than 360°.

A **full angle** is an angle with a degree measure of exactly 360°. This is also a circle.

Review Video: Angles
Visit mometrix.com/academy and enter code: 264624

RELATIONSHIPS BETWEEN ANGLES

Two angles whose sum is exactly 90° are said to be **complementary**. The two angles may or may not be adjacent. In a right triangle, the two acute angles are complementary.

Two angles whose sum is exactly 180° are said to be **supplementary**. The two angles may or may not be adjacent. Two intersecting lines always form two pairs of supplementary angles. Adjacent supplementary angles will always form a straight line.

Two angles that have the same vertex and share a side are said to be **adjacent**. Vertical angles are not adjacent because they share a vertex but no common side.

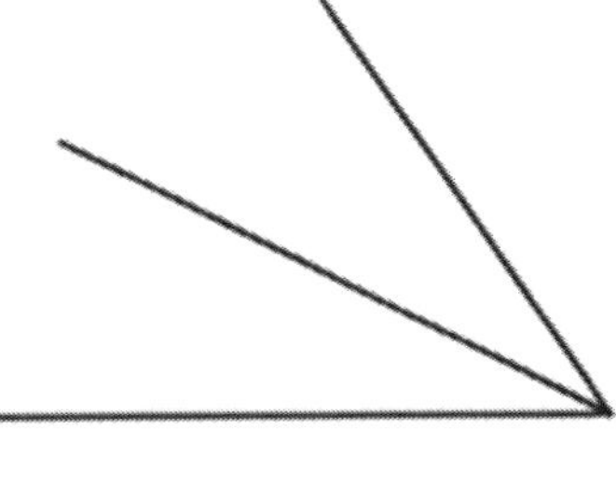

Adjacent
Share vertex and side

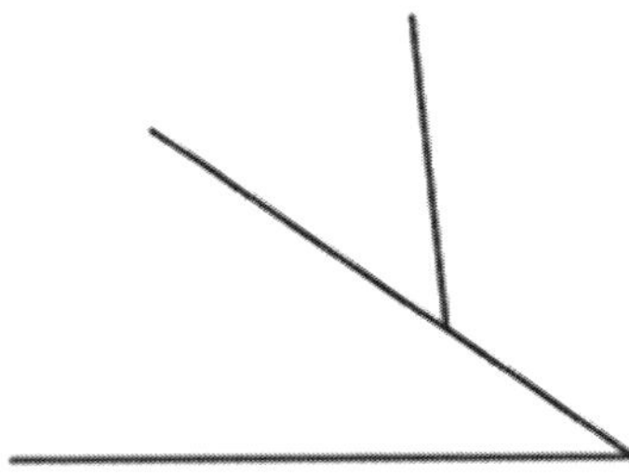

Not adjacent
Share part of a side, but not vertex

When two parallel lines are cut by a transversal, the angles that are between the two parallel lines are **interior angles**. In the diagram below, angles 3, 4, 5, and 6 are interior angles.

When two parallel lines are cut by a transversal, the angles that are outside the parallel lines are **exterior angles**. In the diagram below, angles 1, 2, 7, and 8 are exterior angles.

When two parallel lines are cut by a transversal, the angles that are in the same position relative to the transversal and a parallel line are **corresponding angles**. The diagram below has four pairs of corresponding angles: angles 1 and 5, angles 2 and 6, angles 3 and 7, and angles 4 and 8. Corresponding angles formed by parallel lines are congruent.

When two parallel lines are cut by a transversal, the two interior angles that are on opposite sides of the transversal are called **alternate interior angles**. In the diagram below, there are two pairs of alternate interior angles: angles 3 and 6, and angles 4 and 5. Alternate interior angles formed by parallel lines are congruent.

When two parallel lines are cut by a transversal, the two exterior angles that are on opposite sides of the transversal are called **alternate exterior angles**.

In the diagram below, there are two pairs of alternate exterior angles: angles 1 and 8, and angles 2 and 7. Alternate exterior angles formed by parallel lines are congruent.

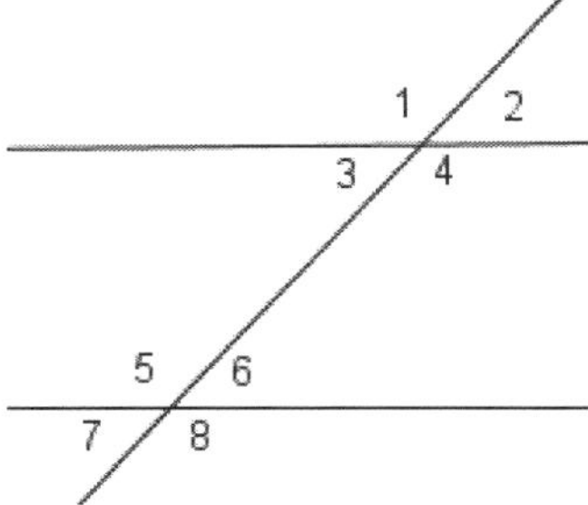

When two lines intersect, four angles are formed. The non-adjacent angles at this vertex are called vertical angles. Vertical angles are congruent. In the diagram, $\angle ABD \cong \angle CBE$ and $\angle ABC \cong \angle DBE$. The other pairs of angles, $(\angle ABC, \angle CBE)$ and $(\angle ABD, \angle DBE)$, are supplementary, meaning the pairs sum to 180°.

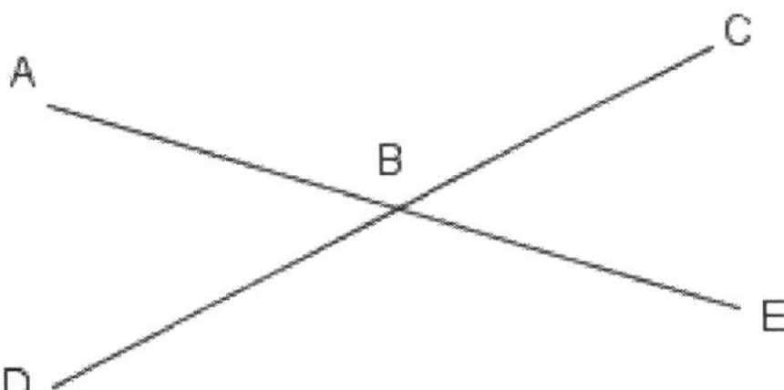

Polygons

A **polygon** is a closed, two-dimensional figure with three or more straight line segments called **sides**. The point at which two sides of a polygon intersect is called the **vertex**. In a polygon, the number of sides is always equal to the number of vertices. A polygon with all sides congruent and all angles equal is called a **regular polygon**. Common polygons are:

$$\text{Triangle} = 3 \text{ sides}$$
$$\text{Quadrilateral} = 4 \text{ sides}$$
$$\text{Pentagon} = 5 \text{ sides}$$
$$\text{Hexagon} = 6 \text{ sides}$$
$$\text{Heptagon} = 7 \text{ sides}$$
$$\text{Octagon} = 8 \text{ sides}$$
$$\text{Nonagon} = 9 \text{ sides}$$
$$\text{Decagon} = 10 \text{ sides}$$
$$\text{Dodecagon} = 12 \text{ sides}$$

More generally, an n-gon is a polygon that has n angles and n sides.

Review Video: Intro to Polygons
Visit mometrix.com/academy and enter code: 271869

The sum of the interior angles of an n-sided polygon is $(n - 2) \times 180°$. For example, in a triangle $n = 3$. So the sum of the interior angles is $(3 - 2) \times 180° = 180°$. In a quadrilateral, $n = 4$, and the sum of the angles is $(4 - 2) \times 180° = 360°$.

Review Video: Sum of Interior Angles
Visit mometrix.com/academy and enter code: 984991

Convex and Concave Polygons

A **convex polygon** is a polygon whose diagonals all lie within the interior of the polygon. A **concave polygon** is a polygon with a least one diagonal that is outside the polygon. In the diagram below, quadrilateral $ABCD$ is concave because diagonal $\overline{AC}$ lies outside the polygon and quadrilateral $EFGH$ is convex because both diagonals lie inside the polygon.

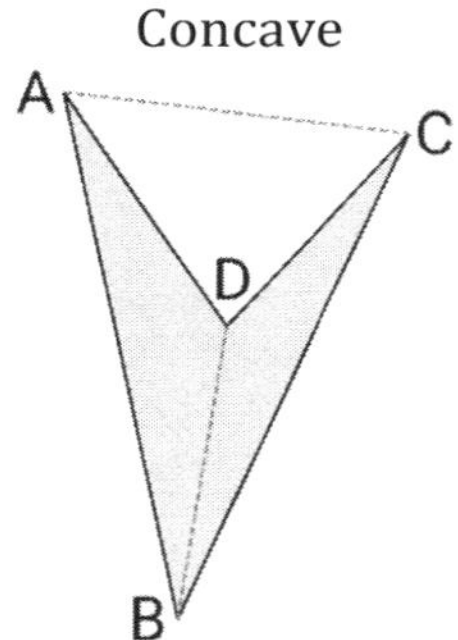

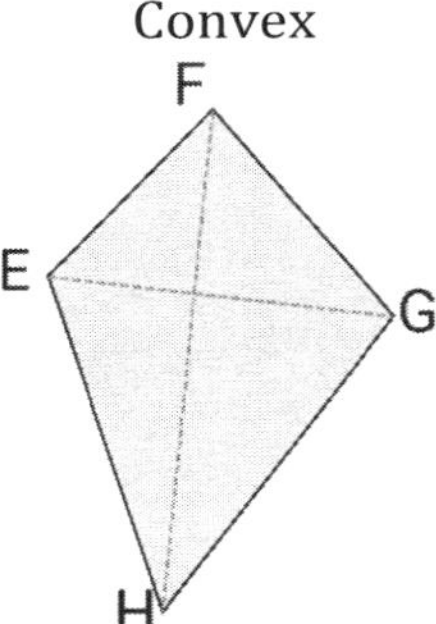

Apothem and Radius

A line segment from the center of a polygon that is perpendicular to a side of the polygon is called the **apothem**. A line segment from the center of a polygon to a vertex of the polygon is called a

radius. In a regular polygon, the apothem can be used to find the area of the polygon using the formula $A = \frac{1}{2}ap$, where a is the apothem, and p is the perimeter.

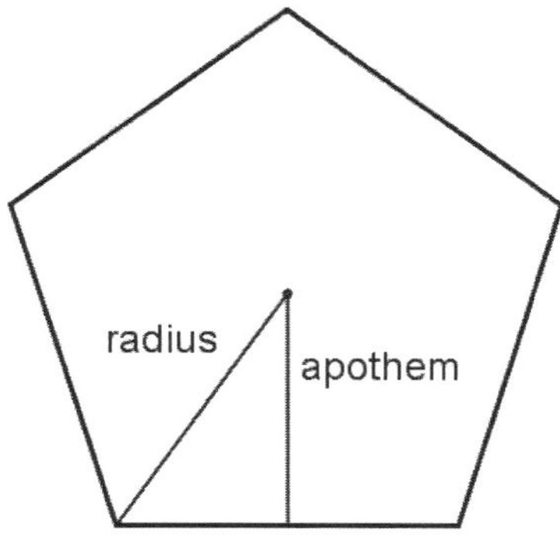

A **diagonal** is a line segment that joins two non-adjacent vertices of a polygon. The number of diagonals a polygon has can be found by using the formula:

$$\text{number of diagonals} = \frac{n(n-3)}{2}$$

Note that n is the number of sides in the polygon. This formula works for all polygons, not just regular polygons.

Congruence and Similarity

Congruent figures are geometric figures that have the same size and shape. All corresponding angles are equal, and all corresponding sides are equal. Congruence is indicated by the symbol $\cong$.

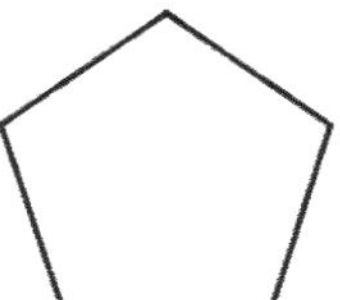
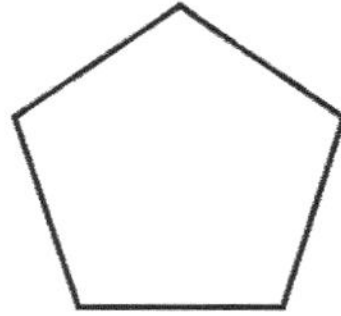

Congruent polygons

Similar figures are geometric figures that have the same shape, but do not necessarily have the same size. All corresponding angles are equal, and all corresponding sides are proportional, but they do not have to be equal. It is indicated by the symbol ~.

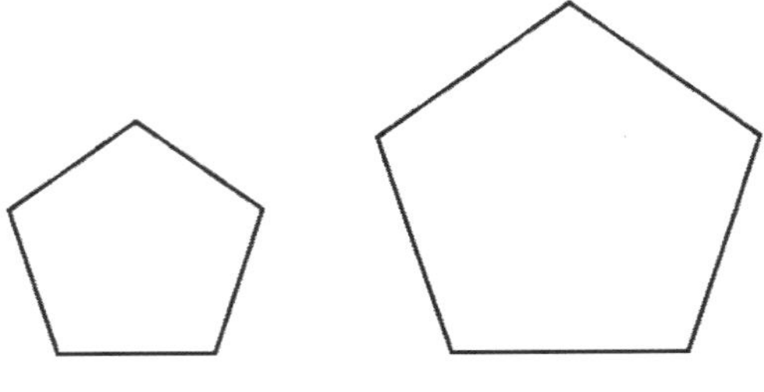

Similar polygons

Note that all congruent figures are also similar, but not all similar figures are congruent.

Review Video: What is a Congruent Shape?
Visit mometrix.com/academy and enter code: 492281

LINE OF SYMMETRY

A line that divides a figure or object into congruent parts is called a **line of symmetry**. An object may have no lines of symmetry, one line of symmetry, or multiple (i.e., more than one) lines of symmetry.

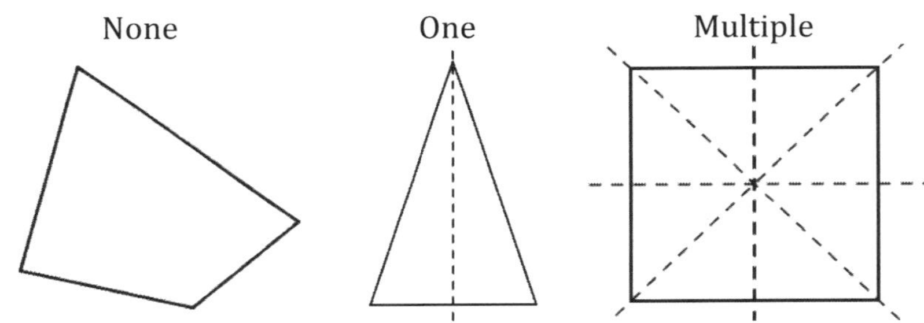

Review Video: Symmetry
Visit mometrix.com/academy and enter code: 528106

TRIANGLES

A triangle is a three-sided figure with the sum of its interior angles being 180°. The **perimeter of any triangle** is found by summing the three side lengths; $P = a + b + c$. For an equilateral triangle, this is the same as $P = 3a$, where a is any side length, since all three sides are the same length.

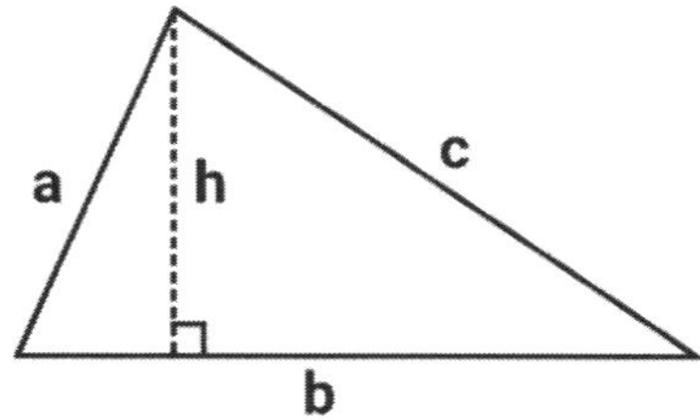

Review Video: Proof that a Triangle is 180 Degrees
Visit mometrix.com/academy and enter code: 687591

Review Video: Area and Perimeter of a Triangle
Visit mometrix.com/academy and enter code: 853779

The **area of any triangle** can be found by taking half the product of one side length referred to as the base, often given the variable b and the perpendicular distance from that side to the opposite vertex called the altitude or height and given the variable h. In equation form that is $A = \frac{1}{2}bh$. Another formula that works for any triangle is $A = \sqrt{s(s-a)(s-b)(s-c)}$, where s is the semiperimeter: $\frac{a+b+c}{2}$, and a, b, and c are the lengths of the three sides. Special cases include isosceles triangles, $A = \frac{1}{2}b\sqrt{a^2 - \frac{b^2}{4}}$, where b is the unique side and a is the length of one of the two congruent sides, and equilateral triangles, $A = \frac{\sqrt{3}}{4}a^2$, where a is the length of a side.

Review Video: Area of Any Triangle
Visit mometrix.com/academy and enter code: 138510

PARTS OF A TRIANGLE

An **altitude** of a triangle is a line segment drawn from one vertex perpendicular to the opposite side. In the diagram that follows, $\overline{BE}$, $\overline{AD}$, and $\overline{CF}$ are altitudes. The length of an altitude is also called the height of the triangle. The three altitudes in a triangle are always concurrent. The point of concurrency of the altitudes of a triangle, O, is called the **orthocenter**. Note that in an obtuse triangle, the orthocenter will be outside the triangle, and in a right triangle, the orthocenter is the vertex of the right angle.

A **median** of a triangle is a line segment drawn from one vertex to the midpoint of the opposite side. In the diagram that follows, $\overline{BH}$, $\overline{AG}$, and $\overline{CI}$ are medians. This is not the same as the altitude, except the altitude to the base of an isosceles triangle and all three altitudes of an equilateral triangle. The point of concurrency of the medians of a triangle, T, is called the **centroid**. This is the same point as the orthocenter only in an equilateral triangle. Unlike the orthocenter, the centroid is always inside the triangle. The centroid can also be considered the exact center of the triangle. Any shape triangle can be perfectly balanced on a tip placed at the centroid. The centroid is also the point that is two-thirds the distance from the vertex to the opposite side.

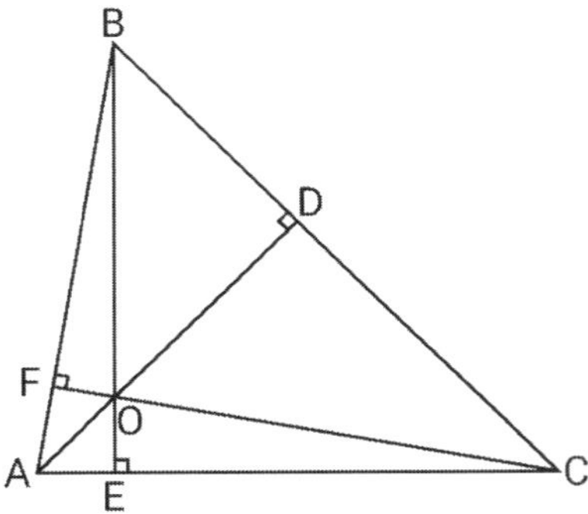

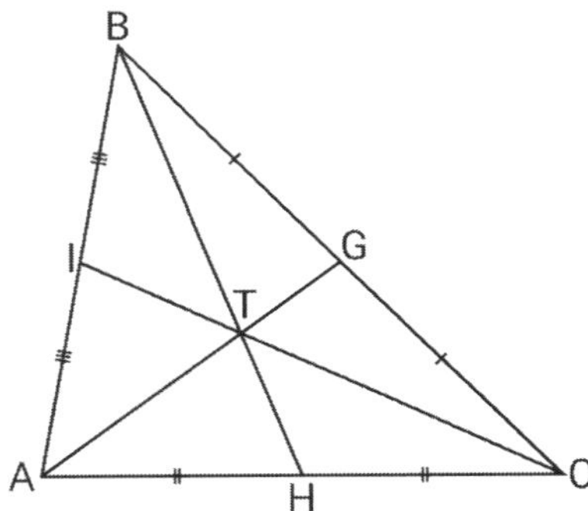

Review Video: Centroid, Incenter, Circumcenter, and Orthocenter
Visit mometrix.com/academy and enter code: 598260

Classifications of Triangles

A **scalene triangle** is a triangle with no congruent sides. A scalene triangle will also have three angles of different measures. The angle with the largest measure is opposite the longest side, and the angle with the smallest measure is opposite the shortest side. An **acute triangle** is a triangle whose three angles are all less than 90°. If two of the angles are equal, the acute triangle is also an **isosceles triangle**. An isosceles triangle will also have two congruent angles opposite the two congruent sides. If the three angles are all equal, the acute triangle is also an **equilateral triangle**. An equilateral triangle will also have three congruent angles, each 60°. All equilateral triangles are also acute triangles. An **obtuse triangle** is a triangle with exactly one angle greater than 90°. The other two angles may or may not be equal. If the two remaining angles are equal, the obtuse triangle is also an isosceles triangle. A **right triangle** is a triangle with exactly one angle equal to 90°. All right triangles follow the Pythagorean theorem. A right triangle can never be acute or obtuse.

The table below illustrates how each descriptor places a different restriction on the triangle:

Angles / Sides	**Acute:** **All angles < 90°**	**Obtuse:** **One angle > 90°**	**Right:** **One angle = 90°**
Scalene: **No equal side lengths**	b, x, z, a, y, c	b, x, z, a, y, c	b, x, z, a, y, c
	$90° > \angle a > \angle b > \angle c$ $x > y > z$	$\angle a > 90° > \angle b > \angle c$ $x > y > z$	$90° = \angle a > \angle b > \angle c$ $x > y > z$
Isosceles: **Two equal side lengths**	b, z, x, a, y, c	b, x, z, a, y, c	b, x, z, a, y, c
	$90° > \angle a, \angle b, or\ \angle c$ $\angle b = \angle c, \quad y = z$	$\angle a > 90° > \angle b = \angle c$ $x > y = z$	$\angle a = 90°$ $\angle b = \angle c = 45°$ $x > y = z$
Equilateral: **Three equal side lengths**	b, z, x, a, y, c		
	$60° = \angle a = \angle b = \angle c$ $x = y = z$		

Review Video: Introduction to Types of Triangles
Visit mometrix.com/academy and enter code: 511711

General Rules for Triangles

The **triangle inequality theorem** states that the sum of the measures of any two sides of a triangle is always greater than the measure of the third side. If the sum of the measures of two sides were equal to the third side, a triangle would be impossible because the two sides would lie flat across the third side and there would be no vertex. If the sum of the measures of two of the sides was less than the third side, a closed figure would be impossible because the two shortest sides would never meet. In other words, for a triangle with sides lengths A, B, and C: $A + B > C, B + C > A$, and $A + C > B$.

The sum of the measures of the interior angles of a triangle is always 180°. Therefore, a triangle can never have more than one angle greater than or equal to 90°.

In any triangle, the angles opposite congruent sides are congruent, and the sides opposite congruent angles are congruent. The largest angle is always opposite the longest side, and the smallest angle is always opposite the shortest side.

The line segment that joins the midpoints of any two sides of a triangle is always parallel to the third side and exactly half the length of the third side.

Review Video: General Rules (Triangle Inequality Theorem)
Visit mometrix.com/academy and enter code: 166488

Similarity and Congruence Rules

Similar triangles are triangles whose corresponding angles are equal and whose corresponding sides are proportional. Represented by AAA. Similar triangles whose corresponding sides are congruent are also congruent triangles.

Triangles can be shown to be **congruent** in 5 ways:

- **SSS**: Three sides of one triangle are congruent to the three corresponding sides of the second triangle.
- **SAS**: Two sides and the included angle (the angle formed by those two sides) of one triangle are congruent to the corresponding two sides and included angle of the second triangle.
- **ASA**: Two angles and the included side (the side that joins the two angles) of one triangle are congruent to the corresponding two angles and included side of the second triangle.
- **AAS**: Two angles and a non-included side of one triangle are congruent to the corresponding two angles and non-included side of the second triangle.
- **HL**: The hypotenuse and leg of one right triangle are congruent to the corresponding hypotenuse and leg of the second right triangle.

Review Video: Similar Triangles
Visit mometrix.com/academy and enter code: 398538

Pythagorean Theorem

The side of a triangle opposite the right angle is called the **hypotenuse**. The other two sides are called the legs. The Pythagorean theorem states a relationship among the legs and hypotenuse of a right triangle: $(a^2 + b^2 = c^2)$, where a and b are the lengths of the legs of a right triangle, and c is the length of the hypotenuse. Note that this formula will only work with right triangles.

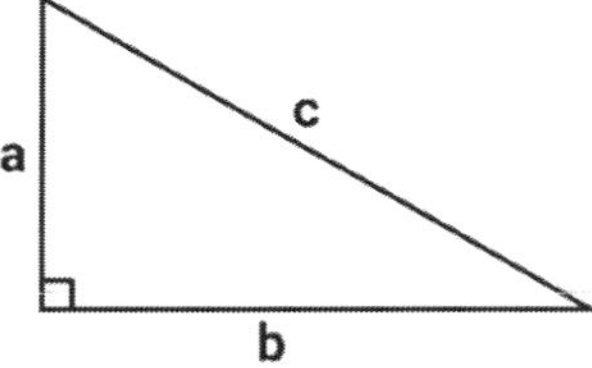

Review Video: Pythagorean Theorem
Visit mometrix.com/academy and enter code: 906576

Trigonometric Formulas

In the diagram below, angle C is the right angle, and side c is the hypotenuse. Side a is the side opposite to angle A and side b is the side opposite to angle B. Using ratios of side lengths as a means to calculate the sine, cosine, and tangent of an acute angle only works for right triangles.

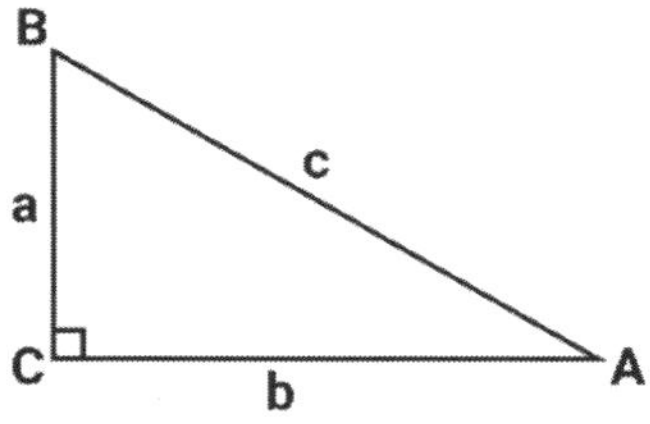

$$\sin A = \frac{\text{opposite side}}{\text{hypotenuse}} = \frac{a}{c} \qquad \csc A = \frac{1}{\sin A} = \frac{\text{hypotenuse}}{\text{opposite side}} = \frac{c}{a}$$

$$\cos A = \frac{\text{adjacent side}}{\text{hypotenuse}} = \frac{b}{c} \qquad \sec A = \frac{1}{\cos A} = \frac{\text{hypotenuse}}{\text{adjacent side}} = \frac{c}{b}$$

$$\tan A = \frac{\text{opposite side}}{\text{adjacent side}} = \frac{a}{b} \qquad \cot A = \frac{1}{\tan A} = \frac{\text{adjacent side}}{\text{opposite side}} = \frac{b}{a}$$

Laws of Sines and Cosines

The **law of sines** states that $\frac{\sin A}{a} = \frac{\sin B}{b} = \frac{\sin C}{c}$, where A, B, and C are the angles of a triangle, and a, b, and c are the sides opposite their respective angles. This formula will work with all triangles, not just right triangles.

The **law of cosines** is given by the formula $c^2 = a^2 + b^2 - 2ab(\cos C)$, where a, b, and c are the sides of a triangle, and C is the angle opposite side c. This is a generalized form of the Pythagorean theorem that can be used on any triangle.

> **Review Video: Law of Sines**
> Visit mometrix.com/academy and enter code: 206844
>
> **Review Video: Law of Cosines**
> Visit mometrix.com/academy and enter code: 158911

Quadrilaterals

A **quadrilateral** is a closed two-dimensional geometric figure that has four straight sides. The sum of the interior angles of any quadrilateral is 360°.

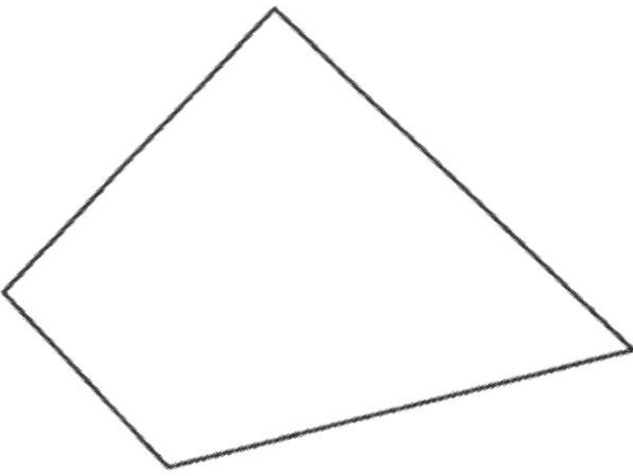

> **Review Video: Diagonals of Parallelograms, Rectangles, and Rhombi**
> Visit mometrix.com/academy and enter code: 320040

Kite

A **kite** is a quadrilateral with two pairs of adjacent sides that are congruent. A result of this is perpendicular diagonals. A kite can be concave or convex and has one line of symmetry.

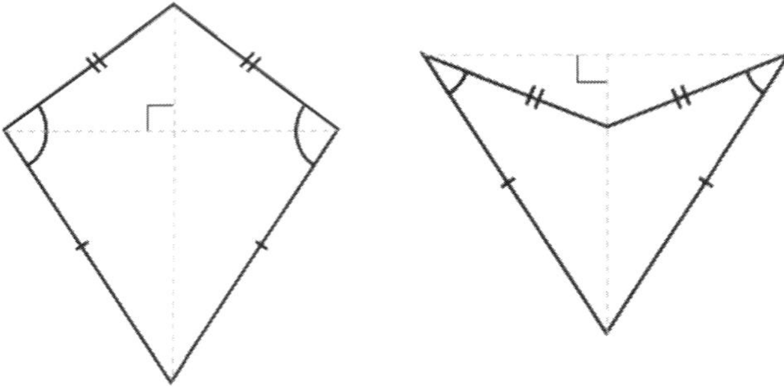

Trapezoid

Trapezoid: A trapezoid is defined as a quadrilateral that has at least one pair of parallel sides. There are no rules for the second pair of sides. So, there are no rules for the diagonals and no lines of symmetry for a trapezoid.

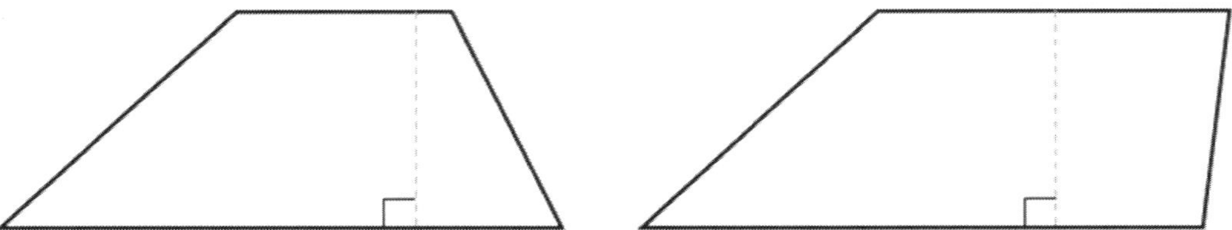

The **area of a trapezoid** is found by the formula $A = \frac{1}{2}h(b_1 + b_2)$, where h is the height (segment joining and perpendicular to the parallel bases), and b_1 and b_2 are the two parallel sides (bases). Do not use one of the other two sides as the height unless that side is also perpendicular to the parallel bases.

The **perimeter of a trapezoid** is found by the formula $P = a + b_1 + c + b_2$, where a, b_1, c, and b_2 are the four sides of the trapezoid.

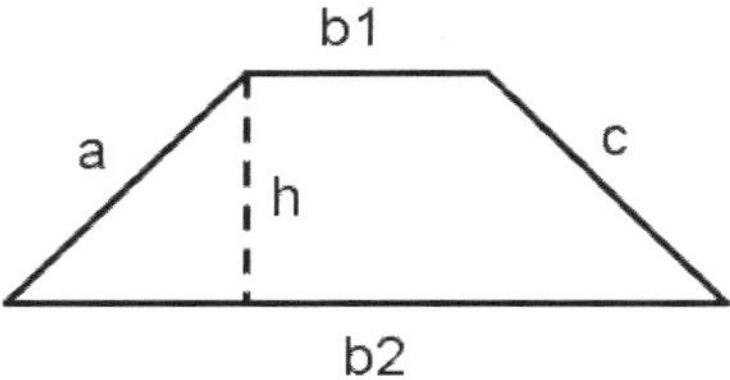

Review Video: Area and Perimeter of a Trapezoid
Visit mometrix.com/academy and enter code: 587523

Isosceles trapezoid: A trapezoid with equal base angles. This gives rise to other properties including: the two nonparallel sides have the same length, the two non-base angles are also equal, and there is one line of symmetry through the midpoints of the parallel sides.

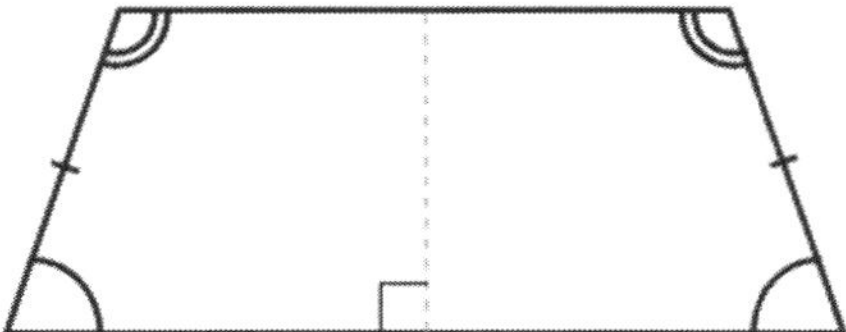

Parallelogram

A **parallelogram** is a quadrilateral that has two pairs of opposite parallel sides. As such it is a special type of trapezoid. The sides that are parallel are also congruent. The opposite interior angles are always congruent, and the consecutive interior angles are supplementary. The diagonals of a parallelogram divide each other. Each diagonal divides the parallelogram into two congruent triangles. A parallelogram has no line of symmetry, but does have 180-degree rotational symmetry about the midpoint.

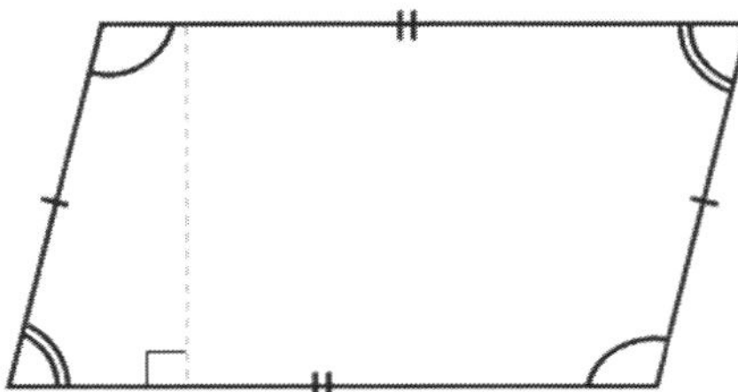

The **area of a parallelogram** is found by the formula $A = bh$, where b is the length of the base, and h is the height. Note that the base and height correspond to the length and width in a rectangle, so this formula would apply to rectangles as well. Do not confuse the height of a parallelogram with the length of the second side. The two are only the same measure in the case of a rectangle.

The **perimeter of a parallelogram** is found by the formula $P = 2a + 2b$ or $P = 2(a + b)$, where a and b are the lengths of the two sides.

Review Video: How to Find the Area and Perimeter of a Parallelogram
Visit mometrix.com/academy and enter code: 718313

Rectangle

A **rectangle** is a quadrilateral with four right angles. All rectangles are parallelograms and trapezoids, but not all parallelograms or trapezoids are rectangles. The diagonals of a rectangle are congruent. Rectangles have two lines of symmetry (through each pair of opposing midpoints) and 180-degree rotational symmetry about the midpoint.

The **area of a rectangle** is found by the formula $A = lw$, where A is the area of the rectangle, l is the length (usually considered to be the longer side) and w is the width (usually considered to be the shorter side). The numbers for l and w are interchangeable.

The **perimeter of a rectangle** is found by the formula $P = 2l + 2w$ or $P = 2(l + w)$, where l is the length, and w is the width. It may be easier to add the length and width first and then double the result, as in the second formula.

RHOMBUS

A **rhombus** is a quadrilateral with four congruent sides. All rhombuses are parallelograms and kites; thus, they inherit all the properties of both types of quadrilaterals. The diagonals of a rhombus are perpendicular to each other. Rhombi have two lines of symmetry (along each of the diagonals) and 180° rotational symmetry. The **area of a rhombus** is half the product of the diagonals: $A = \frac{d_1 d_2}{2}$ and the perimeter of a rhombus is: $P = 2\sqrt{(d_1)^2 + (d_2)^2}$.

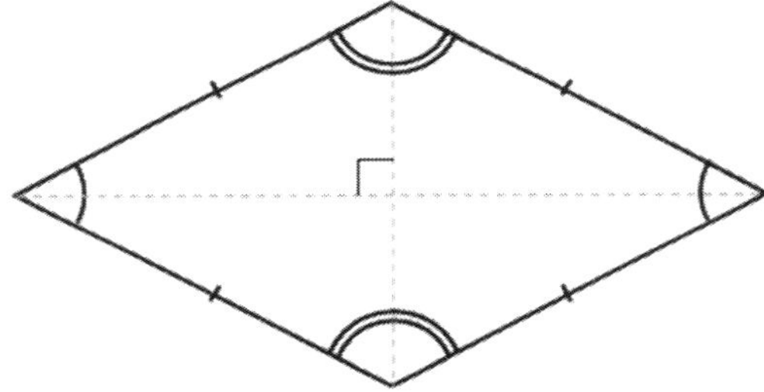

SQUARE

A **square** is a quadrilateral with four right angles and four congruent sides. Squares satisfy the criteria of all other types of quadrilaterals. The diagonals of a square are congruent and perpendicular to each other. Squares have four lines of symmetry (through each pair of opposing midpoints and along each of the diagonals) as well as 90° rotational symmetry about the midpoint.

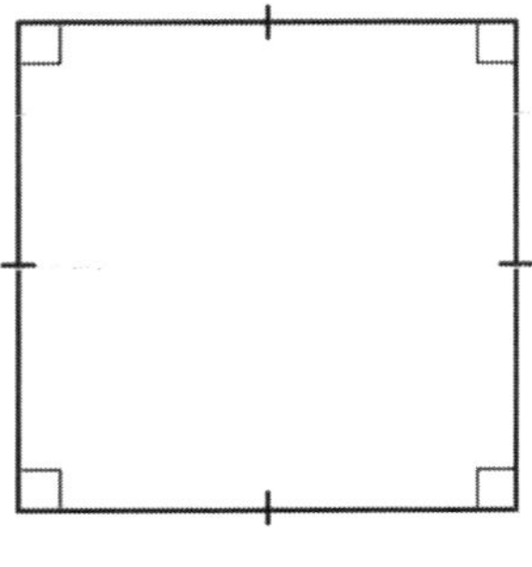

The **area of a square** is found by using the formula $A = s^2$, where s is the length of one side. The **perimeter of a square** is found by using the formula $P = 4s$, where s is the length of one side. Because all four sides are equal in a square, it is faster to multiply the length of one side by 4 than to add the same number four times. You could use the formulas for rectangles and get the same answer.

Review Video: Area and Perimeter of Rectangles and Squares
Visit mometrix.com/academy and enter code: 428109

HIERARCHY OF QUADRILATERALS

The hierarchy of quadrilaterals is as follows:

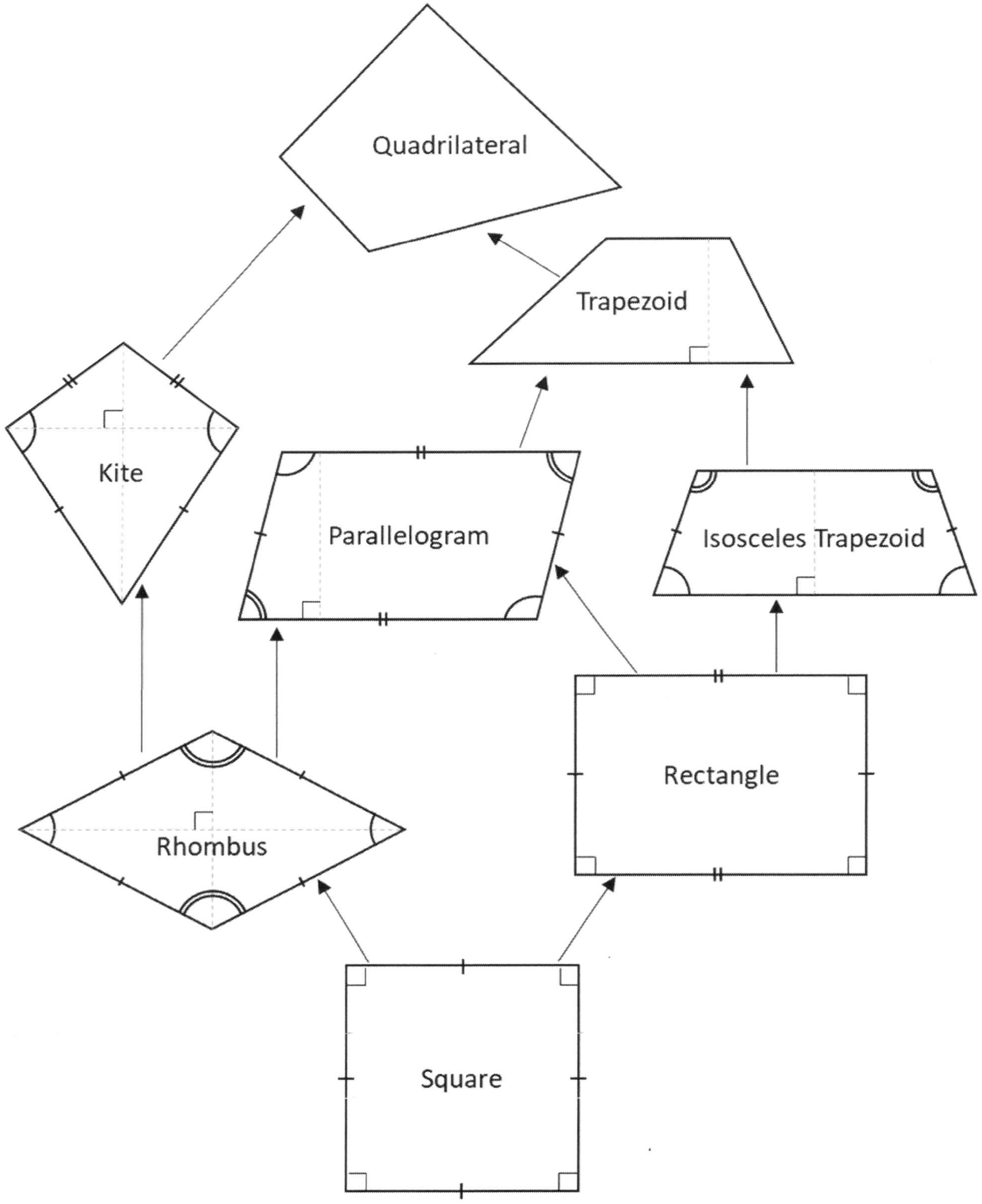

Quadrilateral

Trapezoid

Kite

Parallelogram

Isosceles Trapezoid

Rectangle

Rhombus

Square

CIRCLES

The **center** of a circle is the single point from which every point on the circle is **equidistant**. The **radius** is a line segment that joins the center of the circle and any one point on the circle. All radii of a circle are equal. Circles that have the same center but not the same length of radii are **concentric**. The **diameter** is a line segment that passes through the center of the circle and has both endpoints on the circle. The length of the diameter is exactly twice the length of the radius. Point O in the diagram below is the center of the circle, segments $\overline{OX}$, $\overline{OY}$, and $\overline{OZ}$ are radii; and segment $\overline{XZ}$ is a diameter.

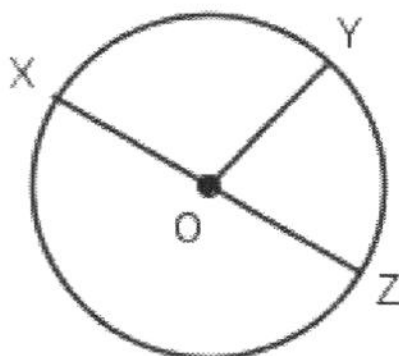

Review Video: Points of a Circle
Visit mometrix.com/academy and enter code: 420746

Review Video: The Diameter, Radius, and Circumference of Circles
Visit mometrix.com/academy and enter code: 448988

The **area of a circle** is found by the formula $A = \pi r^2$, where r is the length of the radius. If the diameter of the circle is given, remember to divide it in half to get the length of the radius before proceeding.

The **circumference** of a circle is found by the formula $C = 2\pi r$, where r is the radius. Again, remember to convert the diameter if you are given that measure rather than the radius.

Review Video: Area and Circumference of a Circle
Visit mometrix.com/academy and enter code: 243015

INSCRIBED AND CIRCUMSCRIBED FIGURES

These terms can both be used to describe a given arrangement of figures, depending on perspective. If each of the vertices of figure A lie on figure B, then it can be said that figure A is **inscribed** in figure B, but it can also be said that figure B is **circumscribed** about figure A. The following table and examples help to illustrate the concept. Note that the figures cannot both be circles, as they would be completely overlapping and neither would be inscribed or circumscribed.

Given	Description	Equivalent Description	Figures
Each of the sides of a pentagon is tangent to a circle	The circle is inscribed in the pentagon	The pentagon is circumscribed about the circle	
Each of the vertices of a pentagon lie on a circle	The pentagon is inscribed in the circle	The circle is circumscribed about the pentagon	

Arcs

An **arc** is a portion of a circle. Specifically, an arc is the set of points between and including two points on a circle. An arc does not contain any points inside the circle. When a segment is drawn from the endpoints of an arc to the center of the circle, a sector is formed. A **minor arc** is an arc that has a measure less than 180°. A **major arc** is an arc that has a measure of at least 180°. Every minor arc has a corresponding major arc that can be found by subtracting the measure of the minor arc from 360°. A **semicircle** is an arc whose endpoints are the endpoints of the diameter of a circle. A semicircle is exactly half of a circle.

Arc length is the length of that portion of the circumference between two points on the circle. The formula for arc length is $s = \frac{\pi r\theta}{180°}$, where s is the arc length, r is the length of the radius, and θ is the angular measure of the arc in degrees, or $s = r\theta$, where θ is the angular measure of the arc in radians (2π radians $=$ 360 degrees).

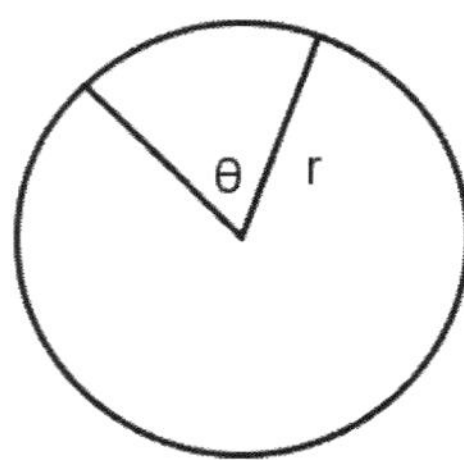

Angles of Circles

A **central angle** is an angle whose vertex is the center of a circle and whose legs intercept an arc of the circle. The measure of a central angle is equal to the measure of the minor arc it intercepts.

An **inscribed angle** is an angle whose vertex lies on a circle and whose legs contain chords of that circle. The portion of the circle intercepted by the legs of the angle is called the intercepted arc. The measure of the intercepted arc is exactly twice the measure of the inscribed angle. In the following diagram, angle ABC is an inscribed angle. $\widehat{AC} = 2(\text{m}\angle ABC)$.

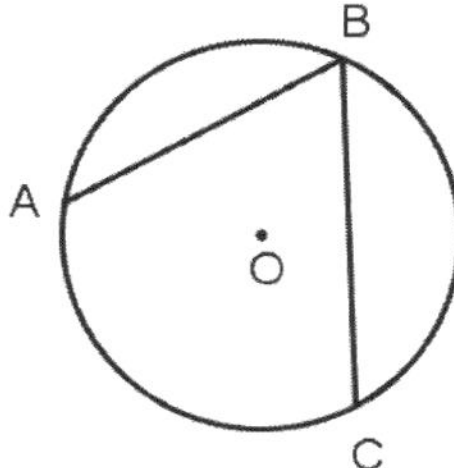

Any angle inscribed in a semicircle is a right angle. The intercepted arc is 180°, making the inscribed angle half that, or 90°. In the diagram below, angle ABC is inscribed in semicircle ABC, making angle ABC equal to 90°.

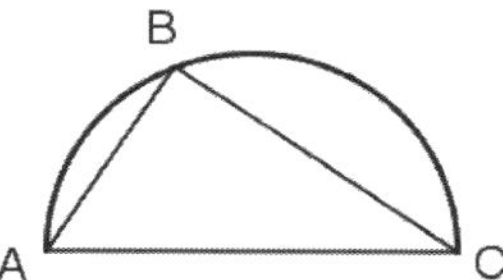

Review Video: Arcs and Angles of Circles
Visit mometrix.com/academy and enter code: 652838

Secants, Chords, and Tangents

A **secant** is a line that intersects a circle in two points. The segment of a secant line that is contained within the circle is called a **chord**. Two secants may intersect inside the circle, on the circle, or outside the circle. When the two secants intersect on the circle, an inscribed angle is formed. When two secants intersect inside a circle, the measure of each of two vertical angles is equal to half the sum of the two intercepted arcs. Consider the following diagram where $\text{m}\angle AEB = \frac{1}{2}(\widehat{AB} + \widehat{CD})$ and $\text{m}\angle BEC = \frac{1}{2}(\widehat{BC} + \widehat{AD})$.

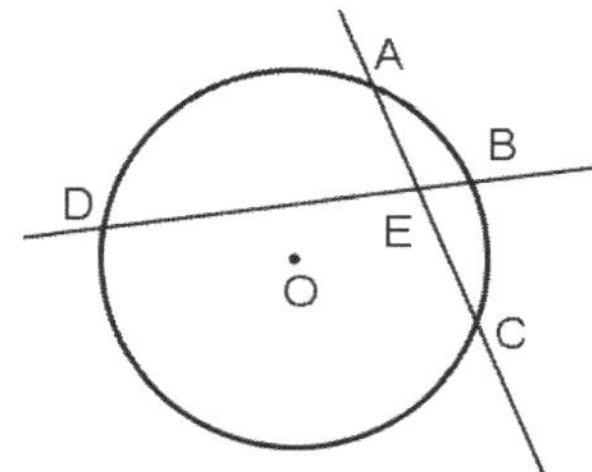

When two secants intersect outside a circle, the measure of the angle formed is equal to half the difference of the two arcs that lie between the two secants. In the diagram below, $m\angle AEB = \frac{1}{2}(\widehat{AB} - \widehat{CD})$.

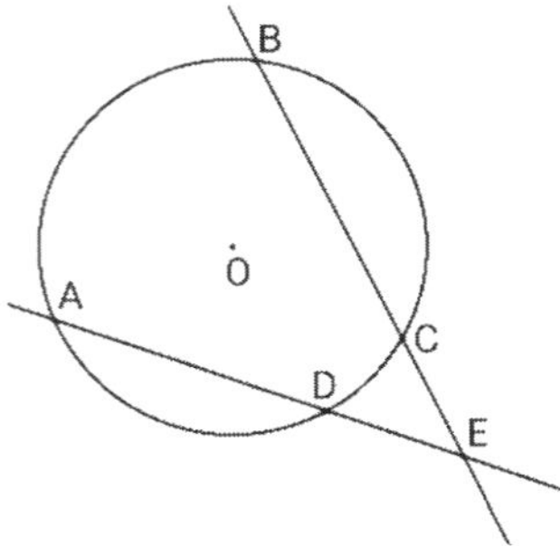

A **tangent** is a line in the same plane as a circle that touches the circle in exactly one point. The point at which a tangent touches a circle is called the **point of tangency**. While a line segment can be tangent to a circle as part of a line that is tangent, it is improper to say a tangent can be simply a line segment that touches the circle in exactly one point.

In the diagram below, $\overleftrightarrow{EB}$ is a secant and contains chord $\overline{EB}$, and $\overleftrightarrow{CD}$ is tangent to circle A. Notice that $\overline{FB}$ is not tangent to the circle. $\overline{FB}$ is a line segment that touches the circle in exactly one point, but if the segment were extended, it would touch the circle in a second point. In the diagram below, point B is the point of tangency.

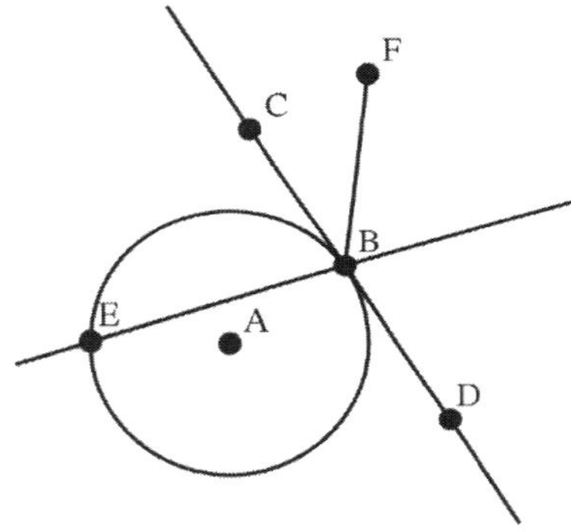

Review Video: Secants, Chords, and Tangents
Visit mometrix.com/academy and enter code: 258360

Review Video: Tangent Lines of a Circle
Visit mometrix.com/academy and enter code: 780167

SECTORS

A **sector** is the portion of a circle formed by two radii and their intercepted arc. While the arc length is exclusively the points that are also on the circumference of the circle, the sector is the entire area bounded by the arc and the two radii.

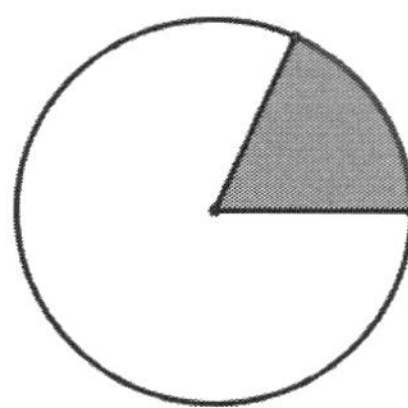

The **area of a sector** of a circle is found by the formula, $A = \frac{\theta r^2}{2}$, where A is the area, θ is the measure of the central angle in radians, and r is the radius. To find the area with the central angle in degrees, use the formula, $A = \frac{\theta \pi r^2}{360}$, where θ is the measure of the central angle and r is the radius.

SOLIDS

The **surface area of a solid object** is the area of all sides or exterior surfaces. For objects such as prisms and pyramids, a further distinction is made between base surface area (B) and lateral surface area (LA). For a prism, the total surface area (SA) is $SA = LA + 2B$. For a pyramid or cone, the total surface area is $SA = LA + B$.

The **surface area of a sphere** can be found by the formula $A = 4\pi r^2$, where r is the radius. The volume is given by the formula $V = \frac{4}{3}\pi r^3$, where r is the radius. Both quantities are generally given in terms of π.

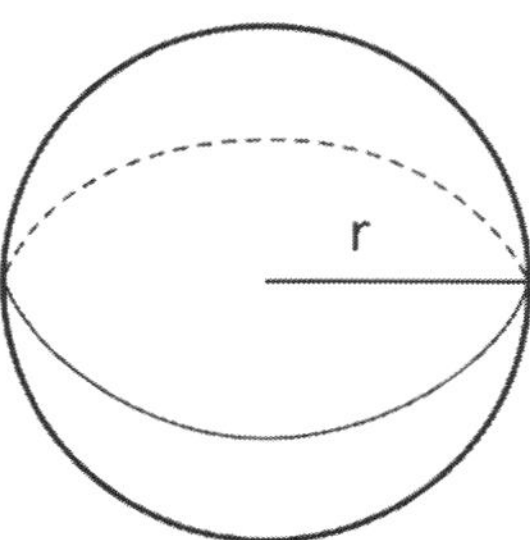

Review Video: Volume and Surface Area of a Sphere
Visit mometrix.com/academy and enter code: 786928

The **volume of any prism** is found by the formula $V = Bh$, where B is the area of the base, and h is the height (perpendicular distance between the bases). The surface area of any prism is the sum of the areas of both bases and all sides. It can be calculated as $SA = 2B + Ph$, where P is the perimeter of the base.

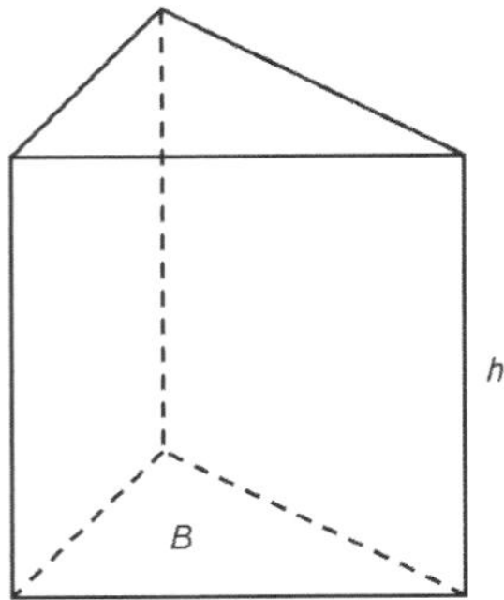

Review Video: Volume and Surface Area of a Prism
Visit mometrix.com/academy and enter code: 420158

For a **rectangular prism**, the volume can be found by the formula $V = lwh$, where V is the volume, l is the length, w is the width, and h is the height. The surface area can be calculated as $SA = 2lw + 2hl + 2wh$ or $SA = 2(lw + hl + wh)$.

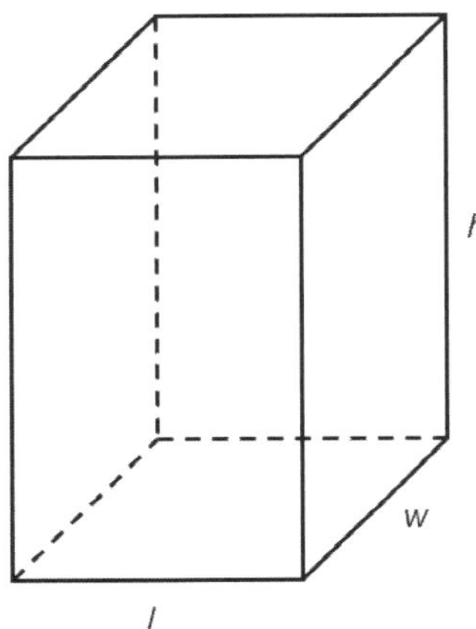

Review Video: Volume and Surface Area of a Rectangular Prism
Visit mometrix.com/academy and enter code: 282814

The **volume of a cube** can be found by the formula $V = s^3$, where s is the length of a side. The surface area of a cube is calculated as $SA = 6s^2$, where SA is the total surface area and s is the length of a side. These formulas are the same as the ones used for the volume and surface area of a rectangular prism, but simplified since all three quantities (length, width, and height) are the same.

Review Video: Volume and Surface Area of a Cube
Visit mometrix.com/academy and enter code: 664455

The **volume of a cylinder** can be calculated by the formula $V = \pi r^2 h$, where r is the radius, and h is the height. The surface area of a cylinder can be found by the formula $SA = 2\pi r^2 + 2\pi rh$. The first term is the base area multiplied by two, and the second term is the perimeter of the base multiplied by the height.

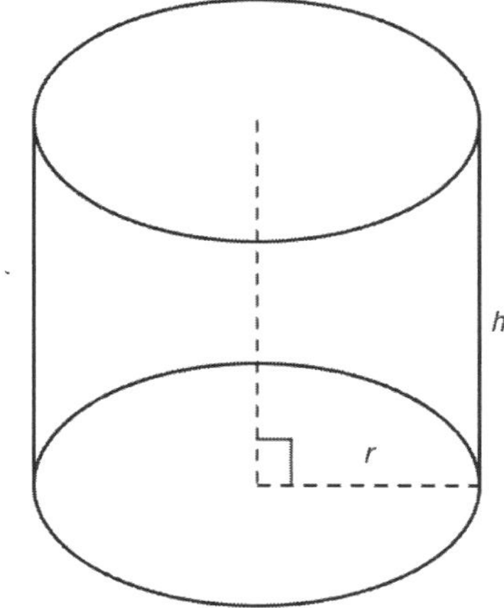

Review Video: Finding the Volume and Surface Area of a Right Circular Cylinder
Visit mometrix.com/academy and enter code: 226463

The **volume of a pyramid** is found by the formula $V = \frac{1}{3}Bh$, where B is the area of the base, and h is the height (perpendicular distance from the vertex to the base). Notice this formula is the same as $\frac{1}{3}$ times the volume of a prism. Like a prism, the base of a pyramid can be any shape.

Finding the **surface area of a pyramid** is not as simple as the other shapes we've looked at thus far. If the pyramid is a right pyramid, meaning the base is a regular polygon and the vertex is directly over the center of that polygon, the surface area can be calculated as $SA = B + \frac{1}{2}Ph_s$, where P is the perimeter of the base, and h_s is the slant height (distance from the vertex to the midpoint of one side of the base). If the pyramid is irregular, the area of each triangle side must be calculated individually and then summed, along with the base.

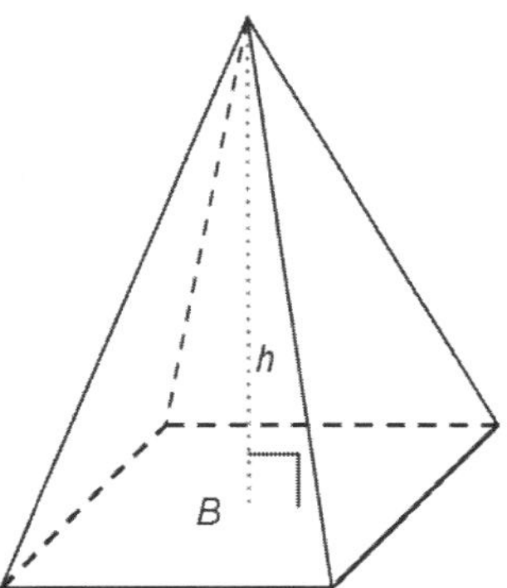

Review Video: Finding the Volume and Surface Area of a Pyramid
Visit mometrix.com/academy and enter code: 621932

The **volume of a cone** is found by the formula $V = \frac{1}{3}\pi r^2 h$, where r is the radius, and h is the height. Notice this is the same as $\frac{1}{3}$ times the volume of a cylinder. The surface area can be calculated as $SA = \pi r^2 + \pi r s$, where s is the slant height. The slant height can be calculated using the Pythagorean theorem to be $\sqrt{r^2 + h^2}$, so the surface area formula can also be written as $SA = \pi r^2 + \pi r\sqrt{r^2 + h^2}$.

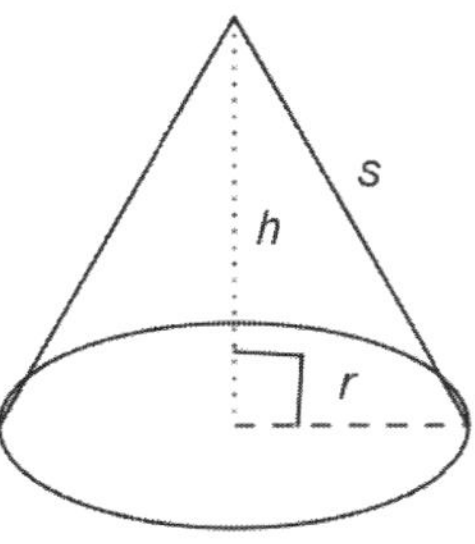

Review Video: Volume and Surface Area of a Right Circular Cone
Visit mometrix.com/academy and enter code: 573574

Degrees, Radians, and the Unit Circle

It is important to understand the deep connection between trigonometry and circles. Specifically, the two main units, **degrees** (°) and **radians** (rad), that are used to measure angles are related this way: 360° in one full circle and 2π radians in one full circle: $(360° = 2\pi \text{ rad})$. The conversion factor relating the two is often stated as $\frac{180°}{\pi}$. For example, to convert $\frac{3\pi}{2}$ radians to degrees, multiply by the conversion factor: $\frac{3\pi}{2} \times \frac{180°}{\pi} = 270°$. As another example, to convert 60° to radians, divide by the conversion factor or multiply by the reciprocal: $60° \times \frac{\pi}{180°} = \frac{\pi}{3}$ radians.

Recall that the standard equation for a circle is $(x - h)^2 + (y - k)^2 = r^2$. A **unit circle** is a circle with a radius of 1 $(r = 1)$ that has its center at the origin $(h = 0, k = 0)$. Thus, the equation for the unit circle simplifies from the standard equation down to $x^2 + y^2 = 1$.

Standard position is the position of an angle of measure θ whose vertex is at the origin, the initial side crosses the unit circle at the point $(1, 0)$, and the terminal side crosses the unit circle at some other point (a, b). In the standard position, $\sin\theta = b$, $\cos\theta = a$, and $\tan\theta = \frac{b}{a}$.

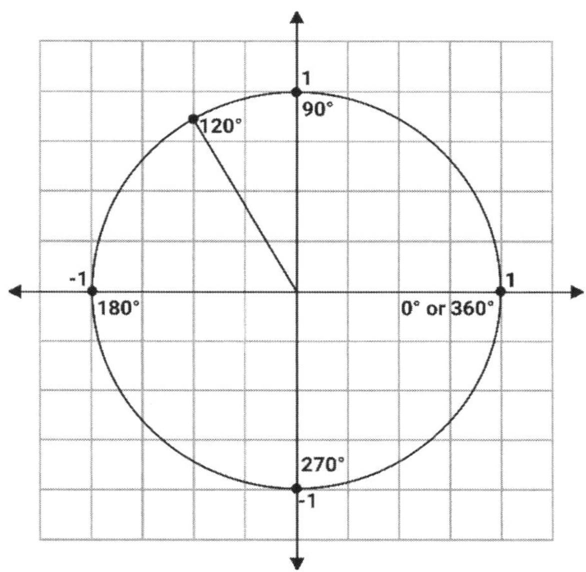

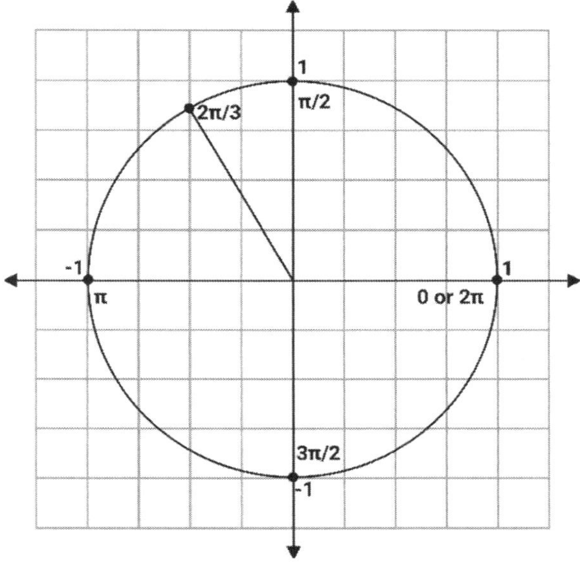

Review Video: Unit Circles and Standard Position
Visit mometrix.com/academy and enter code: 333922

TABLE OF COMMONLY ENCOUNTERED ANGLES

$0° = 0$ radians, $30° = \frac{\pi}{6}$ radians, $45° = \frac{\pi}{4}$ radians, $60° = \frac{\pi}{3}$ radians, and $90° = \frac{\pi}{2}$ radians

$\sin 0° = 0$	$\cos 0° = 1$	$\tan 0° = 0$
$\sin 30° = \frac{1}{2}$	$\cos 30° = \frac{\sqrt{3}}{2}$	$\tan 30° = \frac{\sqrt{3}}{3}$
$\sin 45° = \frac{\sqrt{2}}{2}$	$\cos 45° = \frac{\sqrt{2}}{2}$	$\tan 45° = 1$
$\sin 60° = \frac{\sqrt{3}}{2}$	$\cos 60° = \frac{1}{2}$	$\tan 60° = \sqrt{3}$
$\sin 90° = 1$	$\cos 90° = 0$	$\tan 90° =$ undefined
$\csc 0° =$ undefined	$\sec 0° = 1$	$\cot 0° =$ undefined
$\csc 30° = 2$	$\sec 30° = \frac{2\sqrt{3}}{3}$	$\cot 30° = \sqrt{3}$
$\csc 45° = \sqrt{2}$	$\sec 45° = \sqrt{2}$	$\cot 45° = 1$
$\csc 60° = \frac{2\sqrt{3}}{3}$	$\sec 60° = 2$	$\cot 60° = \frac{\sqrt{3}}{3}$
$\csc 90° = 1$	$\sec 90° =$ undefined	$\cot 90° = 0$

The values in the upper half of this table are values you should have memorized or be able to find quickly and those in the lower half can easily be determined as the reciprocal of the corresponding function.

Defined and Reciprocal Functions

The tangent function is defined as the ratio of the sine to the cosine: $\tan x = \frac{\sin x}{\cos x}$.

To take the reciprocal of a number means to place that number as the denominator of a fraction with a numerator of 1. The reciprocal functions are thus defined quite simply.

Cosecant	$\csc x$	$\frac{1}{\sin x}$
Secant	$\sec x$	$\frac{1}{\cos x}$
Cotangent	$\cot x$	$\frac{1}{\tan x}$

It is important to know these reciprocal functions, but they are not as commonly used as the three basic functions.

Review Video: Defined and Reciprocal Functions
Visit mometrix.com/academy and enter code: 996431

Inverse Functions

Each of the trigonometric functions accepts an angular measure, either degrees or radians, and gives a numerical value as the output. The inverse functions do the opposite; they accept a numerical value and give an angular measure as the output.

The inverse of sine, or arcsine, commonly written as either $\sin^{-1} x$ or $\arcsin x$, gives the angle whose sine is x. Similarly:

The inverse of $\cos x$ is written as $\cos^{-1} x$ or $\arccos x$ and means the angle whose cosine is x.
The inverse of $\tan x$ is written as $\tan^{-1} x$ or $\arctan x$ and means the angle whose tangent is x.
The inverse of $\csc x$ is written as $\csc^{-1} x$ or $\operatorname{arccsc} x$ and means the angle whose cosecant is x.
The inverse of $\sec x$ is written as $\sec^{-1} x$ or $\operatorname{arcsec} x$ and means the angle whose secant is x.

The inverse of $\cot x$ is written as $\cot^{-1} x$ or $\text{arccot}\, x$ and means the angle whose cotangent is x.

Review Video: Inverse Trig Functions
Visit mometrix.com/academy and enter code: 156054

Important Note About Solving Trigonometric Equations

When solving for an angle with a known trigonometric value, you must consider the sign and include all angles with that value. Your calculator will probably only give one value as an answer, typically in the following ranges:

- For $\sin^{-1} x$, $\left[-\frac{\pi}{2}, \frac{\pi}{2}\right]$ or [- 90°, 90°]
- For $\cos^{-1} x$, $[0, \pi]$ or [0°, 180°]
- For $\tan^{-1} x$, $\left[-\frac{\pi}{2}, \frac{\pi}{2}\right]$ or [- 90°, 90°]

It is important to determine if there is another angle in a different quadrant that also satisfies the problem. To do this, find the other quadrant(s) with the same sign for that trigonometric function and find the angle that has the same reference angle. Then check whether this angle is also a solution.

- In the first quadrant, all six trigonometric functions are positive.
- In the second quadrant, sin and csc are positive.
- In the third quadrant, tan and cot are positive.
- In the fourth quadrant, cos and sec are positive.

If you remember the phrase, "ALL Students Take Classes," you will be able to remember the sign of each trigonometric function in each quadrant. ALL represents all the signs in the first quadrant. The "S" in "Students" represents the sine function and its reciprocal in the second quadrant. The "T" in "Take" represents the tangent function and its reciprocal in the third quadrant. The "C" in "Classes" represents the cosine function and its reciprocal.

Trigonometric Identities

Sum and Difference

To find the sine, cosine, or tangent of the sum or difference of two angles, use one of the following formulas where α and β are two angles with known sine, cosine, or tangent values as needed:

$$\sin(\alpha \pm \beta) = \sin\alpha\cos\beta \pm \cos\alpha\sin\beta$$
$$\cos(\alpha \pm \beta) = \cos\alpha\cos\beta \mp \sin\alpha\sin\beta$$
$$\tan(\alpha \pm \beta) = \frac{\tan\alpha \pm \tan\beta}{1 \mp \tan\alpha\tan\beta}$$

HALF ANGLE

To find the sine or cosine of half of a known angle, use the following formulas where θ is an angle with a known exact cosine value:

$$\sin\left(\frac{\theta}{2}\right) = \pm\sqrt{\frac{(1 - cos\theta)}{2}}$$

$$\cos\left(\frac{\theta}{2}\right) = \pm\sqrt{\frac{(1 + \cos\theta)}{2}}$$

To determine the sign of the answer, you must recognize which quadrant the given angle is in and apply the correct sign for the trigonometric function you are using. If you need to find an expression for the exact sine or cosine of an angle that you do not know, such as sine 22.5°, you can rewrite the given angle as a half angle, such as $\sin\left(\frac{45°}{2}\right)$, and use the formula above:

$$\sin\left(\frac{45°}{2}\right) = \pm\sqrt{\frac{(1 - \cos(45°))}{2}} = \pm\sqrt{\frac{\left(1 - \frac{\sqrt{2}}{2}\right)}{2}} = \pm\sqrt{\frac{(2 - \sqrt{2})}{4}} = \pm\frac{1}{2}\sqrt{(2 - \sqrt{2})}$$

To find the tangent or cotangent of half of a known angle, use the following formulas where θ is an angle with known exact sine and cosine values:

$$\tan\frac{\theta}{2} = \frac{sin\theta}{1 + \cos\theta}$$

$$\cot\frac{\theta}{2} = \frac{\sin\theta}{1 - \cos\theta}$$

These formulas will work for finding the tangent or cotangent of half of any angle unless the cosine of θ happens to make the denominator of the identity equal to 0.

The Pythagorean theorem states that $a^2 + b^2 = c^2$ for all right triangles. The trigonometric identity that derives from this principle is stated in this way: $\sin^2\theta + \cos^2\theta = 1$.

Dividing each term by either $\sin^2\theta$ or $\cos^2\theta$ yields two other identities, respectively:

$$1 + \cot^2\theta = \csc^2\theta$$

$$\tan^2\theta + 1 = \sec^2\theta$$

Review Video: Sum and Difference Trigonometric Identities
Visit mometrix.com/academy and enter code: 468838

Double Angles

In each case, use one of the double angle formulas. To find the sine or cosine of twice a known angle, use one of the following formulas:

$$\sin(2\theta) = 2\sin\theta\cos\theta$$

$$\begin{aligned}\cos(2\theta) &= \cos^2\theta - \sin^2\theta \\ &= 2\cos^2\theta - 1 \\ &= 1 - 2\sin^2\theta\end{aligned}$$

To find the tangent or cotangent of twice a known angle, use the formulas where θ is an angle with known exact sine, cosine, tangent, and cotangent values:

$$\tan(2\theta) = \frac{2\tan\theta}{1-\tan^2\theta}$$

$$\cot(2\theta) = \frac{\cot\theta - \tan\theta}{2}$$

Products

To find the product of the sines and cosines of two different angles, use one of the following formulas where α and β are two unique angles:

$$\sin\alpha\sin\beta = \frac{1}{2}[\cos(\alpha-\beta) - \cos(\alpha+\beta)]$$

$$\cos\alpha\cos\beta = \frac{1}{2}[\cos(\alpha+\beta) + \cos(\alpha-\beta)]$$

$$\sin\alpha\cos\beta = \frac{1}{2}[\sin(\alpha+\beta) + \sin(\alpha-\beta)]$$

$$\cos\alpha\sin\beta = \frac{1}{2}[\sin(\alpha+\beta) - \sin(\alpha-\beta)]$$

Review Video: Half-Angle, Double Angle, and Product Trig Identities
Visit mometrix.com/academy and enter code: 274252

Complementary

The trigonometric cofunction identities use the trigonometric relationships of complementary angles (angles whose sum is 90°). These are:

$$\cos x = \sin(90° - x)$$

$$\csc x = \sec(90° - x)$$

$$\cot x = \tan(90° - x)$$

Domain, Range, and Asymptotes in Trigonometry

The domain is the set of all possible real number values of x on the graph of a trigonometric function. Some graphs will impose limits on the values of x.

The range is the set of all possible real number values of y on the graph of a trigonometric function. Some graphs will impose limits on the values of y.

Asymptotes are lines that the graph of a trigonometric function approaches but never reaches. Asymptotes exist for values of x in the graphs of the tangent, cotangent, secant, and cosecant. The sine and cosine graphs do not have any asymptotes.

Domain, Range, and Asymptotes of the Six Trigonometric Functions

The domain, range, and asymptotes for each of the trigonometric functions are as follows:

- In the **sine** function, the domain is all real numbers, the range is $-1 \leq y \leq 1$, and there are no asymptotes.
- In the **cosine** function, the domain is all real numbers, the range is $-1 \leq y \leq 1$, and there are no asymptotes.
- In the **tangent** function, the domain is $x \in \mathbb{R}; x \neq \frac{\pi}{2} + k\pi$, the range is all real numbers, and the asymptotes are the lines $x = \frac{\pi}{2} + k\pi$.
- In the **cosecant** function, the domain is $x \in \mathbb{R}; x \neq k\pi$, the range is $(-\infty, -1]$ and $[1, \infty)$, and the asymptotes are the lines $x = k\pi$.
- In the **secant** function, the domain is $x \in \mathbb{R}; x \neq \frac{\pi}{2} + k\pi$, the range is $(-\infty, 1]$ and $[1, \infty)$, and the asymptotes are the lines $x = \frac{\pi}{2} + k\pi$.
- In the **cotangent** function, the domain is $x \in \mathbb{R}; x \neq k\pi$, the range is all real numbers, and the asymptotes are the lines $x = k\pi$.

In each of the above cases, k represents any integer.

Rectangular and Polar Coordinates

Rectangular coordinates are those that lie on the square grids of the Cartesian plane. They should be quite familiar to you. The polar coordinate system is based on a circular graph, rather than the square grid of the Cartesian system. Points in the polar coordinate system are in the format (r, θ), where r is the distance from the origin (think radius of the circle) and θ is the smallest positive angle (moving counterclockwise around the circle) made with the positive horizontal axis.

To convert a point from rectangular (x, y) format to polar (r, θ) format, use the formula (x, y) to $(r, \theta) \Rightarrow r = \sqrt{x^2 + y^2}; \theta = \arctan\frac{y}{x}$ when $x \neq 0$.

If x is positive, use the positive square root value for r. If x is negative, use the negative square root value for r. If $x = 0$, use the following rules:

- If $y = 0$, then $\theta = 0$.
- If $y > 0$, then $\theta = \frac{\pi}{2}$.
- If $y < 0$, then $\theta = \frac{3\pi}{2}$.

To convert a point from polar (r, θ) format to rectangular (x, y) format, use the formula (r, θ) to $(x, y) \Rightarrow x = r\cos\theta\,; y = r\sin\theta$.

De Moivre's Theorem

De Moivre's theorem is used to find the powers of complex numbers (numbers that contain the imaginary number i) written in polar form. Given a trigonometric expression that contains i, such as $z = r\cos x + ir\sin x$, where r is a real number and x is an angle measurement in polar form, use the formula $z^n = r^n(\cos nx + i\sin nx)$, where r and n are real numbers, x is the angle measure in polar form, and i is the imaginary number $i = \sqrt{-1}$. The expression $\cos x + i\sin x$ can be written $\text{cis}\, x$, making the formula appear in the format $z^n = r^n \text{ cis } nx$.

Note that De Moivre's theorem is only for angles in polar form. If you are given an angle in degrees, you must convert to polar form before using the formula.

Student-Produced Response

This test includes some questions that are not multiple choice. Instead, they require you to solve the problem, then fill the exact number into a grid very similar to the one you used to enter your name and address on the form. The grid has a row of four boxes on top, with a column of numbers 0–9, a slash, and a decimal beneath each box.

To fill in the grid, write your answer in the boxes on top, then fill in the corresponding circle underneath. Use the slash to indicate fractions. It's a machine-scored test, so you don't get any credit for the number you write on top — that's strictly to help you fill in the circles correctly. If your answer doesn't fill up all four columns, that's okay. And it doesn't matter whether you left-justify or right-justify your answers. What does matter is that the circles be filled in correctly.

If You Can't Write It Using the Characters Provided, It's Not Right

No student-produced response will be a negative number or a percentage. If you get a negative number, you've made a mistake. Percentages should be expressed as a ratio or decimal; for example, 50% can be written as .50.

Start on the Left

There are a few reasons to start with the first box every time. For one thing, it's faster. It will also help you be as precise as possible. If your answer is <1, though, don't use a leading 0 before the decimal. This test omits the 0 from column one to help you be as precise as possible. For decimals, use as many columns as you can. Don't round or truncate answers. If you calculate an answer to be .125, enter the full number, not .13.

Repeat a Repeating Decimal

Repeating decimals such as .666666 are only counted correct if you fill all the available columns. Either .666 or .667 will get credit. However, .66 will be counted as wrong.

Don't Use Mixed Numbers

If you try to write 2 ½, the computer will think you've written 21/2 and count it wrong. Instead, use the improper fraction form of such numbers; for example, 2 ½ = 5/2.

Use Your Calculator

You brought a calculator; use it. Work the problem twice to make sure you entered all the numbers correctly.

Check Your Work

More than any other questions in the math section, student-produced responses need to be double-checked. Try working the problem backward, plugging answers back into the original equation.

It's Okay to Get Multiple Answers

Some questions may have more than one answer. In that case, any correct answer will do.

In General

Approach the problem systematically. Take time to understand what is being asked for. In many cases, there is a drawing or graph that you can write on. Draw lines, jot notes, do whatever is necessary to create a visual picture and to allow you to understand what is being asked.

PSAT 8/9 Practice Test #1

Reading Test

Questions 1-8 are based on the following passage.

This passage is adapted from Jane Austen, Pride and Prejudice*, originally published in 1813.*

It is a truth universally acknowledged, that a single man in possession of a good fortune, must be in want of a wife.

However little known the feelings or views of such a man may be on his first entering a neighbourhood, this truth is so well fixed in the minds of the surrounding families, that he is considered the rightful property of some one or other of their daughters.

"My dear Mr. Bennet," said his lady to him one day, "have you heard that Netherfield Park is let at last?"

Mr. Bennet replied that he had not.

"But it is," returned she; "for Mrs. Long has just been here, and she told me all about it."

Mr. Bennet made no answer.

"Do you not want to know who has taken it?" cried his wife impatiently.

"You want to tell me, and I have no objection to hearing it."

This was invitation enough.

"Why, my dear, you must know, Mrs. Long says that Netherfield is taken by a young man of large fortune from the north of England; that he came down on Monday in a chaise and four to see the place, and was so much delighted with it, that he agreed with Mr. Morris immediately; that he is to take possession before Michaelmas, and some of his servants are to be in the house by the end of next week."

"What is his name?"

"Bingley."

"Is he married or single?"

"Oh! Single, my dear, to be sure! A single man of large fortune; four or five thousand a year. What a fine thing for our girls!"

"How so? How can it affect them?"

"My dear Mr. Bennet," replied his wife, "how can you be so tiresome!" You must know that I am thinking of his marrying one of them."

"Is that his design in settling here?"

"Design! Nonsense, how can you talk so! But it is very likely that he may fall in love with one of them, and therefore you must visit him as soon as he comes."

"I see no occasion for that. You and the girls may go, or you may send them by themselves, which perhaps will be still better, for as you are as handsome as any of them, Mr. Bingley may like you the best of the party."

1. Which of the following most nearly matches the meaning of the phrase "It is a truth universally acknowledged" as found in lines 1-3 ("It is ... a wife.")?

A) Everyone knows.
B) The universe has decided.
C) It is a documented fact.
D) It is best to tell the truth.

2. How does Mrs. Bennet feel about the arrival of Mr. Bingley?

A) Mrs. Bennet is excited about the arrival of Mr. Bingley.
B) Mrs. Bennet is nervous about the arrival of Mr. Bingley.
C) Mrs. Bennet is afraid the arrival of Mr. Bingley will upset Mr. Bennet.
D) Mrs. Bennet is indifferent to the arrival of Mr. Bingley.

3. What does Mrs. Bennet expect from Mr. Bingley?

A) Mrs. Bennet expects Mr. Bingley to be interested in marrying one of her daughters.
B) Mrs. Bennet expects Mr. Bingley to be interested in receiving a visit from Mr. Bennet.
C) Mrs. Bennet expects Mr. Bingley to love living at Netherfield Park.
D) Mrs. Bennet expects Mr. Bingley to ask for her help in choosing a wife for himself.

4. Which of the following statements best describes Mrs. Bennet's feelings about her husband as indicated by this selection?

A) Mrs. Bennet is tired of her husband.
B) Mrs. Bennet is exasperated by her husband.
C) Mrs. Bennet is afraid of her husband.
D) Mrs. Bennet is indifferent toward her husband.

5. As used in line 45, the word "design" most nearly means:

A) Intention
B) Drawing
C) Creation
D) Improvisation

6. What is the central idea of this selection?

A) A new neighbor is due to arrive who may become good friends with Mr. and Mrs. Bennet.
B) A new neighbor is due to arrive who may be a prospective husband for one of the Bennet daughters.
C) A new neighbor is due to arrive who may be a good business connection for Mr. Bennet.
D) A new neighbor is due to arrive who has expressed an interest in marrying one of the Bennet daughters.

7. This selection is set in England at the beginning of the 19th century. Drawing on information from the selection, what could you conclude was a primary goal for young women in England during this time period?

A) To marry a man of good character
B) To marry a man with money
C) To entertain the neighbors
D) To be courted by as many men as possible

8. Suppose a subsequent passage indicated that Mr. Bennet was paranoid about his wife being taken by another man. Which of the following selections in the current passage could be seen as providing supporting evidence for this idea?

A) Lines 21-22 ("You want ... hearing it.")
B) Line 36 ("Is he married or single?")
C) Lines 47-49 ("But it ... he comes.")
D) Lines 50-55 ("You and ... the party.")

Questions 9-17 are based on the following passage.

This passage is adapted from Kate Dickinson Sweetser, Ten American Girls from History, *originally published in 1917.*

[Clara has begun her work of ministering to soldiers on the front lines of the civil war. Her tireless efforts and care have taken her to some of the most horrific battles of the war]

Clara Barton!—Only the men who lay wounded or dying on the battle-field knew the thrill and the comfort that the name carried. Again and again her life was in danger—once at Antietam, when stooping to give a drink of water to an injured boy, a bullet whizzed between them. It ended the life of the poor lad, but only tore a hole in Clara Barton's sleeve. And so, again and again, it seemed as if a special Providence protected her from death or injury. At Fredericksburg, when the dead, starving and wounded lay frozen on the ground, and there was no effective organization for proper relief, with swift, silent efficiency Clara Barton moved among them, having the snow cleared away and under the banks finding famished, frozen figures which were once men. She rushed to have an old chimney torn down and built fire-blocks, over which she soon had kettles full of coffee and gruel steaming.

As she was bending over a wounded rebel, he whispered to her: "Lady, you have been kind to me ... every street of the city is covered by our cannon. When your entire army has reached the other side of the Rappahannock, they will find Fredericksburg only a slaughter-pen. Not a regiment will escape. Do not go over, for you will go to certain death."

She thanked him for the kindly warning and later told of the call that came to her to go across the river, and what happened. She says:

"At ten o'clock of the battle day when the rebel fire was hottest, the shells rolling down every street, and the bridge under the heavy cannonade, a courier dashed over, and, rushing up the steps of the house where I was, placed in my hand a crumpled, bloody piece of paper, a request from the lion-hearted old surgeon on the opposite shore, establishing his hospitals in the very jaws of death: "Come to me," he wrote. "Your place is here."

"The faces of the rough men working at my side, which eight weeks before had flushed with indignation at the thought of being controlled by a woman, grew ashy white as they guessed the nature of the summons, ... and they begged me to send them, but save myself. I could only allow them to go with me if they chose, and in twenty minutes we were rocking across the swaying bridge, the water hissing with shot on either side."

"Over into that city of death, its roofs riddled by shell, its every church a crowded hospital, every street a battle-line, every hill a rampart, every rock a fortress, and every stone wall a blazing line of forts."

"Oh, what a day's work was that! How those long lines of blue, rank on rank, charged over the open acres, up to the very mouths of those blazing guns, and how like grain before the sickle they fell and melted away."

"An officer stepped to my side to assist me over the debris at the end of the bridge. While our hands were raised in the act of stepping down, a piece of an exploding shell hissed through between us, just below our arms, carrying away a portion of both the skirts of his coat and my dress, rolling along the ground a few rods from us like a harmless pebble in the water. The next instant a solid shot thundered over our heads, a noble steed bounded in the air and with his gallant rider rolled in the dirt not thirty feet in the rear. Leaving the kind-hearted officer, I passed on alone to the hospital. In less than a half-hour he was brought to me—dead."

She was passing along a street in the heart of the city when she had to step aside to let a regiment of infantry march by. At that moment General Patrick saw her, and, thinking she was a frightened resident of the city who had been left behind in the general exodus, leaned from his saddle and said, reassuringly:

"You are alone and in great danger, madam. Do you want protection?"

With a rare smile, Miss Barton said, as she looked at the ranks of soldiers, "Thank you, but I think I am the best-protected woman in the United States."

9. Lines 8-13 of the passage describe a close call when a bullet whizzed between Clara and a young soldier. Which of the following is the best description of what happened?

A) The bullet killed the soldier, but it only wounded Clara.
B) The bullet wounded both the soldier and Clara.
C) The bullet wounded the soldier, but it missed Clara.
D) The bullet killed the soldier, but it missed Clara.

10. Which of the following best explains why the author referred to one of the soldiers as "the poor lad" in line 12?

A) She wanted to show that the man had little or no material belongings.
B) She wanted to build sympathy for the young man who died.
C) She wanted to show that the soldier had only been a young boy, not a man.
D) She wanted to create an image in the mind of the reader about the soldier.

11. Why is the old surgeon across the river described in lines 47-48 as having "established his hospitals in the very jaws of death"?

A) He was treating wounded soldiers in hospitals which were all destroyed.
B) He was treating wounded soldiers although he was near death himself.
C) He was treating wounded soldiers who all subsequently died.
D) He was treating wounded soldiers directly on the battlefields.

12. What can be inferred from the fact that the men's faces "grew ashy white" in lines 50-56 ("The faces...save myself")?

A) The men were afraid that Clara would be seriously hurt or killed by going to help.
B) The men had not wanted Clara to tend to them or order them around when she first arrived.
C) The men were terrified of the coming war and wanted Clara to escape with them.
D) The men did not want to be moved to the hospital on the other side of the bridge.

13. Which literary device is used in lines 61-65 ("Over into ... of forts")?

A) Alliteration
B) Parallelism
C) Paradoxes
D) Periphrasis

14. Which of the following is the best description of the phrase "with a rare smile" as used in lines 96-99 ("With a rare...the United States")?

A) Miss Barton had an unusually great smile.
B) Miss Barton's smile was fine/precious.
C) Miss Barton did not smile very often.
D) Miss Barton had an admirable smile.

15. Which of the following excerpts provides evidence of Barton's positive feelings for the Union army?

A) Lines 26-28 ("a wounded ... kind to me")
B) Lines 66-68 ("How those ... open acres")
C) Lines 80-81 ("a noble ... gallant rider")
D) Lines 83-85 ("the kind-hearted ... me—dead.'")

16. Why does the author mention the instances when Clara's life had been in danger on the battlefield?

A) To show that Clara was an unwilling participant in the initial war effort.
B) To help the reader picture how Clara seemed to not really be a part of the battle.
C) To compare how many battles she lived through with how many armed men had not.
D) To illustrate how battles were turned through the care she provided.

17. Which of the following might be a good title for the above selection?

A) Clara Barton: The Angel of the Battlefields
B) The Angel of the Civil War
C) Civil War Nurses and the Work of Clara Barton
D) When the Fighting Was Over: Clara Barton, Civil War Hero

Questions 18-25 are based on the following passages.

Passage 1:

Black History Month is unnecessary. In a place and time in which we overwhelmingly elected an African American president, we can and should move to a post-racial approach to education. As *Detroit Free Press* columnist Rochelle Riley wrote in a February 1 column calling for an end to Black History Month, "I propose that, for the first time in American history, this country has reached a point where we can stop celebrating separately, stop learning separately, stop being American separately."

In addition to being unnecessary, the idea that African American history should be focused on in a given month suggests that it belongs in that month alone. It is important to instead incorporate African American history into what is taught every day as American history. It needs to be recreated as part of mainstream thought and not as an optional, often irrelevant, side note. We should focus efforts on pushing schools to diversify and broaden their curricula.

There are a number of other reasons to abolish it: first, it has become a shallow commercial ritual that does not even succeed in its (limited and misguided) goal of focusing for one month on a sophisticated, intelligent appraisal of the contributions and experiences of African Americans throughout history. Second, there is a paternalistic flavor to the mandated bestowing of a month in which to study African American history that is overcome if we instead assert the need for a comprehensive curriculum. Third, the idea of Black History Month suggests that the knowledge imparted in that month is for African Americans only, rather than for all people.

Passage 2:

Black History Month is still an important observance. Despite the election of our first African American president being a huge achievement, education about African American history is still unmet to a substantial degree. Black History Month is a powerful tool in working towards meeting that need. There is no reason to give up that tool now, and it can easily coexist with an effort to develop a more comprehensive and inclusive yearly curriculum.

Having a month set aside for the study of African American history doesn't limit its study and celebration to that month; it merely focuses complete attention on it for that month. There is absolutely no contradiction between having a set-aside month and having it be present in the curriculum the rest of the year.

Equally important is that the debate *itself* about the usefulness of Black History Month can, and should, remind parents that they can't necessarily count on schools to teach African American history as thoroughly as many parents would want.

Although Black History Month has, to an extent, become a shallow ritual, it doesn't have to be. Good teachers and good materials could make the February curriculum deeply informative, thought-provoking, and inspiring. The range of material that can be covered is rich, varied, and full of limitless possibilities.

Finally, it is worthwhile to remind ourselves and our children of the key events that happened during the month of February. In 1926, Woodson organized the first Black History Week to honor the birthdays of essential civil rights activists Abraham Lincoln and Frederick Douglass. W. E. B. DuBois was born on February 23, 1868. The 15th Amendment, which granted African Americans the right to vote, was passed on February 3, 1870. The first black U.S. senator,

Hiram R. Revels, took his oath of office on February 25, 1870. The National Association for the Advancement of Colored People (NAACP) was founded on February 12, 1909. Malcolm X was shot on February 21, 1965.

Table 1

African Americans Age 25 and older with a Bachelor's Degree or Higher

Year	1970	1980	1990	2000	2010	2020
Percent	5%	8%	11%	16%	20%	25%

18. The author's primary purpose in Passage 1 is to:

A) Argue that Black History Month should not be so commercial.
B) Argue that Black History Month should be abolished.
C) Argue that Black History Month should be maintained.
D) Suggest that African American history should be taught in two months rather than just one.

19. It can be inferred that the term "post-racial" in lines 1-5 of Passage 1 ("In a ... to education") refers to which of the following approaches?

A) One that treats race as the most important factor in determining an individual's experience
B) One that treats race as one factor, but not the most important, in determining an individual's experience
C) One that considers race after considering all other elements of a person's identity
D) One that is not based on or organized around concepts of race

20. Which of the following does the author of Passage 1 NOT give as a reason for abolishing Black History Month?

A) It has become a shallow ritual.
B) There is a paternalistic feel to being granted one month of focus.
C) It suggests that the month's education is only for African Americans.
D) No one learns anything during the month.

21. Why does the author of Passage 2 believe that the debate itself about Black History Month can be useful?

A) The people on opposing sides can come to an intelligent resolution about whether to keep it.
B) African American history is discussed in the media when the debate is ongoing.
C) The debate is a reminder to parents that they can't count on schools to teach their children about African American history.
D) Black History Month doesn't have to be a shallow ritual.

22. What is a possible explanation the author of Passage 2 might give for the information in Table 1?

A) Continued education on black history has supported an increase in the higher education of African Americans over time.
B) Continued debate on black history topics is necessary to support higher education.
C) The election of our first black president has led to an increase in the higher education of African Americans over time.
D) The actions of essential civil rights activists before 1970 led to the first African Americans with bachelor degrees.

23. According to Passage 2, which event happened first?

A) The passing of the 15th Amendment
B) The birth of W.E.B. DuBois
C) The establishment of Black History Month
D) The founding of the NAACP

Pay attention to the years not just days!

24. Which of the following statements is true?

A) The author of Passage 1 thinks that it is important for students to learn about the achievements and experience of African Americans, while the author of Passage 2 does not think this is important.
B) The author of Passage 2 thinks that it is important for students to learn about the achievements and experience of African Americans, while the author of Passage 1 does not think this is important.
C) Neither author thinks that it is important for students to learn about the achievements and experience of African Americans.
D) Both authors think that it is important for students to learn about the achievements and experience of African Americans.

25. The author of Passage 1 argues that celebrating Black History Month suggests that the study of African American history can and should be limited to one month of the year. What is the author of Passage 2's response?

A) Black History Month is still an important observance.
B) Black History Month is a powerful tool in meeting the need for education about African American history.
C) Having a month set aside for the study of African American history does not limit its study and celebration to that month.
D) Black History Month does not have to be a shallow ritual.

Questions 26-34 pertain to the following passage.

Comets

Comets are bodies that orbit the sun. They are distinguishable from asteroids by the presence of comas or tails. In the outer solar system, comets remain frozen and are so small that they are difficult to detect from Earth. As a comet approaches the inner solar system, solar radiation causes the materials within the comet to vaporize and trail off the nuclei. The released dust and gas forms a fuzzy atmosphere called the coma, and the force exerted on the coma causes a tail to form, pointing away from the sun.

Comet nuclei are made of ice, dust, rock, and frozen gases and vary widely in size: from 100 meters or so to tens of kilometers across. The comas may be even larger than the Sun. Because of their low mass, they do not become spherical and have irregular shapes.

There are over 3,500 known comets, and the number is steadily increasing. This represents only a small portion of the total comets existing, however. Most comets are too faint to be visible without the aid of a telescope; the number of comets visible to the naked eye is around one a year.

Comets leave a trail of solid debris behind them. If a comet's path crosses the Earth's path, there will likely be meteor showers as Earth passes through the trail of debris.

Many comets and asteroids have collided into Earth. Some scientists believe that comets hitting Earth about 4 billion years ago brought a significant proportion of the water in Earth's oceans. There are still many near-Earth comets.

Most comets have oval shaped orbits that take them close to the Sun for part of their orbit and then out further into the Solar System for the remainder of the orbit. Comets are often classified according to the length of their orbital period: short period comets have orbital periods of less than 200 years, long period comets have orbital periods of more than 200 years, single apparition comets have trajectories which cause them to permanently leave the solar system after passing the Sun once.

26. Which of the following does the passage NOT list as a component of comet nuclei?

A) Solar radiation
B) Dust
C) Frozen gases
D) Rock

27. Which of the following does the passage claim distinguishes comets from asteroids?

A) The make-up of their nuclei
B) The presence of comas or tails
C) Their orbital periods
D) Their irregular shapes

28. According to the passage, what would a comet with an orbital period of 1,000 years be called?

A) A short period comet
B) A long period comet
C) A single apparition comet
D) An elliptical comet

29. According to the passage, which of the following is true?

A) There are 350 known comets, and the number is steadily increasing.
B) There are 3,500 known comets, and the number is staying the same.
C) There are 3,500 known comets, and many more comets that aren't known.
D) Most comets are visible to the naked eye.

30. What does the passage claim about the size of comets?

A) Some are tens of kilometers across, and the coma can be larger than the sun
B) Some are tens of kilometers across, and the coma is never larger than the Sun
C) Some are 100 meters across, and the coma is never larger than the Sun
D) The smallest comet is at least a kilometer, and the coma can be larger than the Sun

31. According to the passage, what shape is the orbit of most comets?

A) Circular
B) Square
C) Linear
D) Oval

32. In line 45, what does the descriptor "single apparition" indicate about a comet?

A) It only appears during the part of its orbit that is nearest to the Sun.
B) It stays in the solar system even though it only appears once.
C) Its orbital period is so long that it only appears once across millennia.
D) It only remains in the solar system long enough to pass the Sun once.

33. Which of the following does the passage author give as evidence of comets' low mass?

A) Their irregular shapes
B) Their nuclei's content
C) The size of the comas
D) Their variability in size

34. According to the passage, which of the following can cause meteor showers?

A) Multiple comets and asteroids collide into the Earth.
B) Large groups of meteors enter Earth's atmosphere.
C) A comet explodes causing meteors to shower down.
D) The Earth passes through a comet's solid debris trail.

Questions 35-42 pertain to the following passage.

Periodic Table

The periodic table groups elements with similar chemical properties together. The grouping of elements is based on atomic structure. It shows periodic trends of physical and chemical properties and identifies families of elements with similar properties. It is a common model for organizing and understanding elements. In the periodic table, each element has its own cell that includes varying amounts of information presented in symbol form about the properties of the element. Cells in the table are arranged in rows (periods) and columns (groups or families). At minimum, a cell includes the symbol for the element and its atomic number. The cell for hydrogen, for example, which appears first in the upper left corner, includes an "H" and a "1" above the letter. Elements are ordered by atomic number, left to right, top to bottom.

In the periodic table, the groups are the columns numbered 1 through 18 that group elements with similar outer electron shell configurations. Since the configuration of the outer electron shell is one of the primary factors affecting an element's chemical properties, elements within the same group have similar chemical properties. Previous naming conventions for groups have included the use of Roman numerals and upper-case letters. Currently, the periodic table groups are: Group 1, alkali metals; Group 2, alkaline earth metals; Groups 3-12, transition metals; Group 13, boron family; Group 14; carbon family; Group 15, pnictogens; Group 16, chalcogens; Group 17, halogens; Group 18, noble gases.

In the periodic table, there are seven periods (rows), and within each period there are blocks that group elements with the same outer electron subshell (more on this in the next section). The number of electrons in that outer shell determines which group an element belongs to within a given block. Each row's number (1, 2, 3, etc.) corresponds to the highest number electron shell that is in use. For example, row 2 uses only electron shells 1 and 2, while row 7 uses all shells from 1-7.

For example, hydrogen is in the s-block as its highest-energy electron is in the s-orbital. The f-block is organized separately from the rest of the periodic table and includes atoms or ions that have valence electrons in f-orbitals.

Atomic radii will decrease from left to right across a period (row) on the periodic table. In a group (column), there is an increase in the atomic radii of elements from top to bottom. Ionic radii will be smaller than the atomic radii for metals, but the opposite is true for non-metals. From left to right, electronegativity, or an atom's likeliness of taking another atom's electrons, increases. In a group, electronegativity decreases from top to bottom. Ionization energy, or the amount of energy needed to get rid of an atom's outermost electron, increases across a period and decreases down a group. Electron affinity will become more negative across a period but will not change much within a group. The melting point decreases.

35. In lines 28-31, this passage states, "Previous naming conventions for groups have included the use of Roman numerals and upper-case letters." What is the current naming convention for groups in the periodic table?

A) Element name words
B) Lower-case letters
C) Roman numerals
D) Arabic numerals

36. Which of the following selections from the passage provide evidence that the groups in the periodic table contain chemically similar elements?

A) Lines 8-12 ("In the periodic ... the element")
B) Lines 21-24 ("In the periodic ... shell configurations")
C) Lines 24-28 ("Since the ... chemical properties")
D) Lines 65-68 ("Ionization energy ... a group")

37. In which of the following does the author provide a description of periodic trends as they are arranged by period and groups?

A) Lines 8-12 ("In the periodic ... the element.")
B) Lines 24-28 ("Since the ... chemical properties")
C) Lines 38-41 ("In the periodic ... electron subshell")
D) Lines 55-59 ("Atomic radii ... top to bottom.")

38. Which of these is correct regarding information in the passage about how cells are arranged in the periodic table?

A) Periods are vertical; groups are horizontal.
B) Periods are horizontal; groups are vertical.
C) Columns are called periods, rows are called groups.
D) Cells have no vertical/horizontal ordering.

39. The periodic trends described in lines 55-71 ("Atomic radii ... point decreases") mainly depict what kind of relationship?

A) Sequence
B) Cause-effect
C) Parts to whole
D) Comparison-contrast

40. From the description of periodic trends in lines 55-71 ("Atomic radii ... point decreases"), the reader might infer that what kind of relationship between periods and groups is not necessarily or always the case, but occurs often?

A) An inverse relationship
B) A converse relationship
C) A direct relationship
D) No discernible relationship

41. According to the passage, what determines which group an element belongs to within a block?

A) The element's atomic number
B) The number given each period
C) The highest-number electron shell in use
D) The number assigned to that element's group

42. What best identifies the purpose of this passage?

A) To explain the relationship of electron shell configuration to chemical properties
B) To explain the differences between periods and groups within the periodic table
C) To explain why the periodic table exists and is used in chemistry in the first place
D) To explain functions, organization, conventions, and trends of the periodic table

Writing and Language Test

Questions 1–10 are based on the following passage.

1. In medieval times, many careers [1] begun as apprenticeships. This was a way for a youth to learn a trade to support [2] him, as well as a way for an older tradesman to have a reliable assistant for an extended period of time. In more recent times, education has become more available and widespread, so apprenticeships have declined. However, demand for skilled trade has begun to grow, leading to a [3] resurgence of this ancient custom.

2. In the Middle Ages, an apprenticeship included not only training [4] nor basic provisions. The apprentice (who could be as young as ten) lived with the master craftsman, who provided housing and food. Apprenticeships typically lasted for seven years, at which point the apprentice would have the necessary skill to open his own shop or to become a journeyman, working for wages and living on his own.

1.

A) NO CHANGE
B) had begun
C) begin
D) began

2.

A) NO CHANGE
B) his
C) himself
D) themselves

3.

A) NO CHANGE
B) dwindling
C) shrinking
D) forgetting

4.

A) NO CHANGE
B) but also
C) not even
D) and even

3. *1.* [5] <u>Although apprentices in the Middle Ages were primarily male, apprenticeships were also available for females, primarily in sewing and baking.</u> *2.* The advent of the Industrial Revolution brought a shift in career training. *3.* Many traditional trades such as weaving or shoe making were replaced with machines, so the need for trained, knowledgeable workers [6] <u>dramatic decrease</u>. *4.* Additionally, with the growth of white-collar jobs and the prestige that came with them, interest in apprenticeships dwindled.

4. However, in more recent years, apprenticeships have found new popularity. Rather than replacing higher education, [7] <u>education is now linked with apprenticeship</u>. Multiple industries have begun to offer apprenticeships concurrent with schooling, assisting students in obtaining licenses or certifications. Industries such as construction and electricity have been long known for their apprenticeship programs, but now [8] <u>fields</u> like engineering and technology have begun to offer apprenticeship programs to train and cultivate new team members.

5. What is the best location for this sentence?

A) NO CHANGE
B) after sentence 2
C) after sentence 3
D) DELETE, because this sentence does not fit in this paragraph

6.

A) NO CHANGE
B) dramatic decreasing
C) dramatically decreased
D) decreased with drama

7.

A) NO CHANGE
B) education is once again linked with apprenticeship
C) education is now separate from apprenticeship
D) apprenticeships are now linked with education

8.

A) NO CHANGE
B) apprenticeships
C) schools
D) openings

5. [9] A shorter-term form of apprenticeship is an internship, which can be a matter of weeks or months and which can serve either for experience in a career field or a probationary time of training at the beginning of a job. The swing back toward apprenticeships is opening doors for many to learn valuable skills as well as [10] obtaining an education. Today, apprenticeships offer much more freedom in choosing a profession, as they are open to a variety of ages, can vary widely in duration, and may lead to different levels of certification. As more industries are embracing the concept, a new set of opportunities is rising for the upcoming workforce.

9. In which paragraph does this sentence best fit?

A) NO CHANGE
B) Paragraph 2
C) Paragraph 3
D) Paragraph 4

10.

A) NO CHANGE
B) receiving
C) to obtain
D) how to achieve

Questions 11–20 are based on the following passage.

As you walk into a room, you suddenly experience a "blank" moment, forgetting what you were going to do. Or as you sit in front of an algebra exam, you can't recall the formula even though you knew it just moments before. [11] Memory can be elusive and frustrating. Or it can be surprisingly helpful.

The brain stores memories in a [12] zephyr of ways. Short-term, or working, memory allows a person to store a small amount of information for a matter of seconds. This could include overheard [13] conversations; addresses or phone numbers, or a short shopping list. If an effort is not made to retain the information it will quickly pass from your mind.

11. What is the best way to combine these sentences?

A) NO CHANGE
B) Memory can be elusive and frustrating; or it can be surprisingly helpful.
C) Memory can be elusive and frustrating, or it can be surprisingly helpful.
D) Memory can be elusive and frustrating. Or, it can be surprisingly helpful.

12.

A) NO CHANGE
B) plethora
C) zenith
D) magnanimous

13.

A) NO CHANGE
B) conversations—
C) conversations.
D) conversations,

In contrast, long-term memory stores information for longer periods of time, up to an entire lifetime. This includes data that was encoded into the brain through repetition, like memorizing one's street address as a child, as well as episodic memory, which recalls [14] past events that occurred. While short-term memory utilizes only the frontal and parietal lobes of the brain, long-term memory [15] creates connection's all across the brain, encoding the information in a process known as synaptic consolidation.

Even though long-term memory is considered a permanent process, these memories can still fade if they are not refreshed through maintenance [16] rehearsal, this is periodic review of the memorized material. Other factors, such as sleep, stress, and aging, also [17] effect the permanence of memory.

14.

A) NO CHANGE
B) events that were past
C) events that occurred in the past
D) past events

15.

A) NO CHANGE
B) creates connections
C) creating connection's
D) created connections

16.

A) NO CHANGE
B) rehearsal, it is
C) rehearsal, and it is
D) rehearsal; this is

17.

A) NO CHANGE
B) affect
C) effective
D) affecting

[18] Though some memory decline is inevitable, several techniques can be used to enhance retention. Some types of memory are more deeply engrained than others. Topographic memory involves the ability to recognize where you are and find your way to destinations. Another type is flashbulb memory, which is a detailed recollection of what you were doing at a specific moment in time, [19] occasionally an emotionally charged event. While other long-term memories may need repetition to keep from fading, these tend to stay clear.

Though science has uncovered many of the mysteries surrounding memory, much is left to learn. New research gives insight into the intricate connections in the brain but brings up even more questions. So while you may never know why you forgot a formula you recited ten minutes ago, you may be surprised when an [20] almost-forgotten memory resurfaces at just the right moment.

18. Where is the best location for this sentence?

A) NO CHANGE
B) the end of this paragraph
C) the previous paragraph
D) remove from the selection because it is irrelevant

19.

A) NO CHANGE
B) suddenly
C) usually
D) hesitantly

20.

A) NO CHANGE
B) mostly forgotten
C) nearly-forgotten
D) basically forgotten

Questions 21–30 are based on the following passage.

[21] It was evidenced by the famed cave drawings, art is one of mankind's earliest forms of expression. While art is often viewed as a method to capture beauty or memorialize events, it is also one of the most powerful ways of spreading messages. This can be done through conventional [22] methods, for example advertising, or through more unique ways.

One of these ways is through graffiti. Though graffiti is known today for bold colors spray painted on the [23] outer walls of brick on the buildings, its history can be traced back several centuries. The Italian *graffiato*, [24] from where the word *graffiti* is derived, means "scratched." Early examples of graffiti involved carving designs or words with a sharp object. The term was not originally associated with the stigma of modern graffiti but typically involved designs scratched or drawn on walls.

21.

A) NO CHANGE
B) As
C) Although
D) Even when

22.

A) NO CHANGE
B) methods, for example, advertising
C) methods; like advertising
D) methods, such as advertising

23.

A) NO CHANGE
B) sides of brick buildings
C) brick on the outside walls of some buildings
D) outer parts of the brick on buildings

24.

A) NO CHANGE
B) in which
C) from which
D) from as which

[25] Gradually the purposes and styles of graffiti changed. The modern graffiti that is familiar today emerged in the twentieth century. Major events such as World Wars I and II and the Great Depression were partially responsible for the development. Military achievements, the longing for home, and [26] criticizing political figures inspired soldiers to commemorate their time overseas with various pictures and slogans painted on bombed buildings, tunnel walls, and the bunks in [27] there quarters. These drawings and notes served as reminders of home and loved ones, expression of frustration at the conflict, or boasting of superiority over the opposing side.

25. Which of the following is the best way to introduce this paragraph?

A) NO CHANGE
B) World War I was the first appearance of modern graffiti.
C) The military was responsible for the change in graffiti from ancient to modern.
D) The beauty of ancient graffiti, however, was doomed to be replaced with a new kind of image.

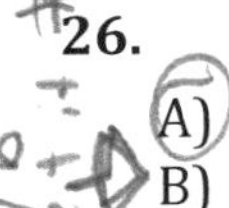

26.

A) NO CHANGE
B) criticism of political figures
C) critically addressing political figures
D) critical viewing political figures

27.

A) NO CHANGE
B) they're
C) their
D) theirs

During the Great Depression, graffiti took a [28] surprising turn. With myriads of people finding themselves unemployed, many traveled by foot to look for work. A system of communication, now known as hoboglyphs, developed among the transient population to share helpful information. For example, an outline of a cat could mean that a sympathetic woman lived on the property and could be approached for a meal, and a shovel could mean that work was available. Conversely, other hoboglyphs warned [29] about: bad-tempered homeowners, dangerous animals, or police officers.

Today, graffiti has a negative connotation, known for its gang associations and for vandalism. But it has a long and rich history, giving glimpses into multiple cultures and time periods. [30] Though not every piece of graffiti tells how to get a free meal, every piece is unique and beautiful.

28.

A) NO CHANGE
B) unusual
C) predictable
D) practical

29.

A) NO CHANGE
B) about—
C) about,
D) about

30. Which of the following would be the best conclusion to the selection?

A) NO CHANGE
B) Graffiti is very different than the earliest examples, and no longer serves a useful purpose.
C) Whether viewed as beauty or vandalism, graffiti is a long-standing and unique way of communicating.
D) Graffiti today is more focused on advertising, rather than the communication that it used to provide.

Questions 31–40 are based on the following passage and supplementary information.

1. Despite the saying, "as American as apple pie," apples [31] origination in Asia. Alexander the Great is said to have found dwarf apples in Kazakhstan in the fourth century BC and brought them back to Europe. From there [32] they were eventually brought, by European colonists, to North America. Since they can be grown in a variety of climates, are hardy, and produce abundant fruit, apple trees flourished in the New World and quickly became a staple on farms. Along with their adaptability to growing conditions, apples can be preserved a variety of [33] ways: drying, canning, and brandy, to name a few.

2. In the late eighteenth century, John Chapman began planting apple trees in Pennsylvania. Traveling west by foot, [34] apple orchards were planted in places he predicted pioneers would settle. Most of these trees bore cider apples rather than fruit that could be eaten fresh, but "Johnny Appleseed" helped spread apples westward.

31.

A) NO CHANGE
B) originally
C) originated
D) origin

32.

A) NO CHANGE
B) European colonists eventually brought them to North America
C) European colonists, to North America, eventually brought them
D) they were eventually brought, to north America, by European colonists

33.

A) NO CHANGE
B) ways; drying, canning, and brandy
C) ways—drying; canning; and brandy
D) ways. Drying, canning, and brandy

34.

A) NO CHANGE
B) he planted apple orchards
C) apple orchards grew
D) apple orchards have been planted

3. Eventually, fruit trees found their way to the west coast, where they thrived. Washington became the nation's apple center, currently producing nearly half of the [35] country's apples (and over half of the fresh apples found in grocery stores). Across the country, farmers began to develop their own breeds, [36] and eventually, thousands of different varieties were grown. Part of this was by selective breeding, and part was a result of growing apples from seed instead of grafting.

4. Grafting allows a person to create a copy of a specific apple tree by taking a small section of the parent tree and grafting it onto another tree or rootstock. Planting seeds, on the other hand, creates a cross between the parent tree and the pollinating tree, which is often unknown, so the apples on these trees are usually different than the apples the seeds came from. While thousands of varieties exist, only 100 are grown [37] commercial and just a handful can be found at the supermarket.

35.

A) NO CHANGE
B) countries
C) countrys
D) countries'

36.

A) NO CHANGE
B) and thousands of different varieties were, eventually, grown
C) eventually growing thousands of different varieties
D) and, eventually, thousands of different varieties were grown

37.

A) NO CHANGE
B) commercially
C) for commercial
D) as commercially

5. Along with their ease of growing, apples offer health benefits. They contain [38] flavonoids, that can help with lowering cholesterol as well as clearing arteries. This fruit can also help prevent heart disease. So while an apple a day [39] is not guaranteed to keep the doctor away, it can help with a healthy lifestyle, as well as participating in an American—and worldwide—tradition.

[40]

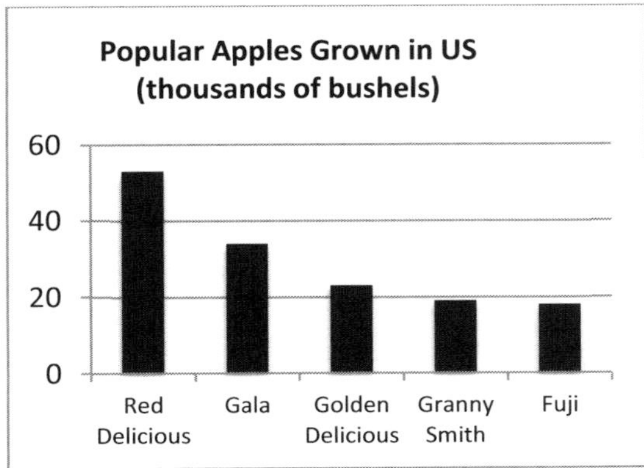

Information in chart taken from US Apple Association, 2011 data.

38.

A) NO CHANGE
B) flavonoids which
C) flavonoids, which
D) flavonoids; that

39.

A) NO CHANGE
B) is no guarantee that the doctor will be kept away
C) does nothing to keep the doctor away
D) does not keep the doctor away, guaranteed

40. Which paragraph is the best location for sharing the information in this chart?

A) NO CHANGE
B) Paragraph 1
C) Paragraph 2
D) Paragraph 4

Math – No Calculator

Questions 1–10 are multiple choice. Questions 11–13 are grid-in.

1. If $6x - 3 = 9$, what is the value of $4x^2$?

A) 4
B) 8
C) 16
D) 64

2. A caterer offers baked chicken, green beans, and rolls. She charges by the following formula, using c for a serving of chicken, b for a serving of green beans, and r for a roll:

$$4c + 2.5b + 1.25r = \text{total cost (in dollars)}$$

What is the cost of 50 servings of chicken, 60 servings of green beans, and 100 rolls?

A) \$475.00
B) \$492.50
C) \$500.00
D) \$525.25

3. Find the ordered pair that solves this system of equations:

$$3x - y = 7$$
$$x + 2y = 0$$

A) $(2, -1)$
B) $(0, -2)$
C) $(-1,3)$
D) $(3, -2)$

4. Find a possible value for m if $x = -3$ and $(3m - x)^2 = 81$.

A) -1
B) 2
C) 3.5
D) 6

5. The graph of a line has a slope of $\frac{1}{2}$ and a y-intercept of -2. A second line has a slope of $-\frac{2}{3}$ and intersects with the first line at $(3, 0)$. What is the y-intercept of the second line?

A) $y = -2$
B) $y = 0$
C) $y = 2$
D) $y = 8$

6. Find the average of the following expressions: $(4 - 2x)$, $(-7 - 3x)$, and $(11x + 6)$.

A) $6x + 3$
B) $2x + 1$
C) $6.3x + 5.6$
D) $7x + 6.5$

7. What is the product of all roots of the equation $2x^2 + 7x - 15$?

A) -8
B) $-\frac{15}{2}$
C) $\frac{3}{2}$
D) 15

8. Given the following data, arrange the mean, mode, and median in increasing order:

15 8 10 8 8 17 12 20 7 9 7

A) Mean, median, mode
B) Mean, mode, median
C) Mode, mean, median
D) Mode, median, mean

9. Zoe works two part-time jobs. The first requires a minimum of 15 hours per week. The second allows a maximum of 18 hours per week. Zoe needs to work at least 30 hours per week to meet her budget needs. Which of the following systems of inequalities represents this information, if x refers to the hours worked at the first job and y refers to the hours worked at the second job?

A) $x + y \geq 30$
$x \geq 15$
$y \leq 18$
B) $30 \leq x + y \leq 33$
$x \geq 15$
$y \leq 18$
C) $x + y = 30$
$x \leq 15$
$y \geq 18$
D) $x + y \leq 30$
$x \leq 15$
$y \geq 18$

10. Tyler's car was worth $6,500 when he purchased it. The car depreciates in value at a constant rate for 10 years, at which point the value is $800. How much is it worth after 3 years?

A) $5,100
B) $4,790
C) $4,460
D) $4,285

11. A company is looking to purchase a robot for their assembly line. Robot A costs $5,000 and produces 3 widgets per hour. Robot B costs $7,250 and produces widgets at a rate 25% faster than Robot A. At $3 of profit per widget, how many hours would it take for Robot B to be worth buying?

Grid your answer.

12. In the system of equations below, x and y are variables while m is a constant. For which value of m does the system have no solution?

$$6x - 3y = 7$$
$$3x - my = 5$$

Grid your answer.

13. What is the value of k in the equation below?

$$4(k - 2) + 5\,(4 - k) = 3k$$

Grid your answer.

Math – Calculator

Questions 1–21 are multiple choice. Questions 22–25 are grid-in.

1. An electronics store tracks the number of Blu-ray players sold. According to the graph below, when was the greatest drop in sales?

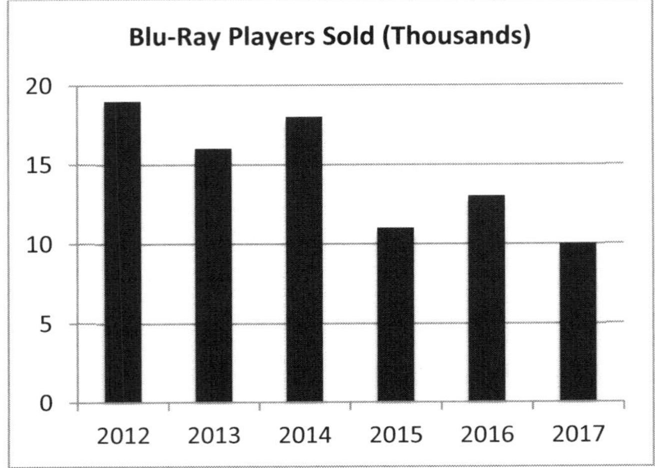

A) 2012–2013
B) 2013–2014
C) 2014–2015
D) 2015–2016

2. Xander takes piano lessons and learns 3 new pieces every month. If he has learned 9 pieces so far, which of the following represents the number of pieces Xander will have learned x months from now?

A) $9 + 3x$
B) $9 - 3x$
C) $3 + 9x$
D) $12 + 3x$

3. Raquel is filling pitchers with juice. If each pitcher holds 2 quarts, how many gallons does she need to fill 28 pitchers? (1 gallon = 4 quarts)

A) 7
B) 14
C) 28
D) 112

4. If $4(x + y) = 6$, what is the value of $x + y$?

A) 2
B) 3
C) $\frac{2}{3}$
D) $\frac{3}{2}$

5. Mackenzie buys a number of tomato and pepper plants for her garden. Tomato plants cost \$3 each and pepper plants cost \$4 each. If she pays a total of \$34 and buys 4 pepper plants, how many tomato plants does she purchase?

A) 7
B) 6
C) 5
D) 4

6. In 4th grade, Juan was 4 feet, 7.5 inches. Now he is 6 feet, 1 inch. How many inches has he grown?

A) 15.5
B) 16.5
C) 17.5
D) 18.5

7. Thomas is planning to sell his collection of vinyl records. He currently has a total of a records and anticipates selling k per month. Which function best represents the number of records, r, Thomas still owns after m months?

A) $r = a + k$
B) $r = a + km$
C) $r = a - k$
D) $r = a - km$

8. Mikayla plots the graph of the equation $y = 3x - 2$. Which of the following equations is perpendicular to this?

A) $-x + 3y = 2$
B) $x + 3y = \frac{3}{2}$
C) $3x - y = 7$
D) $3x + y = \frac{5}{3}$

9. Which of the following ordered pairs satisfies this system of inequalities?

$$y \geq \frac{1}{2}x - 2$$
$$x + y < 5$$

A) $(0,3)$
B) $(-2,7)$
C) $(3,2)$
D) $(4,-1)$

10. Rob had two history projects to complete. The first took half as long as the second. He spent a total of 462 minutes on the two projects. How much time did he spend on the second project?

A) 308 minutes
B) 231 minutes
C) 154 minutes
D) 77 minutes

11. For the system of equations below, what is the value of $x - y$?

$$4x - 7y = 15$$
$$9x + 7y = 11$$

A) 9
B) 6
C) 3
D) 1

12. Which of the following is equivalent to $(3.2a - 4.1)^2 - (3.9a^2 + 2.8)$?

A) $10.24a^2 - 26.24a + 16.81$
B) $6.34a^2 - 26.24a + 14.01$
C) $10.24a^2 - 13.12a + 16.81$
D) $6.34a^2 - 13.12a + 14.01$

13. Sugar cookie dough is shaped into a circle with a diameter of 5.4 cm. When it is baked, its diameter is 6.3 cm. What is the ratio of the perimeter after baking to the perimeter before baking?

A) $1.1\overline{6}$
B) $1.\overline{3}$
C) 1.25
D) $1.\overline{16}$

Questions 14–15 refer to the following information:

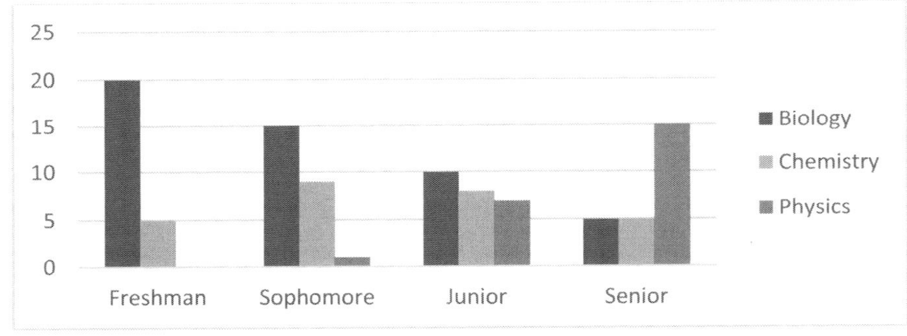

Students at CHS are required to take at least two science classes to graduate. Twenty-five students from each grade are taking science classes this year.

14. How many more of the physics students are seniors than are freshmen?

A) 20
B) 17
C) 12
D) 15

15. Which of the following formulas could be used to describe the change in the number of biology students per year, where y is the number of students taking biology and x is the grade level (Freshman = 1, Sophomore = 2, etc.)?

A) $y = 5x + 20$
B) $y = 5x - 25$
C) $y = -5x + 25$
D) $y = -5x - 0$

16.Find an expression for the area of ΔMNP below.

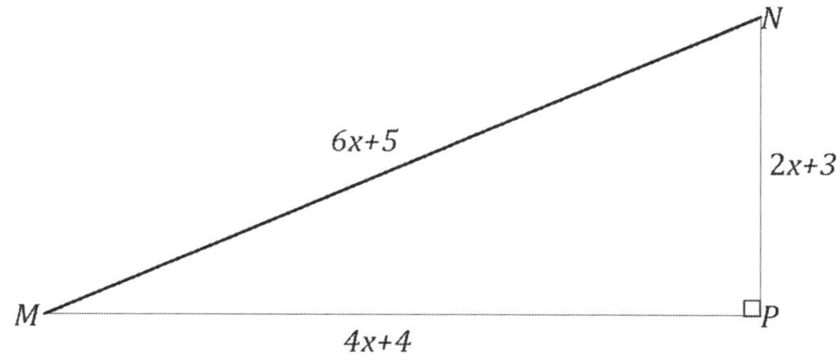

A) $8x^2 + 20x + 12$
B) $12x + 12$
C) $36x^2 + 60x + 25$
D) $4x^2 + 10x + 6$

17. In the equation below, $x < -1$. Which of the following is a possible value for k?

$$\mathbf{k = -2x + 6}$$

A) $k = 9$
B) $k = 8$
C) $k = 7$
D) k can take any value

18. A particular field is shaped such that a semicircle caps each end of a rectangle that is 100 m by 200 m as shown. What is the perimeter of this field to the nearest meter. ($\pi \approx 3.14$)

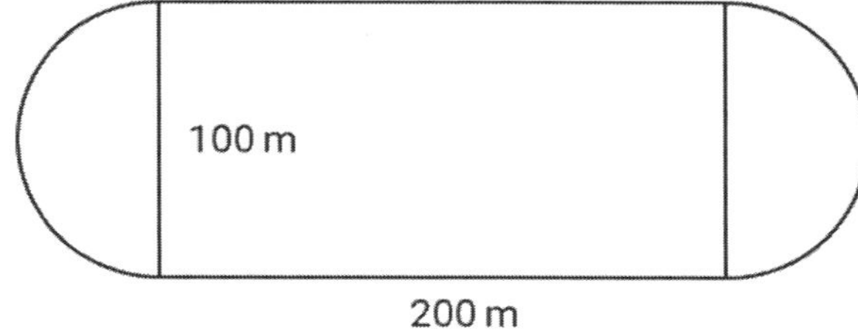

A) 557 m
B) 714 m
C) 8,250 m
D) 27,850 m

19. Trey harvested 24 pumpkins and weighed each one. The mean weight was 7 lb 8 oz and the median weight was 7 lb 9 oz. The largest pumpkin weighed 10 lb 5 oz and the smallest was 7 lb 1 oz. Which of the following conclusions is best supported by the data?

A) The smallest pumpkin is an outlier.
B) The largest pumpkin is an outlier.
C) Most of the pumpkins weighed less than 7 lb 8 oz.
D) Most of the pumpkins weighed more than 7 lb 9 oz.

Questions 20–21 refer to the following information:

Mr. Smith graded his midterm exams and charted them. He also calculated each student's cumulative course grade.

Exam grade	82	83	79	84	68	96
Course grade	86	85	79	92	77	96

20. Based on the chart above, what is the median exam grade?

A) 82
B) 82.5
C) 83
D) 83.5

21. Which of the following conclusions correlates with the data?

A) The exam was more difficult than the rest of the course assignments.
B) The students studied more for this exam than others.
C) The exam was graded on a curve.
D) The exam was a large percentage of the course grade.

22. A class trip cost a total of $414, including a museum ticket and lunch for each student. Three students were sick on the day of the trip and did not attend, so the total cost dropped to $360. How many students went on the trip?

Grid your answer

23. What is the slope of a line that goes through the points $\left(-\frac{15}{2}, 6\right)$, $\left(\frac{3}{2}, -2\right)$, and $(-3, 2)$?

Grid your answer.

24. Each molecule of carbon dioxide has one atom of carbon and two atoms of oxygen. If each atom of oxygen has an atomic weight of approximately 16 atomic mass units (amu), how many amu of oxygen are in 225 molecules of carbon dioxide?

Grid your answer.

25. A swimming pool is being filled by a hose at a rate of 7 gallons per minute. If it takes 28 minutes to fill the last 20% of the pool, how many gallons does the pool hold?

Grid your answer.

Answer Key and Explanations for Test #1

Reading Test

1. Choice A is the best answer. The phrase found in line 1, "It is a truth universally acknowledged" means that something is understood to be true by the general public. A modern version of the same idea is known as a "universal truth."

2. Choice A is the best answer. Mrs. Bennet feels that Mr. Bingley is likely to marry one of her daughters. She tells her husband in lines 37-39 that Mr. Bingley is a "single man of large fortune; four or five thousand a year. What a fine thing for our girls!"

3. Choice A is the best answer. In lines 47-49, Mrs. Bennet remarks to her husband, "But it is very likely that he may fall in love with one of them, and therefore you must visit him as soon as he comes."

4. Choice B is the best answer. Mrs. Bennet is annoyed and fed up with her husband's seeming indifferent to Mr. Bingley. This is supported in lines 41-42, where Mrs. Bennet says: "'My dear Mr. Bennet,' replied his wife, 'how can you be so tiresome!'"

5. Choice A is the best answer. Mr. Bennet is facetiously asking if the idea of marriage (particularly to one of his own daughters) was Mr. Bingley's intention when he agreed to rent Netherfield Park. Choices B, C, and D do not fit the context.

6. Choice B is the best answer. Choices A, C, and D are wrong because there is no indication in the passage that the Bennets are interested in becoming friends with Mr. Bingley, that Mr. Bingley would be a valuable business connection, or that Mr. Bingley has any prior knowledge of the Bennet daughters. In lines 24-26, Mrs. Bennet tells her husband that a new neighbor is moving in: "Mrs. Long says that Netherfield is taken by a young man of large fortune." Mrs. Bennet is sure he will make an excellent husband for one of her daughters: "You must know that I am thinking of his marrying one of them."

7. Choice B is the best answer. The evidence in this selection indicates that marrying a man with money was a primary goal for young women. In lines 37-39, Mrs. Bennet tells Mr. Bennet that Mr. Bingley is "A single man of large fortune; four or five thousand a year." Mrs. Bennet further indicates that she is thrilled with the news because of Mr. Bingley's potential as a husband for one of her daughters in lines 39 and 42-44: "What a fine thing for our girls... You must know that I am thinking of his marrying one of them."

8. Choice D is the best answer. Although the tone of the passage is light-hearted, and there is no indication that Mr. Bennet is concerned about interloping men, one of his statements could be taken to mean that he fears his wife becoming a love interest for another man. In the selection indicated, Mr. Bennet says it may be better for Mrs. Bennet to send their daughters by themselves to visit Mr. Bingley rather than accompanying them, because, as Mr. Bennet states, Mrs. Bennet is "as handsome as any of them" and Mr. Bingley might be more attracted to her than to the daughters.

9. Choice D is the best answer. The sentence found in lines 11-13 provide the evidence: "It ended the life of the poor lad, but only tore a hole in Clara Barton's sleeve." Clara was not wounded; the bullet missed her. The boy, however, was not merely wounded but killed.

10. Choice B is the best answer. While the other choices may have some truth to them, there is no evidence in the text that the soldier had little money (choice A). Choices C and D give only partial answers.

11. Choice D is the best answer. From the context of this passage, the surgeon's hospitals were not all destroyed, as in choice A, as he continued to treat the wounded. The surgeon is described as old, but nothing indicates he was near dying himself, as in choice B. Although a great many soldiers died in the Civil War, not all of them who were treated died, as in choice C, and nothing in the passage indicates all of this particular surgeon's patients died. In this context, "the very jaws of death" refers to treating wounded soldiers on (or directly adjacent to) battlefields, as is indicated in choice D.

12. Choice A is the best answer. In lines 40-48 the text indicates that the "rebel fire was hottest, the shells rolling down every street, and the bridge under the heavy cannonade" and "a courier... placed in my hand a crumpled, bloody piece of paper, a request from the lion-hearted old surgeon on the opposite shore, establishing his hospitals in the very jaws of death." Both indicate that the soldiers knew that the situation was dangerous, no place for an unarmed lady.

13. Choice B is the best answer. The sentence in lines 61-65 ("'Over into that city...blazing line of forts.") uses parallelism/parallel structure in a series of phrases beginning with *every*; i.e., "its every church a crowded hospital, every street a battle-line, every hill a rampart..." The repeated structure and words reinforce the description, emphasizing the visual evidence that the *city of death* was a war zone. Alliteration, choice A, is repeating the same sounds across words. Paradoxes, choice C, combine contradictory concepts to convey deeper insight. Periphrasis, choice D, is deliberately using verbiage for grandiose effect, embellishment, and/or distraction from meaning.

14. Choice C is the best answer. In the context of lines 96-99 ("With a rare...United States."), "rare" means occurring seldomly or infrequently. As in choice A, unusually great is another meaning of "rare," e.g., a rare show of bravery. Fine or precious and admirable as found in choices B and D are other meanings of "rare," but the context describing Barton's courage, dedication, and seriousness informs the correct meaning here.

15. Choice C is the best answer. *Noble* and *gallant* are evidence of positive feelings toward the North. Choice A is evidence of Barton's care for both sides' soldiers. Choice B is evidence of the large numbers and unceasing action of Union troops, not positive feelings toward them. Choice D is evidence of personal experience with war casualties.

16. Choice C is the best answer. The author mentions that men had been shot while Clara lived, demonstrating an interesting dichotomy of her life: the unarmed nurse who was protected on the battlefield, while the armed men did not seem to be.

17. Choice A is the best answer. The text mentions Clara being helpful during several battles. While she may have helped throughout the Civil War, it is not the topic here. Choice C focuses more on other nurses in the war, and choice D doesn't make sense because Clara was on the battlefield when the fighting was taking place.

18. Choice B is the best answer. The entire passage makes the argument that Black History Month should be abolished, offering various reasons why this is the best course of action. One example can be found in lines 37-39 ("knowledge imparted...for all people").

19. Choice D is the best answer. The context of the sentence suggests that post-racial refers to an approach in which race is not a useful or positive organizing principle.

20. Choice D is the best answer. The author of Passage 1 never suggests that people do not learn about African American history during Black History Month.

21. Choice C is the best answer. The author points out in lines 20-25 of Passage 2 ("Equally important…parents would want.") that the debate about how to meet the need to teach children about African American history can remind parents that this need is not yet fully met.

22. Choice A is the best answer. The author of Passage 2 believes that including Black History Month in the curriculum is very important and could suggest that continued education on black history has helped pushed more African Americans to pursue higher education as understanding has spread. The other answer choices are not directly supported by either the passage or the information contained in the table.

23. Choice B is the best answer. The evidence for this answer can be found in lines 37-49 ("In 1926…February 21, 1965.") of Passage 2, where it states that W.E.B. DuBois was born in 1868; his birth was therefore the first of the identified events. The 15th amendment, choice A, was passed in 1870. The establishment of Black History Month, choice C, took place in 1926. Finally, choice D, the NAACP was founded in 1909. This places the birth of W.E.B. DuBois, choice B, first chronologically.

24. Choice D is the best answer. Clearly both authors think it is important for students to learn about the achievements and experience of African Americans; their debate is whether observing Black History Month is the best way to achieve this goal.

25. Choice C is the best answer. The author of Passage 2 points out that just because there is a month focused on African American history, this doesn't mean that African American history must be ignored for the rest of the year.

26. Choice A is the best answer. Solar radiation is not listed as a component of comet nuclei, but dust, frozen gases, and rock are each mentioned in lines 13-16 ("Comet nuclei…kilometers across.").

27. Choice B is the best answer. Lines 2-3 ("They are distinguishable…comas or tails") note that comets are distinguishable from asteroids by the presence of comas or tails. Choices A, C, and D are not mentioned as an explanation of the differences between comets and asteroids.

28. Choice B is the best answer. A comet with an orbit of longer than 200 years is a long period comet, according to lines 43-45, where it states that "…long period comets have orbital periods of more than 200 years."

29. Choice C is the best answer. Line 20 notes that "there are over 3,500 known comets." Lines 21-23 also state that this represents only a small portion of those in existence.

30. Choice A is the best answer. Lines 13-16 ("Comet nuclei…kilometers across") state that some comets may be tens of kilometers across. The passage also notes that comas may be larger than the sun.

31. Choice D is the best answer. Line 37 notes that most comets have oval shaped orbits.

32. Choice D is the best answer. The passage defines single apparition comets as those whose trajectories make them pass the Sun once and then exit our solar system permanently. It also describes most comets as having oval orbits wherein they are nearer to the Sun during part of their orbit, and then move farther away from the Sun *within the solar system* for the rest of the orbit;

hence, choice A is incorrect. While single apparition comets are only apparent once, they are NOT still in the solar system.

33. Choice A is the best answer. Lines 17-19 state, "Because of their low mass, they do not become spherical and have irregular shapes." Lines 13-16 ("Comet nuclei...kilometers across") identify the content of comet nuclei, but these contents are not given as evidence of low mass. Lines 19-21 states that "the comas may be even larger than the sun"), identifying how large the comas can be, but does not use size as evidence of low mass. Lines 13-16 ("Comet nuclei...kilometers across") indicate variability in size, but this is not given as evidence of low mass.

34. Choice D is the best answer. Lines 28-30 in the passage state, "If a comet's path crosses the Earth's path, there will likely be meteor showers as Earth passes through the trail of debris." Lines 31-32 state that "many comets and asteroids have collided with the Earth" (choice A), but they do not say this can cause meteor showers. Nothing in the passage identifies large groups of meteors entering Earth's atmosphere (choice B) as causing meteor showers. Choice C is wrong because there is no mention of a comet exploding.

35. Choice D is the best answer. Following the quoted sentence, the passage author identifies the current periodic table groups by their numbers, which are Arabic numerals 1-18. The names of individual elements (choice A), e.g., helium, calcium, gold, silver, argon, etc., are NOT the current group naming convention; their *group numbers* are. The groups are not named using lower-case letters (choice B). Roman numerals (choice C) are identified as a *previous* group naming convention, but not the current one.

36. Choice C is the best answer. This selection first explains that the outer electron shell's configuration has a primary effect on the chemical properties of an element and then concludes that the periodic table's groups contain chemically similar elements. Choice B identifies the groups as containing elements with similar outer electron shell configurations; but without the explanation from Choice C that those similar configurations of their outer electron shells signify similar chemical properties, this sentence alone is not evidence that groups in the periodic table are chemically similar. Choice A describes cells, not groups, in the periodic table. Choice D describes how one chemical property, ionization energy, increases across periods and decreases down groups, not how groups are chemically similar.

37. Choice D is the best answer. Lines 55-71 ("Atomic radii ... point decreases") describe the change of atomic radii with the arrangement of both group and period. Choice A is wrong because the selection describes what information can be found on a single cell of the periodic table. Choices B and C do not describe the relationship between a property and its arrangement in both groups and periods.

38. Choice B is the best answer. Lines 12-14 ("Cells in the table ... (groups or families)") define rows as periods and columns as groups. Since rows are horizontal and columns are vertical, the reader infers the directionality of periods and groups from this information. Choice A is the reverse of the correct choice. Cells are not called periods or rows called groups (Choice C); the description in lines 12-14 states that cells are arranged in periods, which are rows, and in groups, which are columns. Therefore, Choice D is incorrect.

39. Choice A is the best answer. The periodic trends described are mainly patterns of increasing or decreasing across periods and from top to bottom in groups. Since increases and decreases are progressive linear changes, and since these occur in horizontal or vertical order, the relationship they depict is sequential. Although cause-and-effect underlies these trends, meaning that they occur because of the elements' atomic structures and periodic nature and the periodic table's corresponding arrangement, the trends themselves do not show a cause-effect relationship. For example, electronegativity or other properties named increase or decrease in sequence across periods/down groups; a change in the quantity or quality of a property in one cell of a period or group is not an effect caused by the previous cell. The relationship is not parts to whole, which might involve something like the similar chemical properties of all elements within one group rather than sequences of change throughout groups and periods. Comparison-contrast would involve distinct similarities and differences between/among parts of the table rather than progressive sequences of increasing or decreasing properties.

40. Choice A is the best answer. Based on the descriptions in lines 55-71 ("Atomic radii ... point decreases"), an inverse relationship often occurs between periods and groups in terms of periodic trends; i.e., as one increases, the other decreases and vice versa. The reader might infer this from the information that atomic radii decrease across rows but increase down groups, electronegativity increases across periods but decreases down groups, and ionization energy increases across periods but decreases down groups. The information that electronic affinity increases in negativity across periods but changes little within groups shows that an inverse relationship is not necessarily or always the case. In a converse relationship, such properties would both increase or both decrease both across periods and down groups. The passage does not identify this.

41. Choice C is the best answer. The lines 38-42 ("In the periodic ... next section)" identify the number of electrons in the outer shell as determining which group an element belongs to in a block. The passage never identifies an element's atomic number as determining an element's group. The number assigned to each period does not *determine* an element's group in a block; rather, as the passage states, this period number *corresponds to* and represents the highest-numbered (outer) electron shell in use. Group numbers label each group for reference; the passage does not identify group numbers as *determining* the group where an element belongs.

42. Choice D is the best answer. The purpose of this passage is to explain how the periodic table works, how it is organized, the conventions it uses, and some trends in chemical properties that can be identified in its organization. The other choices are all subordinate topics within this main purpose. For example, Choice A is addressed in lines 21-28 ("In the periodic ... chemical properties"). Choice C is addressed in one sentence: "It is a common model for organizing and understanding elements." Periods and groups are major organizational features of the periodic table and are discussed throughout, but they are still individual components within the larger purpose of explaining the periodic table overall.

Writing and Language

1. Choice D is the best answer. This sentence is in past tense, so only "began" fits grammatically. "Begun" (A) is a past participle and must be used with an auxiliary verb such as "have." "Had begun" (B) is also a past participle, which indicates an ongoing action, and "begin" (C) is present tense.

2. Choice C is the best answer. The reflexive pronoun "himself" is needed here since the subject and object of the sentence are the same. "Him" (A) would refer to a different object, "his" (B) is a possessive pronoun and not appropriate as the object, and "themselves" (D) is plural rather than singular.

3. Choice A is the best answer. The sentence is saying that the custom of apprenticeship is making a comeback due to the need for trade skills, and "resurgence" accurately describes this. It would be incorrect to say that the custom is dwindling (B), shrinking (C), or being forgotten (D).

4. Choice B is the best answer. The correct verbiage to pair with "not only" is "but also." It conveys addition rather than contrast (A and C). The phrase "and even" (D) gives the idea of addition but is not grammatically correct.

5. Choice D is the best answer. This paragraph focuses on the decrease in apprenticeships, so information about apprenticeships in the Middle Ages is irrelevant, though it might have been appropriate in the previous paragraph.

6. Choice C is the best answer. The subject of the clause (need) must have a verb to be complete, and the verb needs to be past tense to fit with the rest of the sentence. Additionally, this verb can only be modified by an adverb. Thus only "dramatically decreased" can be correct. Answer choice A is an adjective and a noun. Answer choice B is an adjective and a participle. Answer choice D uses a past tense verb but states it in an awkward and confusing way.

7. Choice D is the best answer. The introductory clause seems to be modifying "education," but it should be modifying "apprenticeships." We can see that it is referring to something other than education, something that used to take the place of education. Thus "education" cannot be the subject, making A, B, and C incorrect. The subject is "apprenticeship," so this subject must be stated first after the comma.

8. Choice A is the best answer. The sentence is referring to the industries, or fields, of engineering and technology. It is not making reference to specific apprenticeships (B), schools (C), or job openings (D).

9. Choice D is the best answer. The information about internships best fits in the 4th paragraph, which discusses present-day apprenticeships. The 2nd and 3rd paragraphs (B and C) discuss the past history of apprenticeships. The current paragraph (A) is the summary paragraph, which is not a good time to introduce new information.

10. Choice C is the best answer. Using the infinitive (to obtain) matches the structure earlier in the sentence (to learn). "Obtaining" (A) or "receiving" (B) is a participle rather than the necessary verb. "How to achieve" (D) changes the meaning, as the sentence is not discussing how the education is achieved but merely that apprenticeships aid in the achievement.

11. Choice C is the best answer. Separating it into two sentences (A and D) makes it choppy, and starting with a conjunction creates a dependent clause, which should not be a standalone sentence.

Combining the two clauses with a semicolon (B) is incorrect because the second clause is dependent and semicolons are used to separate independent clauses (stand-alone sentences).

12. Choice B is the best answer. The sentence is discussing that memories can be stored in a variety of ways. The word "plethora" (B) means a large amount, so it makes sense. "Zephyr" (A) means a gentle breeze, "zenith" (B) means the high point of the sun as it travels across the sky, and "magnanimous" (D) means generous. None of these choices makes sense with the sentence.

13. Choice D is the best answer. This sentence lists three examples of short-term memory. They should be separated by commas. A semicolon (A) should only be used in a list for clarity if components of the list have internal commas. A dash (B) is inappropriate because the clause following the dash is not a definition or explanation of the previous part. A period (C) is inappropriate because the part after the punctuation is not a complete sentence.

14. Choice D is the best answer. It is redundant to say "past events that occurred" (A), since by definition past events are events that have occurred. Answer choices B and C are also unnecessarily verbose. Answer choice D is the only one that is succinct.

15. Choice B is the best answer. The sentence is referring to plural connections, not to anything the connections possess, so answer choices A and C are incorrect. The sentence is in present tense, so answer choice D is incorrect.

16. Choice D is the best answer. The parts of the sentence before and after the punctuation are both complete sentences, so they should be separated by a semicolon or period. Separating with a comma (A and B) makes them comma-splices. Using a comma with a conjunction (C) is grammatically correct, but the sentence does not make sense with this wording so it is incorrect.

17. Choice B is the best answer. "Affect" is a verb, while "effect" (A) is a noun. Since it is used as a verb here, answer choice B is correct. The words "effective" (C) and "affecting" (D) are an adjective and participle, respectively, and do not fit grammatically.

18. Choice C is the best answer. The previous paragraph discusses the problem of memory decline, so it would be a fitting location for a discussion on retention techniques.

19. Choice C is the best answer. The sentence is describing a type of event that typically evokes strong emotions. The best word to describe this is "usually." The other words do not fit the meaning.

20. Choice A is the best answer. The words "almost" and "forgotten" are combined to create an adjective. A hyphen is typically used to connect the words in this case. Answer choices B, C, and D are incorrect because they all start with consonants, which are improper following "an."

21. Choice B is the best answer. Answer choice A is incorrect because it is a comma splice. Each clause is independent, or a complete sentence, so they cannot be connected by a comma. Answer choices C and D are incorrect because the meaning does not fit. The first clause is providing support for the main idea in the second clause, and using "Although" or "Even so" sets up a contrast. Answer choice B is the only one that fits grammatically and logically.

22. Choice D is the best answer. The phrase "for example" is a conjunctive adverb and must be preceded by a semicolon, so answer choices A and B are incorrect. The preposition "like," (C) on the other hand, should be preceded by a comma. The phrase "such as" is also a preposition and should be preceded by a comma, so answer choice D is correct.

23. Choice B is the best answer. This answer choice is clear and concise. The other choices all contain excess verbiage and convoluted structure, making them difficult to understand.

24. Choice C is the best answer. The correct phrase is "from which." Using the word "where" (A) is incorrect because the sentence is not referring to a location. Using "in which" (B) is incorrect because it refers to a location or situation. The phrase "from as which" (D) is not grammatically correct.

25. Choice A is the best answer. The previous paragraph discusses the origins of graffiti in ancient times, and the current paragraph discusses the beginning of modern graffiti, specifically in wartime. So the paragraph introduction should transition between these two subjects. Answer choices B and C make unsupported claims and do not acknowledge the previous paragraph. Answer choice D states an opinion, namely that ancient graffiti was beautiful and modern graffiti is not. Answer choice A signals a change from the previous topic and sets up a new topic.

26. Choice B is the best answer. This sentence begins with a list of nouns or clauses acting as nouns. Answer choice A serves as a verb, so it does not fit with the rest of the list. Answer choice C also serves as a verb and is not logical, since most of the graffiti artists were not actually addressing political figures. Answer choice D is grammatically incorrect without "of" following "viewing." Answer choice B serves as a noun, fitting with the rest of the list.

27. Choice C is the best answer. Here, the term is possessive, so "their" is the correct choice. "There" (A) refers to a specific location and "they're" (B) is a contraction of "they are." "Theirs" (D) is also possessive but functions as an object (e.g., "Those bunks are *theirs*.") rather than an adjective.

28. Choice D is the best answer. The point of the sentence is that during the Great Depression, graffiti was used not just for artistic expression but for passing messages. This is a practical use. It could possibly be considered surprising (A) or unusual (B), but this is conjecture and rather vague. The change is not predictable (C), as the Great Depression and the consequent use of graffiti were not expected by many.

29. Choice D is the best answer. It is common to precede a list with a colon (A), but this is only correct if the part of the sentence before the colon is an independent clause (a stand-alone sentence). In fact, no punctuation is necessary or correct after a preposition, so answer choice D is the only possibility.

30. Choice C is the best answer. To write an effective closing statement, it is helpful to look back to the opening and the main ideas from the body paragraphs. The opening paragraph speaks of art as a way to pass messages. The body paragraphs give the history of ancient graffiti and uses during war and the Great Depression. There is also discussion of the changing purposes and views of graffiti. Answer choice A refers back to the paragraph about the Great Depression but does not connect to the main idea of graffiti as a way of spreading a message. Answer choice B restates the idea that graffiti has changed over time but adds an opinion statement that is neither justified nor applicable in this selection. Answer choice D makes a statement that is unsupported and does not capture the main idea. Only answer choice C restates the main idea of graffiti as a way to share a message.

31. Choice C is the best answer. We need a past-tense verb to complete the sentence. An adverb (B) or noun (A, D) does not fit. Only choice C is a past-tense verb.

32. Choice B is the best answer. Good writing is clear and concise. Answer choices A and C use confusing sentence structure, which makes it difficult for the reader to understand. Answer choice D would be fairly clear without the commas but is written in passive voice, so it is not as strong as answer choice B.

33. Choice A is the best answer. This list should be preceded by a colon since the part of the sentence before the list is an independent clause. Items in a list are separated by commas unless one or more of the items has an embedded comma.

34. Choice B is the best answer. As written (A), this sentence has a dangling modifier. The subject referenced in "Traveling west by foot" is John Chapman, so his name or a pronoun referring to him needs to be the subject of the following clause. Only answer choice B correctly uses "he" as the subject, rather than "apple orchards."

35. Choice A is the best answer. A possessive singular adjective is needed in this sentence. It is not referring to multiple countries (B and D), and answer choice C is grammatically incorrect.

36. Choice C is the best answer. Answer choices A, B, and D each use passive voice rather than a strong verb. This is not only weaker writing but can make comprehension more difficult. In addition, each of these choices uses unnecessary commas, which can also make comprehension more challenging.

37. Choice B is the best answer. We need an adverb to modify the verb "grown." Answer choice A is an adjective, as is answer choice C (though "for commercial purposes" would be acceptable). Answer choice D includes an adverb, but with "as" it does not fit grammatically.

38. Choice C is the best answer. "That" is considered a *restrictive* term. In other words, it is used to introduce information that is essential to the meaning and grammatical structure of the sentence. Because it is an essential part of the sentence, no comma or other punctuation precedes these restrictive clauses, so answer choices A and D are incorrect. "Which" often introduces a *nonrestrictive* clause—information that is relevant but not essential. In the sentence in question, the first clause ("They contain flavonoids") is a stand-alone sentence. The second clause adds meaning but is not essential, so it is nonrestrictive. Thus we use "which." Nonrestrictive clauses are preceded by commas, so answer choice B is incorrect.

39. Choice A is the best answer. Answer choice A is the most straightforward and clear. Answer choice B words the information in a more confusing and passive way. Answer choice C contradicts the information in the previous sentences, as does answer choice D.

40. Choice D is the best answer. The chart gives information on what kinds of apples are most grown in the US, as of 2011. The two paragraphs that mention the varieties of apples are paragraphs 3 and 4. Since paragraph 3 is not an answer choice, we know that paragraph 4 is the correct answer. Also, examination of those two paragraphs shows that paragraph 3 refers more to varieties developed over the years on farms, while paragraph 4 refers to the number of varieties that can currently be found at grocery stores, so the chart is more relevant to paragraph 4.

Math – No Calculator

1. Choice C is correct. First, we solve for x with the first equation. We add 3 to each side to yield $6x = 12$, then divide each side by 6 to find that $x = 2$. Then we plug in 2 for x in the second equation. We first square 2, which is 4, and then multiply by 4, which yields 16.

2. Choice A is correct. We fill in 50 for c, 60 for b, and 100 for r in the equation, so $4(50) + 2.5(60) + 100(1.25) = 475$, or $475.00.

3. Choice A is correct. We can solve the system of equations by elimination. Because the y-value is positive in one equation and negative in the other, and the values are small, it is the easiest variable to eliminate. We begin by multiplying every term in the top equation by 2 to obtain $6x - 2y = 14$. Then we add the two equations together so that the y-terms are eliminated and we are left with $7x = 14$. We divide each side by 7 to find that $x = 2$. Then we can plug 2 in for x in one of the original equations. Using the first equation: $3(2) - y = 7$, or $6 - y = 7$. We then subtract 6 from each side and switch the sign to find that $y = -1$. We can plug the pair $(2, -1)$ into the second equation to verify: $2 + 2(-1) = 0$.

4. Choice B is correct. We solve by first taking the square root of each side, yielding:

$$3m - x = \pm 9$$

We can plug in –3 for x to obtain:

$$\begin{aligned} 3m - (-3) &= \pm 9 \\ 3m + 3 &= \pm 9 \end{aligned}$$

We solve for the 2 possible solutions:

$$\begin{aligned} 3m + 3 &= 9 \\ 3m &= 6 \\ m &= 2 \end{aligned} \qquad \begin{aligned} 3m + 3 &= -9 \\ 3m &= -12 \\ m &= -4 \end{aligned}$$

Only 2 is a possible answer choice, so B is the correct choice.

5. Choice C is correct. The information in the first sentence is unnecessary to solve the problem. We have the slope of a line and a point it goes through, so we can find the y-intercept with no other information. We first find the equation of the line, using the formula $y = mx + b$. The slope is m, and we plug in the values from the point for x and y: $0 = \left(-\frac{2}{3}\right)(3) + b$. When we solve for b, which is the y-intercept, we find that $b = 2$. So, the y-intercept is $y = 2$.

6. Choice B is correct. To find the average, we must first add the expressions together and then divide by the number of expressions:

$$\frac{(4 - 2x) + (-7 - 3x) + (11x + 6)}{3}$$

Combine like terms and simplify:

$$\frac{(-2x - 3x + 11x) + (4 - 7 + 6)}{3} = \frac{6x + 3}{3} = 2x + 1$$

7. Choice B is correct. We need to solve the equation for the roots, so first we check to see if the equation can be factored. We can write $(2x\pm?)(x\pm?)$. Then we find the factors of –15 to test. For instance, we could write $(2x+15)(x-1)$, since $15(-1)=-15$, but multiplying this out with FOIL for the middle terms will not yield $7x$. When we multiply $(2x-3)(x+5)$, the middle terms are $10x$ and $-3x$, which add up to $7x$, so this is our solution. We then take the two terms and set them equal to zero to solve for the roots:

$$\begin{aligned} 2x-3&=0 \\ 2x&=3 \\ x&=\frac{3}{2} \end{aligned} \qquad\qquad \begin{aligned} x+5&=0 \\ x&=-5 \end{aligned}$$

Finally, we multiply the roots to find the product: $\frac{3}{2}(-5)=-\frac{15}{2}$.

8. Choice D is correct. We need to find each of the values. The mean (average) of the data is the sum of the values divided by the number of values:

$$\frac{15+8+10+8+8+17+12+20+7+9+7}{11}=\frac{121}{11}=11$$

The mode is the most frequently occurring value, which in this case is 8. The median is the middle of the data when it is put in order:

$$7 \quad 7 \quad 8 \quad 8 \quad 8 \quad \underline{9} \quad 10 \quad 12 \quad 15 \quad 17 \quad 20$$

In this case, the median is 9. Since $8<9<11$, the order is mode, median, mean.

9. Choice A is correct. The first job (x) requires 15 or more hours per week. We can represent this with $x\geq 15$. Conversely, the second job (y) requires 18 or fewer hours per week, so $y\leq 18$. Zoe needs a total of 30 hours or more from the jobs combined, so $x+y\geq 30$.

10. Choice B is correct. The car drops in value by the same amount every year for 10 years, from \$6,500 to \$800. We subtract these two numbers to find that the car loses a total of \$5,700 in value. We can divide this value by 10 to find that the car loses \$570 in value every year. In 3 years, it would lose $570(3)=\$1{,}710$. We can subtract this amount from the original value to obtain $\$6{,}500-\$1{,}710=\$4{,}790$.

11. The correct answer is 1000. First, we need to find the rate at which Robot B produces widgets: $1.25\times 3=3.75$ widgets per hour. Now, if we set h as the number of hours the robots operate, we can set up the two equations and find when they are equivalent using the form, (profit per widget) × (widgets per hour) × (hours) – (robot cost) = net income:

$$\frac{\$3}{\text{widget}}\times\frac{3\text{ widgets}}{\text{hour}}\times h-\$5000=\frac{\$3}{\text{widget}}\times\frac{3.75\text{ widgets}}{\text{hour}}\times h-\$7250$$

$$\frac{\$9}{\text{hour}}\times h-\$5000=\frac{\$11.25}{\text{hour}}\times h-\$7250$$

$$\$2250=\frac{\$2.25}{\text{hour}}\times h$$

$$1000\text{ hours}=h$$

12. The correct answer is $\frac{3}{2}$. The solution to a system of equations is the point at which the two lines cross. If a system does not have a solution, it means that the two lines never cross. In other words, they are parallel and thus have equal slopes. We can find the slope for the top equation by moving the x-variable to the right side of the equation and solving for y:

$$-3y = -6x + 7$$
$$y = 2x - \frac{7}{3}$$

The slope is the value in front of the x, so now we need to find a value for m that will result in a slope of 2. Again, we move the x-variable to the right and solve for y:

$$-my = -3x + 5$$
$$y = \frac{3}{m}x - \frac{5}{m}$$

We can solve for m by setting $\frac{3}{m}$ equal to 2:

$$\frac{3}{m} = \frac{2}{1}$$
$$2m = 3(1)$$
$$m = \frac{3}{2}$$

13. The correct answer is 3. We begin by expanding the equation and multiplying through: $4(k) - 4(2) + 5(4) + 5(-k) = 3k$. We can rewrite this as $4k - 8 + 20 - 5k = 3k$. We then combine all the k-terms on the left side of the equation and all the numerical values on the right side: $4k - 5k - 3k = 8 - 20$, or $-4k = -12$. We divide each side by –4 to find that $k = 3$.

Math – Calculator

1. Choice C is correct. From the graph we can see the biggest distance between two years comes between 2014 and 2015, when production drops from approximately 18,000 to approximately 11,000.

2. Choice A is correct. So far Xander has learned 9 pieces, so any he learns in the next x months are added onto that. He learns 3 every month, or 3 times the number of months. So, we can represent the number of pieces Xander will learn as $9 + 3x$.

3. Choice B is correct. Raquel fills 28 glasses with 2 quarts of liquid each, so we can multiply 28 by 2 to find the total number of quarts: $28(2) = 56$ quarts. Then we convert quarts to gallons by dividing by 4: $56 \div 4 = 14$. So, Raquel needs 14 gallons of juice.

4. Choice D is correct. To solve for $x + y$, we must isolate the parenthetical term. We divide both sides by 4: $x + y = \frac{6}{4}$. We then reduce by dividing numerator and denominator by 2 to obtain $\frac{3}{2}$.

5. Choice B is correct. We can set up a system of equations to solve. We let t represent tomato plants and p represent pepper plants:

$$3t + 4p = 34$$
$$p = 4$$

We can use substitution, plugging in 4 for p in the first equation to obtain $3t + 4(4) = 34$, or $3t + 16 = 34$. We then subtract 16 from each side: $3t = 18$. Finally, we divide each side by 3 to find that $t = 6$.

6. Choice C is correct. We need to subtract 4 feet, 7.5 inches from 6 feet, 1 inch. Since we cannot subtract 7.5 from 1, we need to borrow 1 foot, or 12 inches. We can rewrite 6 feet, 1 inch as 5 feet, 13 inches. Then we can subtract both feet and inches to obtain 1 foot, 5.5 inches. This is a total of $12 + 5.5 = 17.5$ inches.

7. Choice D is correct. The number of records left after any given number of months, r, can be found by subtracting the number sold from the original number, a. The number sold can be calculated by multiplying the number sold each month by the number of months, or multiplying k by m. So, we can write our equation as $r = a - km$.

8. Choice B is correct. The slope of Mikayla's first graph is 3. To find the perpendicular line, we need to find the equation with a slope that is the negative reciprocal of the first. The negative reciprocal of 3 is $-\frac{1}{3}$. We can find the slope of each equation in the answer choices. We do this by moving the x-variable to the right side of the equation and dividing by the constant in front of the y. Answer choice A has a slope of $\frac{1}{3}$. Answer choice B has a slope of $-\frac{1}{3}$. Answer choice C has a slope of 3 (which makes it parallel to the original equation, not perpendicular). Answer choice D has a slope of –3. So, B is the only possibility.

9. Choice A is correct. We can plug in each set of points to see which one fits. Plugging in (0,3) to the top equation yields $3 \geq 0 - 2$, which is true. The bottom equation would be $0 + 3 < 5$, which is also true, so we know A must be the answer. To make sure, we can test each of the other points. For answer choice B: plugging in $(-2,7)$ yields $7 \geq -1 - 2$, which is true, and $-2 + 7 < 5$, which is not true. For answer choice C: plugging in (3,2) yields $2 \geq \frac{3}{2} - 2$, which is true, and $3 + 2 < 5$, which is not true. For answer choice D: plugging in $(4, -1)$ yields $-1 \geq 2 - 2$, which is not true, and $4 + (-1) < 5$, which is true. So only answer choice A satisfies both equations.

10. Choice A is correct. We can write two equations with the information given and then solve. Since the first project (f) took half the time of the second (s), we can write: $f = \frac{1}{2}s$, or $s = 2f$. Since both projects add up to 462, we can write $f + s = 462$. Then we can substitute $2f$ for s in the second equation: $f + 2f = 462$, or $3f = 462$. We divide both sides by 3 to find that $f = 154$. Since $s = 2f$, we know that $s = 2(154) = 308$ minutes.

11. Choice C is correct. We can solve the system of equations by eliminating the y-variable. To do this, we add the two equations together, which will cancel out the two y-terms and yield: $13x = 26$. Then we divide each side by 13 to find that $x = 2$. We plug this value in to one of the equations to find y. Using the top equation, we can write: $4(2) - 7y = 15$, or $8 - 7y = 15$. We then subtract 8 from each side: $-7y = 7$. Dividing each side by -7 yields: $y = -1$. So our solution is $(2, -1)$. Now we can find the value of $x - y$: $2 - (-1) = 2 + 1 = 3$.

12. Choice B is correct. We need to expand the equation to simplify it:

$$(3.2a - 4.1)(3.2a - 4.1) - 3.9a^2 - 2.8$$

Then we multiply the parenthetical terms, using FOIL:

$$(3.2a)(3.2a) - (3.2a)(4.1) - (3.2a)(4.1) + (4.1)^2 - 3.9a^2 - 2.8$$

$$10.24a^2 - 13.12a - 13.12a + 16.81 - 3.9a^2 - 2.8$$

Finally, we combine like terms to obtain $6.34a^2 - 26.24a + 14.01$.

13. Choice A is correct. The ratio of the perimeters can be expressed:

$$\frac{\pi d_{\text{after}}}{\pi d_{\text{before}}}$$

Since π is in both the numerator and the denominator, it cancels out and we are left with just a ratio of the diameters:

$$\frac{d_{\text{after}}}{d_{\text{before}}} = \frac{6.3}{5.4} = 1.1\overline{6}$$

14. Choice D is correct. According to the chart, fifteen seniors and zero freshmen are taking physics. So, $15 - 0 = 15$.

15. Choice C is correct. The number of biology students drops by 5 each year, starting with 20 and ending with 5. So, we know the slope of the equation, the coefficient of the x-variable, must be -5. So, our equation is $y = -5x + b$, where b is the y-intercept. To find b, we can plug in one of the known values of (x, y). For example, for the freshman class, $x = 1$ and $y = 20$, so $20 = -5(1) + b$. We simplify to find that $b = 25$. So, our equation is $y = -5x + 25$.

16. Choice D is correct. To find the area of a triangle, we multiply the base by the height and divide by 2:

$$\text{Area} = \frac{bh}{2} = \frac{(4x+4)(2x+3)}{2}$$

Apply the FOIL method to expand the numerator:

$$\frac{8x^2 + 8x + 12x + 12}{2} = 4x^2 + 10x + 6$$

17. Choice A is correct. The first thing to do is solve for x in the given equation:

$$\boldsymbol{k = -2x + 6}$$
$$\boldsymbol{k - 6 = -2x}$$
$$\boldsymbol{\frac{k-6}{-2} = x}$$

Since we are given that $x < -1$, we can apply this to the equation:

$$\frac{k-6}{-2} < -1$$

Now we can reverse the steps to find an acceptable range for k:

$$\frac{k-6}{-2} < -1$$

$$k - 6 > 2$$

(Note: the direction of the inequality flips when we divide by a negative value.)

$$k > 2 + 6$$

$$k > 8$$

This indicates that k must be greater than 8, thus only 9 is correct.

18. Choice B is correct. To find the perimeter, we can start by finding the distance around each of the semicircles. They each have a diameter of 100 m and they are half the circumference of the a full circle, $(\pi \times d)/2$. There are two of them, so the portion of the perimeter from the semicircles is $\pi \times d = 3.14 \times 100 \text{ m} = 314 \text{ m}$. The rest of the perimeter consists of two lengths of 200 m, which means the full perimeter is $314 \text{ m} + 2 \times 200 \text{ m} = 714 \text{ m}$.

19. Choice B is correct. The data shows a mean and median very close together, with the smallest pumpkin not much less than these values. This tells us that the majority of the pumpkins are close to the same size. Thus, the largest pumpkin must be an outlier since it is much heavier than the mean, median, and smallest pumpkin. The smallest pumpkin cannot be an outlier (A) because it is close in weight to the mean and median. Most of the pumpkins do not weigh less than 7lb 8oz (C), because the median is 7lb 9oz, meaning that half the pumpkins weigh less than or equal to 7lb 9oz and half weigh more than or equal to 7lb 9oz. Similarly, the majority of pumpkins cannot weigh more than the median (D).

20. Choice B is correct. The median is the number in the middle when the scores are arranged from least to greatest. We first reorganize them: 68, 79, 82, 83, 84, 96. Since there is an even number of grades, we take the average of the two in the middle. The average of 82 and 83 is $\frac{82+83}{2} = 82.5$.

21. Choice A is correct. Every student's exam grade was lower than or equivalent to his/her course grade. A logical explanation would be that the exam was harder than the other assignments. If the students studied more for this exam than others, this would likely result in higher exam grades rather than lower ones, so answer choice B is illogical. Answer choices C and D have no evidence in the data to support them.

22. The correct answer is 20. The cost of the trip changed from $414 to $360, or a drop of $54. Since three students did not attend, we divide 54 by 3 to find that the cost per student was $18. To find how many students did attend, we divide the total cost by the cost per student. Dividing 360 by 18 yields 20, so 20 students went on the trip.

23. The correct answer is $-\frac{8}{9}$.To find the slope, we need two points, so we can choose which two to use. The second and third points are simpler numbers for subtracting and dividing, so it is easiest to pick them. We find the difference in the y-values and then the x-values and divide them: $\left(2-(-2)\right) \div \left(-3-\frac{3}{2}\right)$, which simplifies to $4 \div \left(-\frac{9}{2}\right)$. We divide by finding the reciprocal and multiplying: $\frac{4}{1} \times \left(-\frac{2}{9}\right) = -\frac{8}{9}$.

24. The correct answer is 7200. Since each molecule of carbon dioxide has 2 atoms of oxygen, and there are 225 molecules total, we multiply 225 by 2 to find that there are 450 atoms of oxygen. Each of these weighs 16 amu, so we multiply 450 by 16 to find that there are 7,200 amu of oxygen in the carbon dioxide.

25. The correct answer is 980. If the hose is filling the pool at 7 gallons per minute, then in 28 minutes the pool will receive $7(28) = 196$ gallons. This is 20% of the pool, so we can set up a proportion to solve for 100%: $\frac{196}{x} = \frac{20}{100}$. We then cross-multiply and divide: $20(x) = (196)(100)$, or $20x = 19{,}600$. Finally, we divide 19,600 by 20 to find that $x = 980$, so the pool holds 980 gallons.

PSAT 8/9 Practice Test #2

Reading Test

Questions 1–8 are based on the following passage.

This passage is adapted from Charlotte Brontë, Jane Eyre, *originally published in 1897.*

Mr. Rochester, as he sat in his damask-covered chair, looked different to what I had seen him look before; not quite so stern—much less gloomy. There was a smile on his lips, and his eyes sparkled, whether with wine or not, I am not sure; but I think it very probable. He was, in short, in his after-dinner mood; more expanded and genial, and also more self-indulgent than the frigid and rigid temper of the morning; still he looked preciously grim, cushioning his massive head against the swelling back of his chair, and receiving the light of the fire on his granite-hewn features, and in his great, dark eyes; for he had great, dark eyes, and very fine eyes, too—not without a certain change in their depths sometimes, which, if it was not softness, reminded you, at least, of that feeling.

He had been looking two minutes at the fire, and I had been looking the same length of time at him, when, turning suddenly, he caught my gaze fastened on his physiognomy.

"You examine me, Miss Eyre," said he: "do you think me handsome?"

I should, if I had deliberated, have replied to this question by something conventionally vague and polite; but the answer somehow slipped from my tongue before I was aware—"No, sir."

"Ah! By my word! there is something singular about you," said he: "you have the air of a little *nonnette**; quaint, quiet, grave, and simple, as you sit with your hands before you, and your eyes generally bent on the carpet (except, by-the-bye, when they are directed piercingly to my face; as just now, for instance); and when one asks you a question, or makes a remark to which you are obliged to reply, you rap out a round rejoinder, which, if not blunt, is at least brusque. What do you mean by it?"

"Sir, I was too plain; I beg your pardon. I ought to have replied that it was not easy to give an impromptu answer to a question about appearances; that tastes mostly differ; and that beauty is of little consequence, or something of that sort."

"You ought to have replied no such thing. Beauty of little consequence, indeed! And so, under pretence of softening the previous outrage, of stroking and soothing me into placidity, you stick a sly penknife under my ear! Go on: what fault do you find with me, pray? I suppose I have all my limbs and all my features like any other man?"

"Mr. Rochester, allow me to disown my first answer: I intended no pointed repartee: it was only a blunder."

*nun

1. Mr. Rochester's "after-dinner mood," as found in lines 7–8, can best be described as which of the following?

A) Mellow
B) Depressed
C) Jubilant
D) Generous

2. What is the author's probable intent in describing Mr. Rochester's eyes in lines 14–19?

A) To show that he is good-looking
B) To show that he is powerful
C) To show that he is capable of emotion
D) To show that he can see well

3. What is Mr. Rochester's attitude regarding Jane Eyre, as seen in lines 31–42?

A) He is annoyed and repulsed.
B) He is surprised and intrigued.
C) He is puzzled and concerned.
D) He is reproving and dismissive.

4. What does Mr. Rochester mean by "stick[ing] a sly penknife under my ear" (lines 53–54)?

A) Delighting in insulting his appearance
B) Seeming to apologize but actually furthering the insult
C) Threatening his well-being
D) Damaging his hearing

5. As used in line 23, the word "physiognomy" most nearly means:

A) Eyes
B) Face
C) Clothing
D) Character

6. What is the central idea of this selection?

A) The two characters are slyly insulting each other.
B) The author is showing the great contrast between the two characters.
C) The two characters are battling to see who will be the dominant one in the relationship.
D) The two characters are drawing conclusions as to each other's character based on appearance and conversation.

7. What could you conclude about Mr. Rochester's expectations of Jane as a young female in a subservient position (governess)?

A) To be meek and unassuming
B) To be clever and witty
C) To be knowledgeable and talkative
D) To be beautiful and accomplished

8. Suppose a subsequent passage indicated that Mr. Rochester spent a great deal of time caring for a young child. Which of the following selections in the current passage best provides background for this?

A) Lines 32–35 ("you have ... carpet")
B) Lines 24–25 ("You examine ... handsome?")
C) Lines 16–19 ("a certain ... feeling.")
D) Lines 54–55 ("Go on ... pray?")

Questions 9–17 are based on the following passage.

This passage is adapted from Horatio Alger, Jr., From Farm Boy to Senator, *originally published in 1882.*

[The following is a scene from the life of Daniel Webster at age 14.]

Judge Webster determined to take Daniel [to Exeter Academy], and provide for his expenses by domestic self-denial. It was not till he had fully made up his mind that he announced his determination to the boy.

"Dan," he said one evening, "you must be up early to-morrow."

"Why, father?"

Daniel supposed he was to be set at some farm work.

"We are going to make a journey," answered Judge Webster.

"A journey!" repeated the boy in surprise. "Where are we going?"

"I am going to take you to Exeter, to put you at school there."

The boy listened with breathless interest and delight, mingled perhaps with a little apprehension, for he did not know he would succeed in the untried scenes which awaited him.

"Won't it be expensive, father?" he asked after a pause, for he knew well his father's circumstances, and was unusually considerate for a boy.

"Yes, my son, but I look to you to improve your time, so that I may find my investment a wise one."

"How are we to go, father?"

"On horseback."

Dan was a little puzzled, not knowing whether he and his father were to ride on one horse or not, as was a frequent custom at that time. It would have been hard upon any horse, for the judge was a man of weight, and the boy though light would have considerably increased the burden.

The next morning Daniel's curiosity was gratified. In front of the farmhouse stood two horses, one belonging to his father, the other filled out with a side-saddle.

"Is that horse for me?" asked Daniel in surprise.

"Yes, my son."

"What do I want of a side-saddle? I am not a lady."

"Neighbor —— is sending the horse to Exeter for the use of a lady who is to return here. I agreed to take charge of it, and it happens just right, as you can use it."

"I don't know how I can get along with it. It will look strange for me to be riding on a lady's saddle."

"If a lady can ride on it probably you can."

So Dan and his father set out on their journey from the quiet country town to Exeter, the boy mounted on a lady's horse. When in his later life he had occasion to refer to this journey, Mr. Webster recalled with great merriment the figure he must have cut as he rode meekly behind his father.

No doubt as they rode along father and son conversed together about the important step which had been taken. Judge Webster already had formed the plan of sending Daniel to college, after he should have completed a course of preparation at Exeter, but upon this part of his plan he did not think it best yet to speak to his son, very probably because he had not yet made up his mind as to whether his circumstances would allow him to incur so heavy an expense.

"My son," said the father gravely, "I hope you will improve to the utmost the advantages I am securing for you. You must remember how much depends upon yourself. A boy's future is largely in his own hands."

"Yes, father, I will do the best I can."

"Mr. Thompson thinks you can make a good scholar."

"I will try, father."

"I shall have no money to leave you, Daniel, but I hope to give you an education, which is better than a fortune."

9. Which of the following can be gathered from lines 3–18?

A) Daniel was hoping to work on the farm.
B) Daniel was not expecting to be able to further his education.
C) Daniel was planning to work hard on the farm to save money for school.
D) Daniel was surprised that his father chose a school far from home.

10. What does Daniel's father mean by "I may find my investment a wise one" in lines 29–30?

A) He expected Daniel to pay him back for his tuition.
B) He expected the long-term effects of Daniel's education to be worth the financial sacrifice.
C) He expected Daniel to work harder when he completed his education.
D) He expected that Daniel would become wise as he studied.

11. Why does Daniel later remember his trip to school "with great merriment" (lines 61–62)?

A) He rode in an obviously female position, humiliating at the time but humorous later.
B) He was joyful about the unexpected chance to obtain an education.
C) He was so excited to go to school that he accidentally put a lady's saddle on his horse.
D) He was later amused that he absent-mindedly rode behind his father instead of side by side.

12. What can be inferred from Judge Webster's encouragement to "improve to the utmost the advantages I am securing for you" in lines 76–77?

A) He wants Daniel to spend the school money wisely.
B) He wants Daniel to thank him for the sacrifice he is making in sending him to school.
C) He is reminding Daniel that he has a future in farming.
D) He knows he cannot afford everything that could help Daniel.

13. Why might the author have added that Daniel's joy in education is mixed with "apprehension" (line 21)?

A) To show his willingness to face unknown circumstances for the sake of education.
B) To show that he is not perfect and has fears like any other person.
C) To show that he secretly doesn't want to go to school.
D) To show that education is a frightening prospect for anyone.

14. Which of the following is the best description of the phrase "the figure he must have cut" as used in line 62?

A) His physical appearance
B) His size
C) His facial expression
D) The people who were watching him

15. Which of the following excerpts best provides evidence of Daniel's attitude toward school?

A) Lines 85–86 ("I hope ... a fortune.")
B) Lines 61–62 ("Mr. Webster ... great merriment")
C) Lines 19–20 ("The boy ... interest and delight")
D) Line 15 ("'A journey!' ... in surprise.")

16. Why does the author mention multiple times that Daniel's father could not easily afford an education?

A) To emphasize that Daniel was not expecting to go to school.
B) To show that Daniel's father was uneducated.
C) To show the sacrifice that was made for Daniel to be educated.
D) To show that Daniel's father constantly worried about money.

17. Which of the following might be a good title for the above selection?

A) Daniel's School Days
B) The Price of Education
C) Riding Side-Saddle to School
D) Daniel Webster: Exeter Student

Questions 18–25 are based on the following passages.

Passage 1:

In an age of innumerable global issues and national budget deficits, focusing resources on space exploration is not only unnecessary, but also irresponsible. While relief agencies are overwhelmed and underfunded, it is unwise to spend staggering sums on research that has few practical applications for the average citizen. This is not to say that research is unimportant—it is valuable to learn and progress, and space offers many research opportunities. Thus, private investors are encouraged to fund these endeavors, but public funds must be used for the public good; i.e., programs and efforts that will provide the highest good for the greatest number of people. It is impossible to compare potential knowledge advances with providing food, clothing, and shelter to those in need.

Some may argue that it is important to look to our future and not merely solve today's issues. But how can we plan a future when our present is in jeopardy? Our children must have basic needs met before we can justify competing with other nations in the space race on the public dime.

Learning and exploring is an important part of the human experience, and we should never stop seeking new information. But there is much still to learn about our own planet, information that is much more relevant to humanity than what we can learn about other planets. It is absurd to spend tax dollars researching potential life forms on Mars when our own Earth contains yet undiscovered life that could have meaningful applications to humanity.

The coming generation needs us to focus our efforts and resources on pertinent research, placing their wellbeing above unnecessary wondering about what lies beyond our atmosphere.

Passage 2:

It is shortsighted to say that space exploration is irrelevant. There are always urgent needs and public funding is finite, but if we focus only on today's needs, we cannot progress as a society. It is imperative to look ahead, to tackle long-term problems, to continue to foster human curiosity and learning.

Space exploration involves making advances in technology and other areas of learning. It creates jobs and teaches valuable life skills. Additionally, it contributes to good relationships between nations. While much funding for space exploration can and does come from private sources, it is important to have a steady source of funding so that continual research can be conducted. Also, it means that every taxpayer is involved in this important research, giving them a stake in the operation.

While it may seem far less necessary than providing food for hungry children, space exploration takes only a small part of the national budget. Much higher amounts are allocated to addressing hunger, environmental issues, and other relief efforts. More importantly, the research that is done in space may be able to help address some of these global problems, offering continuing returns. As a society, we will cripple ourselves and darken our future if we don't look beyond today's concerns and seek to grow by studying, learning, and challenging the boundaries of our understanding.

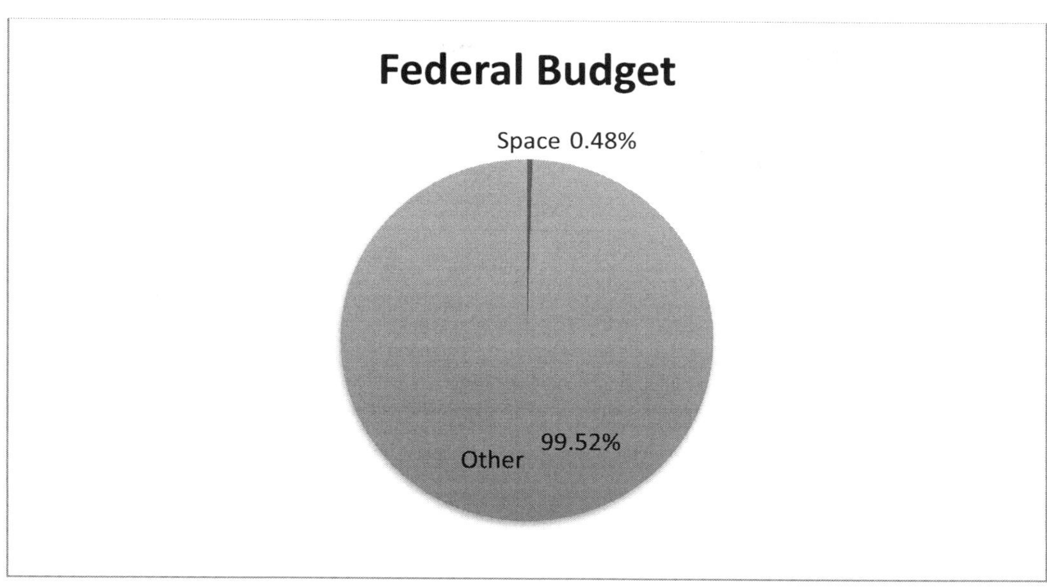

18. The author's primary purpose in Passage 1 is to:

A) Argue that space exploration should be stopped.
B) Argue that space exploration should be maintained.
C) Argue that space exploration should not be funded by the government.
D) Suggest that space funding should be cut in half.

19. It can be inferred that the term "public funds" in line 13 of Passage 1 refers to:

A) Money for which the public can decide the use
B) Taxes and other funds used for government purposes
C) The portion of federal funds that are disclosed to the public
D) Funds that are publicly raised for a specific purpose such as space travel

20. Which of the following does the author of Passage 1 NOT give as a reason for stopping funding for space exploration?

A) The funds are more greatly needed elsewhere.
B) There is more to learn about our planet before exploring further.
C) There is no life on Mars.
D) Scientific advances are less important than providing basic needs.

21. Why does the author of Passage 2 believe we cannot focus only on immediate needs?

A) For humanity to progress, exploration is key.
B) The budget is more than sufficient to cover immediate needs.
C) Most of the funding for space exploration is from private gifts, not public funding.
D) It's better to give people a job, like space exploration provides, than just food.

22. How does the information in the pie chart support the argument in Passage 2?

A) It shows that only a very small percentage of the federal budget is allocated to space exploration.
B) It shows that large amounts of funds are allocated to meeting immediate needs of food, clothing, and shelter.
C) It shows that the federal budget prioritizes space exploration.
D) It shows that the federal budget allocation for space exploration should be increased.

23. According to Passage 1, which of the following should come first?

A) Researching other planets
B) Competing with other countries to explore space
C) Looking for life forms on Mars
D) Exploring ocean life forms

24. Which of the following statements is true?

A) The author of Passage 1 thinks space exploration should continue, while the author of Passage 2 thinks space exploration should cease.
B) The author of Passage 2 thinks space exploration should continue, while the author of Passage 1 thinks space exploration should cease.
C) Neither author thinks space exploration should continue.
D) Both authors think space exploration should continue.

25. The author of Passage 1 argues that space exploration should only receive private funding. What is the author of Passage 2's response?

A) It is not right to use private funds for space exploration.
B) Space programs should also receive steady public funding so they can work steadily.
C) Public funding is the only way to get Americans involved in the important work of space exploration.
D) Space exploration is more important than many of the other programs that are publicly funded.

Questions 26–34 pertain to the following passage.

Mushrooms

Mushrooms, also known as toadstools, are some of the most recognizable members of the fungi kingdom, growing on every continent on earth (even Antarctica). They can be found in backyards, growing on tree branches, and even pushing up through asphalt roads.

A typical mushroom consists of a stem, a cap, and gills—the soft, close-set flaps on the underside of the cap. However, there are over 50,000 species of mushrooms, some in the traditional button mushroom shape and some vastly different, some so tiny they are nearly invisible and some weighing hundreds of pounds.

Mushrooms produce millions of spores, or basidiospores, on their gills, releasing the spores to reproduce. Spores can also be used to identify mushrooms: placing a mushroom cap on a flat surface with the gills down leaves spore markings in the shape of the gills. The color of this "spore print" indicates the type of mushroom.

Unlike seeds that sprout in soil, mushroom spores grow in substances like wood, sawdust, or manure. Before the recognizable mushroom shape appears, a thin, threadlike mycelium begins to grow. This is the actual living part of the organism, not the part that will be eaten eventually. It is composed of tiny filaments, called hyphae, that twine together and can spread over vast distances, adding more than half a mile of length per day. This mycelium is considered the body of the fungus, while the visible mushrooms that are cut and eaten are the fruit.

Mycelium survives on organic material, but typically dead material, which is why mushrooms are often found on rotting tree trunks. It absorbs nutrients, storing them away until it has enough surplus to fruit. This is when mushrooms appear, tiny pinheads. Because it expands its cells with water to grow, a mature mushroom is typically over 90% water. Edible mushrooms are rich in vitamins, and in particular are one of the only foods that naturally contain Vitamin D when they have been exposed to sunlight.

Neither plant nor animal, mushrooms hold a unique place in our ecosystem. Though small and unassuming, they play a valuable role in decomposition and even assisting plants in accessing nutrients. These behind-the-scenes workers help keep nature functioning and producing well.

26. Which of the following does the passage NOT list as a component of mushrooms?

A) The stem
B) The gills
C) The roots
D) The cap

27. Which of the following does the passage state is the body of a mushroom?

A) The hyphae
B) The basidiospores
C) The gills
D) The mycelium

28. According to the passage, what can be used to identify mushrooms?

A) The stem
B) The spores
C) The mycelium
D) The hyphae

29. According to the passage, which of the following is true?

A) Mushrooms are rich in Vitamin C.
B) Mushrooms tend to feed on dead organic material.
C) The mycelium is the fruit of the mushroom.
D) The mycelium is made up of basidiospores.

30. What does the passage claim about the classification and role of mushrooms?

A) They are actually plants, and they help in decomposition.
B) They are actually animals, and they add Vitamin D to the diet.
C) They are neither plants nor animals, and they help plants access nutrients.
D) They can be either plants or animals, and they work behind the scenes to keep nature working smoothly.

31. According to the passage, how many varieties of mushrooms exist?

A) Over 500
B) Over 5,000
C) Over 50,000
D) Over 500,000

32. In line 49, what does the term "surplus" refer to?

A) Water
B) Nutrients
C) Fruit
D) Mushrooms

33. Which of the following does the passage author give as evidence of mushroom's high water content?

A) Their hyphae spread over vast differences, enabling them to soak up water.
B) They grow by absorbing nutrients from dead organic matter.
C) They grow by taking in water to expand their cells.
D) They grow in dark, damp places.

34. According to the passage, which of the following is necessary for mushrooms to form?

A) A surplus of stored nutrients
B) Cool, damp conditions
C) Sawdust, wood, or manure
D) Dead organic material

Questions 35–42 pertain to the following passage.

Types of Chemical Compounds

While there are 118 known elements found in nature and listed in the periodic table, these combine in an innumerable array of chemical compounds to form every substance in our world, from water and the air we breathe, to our body parts, to dangerous poisons. Any time two or more different kinds of atoms join together to create a molecule or formula unit, this is a chemical compound.

Compounds come in two basic types: covalent (or molecular) and ionic. Molecular compounds are simply composed of neutral atoms that join together in covalent bonds, with their atoms sharing electrons. Molecular compounds are typically gases, liquids with low boiling points, or solids with low melting points. Ionic compounds, on the other hand, are formed when two atoms join with a transfer of electrons. This is typically a combination of a metal element and a nonmetal, as the metal transfers electrons to the nonmetal. Ionic compounds are solids, typically with high melting points.

The particles that compose ionic compounds are ions, with either a positive or negative charge. When a neutral atom loses an electron, so that it now has more protons than electrons, it becomes a positively charged cation. When a neutral atom gains an electron, it has more electrons than protons and becomes a negatively charged anion. Cations and anions are attracted to each other and can join to form compounds such as table salt, which is created when sodium cations (Na^+) and chloride anions (Cl^-) are near each other and bond together as the compound NaCl. This transfer of electrons tends to create strong bonds, more so than the typical covalent bond. And unlike covalent compounds, in which two or more neutral atoms join to create a single molecule of a compound, ionic bonds do not create single molecules. Rather, they create joined groups of bonds referred to as formula units.

In covalent compounds, two atoms share electron pairs rather than transferring them. They hold together by the strength of their shared electrostatic attraction. For example, hydrogen peroxide is formed when two oxygen atoms come in contact with two hydrogen atoms and they join to create a molecule of H_2O_2. These bonds are often weaker than ionic bonds and may be broken down, or decomposed.

35. In lines 25–27, this passage states, "The particles that compose ionic compounds are ions, with either a positive or negative charge." What is the term for ions with a positive charge?

A) Cations
B) Anions
C) Covalent ions
D) Formula units

36. Which of the following selections from the passage provide evidence that ionic bonds are the strongest of the ones discussed in this passage?

A) Lines 23–24 ("Ionic compounds ... melting points.")
B) Lines 33–38 ("Cations and ... compound NaCl.")
C) Lines 38–40 ("This transfer ... covalent bond.")
D) Lines 48–49 ("They hold ... electrostatic attraction.")

37. In which of the following does the author provide a description of how molecular compounds are formed?

A) Lines 15–17 ("Molecular compounds ... melting points.")
B) Lines 27–30 ("When a ... charged cation.")
C) Lines 33–38 ("Cations and ... compound NaCl.")
D) Lines 46–49 ("In covalent ... electrostatic attraction.")

38. Which of these is correct regarding information in the passage about how ionic and covalent compounds differ?

A) Ionic compounds share electrons; in covalent compounds they are transferred.
B) Covalent compounds share electrons; in ionic compounds they are transferred.
C) Ionic compounds are made of negatively charged particles; covalent compounds are made of positively charged particles.
D) Covalent compounds are made of negatively charged particles; ionic compounds are made of positively charged particles.

39. This passage can best be described as ________________.

A) Sequence
B) Cause-effect
C) Parts to whole
D) Comparison-contrast

40. What can the reader infer from the passage?

A) Molecular compounds are more prevalent than ionic compounds.
B) There are an equal number of cations and anions.
C) Electrostatic attraction is not the strongest type of attraction between particles.
D) There are likely more than 118 elements.

41. According to the passage, a gas is typically what kind of compound?

A) Ionic
B) Molecular
C) Either ionic or molecular
D) Neither ionic nor molecular

42. What best identifies the purpose of this passage?

A) To explain two types of compounds and how they compare
B) To explain the types of elements that make up the world
C) To explain why some chemical bonds are stronger than others
D) To explain how particles become positive or negative

Writing and Language Test

Questions 1–10 are based on the following passage.

1. While driving through McDonald's is a relatively modern construct, [1] the concept of restaurants have existed for millennia. Ancient Rome had *thermopolia* that served food and drink on long bars, ready to be purchased and taken to-go rather than eaten on site. China is the first location in recorded history to open public, sit-down eating locations. In these early restaurants, [2] waiters referred to as "pot masters," took orders from a "menu" of demonstration dishes.

2. A few hundred years later, a type of restaurant began to [3] emerge in the West, serving a prepaid meal at a specific time each day. This *table d'hôte* was part of an inn, open to both [4] guests or locals alike, who could sit down for a hot meal before traveling or going back to work. Rather than choosing from a list of entrées, each patron was served the same dish. Similar establishments can be found today in farm-to-table restaurants. Later, dinner houses sold "ordinaries," simple meals geared toward working men who would lunch together.

1.

A) NO CHANGE
B) had existed
C) has existed
D) exists

2.

A) NO CHANGE
B) waiters, referred to as "pot masters"
C) waiters, referred to as pot masters
D) waiters referred to as "pot masters"

3.

A) NO CHANGE
B) resurrect
C) dwindle
D) falter

4.

A) NO CHANGE
B) guests and locals alike
C) guests nor locals alike
D) guests and even locals alike

3. *1.* [5] A few decades later, soup shops began to open. *2.* In France, a guild of cooks-caterers formed in the sixteenth century, preparing and delivering food to wealthy clients. *3.* From these the word "restaurant" arose, as this soup was known as *bouillon restaurant*. *4.* [6] Gradual, the menus expanded until these restaurants were similar in format to today's fine dining. *5.* La Grande Taverne de Londres, located in Paris, is counted as the first "real" restaurant.

4. [7] Oyster houses and coffee shops, in the United States, sprang up in the late nineteenth century. As the middle class grew more affluent, restaurants likewise [8] flourished. American contributions to restaurant culture include the cafeteria, where food is laid out and customers make their own selection. Drive-in and fast-food establishments also originated in the US. Additionally, the idea of fine dining on the go first took hold in the US, with Pullman dining cars on trains and elegant dining rooms on steamboats.

5. What is the best location for this sentence?

A) NO CHANGE
B) after sentence 2
C) after sentence 3
D) DELETE, because this sentence does not fit in this paragraph

6.

A) NO CHANGE
B) The menus gradual expanded
C) Gradually, the menus expanded
D) The menus expanded, gradually

7.

A) NO CHANGE
B) In the United States, oyster houses, and coffee shops
C) Oyster houses, in the United States, and coffee shops
D) In the United States, oyster houses and coffee shops

8.

A) NO CHANGE
B) improved
C) settled
D) struggled

5. Restaurants evolved from simple offerings, such as a single meal that all customers shared, to elegant and extravagant dining, with myriads of choices and sophisticated décor. [9] Restaurants in medieval times offered camaraderie as weary laborers halfway through their workday sat down beside tired travelers for a rare chance to hear about the outside world. Yet today, there is somewhat of a return to the origins of [10] eating out, with an emphasis on homey atmospheres and simpler food.

9. In which paragraph does this sentence best fit?

A) NO CHANGE
B) Paragraph 1
C) Paragraph 2
D) Paragraph 3

10.

A) NO CHANGE
B) to eat out
C) having eaten out
D) eat out

Questions 11–20 are based on the following passage.

Beginning in the mid-1500s, more and more men went to sea as the Age of Sail began. Exploration, trade, and warfare were hugely dependent on ships, and there was an increasing need for sailors. [11] However, sailing was a dangerous life. And not just because of storms and pirates. On long trips, as many as 50% of the crew could die from the dreaded disease of scurvy. Yet the cure is simple: Vitamin C.

Vitamin C, or ascorbic acid, is found in [12] a superfluous of foods. Fruits such as lemons, oranges, and kiwi contain high amounts, but it can also be found in many other fruits, as well as vegetables such as [13] broccoli; potatoes and sweet potatoes; and bell peppers. Because the body does not store Vitamin C, it is crucial to maintain an adequate daily intake rather than simply "stocking up" from time to time.

11. What is the best way to combine these sentences?

A) NO CHANGE
B) However, sailing was a dangerous life; and not just because of storms and pirates.
C) However, sailing was a dangerous life, and not just because of storms and pirates.
D) However, sailing was a dangerous life. And, not just because of storms and pirates.

12.

A) NO CHANGE
B) an abundance
C) a multitudinous
D) a marginal number

13.

A) NO CHANGE
B) broccoli—potatoes and sweet potatoes—
C) broccoli, potatoes and sweet potatoes.
D) broccoli, potatoes and sweet potatoes,

The body relies heavily on collagen, a component of bones, skin, tendons, blood vessels, and other important body parts. Vitamin C assists in production of collagen, so without this vitamin, a body is prone to gum disease, decrease in red blood cells, and [14] deficient lack of ability to heal wounds, which is the reason scurvy can be deadly. On the other hand, people with [15] healthy amount's of Vitamin C in their diet tend to heal cuts more quickly, as well as to fight off infections better.

One of the best-known properties of Vitamin C is that it is an [16] antioxidant, this is a particle that helps protect the body against stress due to oxidation. Antioxidants work by giving electrons to various reactions, converting the vitamin to an oxidized state. This has the effect of protecting against free radicals, unstable particles that can damage the body. Vitamin C donates electrons to these particles, stabilizing them as the free radicals [17] except the electrons.

14.

A) NO CHANGE
B) deficiency in lack of ability
C) deficient lacking of ability
D) lack of ability

15.

A) NO CHANGE
B) amount's of healthy
C) healthy amounts
D) health-wise amounts

16.

A) NO CHANGE
B) antioxidant; this is
C) antioxidant, and it is
D) antioxidant, it is

17.

A) NO CHANGE
B) accept
C) excepting
D) accepted

Today Vitamin C deficiency is uncommon in much of the world. People with certain chronic diseases, smokers, and many in undeveloped countries are at risk. Vitamin C is also particularly necessary for those with anemia, to help with absorption of iron, or diabetes, to avoid kidney and eye deterioration. [18] Kidney function is critical and is endangered by diabetes.

While "an apple a day" may not be sufficient to keep the doctor away, it can help in building the immune system, along with a diet high in other [19] vitamin-rich fruits and vegetables. Today it is simple not only to avoid life-threatening scurvy, but also to [20] admire a multitude of benefits with the simple addition of Vitamin C.

18. Where is the best location for this sentence?

A) NO CHANGE
B) The beginning of this paragraph
C) The previous paragraph
D) Remove from the selection because it is irrelevant

19.

A) NO CHANGE
B) vitamin rich
C) richly vitamin
D) high in vitamins

20.

A) NO CHANGE
B) attain
C) question
D) lose

Questions 21–30 are based on the following passage.

[21] Accordance with some of the earliest recorded history, silver has been treasured for much of human history in cultures across the world. It was likely one of the earliest forms of currency and in ancient Egypt was considered more valuable than gold. This changed with the discovery of methods to separate silver from other [22] metals, however silver was still considered of great value. Today silver has a variety of uses, including in electronics, [23] for use in developing photography, and for x-ray vacuum tubes.

[24] In the Bronze Age, in which mankind discovered how to separate silver from other metals in a process called *cupellation*. This process, which is still used in various forms today, involved heating the raw materials in a furnace. Silver melts at a higher temperature than the other materials it is typically mixed with, so melting the alloy at a high temperature allows these other materials to evaporate or be absorbed by the lining of the cupel (a vessel made of bone ash), leaving the pure silver behind.

21.

A) NO CHANGE
B) Accordingly with
C) According to
D) In accordance to

22.

A) NO CHANGE
B) metals; however silver
C) metals, however, silver
D) metals; however, silver

23.

A) NO CHANGE
B) for using in developing photographs
C) to develop photographs
D) in development of photography

24.

A) NO CHANGE
B) In the Bronze Age, during which
C) In which the Bronze Age
D) During the Bronze Age,

[25] Since cupellation is now outdated, new processes have taken its place. For example, the cyanide process, also known as heap leaching, begins by crushing the ore so that it will be porous. Then lime is added, water or a cyanide solution [26] is mixed in, and it is left to cure for 1–2 days. The ore is then poured onto pads that are sloped for drainage. Then a mixture of water and sodium cyanide is misted onto the ore, dissolving the silver, which sinks to the bottom. Zinc dust is then sprinkled on to react with the silver, turning it back to solid form to be collected.

Once the silver is collected it is purified through electrolysis, using nitric acid. The resulting metal, to be commercial grade, must be at least 99.9% pure. After all this the silver is finally ready to be made [27] into: jewelry, coins, or cutlery. However, since silver is very [28] resilient, it is often mixed, or alloyed with other metals to strengthen it. Sterling silver is 92.5% silver and 7.5% copper or other metal. Sterling silver can be finished with rhodium to keep it from tarnishing.

25. Which of the following is the best way to introduce this paragraph?

A) NO CHANGE
B) Along with cupellation, several processes are used today to extract silver from the ores.
C) The most effective method of extracting silver is the cyanide process.
D) As the use of cupellation waned, a new method took its place.

26.

A) NO CHANGE
B) mixing in
C) being mixed in
D) mixes with it

27.

A) NO CHANGE
B) into—
C) into,
D) into

28.

A) NO CHANGE
B) malleable
C) robust
D) tenacious

While most coins today have little or no silver in them, silver bullion coins are still minted, with a purity of 99.9%. To create these coins, silver is melted and poured into a billet, or tube, to create a solid cylinder of silver. Then the silver is put through an extruder to give thin strips. Next, these strips are pressed and cut into coin shapes. After a cleaning, [29] <u>their</u> "struck"—the coin design is pressed into the coins' fronts and backs.

Silver still has worldwide value, as it has since humanity's early days. It has maintained its purchase power through the millennia. [30] <u>Its use has grown, expanding from mere currency to technology and other areas, and thus silver continues to be one of the world's most valuable substances.</u>

29.

A) NO CHANGE
B) they're
C) there
D) there are

30. Which of the following would be the best conclusion to the selection?

A) NO CHANGE
B) While there are many ways of extracting silver, there are even more ways of using it.
C) From ancient coins to modern coins, silver has endured the test of time.
D) Although the use of silver is waning, it still has several applications and thus is still of value.

Questions 31–40 are based on the following passage and supplementary information.

1. Whether you're wanting a sandwich to please a picky child or a gourmet spread to serve at a dinner party, the answer is easy: cheese. This food has been eaten for so long that there is no clear [31] recorded of its origin. A theory is that cheese was discovered by accident when [32] milk was one time stored by someone in a container which had rennet in it, because it was made from an animal's stomach. However it was discovered, cheese quickly became a staple in many cultures as it could be preserved more easily than milk. Today there are over 1,000 types of cheese made from a variety of animals' [33] milk; cows, goats, and sheep, among others.

2. Cheese is made by first souring the milk and adding rennet to separate it into curds (solid) and whey (liquid). Composed of enzymes from a calf's stomach, [34] the cheese is held together by rennet in a rubbery, cohesive consistency.

31.

A) NO CHANGE
B) recording
C) record
D) recordance

32.

A) NO CHANGE
B) someone stored in a container made from an animal's stomach (which had rennet in it) milk
C) someone at one time took an animal's stomach, which had rennet in it, and made a container and stored milk in it
D) someone stored milk in a container made from an animal's stomach, which had rennet in it

33.

A) NO CHANGE
B) milk: cows, goats, and sheep
C) milk—cows; goats; and sheep
D) milk. Cows, goats, and sheep

34.

A) NO CHANGE
B) holding the cheese together with rennet
C) rennet holds the cheese together
D) rennet holding the cheese together

3. A fresh-made cheese (called "newborn") is typically not very flavorful. It must "ripen," giving the [35] enzyme's and microbe's time to achieve the familiar texture and flavor. This may be anywhere from a few weeks to a year or even more, depending on the type. Brie is ready for consumption in about a month, while some varieties of cheddar can be aged for seven years. Some cheeses, however, do not need aging. One can purchase or make fresh ricotta or cream cheese, [36] immediately enjoying their flavors rather than waiting for them to ripen.

4. In the US, cheese is produced across the country, but Wisconsin is the production leader with more than 2.5 billion pounds of cheese [37] annual. This vast amount is necessary as Americans consume, on average, over 35 pounds of cheese per person every year. Mozzarella is the most popular type, thanks to pizza, followed by cheddar.

35.

A) NO CHANGE
B) enzymes' and microbes'
C) enzymes and microbe's
D) enzymes and microbes

36.

A) NO CHANGE
B) immediately, their flavors can be enjoyed
C) and their flavors can be, immediately, enjoyed
D) and their flavors can be enjoyed, immediately,

37.

A) NO CHANGE
B) annually
C) for annual
D) as annually

5. Although cheese isn't necessarily known as a nutritional powerhouse, it has its benefits. It's a good source of calcium and protein and can help guard against osteoporosis. And while fat should be consumed in moderation, cheese can help provide essential healthy fats such as unsaturated [38] fats, which are the most beneficial. So while making a meal of cheese (especially processed cheese) [39] is not, for a healthy diet, recommended, it can help to provide daily amounts of nutrition essentials. So whether you like gouda, gruyere, or the list-topping mozzarella, there are plenty of choices for getting your calcium.

[40]

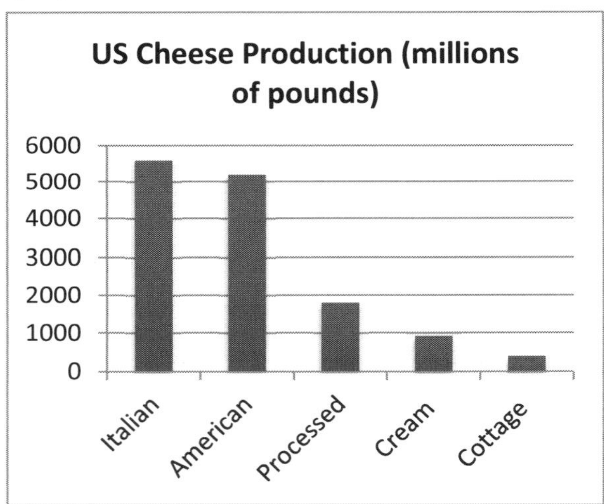

38.

A) NO CHANGE
B) fats which
C) fats, that
D) fats; that

39.

A) NO CHANGE
B) is vital to a healthy diet
C) is an occasional part of a healthy diet
D) is not recommended for a healthy diet

40. Which paragraph is the best location for sharing the information in this chart?

A) NO CHANGE
B) Paragraph 1
C) Paragraph 3
D) Paragraph 4

Math – No Calculator

Questions 1–10 are multiple choice. Questions 11–13 are grid-in.

1. If $4x + 7 = -13$, what is a value of $\sqrt{14 + x} - 6$?

A) 4
B) 0
C) -3
D) -5

2. A food stand sells hot dogs, nachos, and popcorn. Cost is based on the following formula, using h for the price of a hot dog, n for the price of nachos, and p for the price of popcorn:

$$3h + 2.5n + 1.75p = \text{total cost (in dollars)}$$

If Bernardo and his friends bought 16 hot dogs, 10 plates of nachos, and 8 bags of popcorn, how much did they pay?

A) $85.50
B) $87.00
C) $91.25
D) $93.00

3. Find the ordered pair that solves this system of equations:

$$x - 3y = 11$$
$$2x + 4y = -8$$

A) $(2, -3)$
B) $(0, -2)$
C) $(-1, 3)$
D) $(3, -2)$

4. Find a possible value for a if $b = 2$ and $(ab - 2)^2 = 64$.

A) -3
B) 2
C) 1.5
D) 6

5. The graph of a line has a slope of –2 and a y-intercept of 1. A second line has a slope of $\frac{1}{3}$ and intersects with the first line at $(-3, 7)$. What is the y-intercept of the second line?

A) $y = -2$
B) $y = 0$
C) $y = 6$
D) $y = 8$

6. Find the mean of the following: $4x$, $7x$, $11x$, 2, $8x$, and 4.

A) $30x + 6$
B) $10x + 3$
C) $5x + 1$
D) $6x + 1.2$

7. What is the product of all roots of the equation $3x^2 - 10x - 8$?

A) -8
B) $-\frac{8}{3}$
C) -1
D) $\frac{3}{4}$

8. Given the following data, which is the greatest: the mean, mode, or median?

4 22 23 6 2 11 8 11 12

A) Mean
B) Median
C) Mean and mode are equal
D) Mean, mode, and median are equal

9. Mr. Morgan needs to buy basic and graphing calculators for his classroom. He is approved to purchase a maximum of 20 graphing calculators, and his largest class is 32 students. If x refers to the number of basic calculators and y refers to the number of graphing calculators, which of the following systems of inequalities represents the number of calculators Mr. Morgan needs to purchase to make sure each student has a calculator?

A) $x + y \geq 32$
$x \geq 12$
$y \leq 20$
B) $32 \leq x + y \leq 35$
$x \geq 12$
$y \leq 20$
C) $x + y = 32$
$x \leq 12$
$y \geq 20$
D) $x + y \leq 32$
$x \leq 12$
$y \geq 20$

10. Javier bought a new laptop for \$775. If it depreciates in value at a constant rate, so that in 3 years it is worth \$535, how much will it be worth 5 years after purchasing?

A) \$515
B) \$400
C) \$375
D) \$225

11. Josh is deciding between two mowers for his lawn business. Mower X costs \$350, and Josh can mow 0.5 lawns per hour with it. Mower Y costs \$475, and Josh can mow 20% faster with it. After how many hours of mowing would it be more profitable to purchase Mower Y instead of Mower X, if Josh makes a profit of \$25 per lawn?

Grid your answer.

12. In the system of equations below, x and y are variables while m is a constant. For which value of m does the system have no solution?

$$3x + 4y = 11$$
$$mx - 6y = 9$$

Grid your answer.

13. What is the value of z in the equation below?

$$3(2 - z) + 2(z + 4) = 6z$$

Grid your answer.

Math – Calculator

Questions 1–21 are multiple choice. Questions 22–25 are grid-in.

1. A school tracks the number of new students each year. According to the graph below, when was the greatest increase in new students?

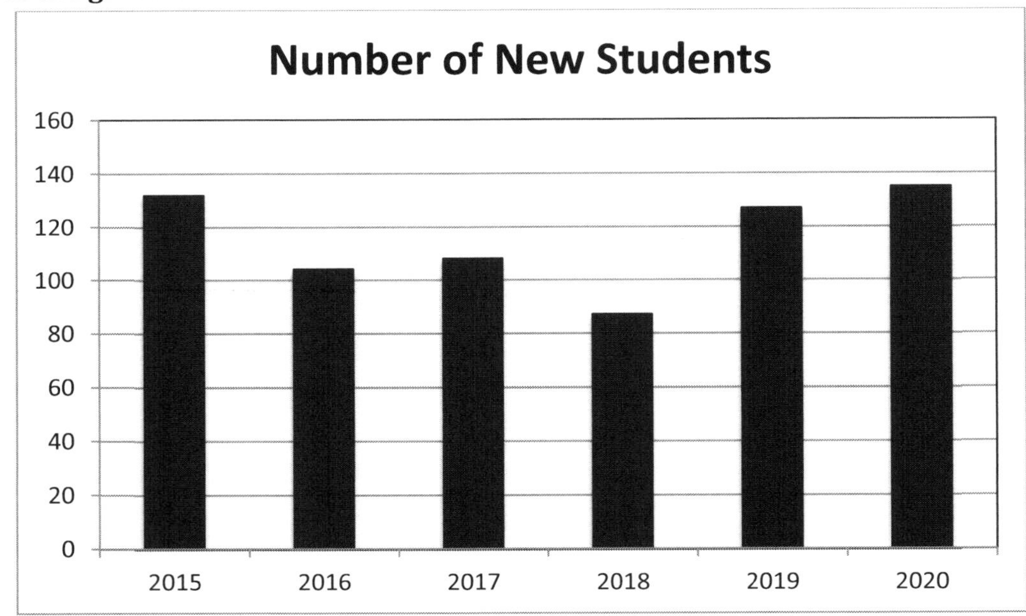

A) 2015–2016
B) 2017–2018
C) 2018–2019
D) 2019–2020

2. Lola attends art class twice a week. If she has attended 6 classes so far, how many classes will she have attended in x weeks?

A) $6 - 2x$
B) $2 - 6x$
C) $2 + 6x$
D) $6 + 2x$

3. If a water bottle holds 3 cups, how many gallons would be needed to fill 32 water bottles?

$$(1 \text{ gallon} = 4 \text{ quarts}, 1 \text{ quart} = 2 \text{ pints}, 1 \text{ pint} = 2 \text{ cups})$$

A) 6
B) 8
C) 9
D) 12

4. If $9(a - b) = 6$, what is the value of $a - b$?

A) 2
B) $\frac{3}{4}$
C) $\frac{2}{3}$
D) $\frac{3}{2}$

5. At a bakery, muffins cost \$4 each and cookies cost \$1.50 each. If Jamie places an order totaling \$63, including 12 muffins, how many cookies does she buy?

A) 7
B) 10
C) 12
D) 15

6. Alejandro is 5 feet, 10 inches. His younger sister is 3 feet, 11.5 inches. How much taller is Alejandro than his sister?

A) 22.5 inches
B) 21.5 inches
C) 20.5 inches
D) 19.5 inches

7. Kyra has a coffee shop gift card with *d* dollars on it. She spends *a* dollars per week at the coffee shop. Which function best represents the amount of money in dollars, *m*, that are still on Kyra's card after *w* weeks?

A) $m = a + w$
B) $m = d - aw$
C) $m = d - a$
D) $m = aw - d$

8. Which of the following equations is perpendicular to $y = \frac{1}{2}x + 3$?

A) $x + 2y = 2$
B) $-x + 2y = \frac{3}{2}$
C) $2x + y = 7$
D) $-2x + y = -3$

9. Which of the following ordered pairs satisfies this system of inequalities?

$$y \leq \frac{3}{2}x + 1$$
$$-x - y < 3$$

A) $(0,2)$
B) $(-2,1)$
C) $(3,-7)$
D) $(4,-4)$

10. Kevin mowed two lawns. The first took 2.5 times as long as the second. If he spent a total of 154 minutes mowing, how long did he spend on the first lawn?

A) 124 minutes
B) 110 minutes
C) 88 minutes
D) 44 minutes

11. For the system of equations below, what is the value of $x + y$?

$$3x + 2y = 9$$
$$x + 4y = 23$$

A) 5
B) 7
C) 10
D) 13

12. Which of the following is equivalent to $(6.7x^2 - 2.1) - (1.2x - 5.7)^2$?

A) $8.14x^2 + 13.68x - 30.39$
B) $5.26x^2 - 13.68x - 30.39$
C) $8.14x^2 - 13.68x + 34.59$
D) $5.26x^2 + 13.68x - 34.59$

13. A cross-section of a tree trunk has a radius of 12.3 in. When the edge is trimmed to make a platter, the radius is 8.2 in. What is the ratio of the area after the edge is trimmed to the area before the trimming?

A) $\frac{9}{4}$
B) $\frac{2}{3}$
C) $\frac{4}{9}$
D) $\frac{2}{9}$

Questions 14–15 refer to the following information:

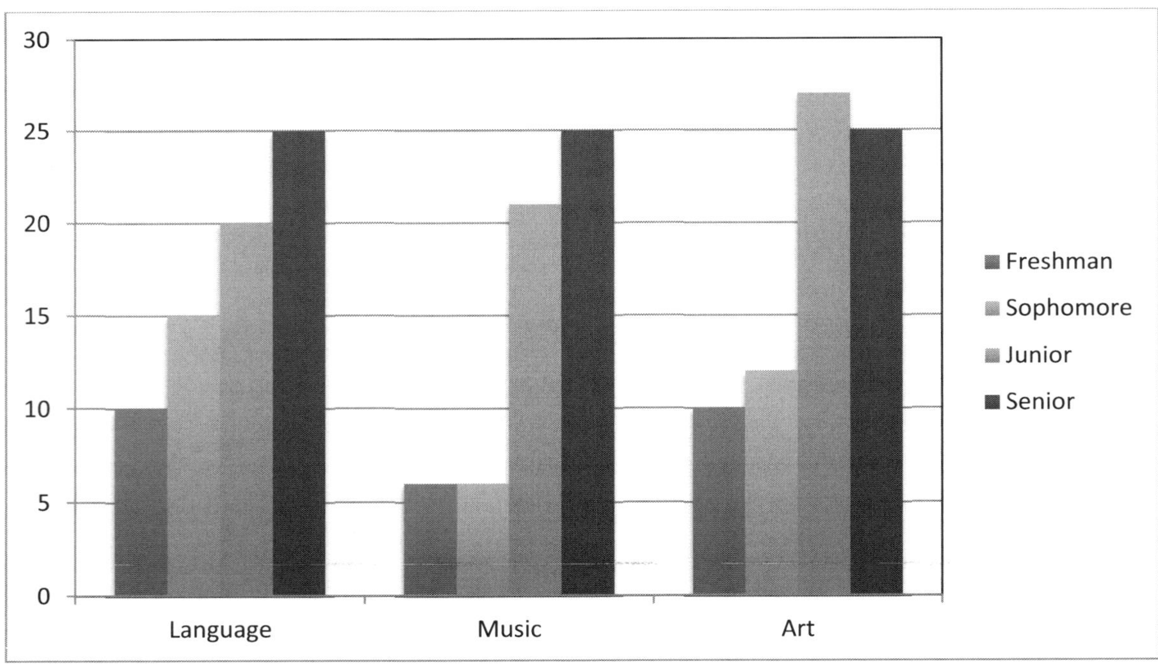

A school requires students to take electives in three areas to graduate with honors: language, music, and art. The chart above shows the number of students currently taking electives.

14. How many more of the art students are seniors than are freshmen?

A) 20
B) 17
C) 12
D) 15

15. Which of the following formulas could be used to describe the change in the number of language students per year, where y is the number of students taking a language elective and x is the grade level (Freshman = 1, Sophomore = 2, etc.)?

A) $y = 5x$
B) $y = 5x + 5$
C) $y = 5x + 10$
D) $y = -5x + 10$

16. Find an expression for the area of the right triangle below.

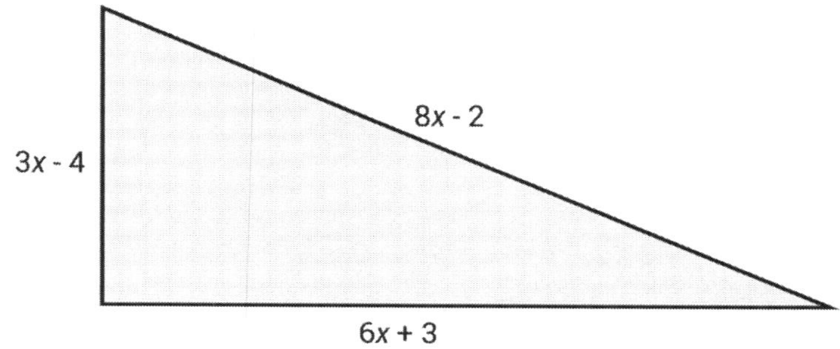

A) $18x^2 - 15x - 12$
B) $17x - 3$
C) $9x^2 - \frac{15}{2}x - 6$
D) $24x^2 - 38x + 8$

17. In the equation below, $x > 4$. Which of the following is a possible value for k?

$$k = -\frac{1}{2}x + 5$$

A) $k = 6$
B) $k = 4$
C) $k = 2$
D) k can take any value

18. A mural is to be painted on a rectangular wall and a base coat of primer needs to be applied to prepare the surface. The wall is 8 feet tall and three times as wide as it is tall. If one can of primer covers 100 square feet, what is the minimum number of cans required to apply the base coat?

A) 1
B) 2
C) 3
D) 4

19. The mean weight of babies born on a single day at a hospital was 7 lb 10 oz. The median weight was 7 lb 8 oz. The smallest baby weighed 6 lb 11 oz and the largest weighed 8 lb 5 oz. Which of the following conclusions is best supported by the data?

A) The smallest baby is an outlier.
B) The largest baby is an outlier.
C) Most of the babies weighed less than 7 lb 10 oz.
D) Most of the babies weighed more than 7 lb 8 oz.

Questions 20–21 refer to the following information:

A group of basketball players charted their heart rates at two different points, as seen in the chart below.

1st heart rate	72	76	65	79	68	81
2nd heart rate	106	105	99	122	103	116

20. Based on the chart above, what is the median heart rate for the first measurements?

A) 72.5
B) 73
C) 73.5
D) 74

21. Which of the following conclusions correlates with the data?

A) The players were more active just before the second measurement than the first.
B) The players were more active just before the first measurement than the second.
C) The second measurement was taken just before a practice.
D) The first measurement was taken during practice and the second measurement was taken during an actual game.

22. Several families made reservations for a camping trip. The total cost of campsite reservations was $180, and the total cost of kayak rentals (1 per family) was $540. Four families canceled their reservations before the trip, and the total cost dropped to $480. How many families went on the camping trip?

Grid your answer.

23. What is the slope of a line that goes through the points $\left(-\frac{3}{2}, -5\right)$, $\left(1, -\frac{3}{2}\right)$, and $\left(3, \frac{13}{10}\right)$?

Grid your answer.

24. Each molecule of sodium carbonate has two atoms of sodium, one atom of carbon, and three atoms of oxygen. If each atom of sodium has an atomic weight of approximately 23 atomic mass units (amu), how many amu of sodium are in 75 molecules of sodium carbonate?

Grid your answer.

25. Jodi pours lemonade into a glass at a rate of 1.5 ounces per second. If it takes 3 seconds to fill 25% of the glass, how much lemonade can the glass hold?

Grid your answer.

Answer Key and Explanations for Test #2

Reading Test

1. Choice A is the best answer. The first paragraph describes his mood as less stern and gloomy, though still "preciously grim." So we could say that his mood is mellow, though not fully jubilant (C). Since his mood is described as less gloomy, *depressed* is not the best choice (B). He is described as "more self-indulgent," but not necessarily generous (D).

2. Choice C is the best answer. The author describes Mr. Rochester's "massive" head and "granite-hewn" features, but follows by describing his eyes that are almost "soft." This shows that while he appears impassive and powerful (B), he actually has depths of emotion. While his eyes are described as *fine*, the emphasis in this description is not that he is good-looking (A). Also, *fine* does not mean that he can literally see well (D).

3. Choice B is the best answer. Mr. Rochester remarks that she is "singular," or unique, because she seems quiet and demure but is able to make a stinging remark. He is surprised by her answer to his previous question and wants to know more about her. He is not annoyed, despite her seeming insult, and is attracted rather than repulsed, so answer choice A is incorrect. He is puzzled but not concerned (C). He does not reprimand Jane, at least not seriously, and is intrigued rather than dismissive (D).

4. Choice B is the best answer. Jane Eyre has just apologized for criticizing Mr. Rochester's appearance, following her apology with the comment that "beauty is of little consequence," which only emphasizes that she does not see beauty in him. He jokingly complains that the apology followed by a further insult is painful, like being pricked by a knife that got past his defenses. There is no indication that she delights in giving insults (A). She does not use a literal knife to threaten him (C) or damage his hearing (D).

5. Choice B is the best answer. Physiognomy refers to a person's facial features or expression.

6. Choice D is the best answer. Jane Eyre, the narrator, is silently observing Mr. Rochester and noticing that he looks more cheerful and that his eyes show a depth of feeling. When he notices her looking, he also observes her appearance and comments on what he learned from her looks and conversation. While Mr. Rochester seems to think Jane is insulting him (A) it is unintentional on her part. This passage does show some contrast between the characters (B), but that is not the main idea. The characters are not battling for power (C); Jane clearly says in lines 68–69 that she "intended no pointed repartee."

7. Choice A is the best answer. The evidence in this selection indicates that Mr. Rochester expected Jane to be quiet and unassuming. He says that she appears to be "quaint, quiet, grave, and simple...with [her] eyes generally bent on the carpet" (lines 33–35) and is surprised at her direct speech.

8. Choice C is the best answer. The description of Mr. Rochester's eyes in the first paragraph shows that while he seems stern and cold, not like a person who would spend time with a child, he actually has the capability of feeling tender emotion.

9. Choice B is the best answer. The first paragraph states that Daniel's father decided to send him to Exeter Academy but did not tell him at first. We then read that Daniel was expecting to work on the farm (there is no indication that he was hoping for this, or that he was working to save up for school, so choices A and C are incorrect), so we can assume that he was not expecting to attend school. While the academy was far enough to take "a journey" (line 13), there is no indication that Daniel was surprised to be sent to a distant school (D), as there was likely no institute of higher education close to home.

10. Choice B is the best answer. While Daniel's father may have expected that Daniel would become wise (D), or possibly that he would work even harder out of gratitude (C), the best-supported choice is that Daniel will use his education for long-term good, making his father's sacrifice worthwhile.

11. Choice A is the best answer. The previous paragraphs explain that Daniel rode to school on a lady's horse and saddle. This would have been embarrassing at the time but he later remembered it with amusement. While he was undoubtedly joyfully anticipating his education (B), this did not cause amusement. The lady's saddle was not put on by accident (C), and he rode behind his father "meekly" (line 63), not absent-mindedly.

12. Choice D is the best answer. The previous sentence states that Daniel's father does not yet know if he will be able to afford college for Daniel. So he is telling Daniel to work hard and make the most of what he has, implying that he cannot give Daniel everything for success. There is no indication that he is giving Daniel the money for school (A). While Daniel is doubtless thankful (B) and will probably have a future in farming if he doesn't work hard at school (C), these are not what Judge Webster is implying.

13. Choice A is the best answer. The entire passage focuses on Daniel's desire for education and his willingness to undergo embarrassment and fear to achieve it. The passage does not imply that Daniel is perfect, so there is no need to prove his imperfection (B). There is no foundation to the idea that he secretly doesn't want to go to school (C); rather, he is willing to go to great lengths to attend. And while the thought of school makes Daniel a little nervous, since he has less experience than many, this is likely not true of everyone (D).

14. Choice A is the best answer. *Figure* refers to a person's physical shape. The author is referring to how Daniel would have appeared as he rode the lady's horse.

15. Choice C is the best answer. The words *interest* and *delight* on lines 19–20 show what Daniel thought of the opportunity to go to school. Lines 85–86 (A) show his father's attitude but not his own. Lines 61–62 (B) show Daniel's later attitude toward his trip to school but not to school itself. Line 15 (D) shows Daniel's reaction to being told he is going somewhere, but he doesn't know where yet so his attitude cannot be in response to school.

16. Choice C is the best answer. The first paragraph mentions that Daniel's father plans to make sacrifices to be able to pay for school. The topic is mentioned several other times, emphasizing that it is a challenge but that Judge Webster thinks it a worthwhile investment. While Daniel was not expecting to go to school (A), this is not the emphasis. Daniel's father may have been uneducated (B), as he worked a farm and was hoping for better things for his son, but this is not certain. He may likely have worried about money (D), but we cannot infer this from the information given.

17. Choice B is the best answer. The emphasis throughout the selection is on the price to pay for education. Daniel's father makes financial sacrifice to pay for his son's education, and Daniel sacrifices his pride by riding in a lady's saddle to go to school. Choices A and D focus on Daniel as a student, while the passage is about his preparation for school. Choice C is humorous and descriptive, but refers to one part of the passage rather than the main idea.

18. Choice C is the best answer. The entire passage makes the argument that space exploration should not be funded by the government, offering various reasons why this is the best course of action. However, it does NOT make the argument that all space exploration should be stopped; lines 11–13 suggest that it can still be funded privately.

19. Choice B is the best answer. The context of the sentence (contrasting with "private" funding mentioned earlier in the sentence) shows that public funds refer to the money at the government's disposal, including taxes and other funds.

20. Choice C is the best answer. The author of Passage 1 never claims that there is no life on Mars but rather refers skeptically to "potential life forms on Mars" (lines 34–35).

21. Choice A is the best answer. The author points out in lines 4–5 of Passage 2 ("if we focus...as a society") that exploration and learning is necessary for humanity to progress.

22. Choice A is the best answer. The author of Passage 2 points out that space exploration takes a tiny fraction of the federal budget. This is supported by the pie chart.

23. Choice D is the best answer. The evidence for this answer can be found in lines 29–33 ("But there...other planets.") of Passage 1, where it states that we should focus on learning about our own planet before looking to space. Since only answer choice D involves research on our planet, it should come first, according to the author of Passage 1.

24. Choice D is the best answer. Clearly both authors think that space exploration is valuable, but they disagree on how it should be funded.

25. Choice B is the best answer. The author of Passage 2 points out that in addition to private funding, it is important to have steady public funding so that research can continue at a steady pace (lines 13–17).

26. Choice C is the best answer. Roots are not listed as a component of mushrooms, but stems, gills, and caps are each mentioned in lines 8–9 ("A typical...and gills").

27. Choice D is the best answer. Lines 34–35 ("This mycelium...the fungus") note that the mycelium is the body of the mushroom. Choices A, B, and C are other parts of the fungus.

28. Choice B is the best answer. Lines 18–19 state that "spores can also be used to identify mushrooms."

29. Choice B is the best answer. Lines 38–39 note that mushrooms absorb nutrients from dead organic material.

30. Choice C is the best answer. Lines 50–51 ("Neither plant...our ecosystem") states that mushrooms are not plants or animals. Lines 52–54 ("they play...accessing nutrients") state that mushrooms help plants in accessing nutrients.

31. Choice C is the best answer. Lines 10–11 note that there are more than 50,000 species of mushrooms.

32. Choice B is the best answer. Lines 41–42 state that mycelium absorbs nutrients and stores them until it has a surplus.

33. Choice C is the best answer. Lines 44–46 state, "Because it expands its cells with water to grow, a mature mushroom is typically over 90% water." Choices A, B, and D are all mentioned in the passage but not in connection with the high water content.

34. Choice A is the best answer. Lines 41–42 in the passage state, "It absorbs nutrients, storing them away until it has enough surplus to fruit." Choices B, C, and D are all conditions that are ideal for mushroom growth, but only the surplus of stored nutrients is listed in the passage as necessary for the mycelium to produce mushrooms.

35. Choice A is the best answer. Following the quoted sentence, the passage identifies a positively charged particle as a cation. Anions (B) are negatively charged. The term *covalent ions* (C) is coined from other terms in the article but is not something that is actually discussed. Formula units (D) have neutral charge.

36. Choice C is the best answer. This selection first explains that ionic bonds tend to be strong and then concludes that they are stronger than most covalent bonds. Choice A merely describes ionic compounds without referring to their strength. Choice B explains how ionic compounds are formed but again does not mention their strength. Choice D describes the strength of covalent bonds, not ionic.

37. Choice D is the best answer. Lines 46–49 ("In covalent ... electrostatic attraction.") describe how covalent compounds are formed. We know from line 6 that *molecular compound* is another term for covalent compound, so this is the correct answer. Choice A describes molecular compounds but does not explain their formation. Choices B and C describe the formation of a cation and an ionic compound, respectively.

38. Choice B is the best answer. Lines 38–40 ("This transfer ... covalent bond") and lines 46–47 ("In covalent ... transferring them") state that ionic compounds transfer electrons while covalent bonds share them. Choice A is the reverse of the correct choice. Ionic compounds are made of BOTH positively and negatively charged particles, according to lines 33–38 ("Cations and ... compound NaCl"), so choices C and D cannot be correct.

39. Choice D is the best answer. The passage focuses on two types of chemical compounds: ionic and covalent (molecular). They are compared and contrasted, showing their similarities and differences.

40. Choice C is the best answer. Lines 48–49 state that covalent compounds are held together by electrostatic attraction. Lines 53–54 state that covalent bonds are often weaker than ionic bonds. Thus, electrostatic attraction can be inferred to be weaker than the transference of electrons that causes ionic bonds. Molecular compounds may appear to be more numerous than ionic (A) because lines 15–21 mention three types of molecular compounds but only one of ionic, but this is not a safe assumption to make since we do not know the total number of each type. Cations and anions balance each other out, in a sense, but there is no evidence in this passage to suggest that they are equal in number (B). The passage mentions "118 known elements" (line 1) but does not suggest that more exist (D).

41. Choice B is the best answer. Lines 15–17 ("Molecular compounds ... melting points") list gases as types of molecular compounds. Gases are not mentioned as types of ionic compounds.

42. Choice A is the best answer. The purpose of this passage is to describe two types of chemical compounds: ionic and covalent. Choice B is addressed in lines 1–7 ("While there ... dangerous poisons"), but these lines mention the elements without explaining the types of elements. Choice C is addressed a couple of times, such as in lines 38–40 ("This transfer ... covalent bond") but it is not the main idea of the passage. The idea of positive and negative particles (D) is discussed in lines 25–30 ("The particles ... charged anion"), but again, it is not the main idea of the passage.

Writing and Language

1. Choice C is the best answer. The subject of the clause (*concept*, not *restaurants*) is singular, so *have* (A) is incorrect. This sentence is in present tense, so choice B is incorrect. It is referring to ongoing events that began in the past, so present perfect tense is needed rather than simply present tense (D).

2. Choice D is the best answer. The clause *referred to as "pot masters"* is dependent, so it either needs a comma both before and after or neither. Since choices A, B, and C each have only one comma, they are incorrect.

3. Choice A is the best answer. The sentence is saying that restaurants first appeared in the West a few hundred years after they did in China. *Emerge* accurately describes this. *Resurrect* (B) implies that they had existed before and were reappearing. *Dwindle* and *falter* (C and D) imply that restaurants were dying out, not being established.

4. Choice B is the best answer. The correct verbiage to pair with *both* is *and*. It conveys addition rather than contrast (A and C). The phrase *and even* (D) gives the idea of addition but is redundant.

5. Choice B is the best answer. Sentence 2 introduces the subject of France, so it should be the first sentence. Sentence 3 refers to the soup shops, so it needs to come after the underlined sentence. Thus, this sentence should be after sentence 2.

6. Choice C is the best answer. The word *gradual* is used as an adverb here, so it must be *gradually*, making choices A and B incorrect. Choice D is incorrect because of the misplaced comma.

7. Choice D is the best answer. The phrase *In the United States* introduces the subject of the new paragraph. Placing this clause in the middle of the sentence is confusing and distracts from the main point, so choices A and C are incorrect. Choice B is incorrect because of the misplaced comma.

8. Choice A is the best answer. The sentence is saying that with the growth in affluence, or wealth, of the middle class, restaurants also prospered. *Improved* (B) is too vague, because it could be referring to improvement in quality of food or a number of other things. *Settled* (C) and *struggled* (D) imply stagnation or backward movement, which is the opposite of what the sentence means.

9. Choice C is the best answer. The information about medieval restaurants best fits in the second paragraph. The first paragraph (B) discusses ancient restaurants before medieval times, the third paragraph (D) discusses French restaurants after the medieval period, and the current paragraph (A) is a summary paragraph, not focusing on any one time period.

10. Choice A is the best answer. The correct answer is a gerund phrase, changing a verb to noun form. Choices A, B, and C are all verb forms.

11. Choice C is the best answer. Separating it into two sentences (A and D) makes it choppy, and starting with a conjunction creates a dependent clause, which should not be a standalone sentence. Combining the two clauses with a semicolon (B) is incorrect because the second clause is dependent and semicolons are used to separate independent clauses (stand-alone sentences).

12. Choice B is the best answer. The sentence is discussing that many foods contain Vitamin C. The word *abundance* (B) means a large amount, so it makes sense. *Superfluous* (A) and *multitudinous* (C) are adjectives instead of nouns, so they do not fit grammatically. *Marginal number* (D) functions as a noun but implies a small amount.

13. Choice D is the best answer. This sentence lists three examples of foods high in Vitamin C (lumping potatoes and sweet potatoes together). They should be separated by commas. A semicolon (A) should only be used in a list for clarity if components of the list have internal commas. A dash (B) is inappropriate because the clause following the dash is not a definition or explanation of the previous part. A period (C) is inappropriate because the part after the punctuation is not a complete sentence.

14. Choice D is the best answer. It is redundant to say *deficient lack of ability* (A), since by definition *lack* is deficient. Answer choices B and C are also unnecessarily verbose. Answer choice D is the only one that is succinct.

15. Choice C is the best answer. The sentence is referring to plural connections, not possessive, so answer choices A and B are incorrect. The word *health-wise* means *referring to health*, which is not the same as *healthy* and does not fit the context.

16. Choice B is the best answer. The parts of the sentence before and after the punctuation are both complete sentences, so they should be separated by a semicolon or period. Separating with a comma (A and D) makes them comma-splices. Using a comma with a conjunction (C) is grammatically correct but does not fit because *it* refers to *antioxidant* rather than *Vitamin C.*

17. Choice B is the best answer. *Accept* means *to take*, while *except* (A) means *other than*. Choice B fits the context and thus is correct. The word *excepting* (C) is a participle, and *accepted* (D) is in past tense.

18. Choice D is the best answer. This detail on diabetes is loosely linked to the previous sentence but is off the topic of Vitamin C, so it is best to remove it.

19. Choice A is the best answer. The words *vitamin* and *rich* are combined to create an adjective. A hyphen is typically used to connect the words in this case. Answer choice B is incorrect because it lacks the hyphen. Answer choice C is grammatically incorrect because of improper use of the adverb. Answer choice D is incorrect because it does not use hyphens, as well as using awkward wording.

20. Choice B is the best answer. The sentence is saying that people can gain benefits from adding Vitamin C to their diet. The best word to describe this is *attain*. The other words do not fit the meaning.

21. Choice C is the best answer. Answer choice C is the only one that fits grammatically. Answer choice A needs *In* at the beginning of the phrase to work. Answer choice B incorrectly uses an adverb, and answer choice D incorrectly uses *to* instead of *with*.

22. Choice D is the best answer. The term *however* is a conjunctive adverb and must be preceded by a semicolon and followed by a comma, so only answer choice D can be correct.

23. Choice C is the best answer. This answer choice is clear and concise. The other choices all contain excess verbiage and convoluted structure, making them difficult to understand.

24. Choice D is the best answer. Only answer choice D is a complete sentence. The other three are all sentence fragments.

25. Choice B is the best answer. The previous paragraph discusses the technique of cupellation, and the current paragraph discusses the technique of the cyanide process. So the paragraph introduction should transition between these two subjects. Answer choices A and D claim that cupellation is outdated or no longer in use, which contradicts the previous paragraph ("[cupellation] is still used in various forms today"). Answer choice C makes no reference to the previous paragraph, so it does not transition smoothly. Answer choice B signals a change from the previous topic and sets up a new topic, so it is the correct answer.

26. Choice A is the best answer. This sentence gives a list, so each item in the list needs to match grammatically. The other two items are *is added* and *is left to cure*, so only choice A matches this structure.

27. Choice D is the best answer. It is common to precede a list with a colon (A), but this is only correct if the part of the sentence before the colon is an independent clause (a stand-alone sentence). In fact, no punctuation is necessary after a preposition, so answer choice D is the only possibility.

28. Choice B is the best answer. The point of the sentence is that silver is soft in a pure state and needs another metal mixed in to be strong enough to make jewelry. *Malleable* means pliable or bendable. The other three choices all communicate the opposite idea of strength.

29. Choice B is the best answer. The implied subject of the sentence is the plural *coins*. The sentence uses a pronoun here, so the correct answer is the contraction *they're*, for *they are*. The possessive *their* (A), location *there* (C), and passive verb *there are* (D) are incorrect because the clause needs a subject, and only answer choice B gives a subject.

30. Choice A is the best answer. To write an effective closing statement, it is helpful to look back to the opening. The opening paragraph mentions silver's original use as currency and later use in electronics. Answer choice A reflects these ideas, adding a general statement of closure (that silver continues to be valuable). Answer choice B refers back to the content on methods of extracting silver but is more suitable for opening a paragraph since it does not describe any of the ways of use. Answer choice C mentions the currency from the opening paragraph, as well as the next to last paragraph, but makes no mention of any of the other uses of silver. Answer choice D erroneously states that silver is no longer used as much.

31. Choice C is the best answer. We need a noun to complete the sentence. Choice A is a past-tense verb, choice B, when used as a noun, refers to an audio file, and choice D is not a word.

32. Choice D is the best answer. Good writing is clear and concise. Answer choices B and C use confusing sentence structure, which makes it difficult for the reader to understand. Answer choice A is not too unclear, but it is not as strong as answer choice D because it is written in passive voice.

33. Choice B is the best answer. This list should be preceded by a colon since the part of the sentence before the list is an independent clause. Items in a list are separated by commas unless one or more of the items has an embedded comma. It should not be separated into two sentences (D) because the second part would be a fragment.

34. Choice C is the best answer. In answer choices A and B, this sentence has a dangling modifier. The subject referenced in *Composed of enzymes from a calf's stomach* is *rennet*, so this needs to be the subject of the following clause. Answer choice C correctly places *rennet* as the subject. Answer choice D uses the wrong verb tense.

35. Choice D is the best answer. Plural nouns are needed here, not possessive. Only answer choice D correctly uses plural nouns.

36. Choice A is the best answer. Answer choices B, C, and D each use passive voice rather than a strong verb. This is not only weaker writing but can make comprehension more difficult. In addition, each of these choices uses unnecessary commas, which can also make comprehension more challenging.

37. Choice B is the best answer. We need an adverb here. Answer choice A is an adjective, as is answer choice C. Answer choice D includes an adverb, but with *as*, it does not fit grammatically.

38. Choice A is the best answer. *That* is considered a restrictive term. In other words, it is used to introduce information that is essential to the meaning and grammatical structure of the sentence. Because it is an essential part of the sentence, no comma or other punctuation precedes these restrictive clauses, so answer choices C and D are incorrect. *Which* often introduces a nonrestrictive clause—information that is relevant but not essential. In the sentence in question, the previous clause ("cheese can help provide essential healthy fats such as unsaturated fats") is a stand-alone sentence. The following clause adds meaning but is not essential, so it is nonrestrictive. Thus, we use *which*. Nonrestrictive clauses are preceded by commas, so answer choice B is incorrect.

39. Choice D is the best answer. Answer choice D is the most straightforward and clear. Answer choice A words the information in a more confusing and passive way. Answer choices B and C contradict the information in the previous sentence.

40. Choice D is the best answer. The chart gives information on what kinds of cheese are most produced in the US. Paragraphs 3, 4, and 5 all mention types of cheese. But only paragraph 4 discusses production of cheese in the US, so it is the best choice.

Math – No Calculator

1. Choice C is correct. First, we solve for x using the first equation. We subtract 7 from each side to yield $4x = -20$, then divide each side by 4 to find that $x = -5$. Then we plug in –5 for x in the second equation.

$$\sqrt{14 + (-5)} - 6$$

$$\sqrt{9} - 6$$

From here, there are two possible answers because $\sqrt{9} = \pm 3$.

$$3 - 6 = -3$$

$$-3 - 6 = -9$$

Since only –3 is listed as an answer choice, it is the correct answer.

2. Choice B is correct. We fill in 16 for h, 10 for n, and 8 for p in the equation, so $3(16) + 2.5(10) + 1.75(8) = 87$, or \$87.00.

3. Choice A is correct. We can solve the system of equations by elimination. Because the x-value in the first equation is half of the x-value in the second equation, and the values are small, it is the easiest variable to eliminate. We begin by multiplying every term in the top equation by –2 to obtain $-2x + 6y = -22$. Then we add the two equations together so that the x-terms are eliminated and we are left with $10y = -30$. We divide each side by 10 to find that $y = -3$. Then we can plug in –3 for y in one of the original equations. Using the first equation: $x - 3(-3) = 11$, or $x + 9 = 11$. We then subtract 9 from each side to find that $x = 2$. We can plug the pair $(2, -3)$ into the second equation to verify: $2(2) + 4(-3) = -8$. Since this results in a true statement, the solution is $(2, -3)$.

4. Choice A is correct. We solve by first taking the square root of each side, yielding:

$$ab - 2 = \pm 8$$

We can plug in 2 for b to obtain:

$$2a - 2 = \pm 8$$

We solve for the 2 possible solutions:

$$\begin{aligned} 2a - 2 &= 8 \\ 2a &= 10 \\ a &= 5 \end{aligned} \qquad \begin{aligned} 2a - 2 &= -8 \\ 2a &= -6 \\ a &= -3 \end{aligned}$$

Only –3 is a possible answer choice, so A is the correct choice.

5. Choice D is correct. The information in the first sentence is unnecessary to solve the problem. We have the slope of a line and a point it goes through, so we can find the y-intercept with no other information. We first find the equation of the line, using the formula $y = mx + b$. The slope is m, and we plug in the values from the point for x and y: $7 = \left(\frac{1}{3}\right)(-3) + \text{b}$. When we solve for b, which is the y-intercept, we find that $b = 8$. So, the y-intercept is 8.

6. Choice C is correct. To find the mean, or average, we must first add the expressions together and then divide by the number of expressions:

$$\frac{4x + 7x + 11x + 2 + 8x + 4}{6}$$

Combine like terms and simplify:

$$\frac{(4x + 7x + 11x + 8x) + (2 + 4)}{6} = \frac{30x + 6}{6} = 5x + 1$$

7. Choice B is correct. We need to solve the equation for the roots, so first we check to see if the equation can be factored. We can write $(3x\pm?)(x\pm?)$. Then we find the factors of –8 to test. For instance, we could write $(3x + 8)(x - 1)$, since $8(-1) = -8$, but multiplying this out using the FOIL method will not yield $-10x$ for the middle terms. When we multiply $(3x + 2)(x - 4)$, the middle terms are $-12x$ and $2x$, which add up to $-10x$, so this is our solution. We then take the two terms and set them equal to zero to solve for the roots:

$$\begin{aligned} 3x + 2 &= 0 \\ 3x &= -2 \\ x &= -\frac{2}{3} \end{aligned} \qquad\qquad \begin{aligned} x - 4 &= 0 \\ x &= 4 \end{aligned}$$

Finally, we multiply the roots to find the product: $\left(-\frac{2}{3}\right)(4) = -\frac{8}{3}$.

8. Choice D is correct. We need to find each of the values. The mean (average) of the data is the sum of the values divided by the number of values:

$$\frac{4 + 22 + 23 + 6 + 2 + 11 + 8 + 11 + 12}{9} = 11$$

The mode is the most frequently occurring value, which in this case is 11. The median is the middle of the data when it is put in order:

2 4 6 8 11 11 12 22 23

In this case, the median is 11. Since mean, mode, and median are all 11, they are all equal.

9. Choice A is correct. Added together, the two types of calculators must equal at least 32 to accommodate Mr. Morgan's largest class, so we can represent this as $x + y \geq 32$. He can purchase a maximum of 20 graphing calculators (y), so we can represent this as $y \leq 20$. To have at least 32 total calculators, he must purchase at least 12 basic calculators ($32 - 20 = 12$), so we can represent this as $x \geq 12$.

10. Choice C is correct. The laptop drops in value by the same amount every year for 3 years, from \$775 to \$535. We subtract these two numbers to find that the laptop loses a total of \$240 in value. We can divide this value by 3 to find that it loses \$80 in value every year. In 5 years, it would lose $80(5) = \$400$. We can subtract this amount from the original value to obtain $\$775 - \$400 = \$375$.

11. The correct answer is 50. First, we need to find the rate at which Josh can mow with Mower Y by adding 20% to his rate with Mower X: $1.2 \times 0.5 = 0.6$ lawns per hour. Now, if we set h as the number of hours the mowers operate, we can set up the two equations and find when they are equivalent, using the form (profit per lawn) × (lawns per hour) × (hours) − (mower cost) = net income:

$$\frac{\$25}{\text{lawn}} \times \frac{0.5 \text{ lawns}}{\text{hour}} \times h - \$350 = \frac{\$25}{\text{lawn}} \times \frac{0.6 \text{ lawns}}{\text{hour}} \times h - \$475$$

$$\$125 = \frac{\$2.50}{\text{hour}} \times h$$

$$50 \text{ hours} = h$$

12. The correct answer is $-\frac{9}{2}$. The solution to a system of equations is the point at which the two lines cross. If a system does not have a solution, it means that the two lines never cross. In other words, they are parallel and thus have equal slopes. We can find the slope for the top equation by moving the x-variable to the right side of the equation and solving for y:

$$4y = -3x + 11$$

$$y = -\frac{3}{4}x + \frac{11}{4}$$

The slope is the value in front of the x, so now we need to find a value for m that will result in a slope of $-\frac{3}{4}$. Again, we move the x-variable to the right and solve for y:

$$y = \frac{m}{6}x - \frac{3}{2}$$

We can solve for m by setting $\frac{m}{6}$ equal to $-\frac{3}{4}$:

$$\frac{m}{6} = -\frac{3}{4}$$

$$4m = -18$$

$$m = -\frac{9}{2}$$

13. The correct answer is 2. We begin by expanding the equation and multiplying through: $3(2) - 3(z) + 2(z) + 2(4) = 6z$. We can rewrite this as $6 - 3z + 2z + 8 = 6z$. We then combine all the z-terms on the left side of the equation and all the numerical values on the right side: $-3z + 2z - 6z = -6 - 8$, or $-7z = -14$. We divide each side by -7 to find that $z = 2$.

Math – Calculator

1. Choice C is correct. From the graph, we can see the biggest positive distance between two years comes between 2018 and 2019, when the number of new students rises from approximately 85 to approximately 125.

2. Choice D is correct. So far Lola has taken 6 classes, so any she takes in the next x weeks are added onto that. She attends 2 every week, or 2 times the number of weeks. So, we can represent the number of classes Lola will attend as $6 + 2x$.

3. Choice A is correct. Each water bottle holds 3 cups, so we can multiply 32 by 3 to find the total number of cups: 32 cups × 3 = 96 cups. Then we convert cups to gallons:

$$96 \text{ cups} \times \frac{1 \text{ pint}}{2 \text{ cups}} \times \frac{1 \text{ quart}}{2 \text{ pints}} \times \frac{1 \text{ gallon}}{4 \text{ quarts}} = 6 \text{ gallons}$$

4. Choice C is correct. To solve for $a - b$, we must isolate the parenthetical term. We divide both sides by 9: $a - b = \frac{6}{9}$. We then reduce by dividing both the numerator and denominator by 3 to obtain $\frac{2}{3}$.

5. Choice B is correct. We can set up a system of equations to solve. We let m represent muffins and c represent cookies:

$$4m + 1.5c = 63$$

$$m = 12$$

We can use substitution, plugging in 12 for m in the first equation to obtain $4(12) + 1.5c = 63$, or $48 + 1.5c = 63$. We then subtract 48 from each side.

$$1.5c = 15$$

Finally, we divide each side by 1.5.

$$c = 10$$

Therefore, Jamie bought 10 cookies.

6. Choice A is correct. We need to subtract 3 feet, 11.5 inches from 5 feet, 10 inches. Since we cannot subtract 11.5 from 10, we need to borrow 1 foot, or 12 inches. We can rewrite 5 feet, 10 inches as 4 feet, 22 inches. Then we can subtract both feet and inches to obtain 1 foot, 10.5 inches. This is a total of 12 inches + 10.5 inches = 22.5 inches.

7. Choice B is correct. The number of dollars left after any given number of weeks, m, can be found by subtracting the amount spent from the original number, d. The amount spent can be calculated by multiplying the amount spent each week by the number of weeks that amount is spent, or multiplying a by w. So, we can write our equation as $m = d - aw$.

8. Choice C is correct. The slope of the first graph is $\frac{1}{2}$. To find the perpendicular line, we need to find the equation with a slope that is the negative reciprocal of the first. The negative reciprocal of $\frac{1}{2}$ is –2. We can find the slope of each equation in the answer choices. We do this by moving the x-variable to the right side of the equation and dividing by the constant in front of the y. Answer choice A has a slope of $-\frac{1}{2}$. Answer choice B has a slope of $\frac{1}{2}$ (which makes it parallel to the original equation, not perpendicular). Answer choice C has a slope of –2. Answer choice D has a slope of 2. So, choice C is the only possibility.

9. Choice D is correct. We can plug in each set of points to see which one fits. Plugging in $(4, -4)$ to the top inequality yields $-4 \leq \frac{3}{2}(4) + 1$, which is true. The bottom inequality would be $-4 - (-4) < 3$, which is also true, so choice D must be the answer. We can test each of the other points to verify. For answer choice A: plugging in $(0,2)$ yields $2 \leq \frac{3}{2}(0) + 1$, which is not true, and $0 - 2 < 3$, which is true. For answer choice B: plugging in $(-2,1)$ yields $1 \leq \frac{3}{2}(-2) + 1$, which is not true, and $-(-2) - 1 < 3$, which is true. For answer choice C: plugging in $(3, -7)$ yields $-7 \leq \frac{3}{2}(3) + 1$, which is true, and $-3 - (-7) < 3$, which is not true. So only answer choice D satisfies both inequalities.

10. Choice B is correct. We can write two equations with the information given and then solve. Since the first lawn (f) took 2.5 times the time of the second (s), we can write: $f = 2.5s$. Since both projects add up to 154, we can write $f + s = 154$. Then we can substitute $2.5s$ for f in the second equation: $2.5s + s = 154$, or $3.5s = 154$. We divide both sides by 3.5 to find that $s = 44$ minutes. Since $f = 2.5s$, we know that $f = 2.5(44 \text{ minutes}) = 110$ minutes.

11. Choice A is correct. We can solve the system of equations by eliminating the y-variable. To do this, we multiply the first equation by -2: $-2(3x) - 2(2y) = -2(9)$, or $-6x - 4y = -18$. Then we add the two equations together, which will cancel out the two y-terms and yield: $-5x = 5$. Then we divide each side by -5 to find that $x = -1$. We plug this value in to one of the equations to find y. Using the top equation, we can write: $3(-1) + 2y = 9$, or $-3 + 2y = 9$. We then add 3 to each side: $2y = 12$. Dividing each side by 2 yields: $y = 6$. So, our solution is $(-1,6)$. Thus, $x + y = -1 + 6 = 5$.

12. Choice D is correct. We need to expand the equation to simplify it:

$$6.7x^2 - 2.1 - (1.2x - 5.7)(1.2x - 5.7)$$

Then we multiply the parenthetical terms using the FOIL method.

$$6.7x^2 - 2.1 - [(1.2x)(1.2x) - (1.2x)(5.7) - (1.2x)(5.7) + (5.7)(5.7)]$$

$$6.7x^2 - 2.1 - [1.44x^2 - 6.84x - 6.84x + 32.49]$$

Finally, we combine like terms to obtain $5.26x^2 + 13.68x - 34.59$.

13. Choice C is correct. The ratio of the areas can be expressed:

$$\frac{\pi(r_{\text{after}})^2}{\pi(r_{\text{before}})^2}$$

Since π is in both the numerator and denominator, it cancels out and we are left with just a ratio of the radii squared:

$$\frac{(r_{\text{after}})^2}{(r_{\text{before}})^2} = \frac{8.2^2}{12.3^2} = \frac{67.24}{151.29} = \frac{4}{9} = 0.\overline{4}$$

14. Choice D is correct. According to the chart, 25 seniors and 10 freshmen are taking an art elective. Since $25 - 10 = 15$, there are 15 more senior art students than freshman art students.

15. Choice B is correct. The number of language students rises by 5 each year, starting with10 and ending with 25. So, we know the slope of the equation, or the coefficient of the x-variable, must be 5. Our equation then is $y = 5x + b$, where b is the y-intercept. To find b, we can plug in one of the known values of (x, y). For example, for the freshman class, $x = 1$ and $y = 10$, so $10 = 5(1) + b$. We simplify to find that $b = 5$. So our equation is $y = 5x + 5$.

16. Choice C is correct. To find the area of a triangle, we multiply the base by the height and divide by 2:

$$A = \frac{bh}{2} = \frac{(6x + 3)(3x - 4)}{2}$$

Apply the FOIL method to expand the numerator:

$$\frac{18x^2 - 24x + 9x - 12}{2} = 9x^2 - \frac{15}{2}x - 6$$

17. Choice C is correct. The first thing to do is solve for x in the given equation.

$$k = -\frac{1}{2}x + 5$$

$$k - 5 = -\frac{1}{2}x$$

$$(k - 5)(-2) = x$$

$$-2k + 10 = x$$

Since we are given that $x > 4$, we can apply this to the equation.

$$-2k + 10 > 4$$

Now we can reverse the steps to find an acceptable range for k.

$$-2k + 10 > 4$$

$$6 > 2k$$

$$k < 3$$

This indicates that k must be less than 3, so out of the answer choices only 2 is a possible value.

18. Choice B is correct. Begin by calculating the area of the wall. We are given that the wall is an 8 ft tall by 3×8 ft $= 24$ ft wide rectangle. So, the area of the wall is 8 ft $\times$ 24 ft $= 192$ ft^2. Since each can of paint can cover 100 ft^2, a minimum of 2 cans is required for the base coat.

19. Choice C is correct. The data shows a mean and median very close together. The largest and smallest weights are not greatly different from these values. This tells us that the majority of the babies are close to the same size and that the smallest and largest babies are not outliers. The median is 7 lb 8 oz, meaning that half the babies weigh less than or equal to this weight, and the other half weigh more than or equal to it. Thus, most of the babies cannot weigh more than 7 lb 8 oz, because *most* means more than half. However, most of the babies can weigh less than the mean, since it is higher than the median.

20. Choice D is correct. The median is the number in the middle when the values are arranged from least to greatest. We first reorganize them: 65, 68, 72, 76, 79, 81. Since there is an even number of grades, we take the average of the two in the middle. The average of 72 and 76 is $\frac{72+76}{2} =$ 74.

21. Choice A is correct. Every person's first heart rate was significantly lower than the second. A logical explanation for this is that they were more active just before the second measurement was taken, raising their heart rates. Answer choice B reverses this explanation, so it is illogical. Answer choice C is incorrect because it is unlikely that heart rates would be so elevated before practice even starts. For answer choice D, it is possible that the stress of a game could cause heart rates to be higher than during practice, but it is unlikely to be such a drastic difference since physical activity levels are similar.

22. The correct answer is 8. We find the original cost of the trip by adding \$180 and \$540 to obtain a total cost of \$720. Then we can find the cost difference when four families canceled: $\$720 - \$480 = \$240$. We divide \$240 by 4 to find that the cost per family was \$60. To find how many families did attend, we divide the total cost (after cancelations) by the cost per family. Dividing \$480 by \$60 yields 8, so 8 families went camping.

23. The correct answer is $\frac{7}{5}$. To find the slope, we need two points, so we can choose which two to use. The first and second points are simpler numbers for subtracting and dividing, so it is easiest to pick them. We find the difference in the y-values and then the x-values and divide them: $\left(-\frac{3}{2} - (-5)\right) \div \left(1 - \left(-\frac{3}{2}\right)\right)$, which simplifies to $\frac{7}{2} \div \frac{5}{2}$. We divide by finding the reciprocal and multiplying: $\frac{7}{2} \times \frac{2}{5} = \frac{14}{10} = \frac{7}{5}$.

24. The correct answer is 3450. Since each molecule of sodium carbonate has 2 atoms of sodium, and there are 75 molecules total, we multiply 75 by 2 to find that there are 150 atoms of sodium. Each of these weighs 23 amu, so we multiply 150 by 23 to find that there are 3,450 amu of sodium in the sodium carbonate.

25. The correct answer is 18. If the lemonade is being poured at 1.5 ounces per second, then in 3 seconds, Jodi will pour $1.5(3) = 4.5$ ounces. This is 25% of the glass, so we can set up a proportion to solve for 100%: $\frac{4.5}{x} = \frac{25}{100}$. We then cross-multiply and divide: $25(x) = (4.5)(100)$, or $25x = 450$. Finally, we divide 450 by 25 to find that $x = 18$, so the glass holds 18 ounces.

How to Overcome Test Anxiety

Just the thought of taking a test is enough to make most people a little nervous. A test is an important event that can have a long-term impact on your future, so it's important to take it seriously and it's natural to feel anxious about performing well. But just because anxiety is normal, that doesn't mean that it's helpful in test taking, or that you should simply accept it as part of your life. Anxiety can have a variety of effects. These effects can be mild, like making you feel slightly nervous, or severe, like blocking your ability to focus or remember even a simple detail.

If you experience test anxiety—whether severe or mild—it's important to know how to beat it. To discover this, first you need to understand what causes test anxiety.

Causes of Test Anxiety

While we often think of anxiety as an uncontrollable emotional state, it can actually be caused by simple, practical things. One of the most common causes of test anxiety is that a person does not feel adequately prepared for their test. This feeling can be the result of many different issues such as poor study habits or lack of organization, but the most common culprit is time management. Starting to study too late, failing to organize your study time to cover all of the material, or being distracted while you study will mean that you're not well prepared for the test. This may lead to cramming the night before, which will cause you to be physically and mentally exhausted for the test. Poor time management also contributes to feelings of stress, fear, and hopelessness as you realize you are not well prepared but don't know what to do about it.

Other times, test anxiety is not related to your preparation for the test but comes from unresolved fear. This may be a past failure on a test, or poor performance on tests in general. It may come from comparing yourself to others who seem to be performing better or from the stress of living up to expectations. Anxiety may be driven by fears of the future—how failure on this test would affect your educational and career goals. These fears are often completely irrational, but they can still negatively impact your test performance.

Elements of Test Anxiety

As mentioned earlier, test anxiety is considered to be an emotional state, but it has physical and mental components as well. Sometimes you may not even realize that you are suffering from test anxiety until you notice the physical symptoms. These can include trembling hands, rapid heartbeat, sweating, nausea, and tense muscles. Extreme anxiety may lead to fainting or vomiting. Obviously, any of these symptoms can have a negative impact on testing. It is important to recognize them as soon as they begin to occur so that you can address the problem before it damages your performance.

The mental components of test anxiety include trouble focusing and inability to remember learned information. During a test, your mind is on high alert, which can help you recall information and stay focused for an extended period of time. However, anxiety interferes with your mind's natural processes, causing you to blank out, even on the questions you know well. The strain of testing during anxiety makes it difficult to stay focused, especially on a test that may take several hours. Extreme anxiety can take a huge mental toll, making it difficult not only to recall test information but even to understand the test questions or pull your thoughts together.

Effects of Test Anxiety

Test anxiety is like a disease—if left untreated, it will get progressively worse. Anxiety leads to poor performance, and this reinforces the feelings of fear and failure, which in turn lead to poor performances on subsequent tests. It can grow from a mild nervousness to a crippling condition. If allowed to progress, test anxiety can have a big impact on your schooling, and consequently on your future.

Test anxiety can spread to other parts of your life. Anxiety on tests can become anxiety in any stressful situation, and blanking on a test can turn into panicking in a job situation. But fortunately, you don't have to let anxiety rule your testing and determine your grades. There are a number of relatively simple steps you can take to move past anxiety and function normally on a test and in the rest of life.

Physical Steps for Beating Test Anxiety

While test anxiety is a serious problem, the good news is that it can be overcome. It doesn't have to control your ability to think and remember information. While it may take time, you can begin taking steps today to beat anxiety.

Just as your first hint that you may be struggling with anxiety comes from the physical symptoms, the first step to treating it is also physical. Rest is crucial for having a clear, strong mind. If you are tired, it is much easier to give in to anxiety. But if you establish good sleep habits, your body and mind will be ready to perform optimally, without the strain of exhaustion. Additionally, sleeping well helps you to retain information better, so you're more likely to recall the answers when you see the test questions.

Getting good sleep means more than going to bed on time. It's important to allow your brain time to relax. Take study breaks from time to time so it doesn't get overworked, and don't study right before bed. Take time to rest your mind before trying to rest your body, or you may find it difficult to fall asleep.

Along with sleep, other aspects of physical health are important in preparing for a test. Good nutrition is vital for good brain function. Sugary foods and drinks may give a burst of energy but this burst is followed by a crash, both physically and emotionally. Instead, fuel your body with protein and vitamin-rich foods.

Also, drink plenty of water. Dehydration can lead to headaches and exhaustion, especially if your brain is already under stress from the rigors of the test. Particularly if your test is a long one, drink water during the breaks. And if possible, take an energy-boosting snack to eat between sections.

Along with sleep and diet, a third important part of physical health is exercise. Maintaining a steady workout schedule is helpful, but even taking 5-minute study breaks to walk can help get your blood pumping faster and clear your head. Exercise also releases endorphins, which contribute to a positive feeling and can help combat test anxiety.

When you nurture your physical health, you are also contributing to your mental health. If your body is healthy, your mind is much more likely to be healthy as well. So take time to rest, nourish your body with healthy food and water, and get moving as much as possible. Taking these physical steps will make you stronger and more able to take the mental steps necessary to overcome test anxiety.

Mental Steps for Beating Test Anxiety

Working on the mental side of test anxiety can be more challenging, but as with the physical side, there are clear steps you can take to overcome it. As mentioned earlier, test anxiety often stems from lack of preparation, so the obvious solution is to prepare for the test. Effective studying may be the most important weapon you have for beating test anxiety, but you can and should employ several other mental tools to combat fear.

First, boost your confidence by reminding yourself of past success—tests or projects that you aced. If you're putting as much effort into preparing for this test as you did for those, there's no reason you should expect to fail here. Work hard to prepare; then trust your preparation.

Second, surround yourself with encouraging people. It can be helpful to find a study group, but be sure that the people you're around will encourage a positive attitude. If you spend time with others who are anxious or cynical, this will only contribute to your own anxiety. Look for others who are motivated to study hard from a desire to succeed, not from a fear of failure.

Third, reward yourself. A test is physically and mentally tiring, even without anxiety, and it can be helpful to have something to look forward to. Plan an activity following the test, regardless of the outcome, such as going to a movie or getting ice cream.

When you are taking the test, if you find yourself beginning to feel anxious, remind yourself that you know the material. Visualize successfully completing the test. Then take a few deep, relaxing breaths and return to it. Work through the questions carefully but with confidence, knowing that you are capable of succeeding.

Developing a healthy mental approach to test taking will also aid in other areas of life. Test anxiety affects more than just the actual test—it can be damaging to your mental health and even contribute to depression. It's important to beat test anxiety before it becomes a problem for more than testing.

Study Strategy

Being prepared for the test is necessary to combat anxiety, but what does being prepared look like? You may study for hours on end and still not feel prepared. What you need is a strategy for test prep. The next few pages outline our recommended steps to help you plan out and conquer the challenge of preparation.

Step 1: Scope Out the Test

Learn everything you can about the format (multiple choice, essay, etc.) and what will be on the test. Gather any study materials, course outlines, or sample exams that may be available. Not only will this help you to prepare, but knowing what to expect can help to alleviate test anxiety.

Step 2: Map Out the Material

Look through the textbook or study guide and make note of how many chapters or sections it has. Then divide these over the time you have. For example, if a book has 15 chapters and you have five days to study, you need to cover three chapters each day. Even better, if you have the time, leave an extra day at the end for overall review after you have gone through the material in depth.

If time is limited, you may need to prioritize the material. Look through it and make note of which sections you think you already have a good grasp on, and which need review. While you are studying, skim quickly through the familiar sections and take more time on the challenging parts.

Write out your plan so you don't get lost as you go. Having a written plan also helps you feel more in control of the study, so anxiety is less likely to arise from feeling overwhelmed at the amount to cover.

Step 3: Gather Your Tools

Decide what study method works best for you. Do you prefer to highlight in the book as you study and then go back over the highlighted portions? Or do you type out notes of the important information? Or is it helpful to make flashcards that you can carry with you? Assemble the pens, index cards, highlighters, post-it notes, and any other materials you may need so you won't be distracted by getting up to find things while you study.

If you're having a hard time retaining the information or organizing your notes, experiment with different methods. For example, try color-coding by subject with colored pens, highlighters, or post-it notes. If you learn better by hearing, try recording yourself reading your notes so you can listen while in the car, working out, or simply sitting at your desk. Ask a friend to quiz you from your flashcards, or try teaching someone the material to solidify it in your mind.

Step 4: Create Your Environment

It's important to avoid distractions while you study. This includes both the obvious distractions like visitors and the subtle distractions like an uncomfortable chair (or a too-comfortable couch that makes you want to fall asleep). Set up the best study environment possible: good lighting and a comfortable work area. If background music helps you focus, you may want to turn it on, but otherwise keep the room quiet. If you are using a computer to take notes, be sure you don't have any other windows open, especially applications like social media, games, or anything else that could distract you. Silence your phone and turn off notifications. Be sure to keep water close by so you stay hydrated while you study (but avoid unhealthy drinks and snacks).

Also, take into account the best time of day to study. Are you freshest first thing in the morning? Try to set aside some time then to work through the material. Is your mind clearer in the afternoon or evening? Schedule your study session then. Another method is to study at the same time of day that you will take the test, so that your brain gets used to working on the material at that time and will be ready to focus at test time.

Step 5: Study!

Once you have done all the study preparation, it's time to settle into the actual studying. Sit down, take a few moments to settle your mind so you can focus, and begin to follow your study plan. Don't give in to distractions or let yourself procrastinate. This is your time to prepare so you'll be ready to fearlessly approach the test. Make the most of the time and stay focused.

Of course, you don't want to burn out. If you study too long you may find that you're not retaining the information very well. Take regular study breaks. For example, taking five minutes out of every hour to walk briskly, breathing deeply and swinging your arms, can help your mind stay fresh.

As you get to the end of each chapter or section, it's a good idea to do a quick review. Remind yourself of what you learned and work on any difficult parts. When you feel that you've mastered the material, move on to the next part. At the end of your study session, briefly skim through your notes again.

But while review is helpful, cramming last minute is NOT. If at all possible, work ahead so that you won't need to fit all your study into the last day. Cramming overloads your brain with more information than it can process and retain, and your tired mind may struggle to recall even previously learned information when it is overwhelmed with last-minute study. Also, the urgent nature of cramming and the stress placed on your brain contribute to anxiety. You'll be more likely to go to the test feeling unprepared and having trouble thinking clearly.

So don't cram, and don't stay up late before the test, even just to review your notes at a leisurely pace. Your brain needs rest more than it needs to go over the information again. In fact, plan to finish your studies by noon or early afternoon the day before the test. Give your brain the rest of the day to relax or focus on other things, and get a good night's sleep. Then you will be fresh for the test and better able to recall what you've studied.

Step 6: Take a Practice Test

Many courses offer sample tests, either online or in the study materials. This is an excellent resource to check whether you have mastered the material, as well as to prepare for the test format and environment.

Check the test format ahead of time: the number of questions, the type (multiple choice, free response, etc.), and the time limit. Then create a plan for working through them. For example, if you have 30 minutes to take a 60-question test, your limit is 30 seconds per question. Spend less time on the questions you know well so that you can take more time on the difficult ones.

If you have time to take several practice tests, take the first one open book, with no time limit. Work through the questions at your own pace and make sure you fully understand them. Gradually work up to taking a test under test conditions: sit at a desk with all study materials put away and set a timer. Pace yourself to make sure you finish the test with time to spare and go back to check your answers if you have time.

After each test, check your answers. On the questions you missed, be sure you understand why you missed them. Did you misread the question (tests can use tricky wording)? Did you forget the information? Or was it something you hadn't learned? Go back and study any shaky areas that the practice tests reveal.

Taking these tests not only helps with your grade, but also aids in combating test anxiety. If you're already used to the test conditions, you're less likely to worry about it, and working through tests until you're scoring well gives you a confidence boost. Go through the practice tests until you feel comfortable, and then you can go into the test knowing that you're ready for it.

Test Tips

On test day, you should be confident, knowing that you've prepared well and are ready to answer the questions. But aside from preparation, there are several test day strategies you can employ to maximize your performance.

First, as stated before, get a good night's sleep the night before the test (and for several nights before that, if possible). Go into the test with a fresh, alert mind rather than staying up late to study.

Try not to change too much about your normal routine on the day of the test. It's important to eat a nutritious breakfast, but if you normally don't eat breakfast at all, consider eating just a protein bar. If you're a coffee drinker, go ahead and have your normal coffee. Just make sure you time it so that the caffeine doesn't wear off right in the middle of your test. Avoid sugary beverages, and drink enough water to stay hydrated but not so much that you need a restroom break 10 minutes into the test. If your test isn't first thing in the morning, consider going for a walk or doing a light workout before the test to get your blood flowing.

Allow yourself enough time to get ready, and leave for the test with plenty of time to spare so you won't have the anxiety of scrambling to arrive in time. Another reason to be early is to select a good seat. It's helpful to sit away from doors and windows, which can be distracting. Find a good seat, get out your supplies, and settle your mind before the test begins.

When the test begins, start by going over the instructions carefully, even if you already know what to expect. Make sure you avoid any careless mistakes by following the directions.

Then begin working through the questions, pacing yourself as you've practiced. If you're not sure on an answer, don't spend too much time on it, and don't let it shake your confidence. Either skip it and come back later, or eliminate as many wrong answers as possible and guess among the remaining ones. Don't dwell on these questions as you continue—put them out of your mind and focus on what lies ahead.

Be sure to read all of the answer choices, even if you're sure the first one is the right answer. Sometimes you'll find a better one if you keep reading. But don't second-guess yourself if you do immediately know the answer. Your gut instinct is usually right. Don't let test anxiety rob you of the information you know.

If you have time at the end of the test (and if the test format allows), go back and review your answers. Be cautious about changing any, since your first instinct tends to be correct, but make sure you didn't misread any of the questions or accidentally mark the wrong answer choice. Look over any you skipped and make an educated guess.

At the end, leave the test feeling confident. You've done your best, so don't waste time worrying about your performance or wishing you could change anything. Instead, celebrate the successful completion of this test. And finally, use this test to learn how to deal with anxiety even better next time.

Review Video: Test Anxiety
Visit mometrix.com/academy and enter code: 100340

Important Qualification

Not all anxiety is created equal. If your test anxiety is causing major issues in your life beyond the classroom or testing center, or if you are experiencing troubling physical symptoms related to your anxiety, it may be a sign of a serious physiological or psychological condition. If this sounds like your situation, we strongly encourage you to seek professional help.

How to Overcome Your Fear of Math

Not again. You're sitting in math class, look down at your test, and immediately start to panic. Your stomach is in knots, your heart is racing, and you break out in a cold sweat. You're staring at the paper, but everything looks like it's written in a foreign language. Even though you studied, you're blanking out on how to begin solving these problems.

Does this sound familiar? If so, then you're not alone! You may be like millions of other people who experience math anxiety. Anxiety about performing well in math is a common experience for students of all ages. In this article, we'll discuss what math anxiety is, common misconceptions about learning math, and tips and strategies for overcoming math anxiety.

What Is Math Anxiety?

Psychologist Mark H. Ashcraft explains math anxiety as a feeling of tension, apprehension, or fear that interferes with math performance. Having math anxiety negatively impacts people's beliefs about themselves and what they can achieve. It hinders achievement within the math classroom and affects the successful application of mathematics in the real world.

Symptoms and Signs of Math Anxiety

To overcome math anxiety, you must recognize its symptoms. Becoming aware of the signs of math anxiety is the first step in addressing and resolving these fears.

Negative Self-Talk

If you have math anxiety, you've most likely said at least one of these statements to yourself:

- "I hate math."
- "I'm not good at math."
- "I'm not a math person."

The way we speak to ourselves and think about ourselves matters. Our thoughts become our words, our words become our actions, and our actions become our habits. Thinking negatively about math creates a self-fulfilling prophecy. In other words, if you take an idea as a fact, then it will come true because your behaviors will align to match it.

Avoidance

Some people who are fearful or anxious about math will tend to avoid it altogether. Avoidance can manifest in the following ways:

- Lack of engagement with math content
- Not completing homework and other assignments
- Not asking for help when needed
- Skipping class
- Avoiding math-related courses and activities

Avoidance is one of the most harmful impacts of math anxiety. If you steer clear of math at all costs, then you can't set yourself up for the success you deserve.

LACK OF MOTIVATION

Students with math anxiety may experience a lack of motivation. They may struggle to find the incentive to get engaged with what they view as a frightening subject. These students are often overwhelmed, making it difficult for them to complete or even start math assignments.

PROCRASTINATION

Another symptom of math anxiety is procrastination. Students may voluntarily delay or postpone their classwork and assignments, even if they know there will be a negative consequence for doing so. Additionally, they may choose to wait until the last minute to start projects and homework, even when they know they need more time to put forth their best effort.

PHYSIOLOGICAL REACTIONS

Many people with a fear of math experience physiological side effects. These may include an increase in heart rate, sweatiness, shakiness, nausea, and irregular breathing. These symptoms make it difficult to focus on the math content, causing the student even more stress and fear.

STRONG EMOTIONAL RESPONSES

Math anxiety also affects people on an emotional level. Responding to math content with strong emotions such as panic, anger, or despair can be a sign of math anxiety.

LOW TEST SCORES AND PERFORMANCE

Low achievement can be both a symptom and a cause of math anxiety. When someone does not take the steps needed to perform well on tests and assessments, they are less likely to pass. The more they perform poorly, the more they accept this poor performance as a fact that can't be changed.

FEELING ALONE

People who experience math anxiety feel like they are the only ones struggling, even if the math they are working on is challenging to many people. Feeling isolated in what they perceive as failure can trigger tension or nervousness.

FEELING OF PERMANENCY

Math anxiety can feel very permanent. You may assume that you are naturally bad at math and always will be. Viewing math as a natural ability rather than a skill that can be learned causes people to believe that nothing will help them improve. They take their current math abilities as fact and assume that they can't be changed. As a result, they give up, stop trying to improve, and avoid engaging with math altogether.

LACK OF CONFIDENCE

People with low self-confidence in math tend to feel awkward and incompetent when asked to solve a math problem. They don't feel comfortable taking chances or risks when problem-solving because they second-guess themselves and assume they are incorrect. They don't trust in their ability to learn the content and solve problems correctly.

PANIC

A general sense of unexplained panic is also a sign of math anxiety. You may feel a sudden sense of fear that triggers physical reactions, even when there is no apparent reason for such a response.

Causes of Math Anxiety

Math anxiety can start at a young age and may have one or more underlying causes. Common causes of math anxiety include the following:

The Attitude of Parents or Guardians

Parents often put pressure on their children to perform well in school. Although their intentions are usually good, this pressure can lead to anxiety, especially if the student is struggling with a subject or class.

Perhaps your parents or others in your life hold negative predispositions about math based on their own experiences. For instance, if your mother once claimed she was not good at math, then you might have incorrectly interpreted this as a predisposed trait that was passed down to you.

Teacher Influence

Students often pick up on their teachers' attitudes about the content being taught. If a teacher is happy and excited about math, students are more likely to mirror these emotions. However, if a teacher lacks enthusiasm or genuine interest, then students are more inclined to disengage.

Teachers have a responsibility to cultivate a welcoming classroom culture that is accepting of mistakes. When teachers blame students for not understanding a concept, they create a hostile classroom environment where mistakes are not tolerated. This tension increases student stress and anxiety, creating conditions that are not conducive to inquiry and learning. Instead, when teachers normalize mistakes as a natural part of the problem-solving process, they give their students the freedom to explore and grapple with the math content. In such an environment, students feel comfortable taking chances because they are not afraid of being wrong.

Students need teachers that can help when they're having problems understanding difficult concepts. In doing so, educators may need to change how they teach the content. Since different people have unique learning styles, it's the job of the teacher to adapt to the needs of each student. Additionally, teachers should encourage students to explore alternate problem-solving strategies, even if it's not the preferred method of the educator.

Fear of Being Wrong

Embarrassing situations can be traumatic, especially for young children and adolescents. These experiences can stay with people through their adult lives. Those with math anxiety may experience a fear of being wrong, especially in front of a group of peers. This fear can be paralyzing, interfering with the student's concentration and ability to focus on the problem at hand.

Timed Assessments

Timed assessments can help improve math fluency, but they often create unnecessary pressure for students to complete an unrealistic number of problems within a specified timeframe. Many studies have shown that timed assessments often result in increased levels of anxiety, reducing a student's overall competence and ability to problem-solve.

Debunking Math Myths

There are lots of myths about math that are related to the causes and development of math-related anxiety. Although these myths have been proven to be false, many people take them as fact. Let's go over a few of the most common myths about learning math.

Myth: Men Are Better at Math Than Women

Math has a reputation for being a male-dominant subject, but this doesn't mean that men are inherently better at math than women. Many famous mathematical discoveries have been made by women. Katherine Johnson, Dame Mary Lucy Cartwright, and Marjorie Lee Brown are just a few of the many famous women mathematicians. Expecting to be good or bad at math because of your gender sets you up for stress and confusion. Math is a skill that can be learned, just like cooking or riding a bike.

Myth: There Is Only One Good Way to Solve Math Problems

There are many ways to get the correct answer when it comes to math. No two people have the same brain, so everyone takes a slightly different approach to problem-solving. Moreover, there isn't one way of problem-solving that's superior to another. Your way of working through a problem might differ from someone else's, and that is okay. Math can be a highly individualized process, so the best method for you should be the one that makes you feel the most comfortable and makes the most sense to you.

Myth: Math Requires a Good Memory

For many years, mathematics was taught through memorization. However, learning in such a way hinders the development of critical thinking and conceptual understanding. These skill sets are much more valuable than basic memorization. For instance, you might be great at memorizing mathematical formulas, but if you don't understand what they mean, then you can't apply them to different scenarios in the real world. When a student is working from memory, they are limited in the strategies available to them to problem-solve. In other words, they assume there is only one correct way to do the math, which is the method they memorized. Having a variety of problem-solving options can help students figure out which method works best for them. Additionally, it provides students with a better understanding of how and why certain mathematical strategies work. While memorization can be helpful in some instances, it is not an absolute requirement for mathematicians.

Myth: Math Is Not Creative

Math requires imagination and intuition. Contrary to popular belief, it is a highly creative field. Mathematical creativity can help in developing new ways to think about and solve problems. Many people incorrectly assume that all things are either creative or analytical. However, this black-and-white view is limiting because the field of mathematics involves both creativity and logic.

Myth: Math Isn't Supposed To Be Fun

Whoever told you that math isn't supposed to be fun is a liar. There are tons of math-based activities and games that foster friendly competition and engagement. Math is often best learned through play, and lots of mobile apps and computer games exemplify this.

Additionally, math can be an exceptionally collaborative and social experience. Studying or working through problems with a friend often makes the process a lot more fun. The excitement and satisfaction of solving a difficult problem with others is quite rewarding. Math can be fun if you look for ways to make it more collaborative and enjoyable.

Myth: Not Everyone Is Capable of Learning Math

There's no such thing as a "math person." Although many people think that you're either good at math or you're not, this is simply not true. Everyone is capable of learning and applying mathematics. However, not everyone learns the same way. Since each person has a different learning style, the trick is to find the strategies and learning tools that work best for you. Some people learn best through hands-on experiences, and others find success through the use of visual aids. Others are auditory learners and learn best by hearing and listening. When people are overwhelmed or feel that math is too hard, it's often because they haven't found the learning strategy that works best for them.

Myth: Good Mathematicians Work Quickly and Never Make Mistakes

There is no prize for finishing first in math. It's not a race, and speed isn't a measure of your ability. Good mathematicians take their time to ensure their work is accurate. As you gain more experience and practice, you will naturally become faster and more confident.

Additionally, everyone makes mistakes, including good mathematicians. Mistakes are a normal part of the problem-solving process, and they're not a bad thing. The important thing is that we take the time to learn from our mistakes, understand where our misconceptions are, and move forward.

Myth: You Don't Need Math in the Real World

Our day-to-day lives are so infused with mathematical concepts that we often don't even realize when we're using math in the real world. In fact, most people tend to underestimate how much we do math in our everyday lives. It's involved in an enormous variety of daily activities such as shopping, baking, finances, and gardening, as well as in many careers, including architecture, nursing, design, and sales.

Tips and Strategies for Overcoming Math Anxiety

If your anxiety is getting in the way of your level of mathematical engagement, then there are lots of steps you can take. Check out the strategies below to start building confidence in math today.

Focus on Understanding, Not Memorization

Don't drive yourself crazy trying to memorize every single formula or mathematical process. Instead, shift your attention to understanding concepts. Those who prioritize memorization over conceptual understanding tend to have lower achievement levels in math. Students who memorize may be able to complete some math, but they don't understand the process well enough to apply it to different situations. Memorization comes with time and practice, but it won't help alleviate math anxiety. On the other hand, conceptual understanding will give you the building blocks of knowledge you need to build up your confidence.

Replace Negative Self-Talk with Positive Self-Talk

Start to notice how you think about yourself. Whenever you catch yourself thinking something negative, try replacing that thought with a positive affirmation. Instead of continuing the negative thought, pause to reframe the situation. For ideas on how to get started, take a look at the table below:

Instead of thinking...	Try thinking...
"I can't do this math." "I'm not a math person."	"I'm up for the challenge, and I'm training my brain in math."
"This problem is too hard."	"This problem is hard, so this might take some time and effort. I know I can do this."
"I give up."	"What strategies can help me solve this problem?"
"I made a mistake, so I'm not good at this."	"Everyone makes mistakes. Mistakes help me to grow and understand."
"I'll never be smart enough."	"I can figure this out, and I am smart enough."

Practice Mindfulness

Practicing mindfulness and focusing on your breathing can help alleviate some of the physical symptoms of math anxiety. By taking deep breaths, you can remind your nervous system that you are not in immediate danger. Doing so will reduce your heart rate and help with any irregular breathing or shakiness. Taking the edge off of the physiological effects of anxiety will clear your mind, allowing your brain to focus its energy on problem-solving.

Do Some Math Every Day

Think about learning math as if you were learning a foreign language. If you don't use it, you lose it. If you don't practice your math skills regularly, you'll have a harder time achieving comprehension and fluency. Set some amount of time aside each day, even if it's just for a few minutes, to practice. It might take some discipline to build a habit around this, but doing so will help increase your mathematical self-assurance.

Use All of Your Resources

Everyone has a different learning style, and there are plenty of resources out there to support all learners. When you get stuck on a math problem, think about the tools you have access to, and use them when applicable. Such resources may include flashcards, graphic organizers, study guides, interactive notebooks, and peer study groups. All of these are great tools to accommodate your individual learning style. Finding the tools and resources that work for your learning style will give you the confidence you need to succeed.

Realize That You Aren't Alone

Remind yourself that lots of other people struggle with math anxiety, including teachers, nurses, and even successful mathematicians. You aren't the only one who panics when faced with a new or challenging problem. It's probably much more common than you think. Realizing that you aren't alone in your experience can help put some distance between yourself and the emotions you feel about math. It also helps to normalize the anxiety and shift your perspective.

Ask Questions

If there's a concept you don't understand and you've tried everything you can, then it's okay to ask for help! You can always ask your teacher or professor for help. If you're not learning math in a traditional classroom, you may want to join a study group, work with a tutor, or talk to your friends. More often than not, you aren't the only one of your peers who needs clarity on a mathematical concept. Seeking understanding is a great way to increase self-confidence in math.

Remember That There's More Than One Way To Solve a Problem

Since everyone learns differently, it's best to focus on understanding a math problem with an approach that makes sense to you. If the way it's being taught is confusing to you, don't give up. Instead, work to understand the problem using a different technique. There's almost always more than one problem-solving method when it comes to math. Don't get stressed if one of them doesn't make sense to you. Instead, shift your focus to what does make sense. Chances are high that you know more than you think you do.

Visualization

Visualization is the process of creating images in your mind's eye. Picture yourself as a successful, confident mathematician. Think about how you would feel and how you would behave. What would your work area look like? How would you organize your belongings? The more you focus on something, the more likely you are to achieve it. Visualizing teaches your brain that you can achieve whatever it is that you want. Thinking about success in mathematics will lead to acting like a successful mathematician. This, in turn, leads to actual success.

Focus on the Easiest Problems First

To increase your confidence when working on a math test or assignment, try solving the easiest problems first. Doing so will remind you that you are successful in math and that you do have what it takes. This process will increase your belief in yourself, giving you the confidence you need to tackle more complex problems.

Find a Support Group

A study buddy, tutor, or peer group can go a long way in decreasing math-related anxiety. Such support systems offer lots of benefits, including a safe place to ask questions, additional practice with mathematical concepts, and an understanding of other problem-solving explanations that may work better for you. Equipping yourself with a support group is one of the fastest ways to eliminate math anxiety.

Reward Yourself for Working Hard

Recognize the amount of effort you're putting in to overcome your math anxiety. It's not an easy task, so you deserve acknowledgement. Surround yourself with people who will provide you with the positive reinforcement you deserve.

Remember, You Can Do This!

Conquering a fear of math can be challenging, but there are lots of strategies that can help you out. Your own beliefs about your mathematical capabilities can limit your potential. Working toward a growth mindset can have a tremendous impact on decreasing math-related anxiety and building confidence. By knowing the symptoms of math anxiety and recognizing common misconceptions about learning math, you can develop a plan to address your fear of math. Utilizing the strategies discussed can help you overcome this anxiety and build the confidence you need to succeed.

Tell Us Your Story

We at Mometrix would like to extend our heartfelt thanks to you for letting us be a part of your journey. It is an honor to serve people from all walks of life, people like you, who are committed to building the best future they can for themselves.

We know that each person's situation is unique. But we also know that, whether you are a young student or a mother of four, you care about working to make your own life and the lives of those around you better.

That's why we want to hear your story.

We want to know why you're taking this test. We want to know about the trials you've gone through to get here. And we want to know about the successes you've experienced after taking and passing your test.

In addition to your story, which can be an inspiration both to us and to others, we value your feedback. We want to know both what you loved about our book and what you think we can improve on.

The team at Mometrix would be absolutely thrilled to hear from you! So please, send us an email at tellusyourstory@mometrix.com or visit us at mometrix.com/tellusyourstory.php and let's stay in touch.

Additional Bonus Material

Due to our efforts to try to keep this book to a manageable length, we've created a link that will give you access to all of your additional bonus material:

mometrix.com/bonus948/psat89

Made in the USA
Middletown, DE
24 May 2023

31301330R00197